ADVANCED ORGANIZATIONAL MANAGEMENT

D0768076

CERTIFIED PROFESSIONAL SECRETARY®
CERTIFIED ADMINISTRATION PROFESSIONAL®
EXAMINATION REVIEW SERIES

ADVANCED ORGANIZATIONAL MANAGEMENT

Mark Garrison, Ph.D.
Kentucky State University

Margaret Bly Turner
Edison Community College

Carol Mull
Series Editor

A joint publication of
International Association of Administrative Professionals®

International Association of
Administrative Professionals®

and

PEARSON
Prentice
Hall

Upper Saddle River, New Jersey 07458

Library of Congress Cataloging-in-Publication Data
Garrison, Mark
   Advanced organizational management / Mark Garrison, Margaret Anne Bly Turner.—1st ed.
      p. cm.—(Certified professional secretary, certified administrative professional
examination review series)
   Includes index.
   "A joint publication of [the] International Association of Administrative
Professionals."
   ISBN 0-13-119337-6
   1.   Office management—Examinations, questions, etc. 2. Industrial management—
Examinations, questions, etc. 3. Secretaries—Examinations, questions, etc. 4.
Secretaries—Certification. 5. Administrative assistants—Examinations, questions, etc.
6. Administrative assistants—Certification. I. Turner, Margaret Anne Bly. II.
International Association of Administrative Professionals. III. Title. IV. Series.
   HF5547.G33 2005
   658.4—dc22

                                        2005005892

Director of Production and Manufacturing: Bruce Johnson
Senior Acquisitions Editor: Gary Bauer
Editorial Assistant: Jacqueline Knapke
Marketing Manager: Leigh Ann Sims
Managing Editor—Production: Mary Carnis
Manufacturing Buyer: Ilene Sanford
Production Liaison: Denise Brown
Production Editor: Judy Ludowitz/Carlisle Publishers Services
Composition: Carlisle Communications, Ltd.
Senior Design Coordinator/Cover Design: Christopher Weigand
Cover Printer: Phoenix Color
Printer/Binder: Command Web

Pearson Education, Inc. previously published this book.

Pearson Education Ltd.   Pearson Education Australia PTY, Limited
Pearson Education Singapore, Pte. Ltd.   Pearson Education North Asia Ltd.
Pearson Education Canada, Ltd.   Pearson Educacíon de Mexico, S.A. de C.V.
Pearson Education—Japan   Pearson Education Malaysia, Pte. Ltd.

PEARSON
Prentice
Hall

                                                     10 9 8 7 6 5 4 3 2 1
                                                     ISBN: 0-13-119337-6

Contents

Preface

The Certified Professional Secretary (CPS) and Certified Administrative Professional (CAP) Examination Review Series, a four-volume set of review manuals that consists of one review manual for each of the first three parts of the CPS and CAP Examinations and one for Part 4 of the CAP Examination, is a joint publication of Prentice Hall and the International Association of Administrative Professionals (IAAP). The content of each review manual is based on the current Certification Review Guide published by the IAAP.

CPS and CAP Examinations

The rewards for achieving the Certified Professional Secretary (CPS) and Certified Administrative Professional (CAP) certifications are numerous, as attested to by the more than 65,000 CPS and CAP holders. These rewards include pride in accomplishment, increased self-esteem, greater respect from employers and peers, and confidence to assume greater responsibilities as well as possible college credit toward a degree, pay increases, bonuses, and opportunities for advancement. In today's workplace, having the CPS or CAP credentials can enhance assurance of employability and career advancement.

The CPS Examination is a one-day, three-part examination which includes

 Part 1: Office Systems and Technology

 Part 2: Office Administration

 Part 3: Management

The CAP Examination is a 1½ day, four-part examination which includes

 Parts 1, 2, and 3 above

 Part 4: Advanced Organizational Management

  To apply for the CPS or CAP Examination, the candidate must meet certain educational and professional experience requirements. Visit the IAAP Web site at *www.iaap-hq.org/* to obtain detailed information concerning testing centers, testing dates, application packets, and other information relative to applying for certification candidacy.

CPS and CAP Examination Review Series

The CPS and CAP Examination Review Series provides valuable assistance to the administrative professional preparing for the CPS and CAP Examinations, whether this series is used for group review sessions or self-study. The series provides an excellent learning tool that is focused on key topics necessary for passing the examinations.

The format used in Parts 1, 2, and 3 (Office Systems and Technology, 5E; Office Administration, 5E; and Management, 5E) of the CPS and CAP Examination Review Series is an outline format with multiple-choice review questions. The format used in Part 4, Advanced Organizational Management for the CAP Examination Review, is slightly different based on the scenario-oriented nature of Part 4 of the CAP Examination. The CPS and CAP Examination Review Series provides relevant information to help the candidate prepare for both the CPS and CAP Examinations. However, this does not imply that all information presented in this series will be included on the examinations. Further review is encouraged for the candidate by studying selected titles from the bibliography supplied by IAAP.

Each review manual in the CPS and CAP Examination Review Series includes:

- An overview introducing the reader to the chapter contents.

- Key terms that reinforce essential vocabulary.

- Text in outline form, with examples highlighted in italics, to enhance the explanation given in the text.

- Key examples emphasized.

- Difficult concepts illustrated.

- Check Point sections within each chapter that offer reviews of key concepts.

- For Your Review section at the end of each chapter with practice questions similar to those found on the CPS and CAP Examinations.

- A glossary at the end of each book that provides accessible reference.

- A comprehensive practice exam that simulates the testing environment and provides even more practice.

- Solutions to all check points and review questions, including references to the chapter outline where the answers are explained.

  For example:

  Answer Reference

  1. *(B)*   *[A-2]* (Section of Chapter)

- An index with page references provided in the Office Systems and Technology, 5E, and the Office Administration, 5E, review manuals.

NEW Online eLearning Format for CPS and CAP Examination Review

The NEW online eLearning format includes all material found in Parts 1–3 of the CPS and CAP Examination Review series plus assessment feedback. You can purchase each title separately or receive a quantity discount when all three titles are purchased. Purchase online at www.prenhall.com/cap-cpsreview.

- Office Systems and Technology, 5E, eLearning version

- Office Administration, 5E, eLearning version

- Management, 5E, eLearning version
- CPS Examination Review Series, eLearning version (includes all three titles)

CPS and CAP Examination Review Guide

The Certification Examination Review Guide should be used to direct any course of study. This guide includes the examination outline, sample questions, bibliography of recommended study materials, and suggestions for examination review. The Certification Examination Review Guide is available free of charge on the IAAP Web site: *http://www.iaap-hq.org*, then Professional Certification, Forms.

Acknowledgments

The first edition of the *Certified Administrative Professional Examination Review for Advanced Organizational Management* complements the current revised study outline for the Fourth Level of the Certified Administrative Professional Examination. Like other reviews in the series, *Advanced Organizational Management* will be a successful tool because of the contributions, critiques, and dedicated efforts of many individuals who have helped in one way or another.

The International Association of Administrative Professionals (IAAP), through the Institute for Certification, has not only provided the incentive for the development of this review but also valuable input during the review process. We are sincerely grateful for the continued support and endorsement of IAAP and the Institute in the development and revision of the series.

Specifically, we acknowledge the contributions of Mary E. Barefoot, ECPI College of Technology, Virginia, and Pam Silvers, Asheville-Buncombe Technical Community College for their helpful reviews and critiques of the manuscript. In addition, the continued support of Kathy L. Schoneboom CPS/CAP, Certification Manager, IAAP, is much appreciated. Diane Garrison of Kentucky State University was extremely helpful in setting early versions of the manuscript in the outline feature in which the entire manuscript is organized.

Lastly, we appreciate the editorial staff of, Prentice Hall, and the many contributions of Deborah Hoffman, Project Manager, and Carol Mull, the Series Editor, in coordinating the reviews and critiques of the manuscript. With their help, we were able to identify and interpret the kinds of information needed by secretaries and administrative professionals to appropriately prepare for the CPS and CAP Examinations.

We hope that all the input provided by professionals and incorporated in the manuscript content for this review will help candidates everywhere in their preparation for the CPS and CAP Examinations.

Mark Garrison, Ph.D.

Margaret Bly Turner, Ph.D.

CERTIFIED PROFESSIONAL SECRETARY®
CERTIFIED ADMINISTRATION PROFESSIONAL®
EXAMINATION REVIEW SERIES

ADVANCED ORGANIZATIONAL MANAGEMENT

Chapter 1

Critical Thinking and Decision-Making Processes

OVERVIEW

Decision making is the most important and difficult task that all managers confront. Most decisions are made in an atmosphere in which there is uncertainty, risk, time pressure, imperfect information, and a lack of knowledge as to responses. Decision making is a part of all the management functions: planning, organizing, leading, and controlling. The use or misuse of communications and risk helps one identify those managers who are effective as well as those who are ineffective. Decision making occurs at all levels in an organization, managers and nonmanagers alike.

People make decisions constantly: at home, at work, and at play. Not all decisions made at work, about work, are organizational decisions. The focus here is on those decisions made in the name of the organization by managers. These may be decisions to adopt goals, allocate resources, or appoint persons to positions—all within the organization. The work of the most dedicated and hardworking employees will not produce effective results unless there are creative decisions and plans, appropriate and efficient organization, and coordination of all those hardworking people.

In economies dominated by private enterprise, decisions (economic, legal—political, social–cultural, or technological) that affect the production and distribution of goods and services are almost entirely in the hands of individual managers of business organizations. In countries where major decisions are made by governmental agencies, public bureaucrats perform decision-making processes. In both systems, some of the same factors must be taken into consideration. There is legal and social concern for the competence and social responsibility exhibited by managers when decision-making processes are used in the performance of their managerial functions.

KEY TERMS

A. Organizational Decision Making

The manager's primary function is **decision making**—the process through which he or she identifies and solves problems creatively, a process that involves making appropriate and rational decisions. Managers and other organizational decision makers need to foster the implementation of creative decisions that affect the entire organization. People today are eager to gain more control of the decisions that shape their jobs as well as their lives. However, differences do exist between the way an individual makes personal decisions and what is involved in making an organizational decision.

1. *Theories of Managerial Decision Making:* Perhaps the most commonly applied theories of managerial decision making are the **classical theory of decision making** and the **behavioral (administrative) theory of decision making.** Classical theory represents an *ideal* model of decision making, with maximizing outcomes as a primary goal. **Maximizing** is the process of making a decision that is aimed at realizing the best possible outcome on one dimension—seeking the best answer. Often, the time and resources available do not permit this to occur. Managers known for maximizing their decisions typically are in the middle hierarchical management levels. Maximizing is most often used with nonprogrammed decisions, but some managers try to maximize with programmed decision making as well. Administrative theory describes how managers actually make decisions in business situations with uncertain outcomes where satisficing is necessary.

   EXAMPLE: *Conducting exhaustive studies on the type of upgrade for software packages that the company uses.*

   Satisficing is almost the extreme opposite. In **satisficing,** the manager adopts the solution that minimally meets the objectives, often found in the first acceptable option that arises. Alternatives are not studied much when satisficing is used. Satisficing is very commonly used and appropriate with programmed and recurring decisions.

   EXAMPLE: *Purchasing software without reviewing whether the same needs exist this year as last year.*

   Optimizing involves the selection of the best alternative from a range of options that have been evaluated within the existing time and price constraints. Optimizing involves the use of the classical decision-making model more than the other two types of strategies.

   EXAMPLE: *Selecting a particular brand of computers to buy for use within the entire office from a range of six major options and within the time allotted.*

   a. *Characteristics of classical theory:* Real people in real situations have difficulty applying an ideal model of decision making. Such a model dictates how managers *should* make decisions according to ideal standards under perfect conditions. Managers are expected to make rational decisions, based on complete information, that are in the best economic interests of the organization. They are expected to gather information, examine this information objectively, consider all alternative solutions, and make an appropriate choice of alternatives that will lead to the best possible outcome for the organization. Managers who are "left-brain thinkers" tend to arrive at logical and analytical decisions and perhaps are stronger advocates of classical theory.

1. *Identification of the problem:* A definite problem is clearly stated and defined, with objectives for solving that problem fully developed.

2. *Presence of certainty:* The amount of risk is clearly evident and easily determined. The manager is certain of the amount of risk involved in the decision to be made.

3. *Information about alternatives:* Gathering complete information about the problem is paramount. A full set of information about each alternative becomes available, and the expected outcomes for each alternative are determined. The manager spends considerable time and effort researching the problem and compiling complete information about the problem and the alternatives.

4. *Maximization of outcomes:* The direct application of classical theory results in a rational choice of alternative(s) in relation to the maximization of outcomes. The manager's goal is to attempt to make the *ideal* decision.

The classical model is considered the *normative* model because it defines *how* a particular decision maker should make decisions. The model provides guidelines for reaching an ideal outcome for the organization. The value of applying this model is shown best when relevant information is available, probabilities can be calculated, and decisions can be made with known certainty and risk.

b. *Behavioral (administrative) theory of decision making:* The behavioral (administrative) model, based on the work of Herbert A. Simon, describes *how* managers actually make decisions in business situations. This model incorporates two basic concepts, bounded rationality and satisficing, and is based on assumptions that are different from those pertaining to classical theory. Managers who are "right-brain thinkers" tend to rely more on intuitive and creative pursuits in their decision-making processes and may be more apt to follow a behavioral (administrative) model.

1. *Identification of the problem:* A problem exists and is identified, but there is difficulty in determining clearly what the problem is and defining it. Vagueness engulfs the objectives as well.

2. *Presence of uncertainty and intuition:* This theory appears to be more realistic than the classical model for more complex decisions that are nonprogrammable. Uncertainty about the outcome exists because there is only incomplete information available for the manager to consider in making a decision. Sometimes the manager must use intuition, based on personal experience, without conscious knowledge of possible outcomes.

3. *Information about alternatives:* Only limited information is available about alternative solutions and the expected outcomes of each alternative. Therefore, managers are limited on how rational their decisions can be. They can

only process the information that is available to make decisions. Managers are functioning within **bounded rationality,** recognizing that decisions must be made as rationally as possible with only limited information available.

4. *Satisficing decision making:* Managers select the alternative solution that satisfies *minimal* decision criteria and seems "good enough," although certainly not perfect or ideal. Intuition plays an important part, too, in the manager's decision-making process.

The behavioral (administrative) theory of decision making recognizes human and environmental limitations affecting a manager's ability to make rational business decisions.

Recent research into decision-making processes within business organizations has found classical procedures, based on rational managerial decisions, to be associated with high performance for organizations in stable environments. Behavioral (administrative) procedures have been associated with high performance in unstable environments where decisions must be made under more complex and difficult conditions and within a short period of time.

2. *Types of Decisions:* All individuals and organizations are faced with various decisions on a recurring basis. Some of these decisions require totally new approaches to solving previously unresolved problems. Other decisions can rely on precedents or previously established procedures to help the individuals making them. The two basic types of decisions to be made are **programmed decisions** and **nonprogrammed decisions.**

a. *Programmed decisions:* Decisions made routinely on a recurring basis most often do not require huge expenditures and are less complex in nature. Often, the decision makers recognize the situation and factors involved in programmed decisions. Precedents may have already been established to help these individuals make the appropriate decisions.

EXAMPLES:

> *Buying paper for the copier*
> *Stocking the supply cabinet in each office*

b. *Nonprogrammed decisions:* Decisions that are nonprogrammed have no precedents and represent situations that have not been dealt with previously or, if so, only on a limited basis within the organization. Nonprogrammed decisions have no rules, procedures, or policies for the decision makers to follow. Usually, they are unstructured and require more time as well as creativity and intuition to be solved.

EXAMPLES:

> *A decision needs to be made whether or not to adopt a new artificial intelligence program, which is attractively priced. At present, few individuals within the organization know how to work with such a program.*
> *The board of directors is considering whether or not to liquidate the assets of the corporation and cease doing business or to merge with another company.*

3. *Personal Versus Organizational Decisions:* In making personal decisions, one may choose to behave rationally or irrationally in making personal decisions,—that is, to behave or not to behave by rules of logic. While individuals may set out to act in a fully rational manner, most often emotional forces and interpersonal determinants as well as intuition play significant roles in the decisions that are finally made. There are occasions to make personal decisions at work. The decision to make personal contacts

at work and therefore personal decisions needs to follow careful protocol to make sure that the two areas do not collide.

4. ***Business Decisions:*** When making business decisions, managers and other organization leaders, in contrast, are expected to act in a totally rational manner, emotions notwithstanding. The moral responsibility of management requires the use of one's best capabilities in making decisions that affect the work lives of others in the organization and the well-being of the organization itself. However, at the same time, to imply that managers make decisions based strictly on rational factors is sheer nonsense. Emotions and intuition also enter into the making of business decisions. The higher up the hierarchical ladder that managers go, the more they rely on intuition and less on systematic processes in their decision making. Yet, this intuition may incorporate a "nanosecond version" of the systematic process as well as experience and previously acquired feelings.

   a. *Need for rational behavior:* Managers are expected to behave rationally—to follow a well-established logical process—in making organizational decisions. The ability that managers have to view situations objectively rather than subjectively determines their success, especially in examining facts in a rational, rather than emotional, manner.

   b. *Use of decision-making aids:* Managers are also expected to know and to use computers and appropriate aids to decision making, such as statistics and decision trees. The widespread growth and usage of computers has brought about more sophisticated and accurate tools for providing better information to use in making decisions.

Objective and subjective judgments are frequently necessary in making appropriate decisions. However, the subjectivity involved in perceiving various alternatives and in defining the problem itself cannot be ignored. Thus most decisions combine objectivity and subjectivity.

Check Point—Section A

Directions: For each question, circle the correct answer.

A–1. When a manager collects information, examines the information objectively, considers all alternative solutions, and makes an appropriate choice of the alternatives, the decision-making theory is called

A) behavioral theory
B) personal theory
C) classical theory
D) creative theory

A–2. Managers who are right-brain thinkers tend to rely more on intuitive and creative pursuits and therefore are more apt to use which one of the following theories of decision making?

A) Behavioral (administrative) theory
B) Personal theory
C) Classical theory
D) Logical theory

A–3. After September 11, 2001, many businesses were faced with making decisions about their security that had never been made before. These decisions were

A) programmed decisions
B) personal decisions
C) nonprogrammed decisions
D) hiring decisions

B. Critical Thinking

Critical thinking, by definition, means using evidence and reason to evaluate claims, dilemmas, or choice options. Rational decision making requires critical thinking. Some decisions are made routinely, based on the repetitious occurrence of problems or situations. As previously stated, these are known as programmed decisions. Other scenarios present situations that are unique, unanticipated, have wide implications, and have not been encountered before. A more detailed process is required to define, analyze, and solve these nonprogrammed decisions.

1. *The Scientific Method:* The steps of critical thinking are essentially those usually described as the **scientific method.** This method of research follows scientific rules so that knowledge can be obtained in an unbiased manner. The great power of scientific research and invention over the past few centuries is attributed by many people to increased application of the scientific method in the Western world. The belief in the power of rationality is so deeply held by some people that they assume good decisions will result if the prescribed process is followed.

2. *Logical Reasoning Using the Scientific Process:* The steps in the scientific process are deceptively simple in number and title. The application of these steps, however, can become incredibly complex.

   a. *Identifying and defining the problem:* This is the *most important* step in decision making. Sometimes this step seems easy because the problem is obvious.

      EXAMPLES:

      > *A broken copy machine*
      >
      > *A late shipment of goods*

      The deceptive simplicity can cause one of the major failures in decision making: confusing symptom with cause, then "solving" the symptom.

      EXAMPLE: *If the problem is identified as a broken copy machine, the ensuing decision process will focus on repair or replacement of the machine. A more complete look into the circumstances surrounding the breakdown may reveal the presence of a causal factor which, if not corrected, will predictably cause another machine or the same machine to break again. It must be determined if the copier is not adequate for the use, too old to continue reliably, and so on. Is it possibly human error?*

      1. *Reasons for failure to identify real causes:* A major reason for failing to identify the real causes of problems is haste. Sometimes the person who perceives and defines the problem is pressured into haste by an overload of work. Aside from work pressure, there is in all of us a discomfort with ambiguous, vague, and ill-defined situations.

      2. *Results of failure to identify real cause:* There are many unfortunate outcomes likely to follow the failure to identify the correct cause and address it with a solution:

         a. Obviously, the real cause is neither addressed nor removed.

         b. The decision maker who believes the problem to be solved relaxes her or his guard against a recurrence and thus becomes more vulnerable to its recurrence.

         c. Some person or thing is addressed in the solution of the symptom (the incorrectly defined problem).

     d. Persons who are directly or indirectly affected by the incorrect action are likely to feel proper indignation and to respond with some form of resentful and retaliatory behavior.

     e. Finally, unless the causal factor disappears on its own, it will recreate the same problem at a later date.

The normal desire is to put a name to things, to assign a meaning to the puzzling event by identifying it or associating it with similar events one has known. It takes real psychic effort to resist this tendency to "effect closure"—the psychological term for resolving the cognitive dissonance or inner conflict—by assigning a meaning or making the causal connections that explain what is disturbing the mental peace. Only when a decision maker becomes convinced of the seriousness of jumping to conclusions is she or he likely to be willing to suffer the discomfort of inner uncertainty long enough to gather sufficient information to be more accurate.

b. *Gathering information about the problem:* Great care should be taken to investigate fully the circumstances surrounding the event that is perceived to be the problem. This is the time for challenging all prior assumptions and beliefs about the problematic event.

EXAMPLES:

    In the previous example of the broken copy machine, questions should be raised about whether that machine is even needed. So often the decision is made to fix or correct a deficiency just because the item, procedure, or arrangement has been there in the past. No one ever challenges the necessity for its continued existence.

    At times the problem that arises is a failure to meet a production quota or a quality target in items produced. A hasty acceptance of the fact of the undesirable variance will lead to a search for the "villain" or "villains" who are at fault in order to correct individual performance. Often, the production quota or the quality target was set too high in the first place. The failure in performance, in this case, is a symptom of the real cause.

c. *Developing alternative solutions:* The way the problem was defined and the types of information gathered are guided by an implicit and explicit objective to be attained by solving the problem. Sometimes the objective seems absolutely obvious: repair the broken machine! (As shown above, even that apparently clear-cut imperative should be challenged.) Most decision situations provide far greater latitude for the decision maker to follow individual desires in setting the objective to be achieved. The state of feeling dissatisfaction with current conditions starts the logical process. Clear acknowledgment of what one does *not* want rarely gives the answer to what one *does* want. Any decision to change opens one to the question of changing to what? to where?

    1. *Need for clear objectives:* To develop alternative solutions, a clear statement of the objective, which any alternative action is expected to meet, with more or less appropriate information, must be developed. The objective should have been explicit in the first step, as the problem is defined, in order to guide the collection of appropriate information. The less clear the objective before the information gatherers, the more opportunity they have to affect the possible outcomes through the types of information they do or do not collect.

2. *Need for creative solutions:* Another feature of the human personality that comes into play in this phase of the process with immense significance is **creativity.** Psychology as yet has little exact scientific explanation for the functioning of human creative capacity. It can and does tell us, though, that there are wide differences in human creativity and that there are activities that can predictably increase creativity.

   a. *Brainstorming:* This technique has been designed to help individuals become freer in exercising their creativity. Brainstorming is used to generate ideas in the decision process. The word *brainstorm* properly conjures the image of lightning, flashing from out-of-the-blue, rapid and definite. The expectation is that persons who are provided encouragement and facilitating circumstances will direct their psychic energies into producing new ideas. A major use of the technique is in the development of alternatives in decision situations. The technique is surprisingly simple, the rules and requirements few.

      • Persons who are expected to be motivated to find a solution to the problem are brought together for the purpose of naming as many alternatives as possible in a short period.

      • The rules require that the idea be given by the one who thinks of it.

      • Neither the one making the suggestion nor any other group member may offer any criticism or other discussion of the idea during the brainstorming session's idea-generation stage.

      • A group leader functions to steer the process back into the spontaneous flow of positive ideas if digression into criticism or discussion begins.

      • A recorder captures the ideas as they are presented.

   b. *Brainwriting:* A variation known as brainwriting is used to get individuals to write down their ideas independently before the group's ideas are compiled. The collective list that results is the culmination of every group member's individual creativity. Once the composite list is formed, the entire group can review and critique each of the ideas.

3. *Need for alternative scenarios:* An analytical method that is gaining widespread popularity for futuristic planning is the development of alternative or contingent scenarios. Several alternatives are developed, each one based on a different set of assumptions. A logical sequence is developed for each alternative, with results clearly described. The primary advantage of this method is the ability of the manager to examine a number of possibilities rather than selecting only one path to follow. Different plans can be devised to fit different scenarios. A manager needs a minimum of two alternatives. If only one solution is identified, the search for information relative to other solutions must go on. Computerized tools such as spreadsheets make the use of alternative scenarios a relatively easy and commonplace process.

Whatever technique has been used to generate alternatives, the decision maker or the decision-making group turns next to evaluating the alternatives.

d. *Evaluating alternatives:* The process of decision making is improved when the problem and possible alternative solutions are presented for evaluation. The test of logic requires that each alternative, although based on a different set of assumptions, be evaluated according to the same set of standards. The logical sequence for each alternative must be reviewed as well. Because the purpose of the decision-making process is aimed at achieving the objective, it is at this stage that the objective must be made clear and unambiguous in order to derive clear standards for measuring alternatives. These standards, generally called *decision criteria*, may be stated in quantitative and/or qualitative terms. Where a number of decision criteria must be met, it is usually necessary to prioritize them to clarify the relative significance of each. Many analytic techniques provide help in defining and applying the criteria.

EXAMPLE: *Adams is interviewing applicants for the position of administrator to the vice president of finance. Decision criteria were established first: the level of education required, skills, and personal qualities or traits. Then Adams was ready to examine the applications to begin the evaluation process.*

1. *Statistical analysis:* The term *statistics* is used generally to mean data (characteristics) for a sample (a subset) of a population. The technical meaning of the data is related to the problem being studied. *Statistical analysis* is a set of methods or techniques for collecting, organizing, and interpreting the data. Conclusions may be drawn about their probable meanings. The way data are displayed can aid the reader to derive meanings from the data.

   a. *Graphs:* Data may be organized and presented in terms of two characteristics: the most common plot or the total volume per time period.

      EXAMPLE: *Visual inspection of the line graph can lead one to "draw" an imaginary trend line when data are graphically displayed in this way.*

   b. *Tables:* Data are organized into arrays by chronology, size, location, or some other characteristic.

      EXAMPLE: *When there is a variation in the number of occurrences or events of the factor being studied, a frequency distribution can be very useful. This distribution, as shown in a table, illustrates how many times a certain item appears in comparison to other items. An array of test scores (see Figure 1–1) can be paralleled by a column in which the number of persons earning that score is arrayed.*

FIGURE 1–1　Example of Frequency Distribution.

Test Score	Frequency
100	1
99	0
98	4
97	3
96	7
95	3
94	4
93	2
92	1
91	0
90	2
	27

FIGURE 1–2 Example of Sequential Frequency Distribution.

Number of Cars per Household	Frequency of Households
5+	2,000,000
4	10,000,000
3	15,000,000
2	30,000,000
1	35,000,000
0	10,000,000
	102,000,000

When the frequency distribution is arrayed sequentially by the score, or measured factor, it is possible to see the two extremes and to get a rough idea where the average is likely to fall. One might array data in a hypothetical example as shown in Figure 1–2.

EXAMPLE: *Visual inspection suggests that the average number of cars owned per household is between 1 and 2. A more accurate estimate can be made by calculating a weighted average. The sum of the products of frequency times the number of cars owned, divided by the sum of the frequencies, yields 1.86 cars per household.*

Statisticians have developed rules by which *inferences* and *predictions* about future occurrences can be drawn once a frequency distribution has been developed. Essentially, the rules are derived from assumptions about what occurrences random chance would account for.

EXAMPLE: *In the example above, one might ask: What is the likelihood that the next person I meet will own 1 car? 2 cars? 3 cars? 4 cars? 5 cars? or more?*

Inferential statistics provide techniques for calculating the odds, or probabilities, that certain events will happen.

c. *Payoff tables or matrices:* The results of a comparison of different alternatives can be shown in a payoff table or matrix. Such a matrix arranges information so that comparisons of all possible outcomes of a problem can be examined simultaneously. The reliability of this strategy depends on the accuracy of the values used and the probabilities assigned to the variables identified. Computers have made the preparation of payoff tables and matrices a much simpler process. A sample matrix is shown in Figure 1–3.

2. *Operations research:* Operations research (OR) includes a wide range of mathematical formulas and techniques for analyzing complex decision problems. Sometimes the amount of information about a particular problem is so large that the human mind cannot manipulate it all simultaneously. Operations researchers develop mathematical expressions to represent each major factor in the situation, then solve the resulting formula according to the objective which has been established. *Linear programming* is used to find the best (or optimum) answer to situations where many known elements may be put together in different combinations that may yield different profits.

FIGURE 1–3 Payoff Table or Matrix.

Decision	Outcome				
	1	2	3	4	5
1	$P_{1\text{-}1}$	$P_{1\text{-}2}$	$P_{1\text{-}3}$	$P_{1\text{-}4}$	$P_{1\text{-}5}$
2	$P_{2\text{-}1}$	$P_{2\text{-}2}$	$P_{2\text{-}3}$	$P_{2\text{-}4}$	$P_{2\text{-}5}$
3	$P_{3\text{-}1}$	$P_{3\text{-}2}$	$P_{3\text{-}3}$	$P_{3\text{-}4}$	$P_{3\text{-}5}$
4	$P_{4\text{-}1}$	$P_{4\text{-}2}$	$P_{4\text{-}3}$	$P_{4\text{-}4}$	$P_{4\text{-}5}$

Note: P, payoff value.

EXAMPLE: *With a given amount of cookie dough, labor, and oven space, what mix of plain cookies and iced cookies will produce the highest profit? This is a highly simplified example of the types of problems linear programming routinely solves.*

3. *Qualitative factors:* By definition, *qualitative factors* are those which cannot be measured directly in quantitative terms. Situations or problems can be described in terms of the certainty or uncertainty of the information one has or can get about the situation as well as the risk to be taken when alternatives are considered.

   a. *Certainty:* For the decision maker to be certain, all possible alternatives must be known, direct and predictable methods for comparing the effects of each alternative must be available, and all possible outcomes must be known. Analysis and choice in decision making are simple in these circumstances.

   Unfortunately, very few situations fit these requirements. Questions such as "what is the least expensive way to ship a package from point A to point B?" are in the realm of certainty. Questions of certainty, however, are not the most significant or most troubling of decision problems.

   • *Uncertainty:* At the other extreme of information availability is the condition of uncertainty. In the extreme uncertain condition, we have little or no information about possible alternatives or outcomes.

   EXAMPLE: *An individual is faced with a choice of crossroads in a foreign land, with no map and no one in sight who can be asked for directions.*

   • *Limited certainty:* More frequently, the decision maker has some knowledge about some alternatives but has little information about outcomes or their likelihoods.

   EXAMPLE: *Preparing for a first examination given by a new instructor places a student in this situation. The student is aware of personal capabilities and study habits; the text material is given. Major alternatives are to prepare for an objective exam, a short-answer exam, or an essay exam. Obviously, there are different approaches to studying for each of the three major exam types, carrying different time and effort implications. With no past history or current information on the instructor's plan for the test, the student is in a state of uncertainty.*

   b. *Risk:* Where alternatives, the possible outcomes, and the probabilities of those outcomes occurring are known, the problem can be converted to one of "gambling" or risk.

      EXAMPLE: *If the problem is to drive somewhere in a fixed period of time with two alternative routes, the uncertainty about the necessity of getting there on time can be "cured" by information. Route A requires the most time, but has no known hazards (train crossings and roadwork). Route B is shorter but has a busy train crossing. If experience indicates that there is a 75 percent chance of hazard (train crossing or roadwork) on Route B, and a 25 percent chance on Route A, one can now calculate the odds on each of the routes and know the associated risk one is taking.*

      It is exactly in the condition of uncertainty that most significant decisions must be made. Qualitative factor analysis becomes doubly important in these conditions. Attitudes and preferences of persons who can affect the outcomes are important and can frequently be measured in some fashion.

      EXAMPLE: *A very important area of uncertainty for many industries is the question of when new technological innovation can be expected. Clearly, history cannot answer this question directly. Yet the company that can anticipate changes in technology and take action now to acquire the innovation has a decided advantage.*

4. *Analytical tools for decision making:* Development of decision trees, the use of such techniques as the Delphi technique, or the application of computer software programs may be helpful analytical tools.

   a. *Decision trees:* A decision tree is a powerful method of graphing complex decision problems, particularly those in which one is considering a sequence of decisions to be made across a period of time. The first decision commits one to follow A or B paths; following either has a different impact on the next decision's outcomes. These combined effects get too complex to visualize mentally, so decision trees are used to provide a systematic visualization.

      The most common decision-making tree was developed by Vroom and Yetton. Referred to as the **Vroom model,** this model helps determine the optimal amount of subordinate participation desired in the decision-making process. It has been modified by Vroom and Jago. A decision tree based on a hypothetical example is shown in Figure 1–4.

      As the model has expanded, it has become more complicated. A computer model has been created to assist managers in following the decision model.

      EXAMPLE: *Peterson is considering taking a yearlong CAP review course at a cost of $400. Peterson believes that there is a 90 percent chance of passing the CAP examination. The manager would recognize the achievement with a $2,500 salary increase. On the other hand, the present planned raise is $360 for next year.*

FIGURE 1–4 Decision Tree.

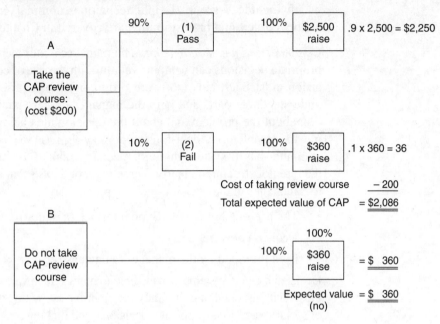

An analysis of the situation starts at the left in Figure 1–4, with the first decision: to take or not to take the CAP review course. Since the desire is to make the decision in light of later occurrences or decisions, Peterson evaluates the expected value of each path.

$$
\begin{array}{lll}
A_1\ (.90 \times 1.00 \times \$2,500) & = & \$\quad 2,250 \\
A_2\ (.10 \times 1.00 \times \$360) & = & +\quad 36 \\
\text{Cost of review course} & = & -\quad 400 \\[1em]
\text{Total expected value of} & & \\
\text{taking CPS exam} & = & \$\quad 1,886 \\[1em]
B_1\ (1.00 \times \$360) & = & \\[1em]
\text{expected value of not} & & \\
\text{taking CPS course} & = & \$\quad 360
\end{array}
$$

Note the $400 expense is incurred whether the exam is passed or not. Without the expense of the review course ($400), the expected value is $2,286 (.90 × 2,500) + (.10 × 360). The $400 expense of taking the review course needs to be subtracted from $2,286 to arrive at the expected value of $1,886.

Of course, there is no estimate of the alternate value of Peterson's use of spare time in the example above. If, for example, Peterson is willing to do contract work in his spare time, that factor would be included as an offset to the $400 investment in A and added to the $360 expected raise in B. As it is, Peterson's decision should be to take the course if qualitative factors are to guide the decision. On the other hand, Peterson may accept the above information but still put a higher value on the qualitative factor of preserving his spare time for leisure or other activities. In that case the aid received from the decision tree is a clearer understanding of the cost of that spare time.

    b. *Decision making using groups:* Group problem-solving techniques, which include T-group, Delphi technique, nominal group technique, quality circles, and brainstorming, are covered in Chapter 8.

    c. *Computerized decision making:* The manager's judgment in making appropriate decisions can be improved through the use of computerized decision aids. Such aids (software programs) break problems into more understandable parts and help the manager process additional information about the problem and about the decision aids being used to examine the problem. A decision support system (DSS) is an interactive computer-based system that aids decision makers in solving problems that are not structured clearly. Three parts of a DSS that are of most help to a manager in the decision-making process are:

- The use of a human–machine interface (a dialog)
- Decision aids (models)
- Data provided by the manager (a database)

Decision support systems provide help to managers in various ways: retrieving data items, obtaining summary information, estimating the consequences of specific decisions, proposing decisions, and making routine decisions.

    e. *Choosing an alternative:* Once the alternatives have been developed as fully as possible, in terms that reveal the probable consequences of each, the final step is to choose among them. Since decisions in organizations almost always require the use of resources for implementation, the chosen alternative is performed by the managers who have authority over those resources. The manager may choose to perform this function alone or through a committee, but the final responsibility will be the manager's.

1. *The use of judgment:* Although quantitative aids may have been used extensively in the prior steps, rarely will the results of such forecasts and calculations make the choice of one alternative over the others clear-cut or automatic. Judgment is almost always needed in addition to the use of quantitative data.

2. *Consideration for possible negative consequences:* In comparing alternatives, possible negative consequences of each alternative should be taken into account, along with the more obvious positive possible outcomes. Sometimes the alternative with the highest possible payoff also has the highest possible risk of adverse consequences. These may be quantitative or qualitative in nature.

EXAMPLE: *An opportunity to win $1 million may have a 95 percent probability, whereas the probability of losing is only 5 percent. But if the price of losing is $50,000, and that amount would be impossible for you to raise, this alternative would not be chosen because of the possible adverse consequences.*

3. *Personal values:* Personal bias, attitude toward risk, ambition, fear of public opinion—these and a whole host of individual psychological predispositions come into play in the act of choosing whenever one alternative is not outstandingly superior. There is really no way to exclude personal values from decision making.

EXAMPLES:

In the case of businesses that are individual proprietorships or partnerships, the overriding goal of the owner–decision maker is to fulfill personal goals.

In corporate forms of business, managers accept the moral obligation to make decisions with the best possible skill to achieve optimum results for the organization.

The more uncertain the decision situation, the more difficult it is for managers to avoid the temptation to follow the dictates of their personal agendas rather than to choose in favor of the organization's objectives.

4. *The use of groups or committees for implementation:* Frequently, the concurrence of a group of people is necessary to implement a decision. Where this is true, a manager will do one of two things to ensure the necessary commitment.

 a. Parties interested in the decision may be consulted prior to making the choice, and the choice will be constrained to those alternatives that are feasible in light of the group's willingness to support them.

 b. On the other hand, the decision maker may frankly acknowledge the power of influential organization members and include them in a committee, which makes the choice on a consensus basis.

 Either way, a political process is being used to arrive at the choice. Compromise, trading votes, filibustering, coalition-building—all the typical techniques made familiar by governmental decision making—are involved in the process of making important decisions.

f. *Implementing the decision:* Once a decision has been made, steps for appropriate implementation need to be developed. The manager's responsibility in implementing the decision to solve an identified problem includes tasks such as the following:

 1. Acquiring resources needed for the implementation

 2. Allocating resources to individuals, departments, or other groups

 3. Establishing schedules and budgets for the implementation to take place

 4. Assigning specific task responsibilities to individuals or to groups

 5. Identifying potential risks during the early stages of implementation

 6. Developing detailed plans for dealing with any risks or uncertainties that may develop

 7. Establishing procedures and schedules for receiving progress reports from individuals or groups involved

 8. Preparing to correct the implementation process if additional problems arise

 A manager needs to take time to reexamine the decision at any point during the implementation phase. A decision is no better than the actions taken to implement that decision and make it a reality.

g. *Monitoring the decision:* Once the decision is implemented, information must be gathered on how well the changed process is working. Any actions taken to implement a decision need to be monitored closely.

 1. *Feedback:* Monitoring is useful whether the feedback is positive or negative. Positive feedback will indicate that the decision was an appropriate one, the process should be continued, or perhaps it should be utilized in other areas of the organization as well. Negative feedback may mean that the decision was a poor one or that implementation requires even more effort, time, or resources.

2. *Internal and external environments:* Monitoring allows managers to examine the internal and external environments carefully to determine what is happening as a result of the decision that has been made. Internally, managers need to find out exactly what subordinates have been doing and generally what the results of implementing the decision are. Externally, the organization needs to be aware of how competing organizations are reacting to the decision.

If the decision appears to have been an appropriate one to make, the process can continue to the final outcome. If the decision seems to have been a poor one, the problem may need to be redefined and the process cycled back to the first step so that the decision process begins again. This process is also referred to as evaluation of decision-making outcomes.

EXAMPLE: *In the example of the broken copy machine, if a repair has been done and it lasts only two days; the decision to repair the machine needs to be reconsidered by starting from the very beginning of the process.*

3. ***Logical Thinking Patterns:*** Logical reasoning results in patterns of thinking that add value to information by increasing the number of facts available that may affect decisions. Most people regard a logical mind as a positive attribute.

    a. *Inductive reasoning:* Sometimes thought processes move from specific premises to one or more general conclusions. Inductive reasoning first of all defines the problem and then moves to identify factors or variables inherent in the problem. Hypotheses are formed that can be supported by primary data, leading to specific findings and one or more general conclusions. In inductive reasoning, thinking moves from specific to general, from known to unknown.

    b. *Deductive reasoning:* In deductive reasoning, thought processes move from a general premise toward specific conclusions. Starting with a thought process that presents a problem very generally, variables are identified, accounted for, and explained one at a time. The process moves from general to specific, from unknown to known, until one or more specific conclusions can be drawn.

    c. *Comparison:* Similar objects or attributes can be compared using a set of criteria established for the observations. The key is to use the same procedures for comparing all objects or attributes being investigated. Otherwise, bias results in the application of the criteria to the entire sample of objects or attributes.

    d. *Causation:* Perhaps the most difficult thought process is one that tries to establish cause and effect. "If A occurs, then [something] happens to B." Specific facts about A and B are obtained through inference. The problem sometimes is to have enough facts about the relationship of A and B for the inference to be accurate.

Logical thinking processes such as those identified here require that the problem be accurately identified, not just symptoms of the problem. More time is required to identify the problem and to be thorough in establishing relationships between specific facts or variables contained in the problem. For example, in deductive reasoning, if the basic premises on which a problem is based are true, then the conclusion drawn will be true, also. However, if these premises are false, then the conclusions drawn will be false, too.

Check Point—Section B

Directions: For each question, circle the correct answer.

B–1. The steps in the scientific method, in order, are

A) evaluate alternatives, choose an alternative, develop solutions, and develop alternatives

B) create responses to problem, ask for advice, and make decisions

C) evaluate economic consequences of business, identify problem, and choose an alternative

D) identify and define the problem, gather information, develop alternative solutions, evaluate alternatives, and choose an alternative

B–2. Which one of the following types of information cannot be quantified?

A) Qualitative data

B) Operations factors

C) Numeric items

D) Limited certainty

B–3. Which one of the following is *not* an analytical tool for decision making?

A) Personal values

B) Decision trees

C) T-groups

D) Computerized decision making

C. Creative Thinking in Organizational Decision Making

The close relationship of creative thinking and innovation is very important in organizational decision making. **Creativity** is the generation of new ideas, whereas **innovation** is the translation of a new idea into a new product, a new service, a new method of production, or even a new organization. Organizations that fail to be creative or innovative probably will not survive. Creativity and innovation need to be encouraged and fostered by individuals and organizations.

1. *Individual Creativity:* The manager has the awesome task of identifying people within the organization who are creative and fostering that creativity for the benefit of the individual and the organization. Highly creative people tend to be:

   a. More original in thought and ideas generated than less creative individuals

   b. Willing to shift from one approach to another when trying to solve a problem

   c. More flexible and less rigid with regard to time, resources, and effort devoted to the problem

   d. More independent in their pursuit of solutions to a problem

   e. More apt to disobey orders that make little or no sense to them

   Highly creative people are often more difficult to manage within most organizations. Because they sometimes question authority, creative people have a difficult time being "yes" people—doing whatever the manager orders or commands them to do. They typically need little supervision in getting a job done and typically prefer tackling complex problems.

2. ***The Creative Process in Organizations:*** From the generation of new ideas through the implementation phase of the process, the talents of individuals or groups within the organization are expressed through the introduction of new products, services, or processes.

   a. *Idea generation:* Ideas may be the response to conditions in the marketplace—a product needed to fill a void or a service to accompany a new product. Dissatisfaction with an existing product may lead to potential demand for a new product. Ideas can be generated from a variety of sources: outside consultants, employees who keep up-to-date on markets and technology, or new employees bringing ideas from the external environment. Brainstorming is a technique often used in the generation of new ideas. Brainstorming is covered in more detail later in this text.

   b. *Idea development or problem solving:* Within an organization, the development of creative ideas can be supported or inhibited, depending on the processes already functioning within the organizational culture. Some organizations are more receptive than others in considering creative ideas for processes and products. If a rational problem-solving approach is used, creative ideas will be recognized and developed more fully than in organizations where creativity is stymied. Technology like decision support systems or expert systems assists with storing ideas, retrieving ideas, and communicating among departments and individuals throughout the organization.

   c. *Implementation of creative ideas:* Often a high degree of integration is required among various units of the organization when new ideas are implemented. Technical specialists, administrative professionals, and financial experts are enlisted to monitor costs, processes, and people. Frequent communication among individuals and groups involved in the implementation relates positively to the rate at which innovative change may occur. Innovation must be introduced on time, within budget, and for an identified market.

   d. *Monitoring of innovation:* As with any other business decision, close monitoring of the implementation of a creative idea is absolutely necessary to ensure that the goals of the organization are met. Monitoring enables the organization to examine the results to see if further research is needed, the number of units being produced needs to be increased, a process needs to be revised, or whether the new idea will generate sufficient profits.

The creative decision-making process in organizations requires a more permissive atmosphere to encourage the exploration of new ideas and new ways of doing things. Managers have the capability of either fostering the intrapreneurial spirit among employees through encouraging creative efforts or stifling the innovative efforts of subordinates who have creative ideas that would benefit the organization greatly.

Check Point—Section C

Directions: For each question, circle the correct answer.

C–1. The generation of new ideas refers to
   A) decision making
   B) creativity
   C) productive thinking
   D) critical thinking

C–2. Which one of the following can be described as the translation of a new idea into a new product, service, or even a new organization?
   A) Innovation
   B) Creativity

C) Critical thinking
D) Entrepreneurial spirit

C–3. A manager takes the view that no matter how good an idea, there must be evidence for it being successful.

This thought explains the importance of which one of the following?

A) Entrepreneurial spirit
B) Creativity
C) Being receptive
D) Monitoring innovation

For Your Review

Directions: For each question, circle the correct answer.

Case 1: Microchip Downturn

Smith and Cho own and manage a midsized microchip manufacturing facility. Although the company has maintained the highest quality ratings for the past several decades, there are emerging problems with employee satisfaction, waste, productivity, and customer satisfaction recently. Worse, a financial downturn has begun and is predicted to last for more than a year. Smith and Cho recognize that the situation must be addressed because just one or two of the problems mentioned can force the company into bankruptcy. They do not believe that they can solve the problems immediately, and they may not be able to take them on all at once.

1. The most important and difficult task that all managers confront is

   A) satisficing
   B) optimizing
   C) bounded rationality
   D) decision making

2. Smith has to make a decision about redesigning the out-of-date plant. The *ideal* model for decision making is

   A) personal decision making
   B) problem solving
   C) optimizing
   D) classical theory of decision making

3. Cho has identified a problem in his engineering of the new plant design. The objectives for solving the problem using classical theory of decision making are determined. The next step is

   A) determining the risks
   B) gathering information on alternatives
   C) making a decision
   D) satisficing

4. It is discovered that the problem is more complex, the problem is unclear, and the objectives are also not clear. Smith uses the behavioral theory of decision making after identifying problems. He discusses the findings with Cho and explains that

   A) they need to take careful observations from everyone
   B) this is a complex decision and only incomplete information is now available
   C) they need to separate each problem because the problems are unrelated
   D) they need to control all actions and allow no intuition into the decisions made

5. Many of the employees in the plant have worked for Smith and Cho since the plant was first built and started production. Cho emphasizes that personal feelings must be set aside for

   A) proper problem solving
   B) results that would be considered satisficing
   C) effective data collection
   D) organizational success

Case 2: Printing Business Woes

Salazar has a large printing business. The business prints, compiles, and mails advertisements for multiple local and regional companies. Most of the production is for local sales events and similar promotions. The mailings go out on specific dates announcing sales and special events. Timing is always crucial for Salazar's clients. The volume is high and the workload very steady.

Recently, one of the large compiling machines has begun to fail in midshift, and sometimes it has remained broken down for days. This unpredictable problem causes production problems and has caused several costly delays. Salazar had anticipated that the machine had another five years of predictable usage, but must now cope with the need to overhaul or replace the machine.

6. Salazar has a broken machine. Salazar should
   A) call in the repair company for an overhaul immediately
   B) send the operator home for the week until the machine is fixed
   C) determine the cause of the machine malfunctions before proceeding
   D) order a new machine immediately

7. Salazar needs a long-term solution. More time is required to use
   A) logical thinking patterns
   B) satisficing
   C) programmed decisions
   D) individual decision making

8. The issues of logical reasoning and systematic investigation imply that Salazar is using which one of the following approaches to solve the problem?
   A) Idea generation
   B) Scientific method
   C) Creativity
   D) Idea development

9. Salazar needs a solution for a critical, unanticipated problem. Since the inception of the company, Salazar has never faced a problem like this. Salazar and the management team are most likely to use what kind of tools in their rational decision making?
   A) Satisficing
   B) Creativity
   C) Analytical tools
   D) Personal biases

10. Salazar has determined that the best approach to decision making will begin with identifying and defining the problem, gathering information, then developing alternatives, evaluating alternatives, and monitoring the decision. This is called
    A) the scientific method
    B) satisficing
    C) creativity
    D) idea generation

Case 3: The New Ideas Corporation

Prior to founding a new company, Baker was known for being a highly innovative leader and creative thinker in the corporation where he formerly worked. The mission of the new company is to facilitate clients who have innovative ideas but need support for bringing the ideas to market, developing manufacturing techniques, and resolving design challenges.

11. Which one of the following characteristics of innovative people will make Baker's company a success at working with customers with unique or highly unconventional problems?
    A) Entrepreneurial spirit
    B) Monitoring of innovation

C) Originality in thought and ideas generated
D) Deductive reasoning

12. Baker was not a manager in the previous job, yet the leadership of the new company may require that he serve that role.

Baker may have a problem with which one of the steps in the creative process?

A) Idea generation
B) Idea development
C) Problem solving
D) Monitoring of innovation

13. Baker's innovative nature may prove more successful in his new company than in other employment situations because

A) there is no pattern of decision making and production to follow
B) most technological innovation proceeds in small steps
C) monitoring will no longer be necessary
D) Baker's entrepreneurial spirit will no longer be suppressed by managers

14. Based on the description of Baker, which one of the following is the greatest strength being brought to the new company?

A) The successful generation of new ideas
B) A tested ability to implement creative ideas
C) Careful monitoring of innovations
D) Strong organizational skills and experience

15. Which one of the following suggests what a client would expect to benefit from Baker's ability to be innovative?

A) Inductive reasoning
B) Entrepreneurial spirit
C) New ways of doing things
D) Critical thinking

Solutions

Solutions to Check Point—Section A

Answer:	Refer to:
A–1. (C)	[A-1-a]
A–2. (A)	[A-1-b]
A–3. (C)	[A-2-b]

Solutions to Check Point—Section B

Answer:	Refer to:
B–1. (D)	[B-2-a–e]
B–2. (A)	[B-2-d-(3)]
B–3. (A)	[B-2-e-(3)]

Solutions to Check Point—Section C

Answer:	Refer to:
C–1. (B)	[C]
C–2. (A)	[C]
C–3. (D)	[C-2-d]

Solutions to For Your Review

	Answer:	*Refer to:*

Case 1:

1.	(D)	[A,B,C]
2.	(D)	[A-1-a]
3.	(A)	[A-1-a-(2)]
4.	(B)	[A-1-b]
5.	(D)	[A-1-b-(4)]

Case 2:

6.	(C)	[A-2 & B-2]
7.	(A)	[B-3]
8.	(B)	[A, B, & C]
9.	(C)	[B-2-d-(4)]
10.	(A)	[B]

Case 3:

11.	(C)	[C-1]
12.	(D)	[C-2]
13.	(A)	[C-1]
14.	(A)	[C-2-a]
15.	(C)	[C]

Chapter 2

Strategic Planning— Mission and Values

OVERVIEW

Planning is the most important and basic management function. Planning involves setting objectives and then establishing the policies, procedures, and action plans necessary to achieve them at all levels of an organization. Strategic planning establishes the direction the organization will take over a long term. Strategic planning involves developing goals for the future that reflect current threats and opportunities and match the strengths and weakness of the organization to these challenges. Planning results in clearly stated goals, from which objectives are created to guide steps and actions that will be taken during the short term. Quality planning also identifies the needed resources, both current and future, including space, materials, equipment, and human. Effective strategic planning leads to a comprehensive planning and implementation process.

Plans must be conveyed to the workforce and accepted by the entire organization, from the top level of management to the entry-level employee. Success comes when the entire organization accepts and endorses the mission and values that guided the formation of the plan and will guide its implementation. An important aspect of corporate values is the ethical standards that govern both individual corporate leaders and the company itself.

KEY TERMS

Contingency planning, 26
Ethics, 38
Gap analysis, 29
Management by
    objectives (MBO), 37
Mission, 27

Objective, 31
Operational planning, 26
Policy, 32
Procedure, 32
Rule, 33
Single-use plans, 33

Stakeholders, 39
Standing-use plans, 33
Strategic planning, 26
SWOT analysis, 28
Tactical planning, 26

A. Organizational Planning

Planning is one of the primary management functions of an organization. It involves organizing a sequence of predetermined actions to accomplish future objectives. More specifically, planning entails establishing objectives and then setting policies, procedures, and action plans to achieve those objectives.

1. *Types of Planning:* There are four main types of planning: strategic planning, tactical planning, operational planning, and contingency planning. Administrative professionals are often engaged in all four types of planning.

   a. *Strategic planning:* Strategic planning is the core of any effective organizational planning process. **Strategic planning** establishes long-term goals agreed upon by the entire organization that define the direction in which the organization will go, establishes clear parameters for recognizing and achieving success, and directs a process of continuous adaptation that is within the corporate objectives and resilient to external challenges.

      Strategic planning: Strategic planning is done by upper-level management. It is a formal process of planning to fit the mission and values of the organization. The plan is followed unless the dynamics of the environment indicate that a change is necessary. Strategic planning does not work without support from the top managers. In addition, the managers at all levels must support the plan. Strategic planning that is participative is more likely to succeed. All managers should be involved in the planning process from the beginning and follow through the implementation.

   b. *Tactical planning:* **Tactical planning** involves setting short-term goals that show how to achieve the broad objectives specified in the strategic plans. Tactical plans include specific actions to be taken to achieve objectives and are the responsibility of middle-level managers.

   c. *Operational planning:* Through **operational planning,** first-line managers conduct day-to-day activities necessary to achieve longer term tactical and strategic goals.

   d. *Contingency planning:* **Contingency planning** involves developing action plans to help an organization cope with any unforeseen events that may arise.

      EXAMPLES:

      > *Security planning post 9/11*
      > *Plans for dealing with natural disasters*
      > *Massive product liability suits*

      Tactical, operational, and contingency planning all emanate from strategic planning. Ineffective or a lack of strategic planning can result in "crisis management," a state in which the organization moves from one crisis to another. Eventually, the organization will fail in such a mode. Setting goals and establishing clear and reasonable objectives is just the first step, however. The organization's management team must lead all the employees toward the goals by approaching each objective in a systematic manner with adequate and appropriate resources for accomplishing each task.

2. *Strategic Planning Process:* The strategic planning process can be structured to involve representatives from every level and division of an organization, or it can be restricted to upper-level management. Sometimes, consultants are used to provide both an objective, external point of view and to undertake data collection and analysis. An

external consulting group might conduct extensive interviews of all stakeholders, including the community and customers of the organization.

a. *First steps:* The first goal is to clarify a vision and a mission of the organization if none exists. If a mission already exists, then the process will undertake either validation of the current statement or revision to match current concerns. Second, strategies for the process are determined. Reaffirmation of the mission, strategy development, and wide-ranging analysis may occur simultaneously.

b. *Mission:* The most broadly stated objective of an organization is called its **mission**. The mission is the basic purpose for the organization's existence. It may appear easy to determine a company's mission. However, this is not always true.

    EXAMPLE: *When the train business in the United States was challenged by trucks, buses, planes, and private cars, it did not change its mission as being the rail system, and thus suffered a loss of recognition as a reliable rail transport service. If the mission had been adjusted to a mission of moving people and things, or using its right of ways, the situation today might be very different.*

    Senior management of the organization determines its mission. All managers are responsible for understanding, communicating, and implementing the mission. The mission statement defines the organization by defining its activities, markets, and consumers.

    EXAMPLES:

    > *The mission of CNN is to provide news around the clock and be the world's source of information.*

    > *The mission of Hewlett-Packard is "To provide reliable and cost effective IT solutions & services, using appropriate technologies, innovation and business expertise."*

c. *Strategy:* The term *strategy,* as used in planning, has both military and sports connotations. Strategy describes the plan the general or team manager or planner has for using the organization's resources to achieve a specific objective. Tactics are specific actions taken by a manager and work group to achieve a specific goal (how a goal will be achieved). There are three levels of strategy.

    1. *Corporate-level strategy:* This level involves the entire corporate organization, and usually implies that the corporation consists of a number of different business interests. General Motors is an excellent example of a corporation with numerous profitable business units ranging from automobile manufacturing to loan companies. The corporate-level strategy guides what kinds of new ventures to undertake and how to distribute financial resources to existing ventures.

    2. *Business-level strategy:* This strategy level involves the independent business unit of a larger company. The Cadillac automobile is made by a division of General Motors. The strategy for Cadillac will follow specific goals of a luxury automobile manufacturer in contrast to the goals of a subcompact division.

    3. *Functional strategy:* Departments within a business unit can also have goals, objectives, and mission statements. The General Motors design engineering group may set a strategy that helps it be more responsive to internal customers, collaborate more smoothly with the stylistic design group, and explore more fuel-efficient options. Department-level strategies are the point at

which businesses maintain their competitive edge because they represent the point at which the customer is reached.

EXAMPLES:

> *A football coach develops a strategy (plan) for improving the team's passing in offensive play. One tactic is to have the quarterback practice with the receivers a minimum of one hour during each practice.*

> *A general, with thin reserves and supplies, may direct a series of short guerrilla-type engagements rather than an all-out offensive action as a means of conserving resources.*

> *A soft-drink manufacturer may restrict its distribution to a regional area, rather than initiate a national sales campaign, in order to use fewer resources in a more concentrated fashion.*

Strategy statements are meant to guide those organization members who have the authority to make plans for the actions of major units of the organization. Corporate vice presidents and division managers are typically individuals who would be expected to make and to be directly affected by strategic decisions.

3. ***Data Collection and Analyses:*** With the initial steps under way, data collection and analyses become crucial to the process of strategic planning. The nearly universal approach to analysis is called *SWOT analysis.* This analysis provides the basis for the formulation of the strategic plan.

    a. *SWOT analysis:* **SWOT** stands for *strengths, weaknesses, opportunities,* and *threats* for the organization. SWOT is a system used to scan the environment and understand the factors that will affect the strategy designed. SWOT analysis is a long-standing technique used by companies for planning. It is an in-depth project that does not always give easy or clear answers. Every aspect of the business—its business activity, goals, resources, and weaknesses—is included in the analysis.

        1. *Conducting SWOT:* Several techniques can be used to conduct a SWOT analysis. Commonly, even with extensive interviews and other data collected from all stakeholders, a task force designated to complete the strategic plan engages in a session that looks like brainstorming or a focus group. A popular technique involves posting lists of strengths, weakness, opportunities, and threats on the walls of a room and giving each participant a set number of votes for each category (such as five votes for strengths, etc.). After the participants vote, a leader guides the group through a discussion of the outcome. Often, this leader is an external consultant. Other methods include using a consulting team to complete the SWOT analysis.

        2. *Tabulating the SWOT:* A SWOT analysis for a large organization with many different business facets can be quite extensive. A trained planner should help orchestrate the extensive data. This includes conducting some data analysis and summary of critical points. Usually this kind of process will involve several drafts that are shared with the team responsible for developing the strategic plan.

    b. *Internal and external audits:* Another method used for analyzing a corporation's strengths and weaknesses is the audit—the internal audit and the external audit.

        1. *Internal audit:* An internal audit reviews the mission statement and the degree of success the business mission has had.

2. *External audit:* The external audit addresses five categories: economic forces, social forces, political forces, technological forces, and competitive forces. Analysis of these forces results in a picture of the opportunities and threats faced by a business.

c. *Gap analysis:* **Gap analysis** measures the gap between perception and reality within the organization as well as between the organization and the broader business environment. An organization might do a Gap analysis on service to customers, or on internal or external communication.

    EXAMPLE: *At an office equipment store, the owners may expect a certain level of sales per month. The sales personnel will attempt to meet that level. The customer may feel pushed into a sale that is later regretted, by personnel who are attempting to meet monthly goals. Management's perception is that everyone is happy. The reality may be something different.*

d. *Other analyses:* Information is collected from external and internal sources to determine if the mission statement will be compatible with the external and internal environment of the business. Scanning the environment in all aspects—social, economic, ethical, and so on—is crucial in designing a plan that ensures success.

    1. *Government data:* Local, state, and federal governments in the United States as well as most major countries and even some emerging industrial nations maintain government data bureaus. World organizations like the United Nations and the World Trade Organization also maintain large data sources that provide information about what is happening at every social, civic, and cultural level.

    2. *Business association data:* Business and professional organizations also maintain research and data collection offices. Tracking and anticipating business trends is often one of the major activities of business associations.

    3. *Research trends:* Governments all over the world fund research, and many universities support scientific research as well. Large corporations, like GM, IBM, AT&T, and Microsoft, have research and development divisions. Many of these companies publish the results of their research in scientific journals. These research activities are often on the cutting edge and indicate future applications.

    EXAMPLES:

    > *An airline has a mission to get every customer's luggage to the customer's destination and on time. An objective that supports that mission is to reduce lost luggage by 5 percent each month. An objective to prevent theft of customers' suitcases by their own employees would not have the same interest to travelers who are now focused on personal security and safety.*

    > *Since the increase in gas prices, auto manufacturers will not likely adopt additional objectives to increase the size of vehicles, though large vehicles have a large customer base. Environmental groups may even protest a mission to increase vehicle size. Market forces will lead to a new mission that blends fuel efficiency with desirable vehicles*

e. *Current trends influencing strategic planning:* The broadest social, economic, and technological trends that affect strategic planning change and evolve at their own pace. However, the strongest current trends include globalization of the marketplace, rapidly changing technology, increasing security needs, and changes in employment and worker patterns. The areas promise to continue to be focal points of concern for years to come.

1. *Globalization of the marketplace:* The marketplace is now worldwide, no matter how small the company or business enterprise. Access to the Internet has made marketing a global concern. Products can be manufactured nearly anywhere and delivered through reliable transportation networks. Services, especially those that include a telecommunications link such as computer customer service or other information technology support, can be delivered from India or the Caribbean without the customer realizing the source.

2. *Technology innovation:* The technology does not present a threat in its own right as much as the rapid pace of technological innovation does. Desktop computers are outdated within only a few years, even though they continue to be serviceable for much longer. Personal data assistants (PDAs) now integrate ever more features, making one just purchased obsolete within the year, again, even though quite functional and adequate. These are only the most visible areas of change in technology.

3. *Security:* After the terrorist attacks of September 11, 2001, security concerns have been extreme. These concerns are for the safety of people, places, and products. Concern begins from the moment a raw material leaves the ground and is transported to a processing plant, is manufactured, and then is shipped to the customer. Human movement also has vulnerabilities. Security has become a driving force in technological change as well.

4. *Employment:* The area of employment includes the changing needs of the workforce as well as the changing patterns of employment. The workforce has become multicultural and global, aging in some areas of the world and becoming younger in others. The cost of human resources will always be a factor for strategic planning. Telecommuting, part-time and temporary employment, outsourcing, and on-site consulting have become major trends in the pattern of employment.

Check Point—Section A

Directions: For each question, circle the correct answer.

A–1. The first step in planning is to formulate a/an

    A) action guideline
    B) value statement
    C) analysis of the situation
    D) mission statement

A–2. After 9/11, organizations in New York City had to perform which kind of planning?

    A) Tactical planning
    B) Contingency planning

    C) Strategic planning
    D) Operational planning

A–3. Which one of the following strategic planning concerns represents a current trend?

    A) Technological innovation
    B) GAP analysis
    C) Business association data
    D) Internal auditing

B. Managing the Strategic Plan

The formulation of a strategic plan involves the preparation of a mission statement and the formulation of a set of goals that connect the mission to the activity of the organization. Objectives are derived from the goals and guide specific business or organizational activity. Objectives are the primary management tool for achieving any plan, whether it is a strategic, tactical, operational, or contingency plan. With objectives developed, a manager or management team can then prepare an action plan.

1. *Objectives:* The primary activities necessary to achieve an organization's mission are identified, and objectives (goals) are established for each of these activities. The term **objective** refers to the end results an organization seeks to attain to fulfill the organization's mission. Objectives are measurable and observable, and they may be written for each unit in the organization. All objectives should be interrelated and should work together to meet the organization's mission.

   EXAMPLE: *A retail bakery must set objectives for purchasing raw materials, mixing and balancing operations, sales, and employment practices.*

   a. *Multiple objectives:* Organizations have multiple objectives. Care must be taken to ensure that the objective set for each activity is compatible with those set for other activities.

   EXAMPLE: *A sales objective to sell 5,000 management textbooks should be matched to a production objective of printing at least 5,000 copies plus the number that would be used to promote the book.*

   b. *Short-term, intermediate, and long-term objectives:* Objectives are established for short- and long-term periods. In addition, intermediate objectives may be established as benchmarks. Most organizations prepare formal plans, such as the annual corporate business plan, to control current operations. The annual plan is then broken down into monthly, weekly, or even daily subplans. The long-term plan is more general; it represents management's intentions about actions in the future—5 to 20 years—if external circumstances and internal performance permit.

   EXAMPLE: *A local company that manufactures and sells briefcases may have a short-term objective of selling 1,000 dozen briefcases in the local region this year. Its long-term objective may be to expand its business nationally over the next five years to a volume of 50,000 dozen.*

   Responsibility for achieving short-term objectives typically rests with supervisors. Intermediate objectives coincide with middle managers' duties and responsibilities. The achievement of long-term objectives is the primary concern of top management.

   c. *Necessary objectives:* Peter Drucker, a noted management theorist, identified eight key areas in which any organization should have specific objectives on which to focus, especially long term. Drucker's objectives are:

   - Market standing
   - Innovation
   - Profitability
   - Productivity

- Physical and financial resources
- Managerial performance and development
- Worker performance and attitude
- Public responsibility

2. *Action Guidelines:* Objectives establish *what* is to be done. To guide the organization's employees in *how* the work is to be performed, management develops a number of different types of action guidelines. Guidelines take the form of policies, procedures, and rules. An action plan then incorporates procedures with a schedule of work.

a. *Policies and procedures defined:* **Policies** are general statements developed by organizational management and communicated to managers and supervisors so they can make consistent decisions in handling certain anticipated problems. Policies define the limits within which supervisors must stay as they make decisions. **Procedures** are sets, or sequences, of steps to be followed in performing specific tasks or actions. Procedures specify behavior for managers to follow in making decisions in specific situations. Punishment is implied if managers fail to follow these steps or guidelines.

EXAMPLES: *Pearson has worked for the Z Corporation for 10 years and is eligible this year for a three-week paid vacation. The company policy states that employees who have worked for the company for 10 to 15 years may have three weeks of paid vacation each year.*

Pearson's supervisor, Miller, will have to schedule each employee's vacation in such a way that the routine work of each position can still be handled. The procedure used in the company allows those employees with seniority to select their vacation dates first. The supervisor then matches these dates with the schedule to see if there is appropriate coverage for the work to be done.

b. *Policy:* Strategy is focused on the resources of the whole organization and on those persons at the upper managerial levels who have the authority to decide how to use those resources. Policy, on the other hand, focuses on a wide range of actions or decisions that may be made by organization members at any level of the organization.

1. *Policy governs:* A policy describes the way actions are completed or decisions are made in particular situations.

2. *Policy directs:* A policy statement represents management's preference or commitments on a subject. Subordinates are expected to follow the policy guideline as they exercise authority, make decisions, or take actions.

EXAMPLE: *Policy statements directing that practices ensure equal opportunity in employment for minorities and women are found in corporate policy manuals.*

It is important to recognize that a policy is not, as a rule, a law or a completely rigid requirement. A policy is intended to be a guideline that is honored in most instances, but leaves room for justified exceptions.

c. *Procedure:* As stated earlier, a procedure is a set, or sequence, of steps to be followed in performing a specific task or action. Activities that are repeated frequently are studied, and the best or preferred ways of responding or performing are identified. The preferred steps are then written into a procedure. Persons performing these activities are guided into a highly consistent pattern of behavior by the requirements of the procedure.

d. *Rule:* A **rule** states exactly what is to be done; it allows for no discretion or deviation. Rules are most commonly established in matters of health, safety, and other areas of major importance.

3. ***Duration of Plans:*** Plans are generally developed by the various levels of management for three specific time periods and degrees of specificity.

a. *Strategic plans:* Upper-level management designs a plan based on the organization's mission and values. This plan is long range and will include methods of review and adjustment that keep the organization responsive to changes, whether they are threats or opportunities.

b. *Tactical plans:* Tactical plans are of shorter duration and are the responsibility of middle management. They are more specific and objective. A tactical plan may last only as long as a specific objective requires. If the plan is to open a new market in Asia, then the tactical plan is complete when that market is open, and a new plan for sustaining or expanding the market should be designed and implemented.

c. *Operational plans:* Operational plans are the responsibility of first-line managers and are specific and objective. An operation may take a few hours or a few days, or it may even have an entire annual cycle. The preparation of an annual financial audit may be completed in several months, but the plan that creates all the necessary documentation and directs how financial records will be maintained is an ongoing, yet annualized process. The completion of a purchase, travel activity, or software upgrade follows a specific operational plan. Each event has a completion date and time, yet the record of that event becomes part of a larger operational plan (like the audit).

d. *Contingency plans:* Contingency plans are designed to assist the organization in dealing with dynamic environments. Evaluation and feedback are used to determine if any alterations need to occur in the plans at any level.

EXAMPLES:

> *Plans to increase company market share (strategic)*
> *Plans to reduce waste through improved quality control (tactical)*
> *Plans to reduce waste through an employee empowerment plan (operational)*
> *Plans for dealing with terrorist acts (contingency)*

4. ***Types of Plans:*** There are two basic types of plans: standing-use plans and single-use plans. Some are aimed at solving problems that occur on a regular basis, whereas others are prepared to deal with one-time emergencies.

a. *Standing-use plans:* **Standing-use plans** guide regular activity of an organization. The plans may be in the form of procedure guidelines, calendars, report cycles, documents, or other tools that can guide and direct the business routine. Any classification of plan—strategic, tactical, operational, and even contingency (if contingencies occur regularly)—could be considered standing-use plans if they guide daily, weekly, or frequent routines. Anyone involved in the actions should be able to review the plan, whether it is in the form of a procedure, policy statement, or other schedule.

b. *Single-use plans:* A **single-use plan** may cover an activity such as a technology transition, a physical move to a temporary location during a renovation, installation of complex machinery or systemwide software, or any singular action that requires concentrated planning. Single-use plans are expected to guide the single activity in a smooth and efficient manner. All parties to the action should be aware of the plan. Each affected group or organizational division should also have a role in developing the details of the plan.

5. ***Evaluation of Plans:*** Every plan must be evaluated. Objectives are measurable because they are the means of determining whether or not a plan was successful.

    a. *Determining success:* Success can be determined by the degree to which an objective was reached, such as a quality objective, where the objective was to reduce customer complaints by a specified percentage. The stated percentage of reduced complaints—the objective—can be reached, exceeded, or not reached.

    b. *Making adjustments:* Plans should be adjusted according to factors determined in the plan. An operational plan that set out to reduce complaints should be adjusted on the basis of the complaint rates. Achieving 95 percent of an objective may be considered acceptable, but the determination of whether the plan of operation is working must be made. Exceeding the objective by 5 or 10 percent is also good, but the plan should be reviewed so that a more accurate forecast can be made. If budgeting is based on meeting objectives, then the savings of 5 or 10 percent can be incorporated earlier if the forecast is more accurate. A strategic plan should be adjusted when the trends are expected to change. A change in complaint rate is not the basis for shifting the strategic plan.

Check Point—Section B

Directions: For each question, circle the correct answer.

B–1. Which one of the following states exactly what must be done and allows for no variation or discretion?

    A) Policy
    B) Procedure
    C) Rule
    D) Objective

B–2. Evaluation of a plan rests on careful measurement of

    A) action plans
    B) objectives
    C) procedures
    D) rules

B–3. To achieve the organization's mission

    A) the organization must move forward quickly
    B) subjective criteria should be established
    C) the mission statement already directs the action
    D) activities to achieve the mission must be established

C. Communicating Mission and Values

The mission and values of an organization must be communicated throughout the organization. No supervisor can fulfill a managerial function like planning, organizing, or controlling without communicating. *Communicating* is the process of sharing ideas in such a way that others will understand and be able to use the transmitted information. The computer and other recent changes in technology have vastly improved ways that organizations can communicate effectively internally and externally. Communications is the process that links all managerial functions.

1. ***The Managerial Role in Communicating Mission and Values:*** In converting mission statements into action, upper managerial levels create policy statements. Policies cover a wide range of actions or decisions; however, they are crucial for guiding change and maintaining focus on the organization's mission and values.

   a. *Controlling interaction:* Policy statements specify how management and employees will work together in the organizational structure. A policy will express a value or specify conduct. A value might be "fairness" when a policy addresses a grievance procedure or the intent of the company to pay employee health insurance premiums. A policy relating to customer service may direct employees to be courteous at all times.

   b. *Clarifying policy with procedure:* Employees are expected to follow policies. In order to implement policies effectively, procedures must be carefully developed and articulated. A procedure for courteous customer service may be as detailed as providing the employee with scripts that cover the initial contact with the customer.

   c. *Determining the extent of policy coverage:* All situations cannot be covered in policies. Policies are guidelines and the intent is to be considered.

   EXAMPLES:

   > *An airline has a policy not to buy tickets for its displaced passengers on competing airlines. A woman misses a connecting flight due to no fault of her own, yet her critical medicine supply has moved on to the next stop. A customer service representative can make an exception to the policy and purchase a ticket for the woman on a competing airline on the basis of compassion, which does not have to be articulated in a policy or procedure.*

   > *A guideline is given that informs employees whether or not they can accept gifts from suppliers, customers, contractors, and so on, and defines gifts very specifically.*

   > *A company's stance on employee dating is usually stated in a policy and procedures for actions to be taken if the policy is violated are articulated in a procedure manual that all employees are expected to read.*

2. ***Policies and Procedures Guide Communication:*** Policies and procedures help communicate the organizational mission and values by providing clear guidelines to employees. Policy statements and the procedures associated with them address relationships with the public as well as the relationship of the organization to the employee. Properly communicated, they help standardize the practices of the organization even as they communicate the role of each organizational member in helping the organization meet its objectives, goals, and mission.

   a. *Formal versus informal policies and procedures:* As vital guides in decision making, policies need to be stated and communicated explicitly to those in the organization who are to apply them. It is desirable that formal policies be written. Having to put policies in writing requires the manager to think them through carefully to develop clear and consistent guides. The wording of a written policy cannot be changed by word of mouth. Written policy helps new supervisors become more familiar with the company and its established policies rather quickly.

b. *Standardization of practice:* Once the policy or procedure is established, the supervisor will be able to apply it in making decisions. Past experience with policies already in existence will serve as precedents in actions to be taken. The development of companywide policies and procedures manuals helps standardize many practices that formerly were hearsay or "carried around in people's heads."

c. *Public and employee relations:* Policies affect every person engaged in business activities for the firm and every person or company served by the firm. Employee relations as well as public relations are very important considerations in establishing appropriate company policies.

1. *Public relations policies:* For firms to be responsive to the needs of customers or clients, public relations policies must be established so that:

    a. Products and services are provided that meet the public demand

    b. Customers and clients are provided with the kinds of service expected

    c. Marketing practices adhere to the requirements of legislation and are directed toward the public benefit

2. *Employee relations policies:* Many company policies are designed to maintain good employee relations throughout the firm. Not only do these provide benefits to employees, but indirectly they also will help increase the morale and motivation demonstrated by the employees.

    a. *Hiring new employees:* Appropriate policies will define the limits for hiring new employees, and procedures will outline the ways in which new employees can be sought and hired.

    b. *Training:* Newly hired employees or employees who are being transferred to new responsibilities may be eligible for certain types of company-sponsored training. Sometimes newly hired employees will receive up to six months of training in special programs designed to assist them in making the transition.

    c. *Promoting employees:* Some organizations prefer to promote employees who have been with the company rather than conduct external searches for managerial personnel.

    d. *Providing employee assistance programs:* Employee assistance programs (EAPs) may be available to employees through special programs established by management. Special services provide help for employees who are having difficulty with stress, drug abuse, alcoholism, finances, or other personal problems.

    e. *Retiring and discharging employees:* Retirement programs support employees who qualify for retirement benefits. Other policies support procedures to be followed in case employees must be discharged.

    f. *Providing employee benefits:* Employers provide employee benefits (often called fringe benefits) as a part of the employment conditions. Company policies may provide for payment of a health insurance plan, dental and vision care, paid vacations, child care, elder care, employee participation in profit-sharing plans, special retirement plans, participation in educational programs, or life insurance programs.

d. *Support of formal authority system:* Policies and procedures in effect within an organization communicate the expectations of the formal authority system. In other words, everyone within the organization is expected to support these policies and procedures or be willing to sever their relationships with the organization. Specific policies that need revision or change to obtain the support of the employees should be examined carefully by management to see if such change is feasible.

EXAMPLE: *Many organizations have initiated suggestion systems whereby employees can submit ideas for changing policies and procedures, without endangering their positions. Usually, these suggestions are collected in boxes distributed throughout the organization or even through electronic mail, (e-mail). Employees are not required to sign their names.*

3. *Management by Objectives* **(MBO): Management by objectives** is a systematic approach to planning and controlling activities whereby superiors and those who report to them (subordinates) collaborate on setting objectives. MBO is one of the more popular management approaches that begin as a planning process. It is specifically designed to gain mutual acceptance of the final plan and objectives. Peter Drucker is generally credited with originating this approach, through his insistence that each person responsible for achieving an objective should have a clear voice in setting that objective.

a. *Mutual setting of objectives:* The employee and supervisor together initiate a set of specific goals for areas of responsibility. These goals, must be specific and measurable. In addition to the objectives, the standard or quality of the actions must be determined jointly. The time for the objectives to be performed must be indicated as well. These goals are discussed, and the supervisor may, work with the subordinate to refine or amend them. Once agreement is reached, work proceeds with both supervisor and subordinate clearly understanding and agreeing on objectives.

b. *Setting of measurable objectives:* Some activities lend themselves to measurement easily.

EXAMPLES:

Increase sales by 10 percent within six months

Decrease use of electricity by 3 percent within one month.

Some activities are not so easy to measure.

EXAMPLES:

Improved public relations

Better customer–salesperson interaction

Nevertheless, it is possible to develop indirect activities that can be measured even in these qualitative areas.

c. *Regular monitoring and performance evaluation:* Part of the task of setting objectives requires establishing times for completion of the activities. These times or dates provide a framework for periodic review of performance. The review can be linked to the reward structure and can reveal areas in which the subordinate needs additional training. Such a review can also lead to revised approaches for setting objectives in the future.

d. *Effectiveness of MBO:* Generally, behavioral science research supports the use of participation in goal setting and timely feedback on performance. There are, however, some problems or limitations with the use of MBO:

1. The MBO process is time consuming.

2. Top management must support MBO and be involved in it.

3. The emphasis is on short-term objectives.

4. Some individuals are not positively motivated by participation.

5. Some managers are reluctant to share the goal-setting process with their subordinates.

6. If an employee emphasizes *personal* MBO goals, work team and corporate goals may be ignored.

4. *Ethics:* **Ethics** refers to the standards of right and wrong behavior that guide people. Common ethical principles generally include honesty, fairness, respect for others, nonviolence, and helpfulness. Corporations often will state their ethical views in their mission statements or in an actual statement called a *code of ethics.* Every profession has a code of ethics. Physicians subscribe to the Hippocratic Oath, a code of ethics that specifies the value of human life. Physicians also address a wide range of concerns in the code published by the American Medical Association. Each professional organization publishes its own code of ethics as well. Many define specific principles that apply to the profession's work. For instance, in medicine, psychology, social work, and other human services professions, sexual relations between doctor and patient or therapist and client is strictly prohibited. Often the punishment for violating the code will be expulsion from the profession. Stockbrokers have codes against using information that was gained from "insiders," people who are in a place to have access to special, not yet available, or confidential information.

Businesses have codes of ethics as well. Some business and organizational groups like publishing and oil companies and insurance groups will prepare statements concerning proper conduct of both corporations and representatives of corporations. These *codes of conduct* indicate types of practices that may create unfair advantage. The government controls some practices, like fair-wage laws, employment practices, and truth-in-advertising laws.

a. *Corporate social responsibility:* Since the Enron scandal in 2001 (which led to new legislation in the United States to protect stockholders from corporate fraud), the public has been skeptical, even cynical, about the social responsibility of businesses. There is concern about the ethical behavior of employees because it reflects on an organization's reputation. In 2001, employees of the Enron Corporation lost their retirement and jobs almost overnight because of the unethical behavior of managers. Ethical behaviors are therefore beneficial to both managers and employees. Guidelines are usually listed in the company policy manual. "Value-driven" is listed as one of the eight attributes of an excellent company by Peters and Waterman in their management book, *In Search of Excellence: Lessons from America's Best-run Companies* (Tom Peters and Robert Waterman, New York: Harper and Row Publishers, 1982). Peters and Waterman, leading writers about management, introduced this concept long before corporate ethics became an issue of national concern. Knowing that your personal values are in agreement with those of your coworkers and employer is an important part of striving for success.

EXAMPLES:

> *McDonald's builds Ronald McDonald houses. Families of very sick children may stay there during their children's hospitalization. It is a home away from home.*

> *Florida Power & Light built a park on the Caloosahatchee River to protect the manatees who visit its power station outside Fort Myers, Florida, every winter because the water is a little warmer there. They have planted the area around the power station in an ecologically sound manner and give wildlife tours so that the public may see the huge manatees up close.*

b. *Responsibility to stakeholders:* Corporations have an ethical responsibility to all of its **stakeholders**—all persons whom the organization is dedicated to serve. Internal responsibility is to all employees, where external responsibility is to stockholders, the community, and to society as a whole. Many organizations state their mission and their views on the organization's corporate responsibilities publicly.

EXAMPLES:

> *Ben & Jerry's Homemade Ice Cream considers itself a business with corporate responsibility that sets high standards for its practices. Its mission statement is clearly stated on its Web site. It states the company's responsibility to all of its stakeholders and the world at large.*

> *EXXON has a Web site with a topic on corporate governance.*

> *IBM has published its mission and policy statement online at its Web site. It covers all areas of how business is to be conducted.*

> *Honda publishes its worldwide vision of corporate responsibility on its Web site.*

> *There is a Web site with news on corporate social responsibility in China and other Asian nations.*

Check Point—Section C

Directions: For each question, circle the correct answer.

C–1. Controlling employee interaction, clarifying policy and procedure, and recognizing the limitation of policies are key components of a manager's effort to

A) develop a management by objectives approach

B) support the formal authority structure

C) communicate mission and values to employees

D) express public and employee relations policies

C–2. MBO (management by objectives) involves

A) superior–subordinate collaboration on setting goals

B) supervisors setting subjective goals

C) workers determining what actions they should perform

D) a small amount of time in meetings with other managers

C–3. Which one of the following is related to public policy statements?

A) Hiring of new employees

B) Retirement and discharge

C) Informal procedures

D) Legal marketing practices

For Your Review

Directions: For each question, circle the correct answer.

Case 1: Terrorist Attack

On September 11, 2001, terrorists launched major attacks against the United States. There were fears that the banks in the area of the attack would be unable to recover lost information as a consequence of the attacks because many investment banking firms were housed in the Twin Towers. Within days after the World Trade Center towers fell, the banking industry both in the United States and worldwide was asked to track money that might be supporting terrorism. Day-to-day activities suddenly had more government oversight. More requirements were placed on banking, nationally and internationally. One apparent goal of the terrorists was to disrupt the financial institutions and wreak havoc on the trade organizations that depend so heavily upon them.

1. Which one of the following types of plans would have been the first examined by the banking industry immediately after September 11, 2001?

   A) Contingency
   B) Tactical
   C) Operational
   D) Strategic

2. Some financial institutions lost personnel and business locations in the attack. Their immediate plans for dealing with an attack worked well, but the changing nature of government oversight means that they may have to consider

   A) rethinking the day-to-day operations
   B) making sure they have done their gap analysis
   C) creating new multiple objectives
   D) reviewing their strategic planning

3. After banking organizations declared new policies to track and detect terrorist organization monies, they needed to develop

   A) contingency plans for another possible attack
   B) action plans to guide the work to be performed

   C) adjusted strategic plans to reflect the new policies
   D) comprehensive gap analyses for successful implementation

4. The terrorist attack resulted in actions that suggest a strong link between which one of the following combinations of strategic trends?

   A) Employment and technology
   B) Technology and security
   C) Globalization and security
   D) Globalization and employment

5. Banking regulations are very slow to change and tend to govern exact methods for collecting, securing, and transferring funds. Based on this description, these regulations would be considered which one of the following?

   A) Rules
   B) Procedures
   C) Policies
   D) Plans

Case 2: Web.com

The Internet-based company Web.com had a few years of excellent growth and development. Without much planning, it was successful. People invested money into the company. Conservative organizational behaviors were absent. Workers did not dress in a traditional, professional manner. The environment for work resembled an unorganized warehouse. Many employees, including top management, were considered arrogant by those outside the computer industry. Employees of Web.com were devoted to their company and spent many hours at work. Then, the "dot.com" crash occurred. Investors stopped offering money to technology businesses in general. However, through the downturn Web.com has survived. Today, the owners and employees have an uncertainty about where they should go from here.

6. What should Web.com do first to go forward with planning?
   A) Use contingency planning
   B) Focus on operational planning
   C) Implement management by objectives
   D) Adjust its strategic plan

7. As Web.com makes needed changes to survive in the new reality, it needs to
   A) perform a complete analysis of internal and external environments
   B) focus its plan on internal operations at this time
   C) emphasize external changes in the environment
   D) create a company policy on professional behavior

8. After Web.com has performed both an internal and an external audit, the next step is to
   A) do operational planning at once
   B) put a single-use plan into place
   C) implement MBO
   D) set objectives to implement the plan

9. Web.com has finished planning and has decided to communicate its new mission and values to the organization at large. Which one of the following will provide the next logical step?
   A) Complete the tactical planning
   B) Undertake a gap analysis
   C) Formulate policy to reflect new values
   D) Adjust its strategic plan

10. Web.com discovered during its analysis of the external environment that the public in general has a negative perception of its corporate image. The company should consider
    A) performing a SWOT
    B) setting objectives for day-to-day operations
    C) revising its MBO plans
    D) stating its corporate values

Case 3: W&M Enterprises

Wu and McGinty have successfully operated a business in their home country of Ireland for five years. They want to expand into more countries and build an international company. They have decided that their company first should expand to the European mainland or to North America. Though they have personal preferences, they have not carefully analyzed which countries would hold the greatest potential for their business. They have also not decided how extensive their expansion should be, although they have a strong financial base to work from.

Wu speaks French as well as English, but McGinty does not speak any language other than English. Both have had little experience in traveling through Europe, though both have visited several of the major cities.

11. Wu and McGinty's first step toward expansion should be to
    A) conduct an external audit of the countries they like
    B) pick a country to expand into and proceed
    C) consider maximizing their business in Ireland before expanding
    D) begin a careful evaluation of their existing strategic plan

12. Wu and McGinty will need to convince their employees that expansion will benefit them as well. Assuming they have a good business plan, which one of the following methods would ensure employee support of the new idea?
    A) Establish clear rules for the new adventure
    B) Conduct a careful internal audit
    C) Use management by objectives to establish participation
    D) Prepare a policy manual with guidelines for international operations

13. A business plan for this expansion should start with
    A) a strategic plan including a mission statement
    B) contingency plans for working in each country
    C) a statement of the duration of the plan
    D) a policy manual in all the languages of Europe

14. Wu and McGinty have a special method of ensuring employee involvement and self-direction. They want to be able to achieve the same level of employee confidence in the new countries they enter. Which one of the following trends must they take into account to respond to their concern?
    A) Standardization of practice
    B) Security
    C) Technological innovation
    D) Globalization of the marketplace

15. As Wu and McGinty develop their strategic plan to enter the market in a new country, which one of the following would be a new component of the plan in comparison to their previous single-country plan?
    A) Their corporate responsibility in the new country
    B) Details of new operational planning
    C) Ethical considerations of being able to avoid Irish taxes
    D) Technological innovations that may influence how they do business

Solutions

Solutions to Check Point—Section A

Answer:	Refer to:
A–1. (D)	[A-2-b]
A–2. (B)	[A-1-d]
A–3. (A)	[A-3-e-(2)]

Solutions to Check Point—Section B

Answer:	Refer to:
B–1. (C)	[B-2-d]
B–2. (B)	[B-1-a–c]
B–3. (D)	[B-2]

Solutions to Check Point—Section C

Answer:	Refer to:
C–1. (C)	[C-1]
C–2. (A)	[C-3]
C–3. (D)	[C-2-c-(1)]

Solutions to For Your Review _____

Answer:	*Refer to:*

Case 1:

1. (A)   [A-1-d]

2. (D)   [A-3-e-(3) & B-3]

3. (B)   [B-1]

4. (C)   [A-3-e-(1) & (2)]

5. (A)   [B-2-d]

Case 2:

6. (D)   [A-2-b]

7. (A)   [A-3-b]

8. (D)   [B-1-a–c]

9. (C)   [C-2-c]

10. (D)   [C-2-C-(1) & C-4-a–b]

Case 3:

11. (D)   [B-5]

12. (C)   [C-3-a]

13. (A)   [A-2 & B-1]

14. (D)   [A-3-e-(1)]

15. (A)   [C-4-a]

Chapter 3
Allocating Resources

OVERVIEW

The resources of an organization need to be carefully allocated in order for the organization to sustain successful operations. Administrative professionals are regularly involved in the operations of the organization that are called the "control process." The control process includes every aspect of the business including human resources, the management of raw materials, standards for manufacturing, assembly processes, service operations, scheduling, delivery, and customer satisfaction.

Planning is an essential part of the control process. Once plans are established, resources can be aligned with the steps from beginning production to the end product. A process of quality assurance can follow the product or service and be used to improve the end result. Effective resource allocation requires continuous reappraisal of the process.

KEY TERMS

Aggregate planning, 50
Computer-aided
   design (CAD), 49
Computer-aided
   manufacturing (CAM), 49
Computer-integrated
   manufacturing (CIM), 49
Concurrent control, 47
Controlling, 46

Critical path method
   (CPM), 52
Economic order
   quantity (EOQ), 54
Feedback control, 47
Feedforward (precontrol)
   control, 47
Master production
   schedule (MPS), 51

Program evaluation and
   review technique
   (PERT), 52
Quality circles, 63
Quality control, 62
Standard, 46
Total quality management
   (TQM), 63

A. Controlling

Controlling focuses on evaluating performance according to the plans that have been established. However, the purpose of controlling is to ensure that the goals set forth during the planning process are realized, even if modifications have to be made along the way. Employee and production performance are measured, evaluated against known standards, and corrected to ensure that plans are being carried out effectively.

1. *The Control Process:* The more effectively management plans, organizes, staffs, and directs, the easier it will be to control business activities and personnel.

   a. *Basic steps:* The four basic steps in the control process are the determination and definition of goals to be evaluated, establishment of standards, comparison of performance against these standards, and correction of any unacceptable deviations.

      1. *The determination and definition of goals:* Goals set during planning are defined in relationship to the control process. Not all goals are equally important. Major goals need to be controlled.

      2. *Establishment of standards:* Appropriate standards of performance must be developed in order to determine whether or not goals have been accomplished. Standards may be established through the MBO (management by objectives) process, and may be industrywide or specific to the organization itself. A **standard** is an expected level of performance. A standard must be very specific and measurable (quantifiable).

         EXAMPLE: *A calculator costs $4.875 to produce and requires 0.15 labor hours to assemble.*

         Or, a standard may be more qualitative in nature.

         EXAMPLE: *The sales staff must be courteous to the customers.*

         The more technical the work is, the easier it is to develop an objective standard. Subordinates must know these standards ahead of time so that they know exactly what performance is expected of them and the bases on which their performance will be judged.

      3. *Comparison of performance with standards:* Actual performance must be compared with established standards for a program. Deviations from standards should be identified as early as possible. Knowing how to measure actual performance is difficult. Some standards are easily measured, while others require custom-made appraisals. Objective evaluation becomes even more difficult the farther up one goes in an organization.

      4. *Correction of deviations:* To correct deviations between standards and actual performance, the supervisory level of management must be aware of the reasons why errors occurred and appropriate action that might be taken.

         (a) *Investigation of errors:* The errors might have occurred as the result of an unforeseen event rather than as one person's fault.

             EXAMPLES:

             Sales may have been lower than anticipated because of an economic downturn. (This example demonstrates that an unforeseen event occurred.)

             Keller was not aware that a persuasive letter must be written with an attention-getting opening statement followed by arguments used to generate the reader's interest. Keller's letter needs to be rewritten. (This example shows that the employee did have a deficiency that needed to be corrected.)

b. *Action determination:* The appropriate action to be taken must be determined. Management may respond with these types of actions:

- Standards change, showing a change in employer behavior
- Performances change, showing a change in employee behavior
- Both standards and employee performances change

Not all deviations occur because an individual or group is at fault. If management tries to assess blame for every error, employee attitudes toward work may suffer. A severe error in judgment may even result in the termination of an individual's employment. At any rate, corrective or remedial action is needed to ensure better results in the future.

b. *Control mechanisms:* Three primary control mechanisms are used to ensure that progress is being made toward achieving certain objectives. They are feedforward (precontrol) controls, concurrent controls, and feedback controls. These mechanisms are classified according to the time factor in which they are implemented.

1. *Feedforward (precontrol) controls:* **Feedforward control** is actively anticipating and preventing problems. The possibility of technology malfunctioning or the event of other mistakes must be anticipated so that preliminary controls (sometimes called preventive controls) can be implemented. This includes materials and employee training. Modern technology built into machinery can now give a warning if it needs attention.

EXAMPLES:

Transistors purchased as part of an electronic appliance are inspected prior to using them in production.

Safety posters on bulletin boards warn employees of possible work hazards.

A preventive maintenance program for certain types of technology keeps equipment in good repair and ready for use.

2. *Concurrent controls:* **Concurrent controls** are also called in-progress controls and apply while operations are actually going on. Their purpose is to monitor and adjust ongoing activities and processes. In most cases, feedforward controls have been set up, too. It is also important to have concurrent controls available to minimize damage that occurs if precontrols should fail.

EXAMPLES:

Automatic switches may be installed in an office so that all power within the office area can be turned off in an emergency situation.

Warning signals may turn on automatically if a precontrol measure fails to operate; for example, a light appears on a computer panel if a particular alarm system is inoperative.

3. *Feedback controls:* After the work process has been completed, postcontrol measures may be used to see if the process can be improved. **Feedback controls**, often known as postcontrol measures, involve checking a completed activity and learning from the mistakes. Feedback controls may be the least desirable if errors did occur during the process.

EXAMPLE: *An examination of various accounting reports to compare net profit for the past two years might yield possible causes for an exceptionally low profit this year.*

Effective control mechanisms must be timely, understandable, economical, and flexible, indicating who is responsible for a given deviation and pointing toward the procedure or part of the process that needs to be corrected.

c. *Resistance to control:* If there were no controls established for a work process, the comparison between what was planned and what was actually accomplished would show a low correlation. Each level of management has a responsibility to keep work activities in line. When there are deviations from expected performance, it is usually the supervisor who must get workers back "on track." The goal, of course, is to have a workforce that can produce good-quality work with minimal controls.

d. *Information control:* Many business activities are reflected in numeric or monetary terms. Certain kinds of information that need to be controlled include accounting, budgetary, cost, inventory, and production information.

  1. *Accounting controls:* Systems are used to track expenses in all aspects of the organization. Summaries of financial information are prepared in the form of financial statements, such as the income statement or the balance sheet.

  2. *Budgetary controls:* A budget is a financial statement that is prepared to reflect proposed expenditures for a period of time. Although the preparation of the budget is a planning function, utilizing the budget in controlling costs is part of the controlling function.

  3. *Cost controls:* Supervisors and middle managers are constantly reminded by top management to reduce costs wherever possible. Open Book management is used in some organizations to share knowledge with each employee or work group as to the financial benefit they provide for the organization. Employees need to be aware of costs involved in certain business procedures so that cost control efforts will result in lower per-unit costs. In times of economic hardship, across-the-board cuts may be necessary to reduce costs. Employees that are aware of costs will be motivated to cut them when they can understand the value.

  EXAMPLES:

  The number of telephone lines coming into the organization may be reduced.

  Certain telephone lines may be restricted to local calls.

  4. *Specialized controls:* Other areas of control exist within organizations. These areas may be supervised by departments designed for that particular business function.

    a. *Inventory control:* Control may be established over raw materials, supplies, work in process, and finished goods.

    b. *Quality control:* Quality standards that are continually tested are maintained for the products or services of an organization. This area of control will be discussed in detail in Section D which follows.

    c. *Production control:* This area of control pertains to activities that are involved in maintaining overall operations on schedule. As work flows through various departments, scheduling and expediting the work flow are primary concerns.

2. ***Contemporary Production Processes:*** In the past, two types of production processes existed: mass production (including the assembly line and job lots for small orders) and flexible production (brought about because of changes in technology, demands of competition, and involvement of teams). While many organizations still rely on characteristics of mass production, more and more firms have adopted flexible processes, consistent with the focus on continuous improvement and the total quality management movement. The customer can now get more satisfaction with the product because it meets specific needs.

EXAMPLES:

> *Clothing manufacturers are now able to produce jeans for an individual customer using a system of personalized measurements that are entered into a computer linked to production facility computers.*

> *Automobile manufacturers are producing uniquely painted cars for individuals.*

3. ***Modern Technology and Control Processes:*** Improved technology has aided many innovations in production and operations processes.

   a. *Robotics:* Programmable machines (robots) can perform numerous tasks, often very repetitive, as long as software programs direct them. Robots are being used in many types and sizes of production and operations facilities. Robots have produced many of the tools used in the past.

      EXAMPLE: *A robot can pick up, reposition, lubricate, drill, or paint and can be used at night, on weekends, and on holidays. Robots can be programmed to deliver mail throughout a building.*

   b. *Computer-aided design (CAD):* With **computer-aided design (CAD)**, a designer conceives and designs parts and items to meet predetermined specifications using specialized computer systems. With CAD, engineers can draw three-dimensional designs, make changes, and allow for testing as well as the integration of various materials, all within specified tolerances. CAD has allowed designers to develop and pretest more sophisticated and advanced products with greater accuracy.

   c. *Computer-aided manufacturing (CAM):* **Computer-aided manufacturing (CAM)** takes the finished design and translates it into a set of programmed instructions that are sent electronically to production processing machines, instructing them to perform specific steps in a given order.

      EXAMPLE: *Boeing Aerospace and General Motors use CAM systems to manufacture products from parts that were first designed using CAD systems.*

   d. *Computer-integrated manufacturing (CIM):* In **computer-integrated manufacturing (CIM)**, production systems are developed to help workers design products, control machines, handle materials, and direct entire manufacturing processes in a systematic manner. While CIM does not require full automation, it does involve different operations that are organized around the computer as well as the integration of people and machines into a production or operations process in an automated manner.

      EXAMPLE: *Deere and Co. manufactures farm equipment by utilizing a computerized system that integrates engineering, planning, and analytical methods for tooling, sequencing, machining, and assembly.*

Many other types of processes and design tools assist in production and operations management. However, an understanding of robots, CAD, CAM, and CIM provides a basis for further study in this area as desired.

4. ***Production Planning and Scheduling:*** Efficiency is the key to planning and scheduling production. It is the customer who sets production goals. The production function is responsible for producing quality products at low cost, timed to be available when the market wants to buy them. This function is concerned with inventories and a stable workforce. Frequently, the production manager must consider making trade-offs among the variables to end up with the most optimal production plan.

   EXAMPLE: *Attempting to balance payroll costs and employment stabilization as well as market timing and employment stabilization can be difficult.*

   Detailed production scheduling proceeds at a level within the constraints of the broad plan. Various methods are available for aggregate planning. Graphic, mathematical, and computer search methods have been developed in an effort to improve on the more traditional methods. Like most other management decisions, production management decisions cannot be made in isolation. Planning meetings should involve marketing, sales, production, and engineering specialists.

   a. *Aggregate planning:* **Aggregate planning** involves making decisions about how the firm's capacity will be used to respond to forecasted sales. Aggregate planning requires the production function to be considered as a whole.

      1 *Effect of aggregate planning:* All decisions as to what, how, and when a business should produce affect the entire organization. The sequential nature of the decisions needs to be a concern.

         EXAMPLE: *A decision about employment levels and production rates for the next six months is not a wrong or right decision. The result is that all decisions the firm makes will be right or wrong, good or bad.*

         Aggregate planning is complex and requires a thorough knowledge of the variables involved in order to plan for an optimal mix of labor, materials, and capital inputs.

      2 *Aggregate planning strategies:* Several strategies (or methods) assist in the development of aggregate plans. All methods give data requiring managerial analysis and interpretation. No one method will, for example, determine the optimal rate of production and levels of personnel. There are basically three methods available: graphic and charting, mathematical, and computer search methods.

         a. *Graphic and charting methods:* Graphic and charting methods deal with a few variables at a time on a trial-and-error basis. By plotting and charting the impact that variables will have on the quantity and timing of the firm's output, various trade-offs can be made to achieve a cost-effective aggregate plan.

            (i) *Advantages:* Graphic methods are basically simple and have the advantage of visualizing alternate programs over a broad planning period.

            (ii) *Disadvantages:* Difficulties with graphic and charting methods stem from the static nature of the graphic model. In addition, the process is not cost or profit optimizing. The graphic and charting methods themselves do not generate good programs, but simply compare program proposals made.

   b. *Mathematical planning methods:* Although mathematical planning methods use charts and graphs to illustrate results, they attempt to refine and improve the trial-and-error approach of charting methods. Mathematical planning methods have a basis for optimizing results. They have been developed in an effort to improve traditional methods of charting and graphing by making the process dynamic, optimum seeking, and representative of the complex nature of the problems involved in aggregate planning. Generally speaking, they are more complex, more difficult to understand, and require interpretation by trained persons.

   (i) *The linear decision rule (LDR):* In 1955 Holt, Modigliani, Muth, and Simon developed the linear decision rule (LDR) as a quadratic programming (a method that creates a multiple variable formula) approach for making aggregate employment and production rate decisions.

   (ii) *Linear programming methods (LPMs):* In 1960, Hanssmann and Hess developed a linear optimization model that is entirely parallel with the linear decision rule in terms of using workforce and production rates as independent decision variables. LPMs are much easier to understand and more flexible than the LDR. The model provides information related to costs of employment, overtime, and ability of inventories to meet projected demand.

   c. *Computer search models (CSMs):* Computer search models seem to offer the most promise of flexibility in aggregate planning. Basically, CSMs search numerous combinations of variables systematically and select the combination that is the most cost effective.

b. *Master production scheduling:* Aggregate plans are comprehensive. The **master production schedule (MPS)** sets detailed schedules for individual end products, facilities, and personnel. The MPS must be developed within the parameters set by the aggregate plan; the aggregate plan constrains the MPS.

   EXAMPLE: *The aggregate plan calls for 1,000 units to be produced in a four-week period. If there were three products, a more detailed master production schedule would indicate quantities of each of three products to be produced in each week of the four-week period.*

   With computer scheduling, production managers have the speed and quantity of information needed to plan and control highly complex production.

   EXAMPLE: *Master production schedules can state in more specific terms the quantities of each individual product to be produced and the time periods for production.*

c. *Project planning and scheduling:* Until now, the discussion has focused on problems related to planning and scheduling inventoriable outputs. A large percentage of workers are involved in noninventoriable work—the building of roads, dams, missiles, ships, and public works activities. The problems of planning and managing such projects stem from their great complexity and the nonrepetitive nature of the activities required.

   1. *Operations with inventoriable output:* Planning operations that produce inventoriable output requires coordinating material needs with production schedules and the planning and control of capacity requirements, among others.

2. *Operations with noninventoriable output:* When output is not inventoriable, problems shift to jobs and tasks, which often have some unique characteristics. A large-scale project by its nature involves many jobs and tasks that have unique features. The required activities or operations flow from the unique design.

   a. Because of the large-scale operation, complexity results in terms of the number of activities, their sequence, and timing.

   b. The risks that result from failure to meet project completion deadlines are high, and the penalties for missing completion dates are usually in terms of higher costs and lower profit margins. Thus the focus in project work is on detailed planning, scheduling, and control of each major activity in relation to the project as a whole. The interdependent nature of the sequence and timing of the activities mandates careful planning.

3. *Network planning methods:* Network planning methods were developed by two different groups to handle the planning of large-scale projects.

   a. *Critical path methods (CPMs):* E. I. du Pont de Nemours and Co. developed critical path methods (CPMs) in 1958 to plan and control equipment maintenance in chemical plants. The **critical path method** is the sequence of events that are most critical as to timing the path of activities in a system.

   b. *Program evaluation and review technique (PERT):* The U.S. Navy, also in 1958, developed the **program evaluation and review technique (PERT)** to plan and control the Polaris missile project. The project involved 3,000 separate contracting organizations and was regarded as the most complex of projects coordinated to that date. PERT is a method for project planning by analyzing the time required for each step.

CPM and PERT are *substantially* based on the same concepts. Network analysis techniques can significantly improve the planning, scheduling, and control of complex projects.

Check Point—Section A

Directions: For each question, circle the correct answer.

A–1. After planning, the next management function is

A) leading
B) organizing
C) controlling
D) planning

A–2. Which one of the following standards would be the easiest to determine and evaluate?

A) Subjective
B) Temporary

C) Long-term
D) Objective

A–3. A technological control process that is *not* a choice for management is

A) CAP (control association process)
B) CAD (computer-aided design)
C) CIM (computer-integrated manufacturing)
D) CAM (computer-aided manufacturing)

B. Materials—Procurement, Processing, and Control

Materials often represent 20 to 30 percent of the total assets of a manufacturing firm. Even in service organizations, inventories for materials and supplies can represent a significant investment. Today's cost-conscious organizations consider the procurement, processing, and control of inventories an important function often requiring daily control.

1. *Authorization and Ordering of Materials:* Effective inventory replenishment policies must include several elements.

   a. *Costs:* Inventories must be adequate without being too large.

   b. *Inventory planning:* Careful inventory planning attempts to accommodate increases or decreases in material needs based on such factors as seasonal variations, projected sales increases, and the need for "buffer" stock.

   c. *Quantity discounts:* Consideration also needs to be given to the opportunity for getting quantity discounts if large quantities of materials are purchased. The advantages must be weighed against the cost involved in storing the goods until they are needed.

   d. *Timing:* Often, materials and supplies need to be available and ready for use at a precise time. If they arrive too late, production may be disrupted and even delayed. If they are available too early, the firm has capital invested unnecessarily in inventory costs.

   Inventory control, timing of orders, production schedules, and projected sales data all need to be coordinated for a firm to maintain a competitive position.

2. *Make or Buy Decisions:* Most manufacturing firms need to decide which of the components and parts included in the products they produce will be made "in-house" or purchased. Improper make or buy decisions can be costly in terms of funds used.

   a. *Make decisions:* Some firms find that producing their own components and parts is wise economically when the finished product's performance is critically dependent on the quality of the subassemblies. By making all parts and components, the firm's control over quality and reliability of the finished product is maximized. If availability of parts and components is uncertain and may cause unreasonable production delays, the organization may find it economically sound to make parts and components.

   b. *Buy decisions:* New businesses usually find that it is more cost effective to purchase most parts and components. Only when special expertise possessed by the firm's personnel is required or special equipment unique to the manufacturing facility is needed should the new firm take on the manufacturing chore. As a firm grows and becomes profitable, it may choose to add the manufacturing of parts and components to its operations.

   c. *Costs of buying from a fixed supplier:* Becoming dependent on one supplier can be detrimental to a business. Also, changing suppliers can have hidden costs, such as training costs. Service for any products also needs to be considered. Often, make or buy decisions are closely tied to the plant's capacity. Does the plant have idle capacity that could be optimized by manufacturing parts and components? Make or buy decisions require many considerations and need to be made in terms of the firm's strategic plan.

3. ***Receiving and Warehousing of Materials:*** Materials management does not end once materials and supplies are ordered. Inventories received from vendors need to be checked to ensure that they are the goods ordered, that the correct quantities have been received, and that the materials received are of the quality required. Receiving systems vary greatly depending on the type of firm.

    a. *Receiving policies and procedures:* Every firm needs to establish policies regarding the procedures to be followed for payment of shipments received and how and where the materials and supplies will be stored or warehoused.

    b. *Warehousing facilities:* Warehousing facilities depend on the type of product being stored.

    EXAMPLES:

        Blood needs to be refrigerated.

        Flammable liquids need to be stored in areas removed from dangerous fumes.

The essence of effective production and operations management is to integrate all the variables in the entire process. Getting materials and supplies from the location where they are stored to the location where they are needed when they are needed is an extremely important materials management task.

4. ***Inventory Management:*** Inventory management policies should be viewed as overall plans that link major functions needed to make the product and serve the customers' needs. Inventory management is responsible for maintaining an optimal balance between the advantages of having the materials and supplies on hand when needed and the costs of having inventories on hand. Effective inventory management policies allow the interdependent functions of marketing, sales production, and engineering to be supplied with the right materials and components at the right time to meet schedules at the lowest costs.

    a. *Economic order quantity (EOQ):* The **economic order quantity (EOQ)** equation is used to determine how much should be ordered to meet estimated demand at the lowest cost. The EOQ formula is widely used for determining optimal order quantities, but it should not be accepted blindly. A firm needs to be mindful that the results of the equation require careful interpretation in terms of real-world problems.

    The most important concept to remember about EOQ is that it is an equation that provides the basis for balancing the costs affected by inventory replenishment decisions.

    b. *Manufacturing versus distribution inventories:* A firm's policies for inventory management must be designed to fit the kinds of inventory to be managed. Two basic types of inventories that need to be maintained are manufacturing inventories and distribution inventories.

        1. *Manufacturing inventories:* Raw materials, parts, and components used in planned manufacturing operations are included in manufacturing inventories. Such inventories are largely predictable based on production plans and schedules.

            a. In many cases, the timely arrival of raw materials to meet production schedules is more important than ordering exactly the right quantity—the economic order quantity. For most businesses, the variables that affect inventory management are not only numerous, but many factors are out of the firm's control.

b.   Delayed shipments by vendors, goods damaged in transit from suppliers, and unexpected shortages of raw materials because of poor weather may, alone or in combination, cause an organization to reevaluate its inventory management policies and practices.

2.   *Distribution inventories:* This type of inventory includes the finished products to satisfy consumer demand.

EXAMPLES:

   Wholesalers and retailers purchase distribution inventories to resell.

   A manufacturer of business forms contracts with customers to produce large quantities of needed forms. Customers do not always have the warehousing space to store large quantities, so the manufacturer stores the finished goods until the customer needs a partial shipment. This procedure allows the manufacturer to produce goods in more - cost-effective quantities and to assist the customer by storing the forms until needed.

a.   Distribution inventories are frequently more difficult to manage because they are dependent on consumer wants and needs. The manager of distribution inventories needs to predict consumer needs and study consumer trends.

b.   The uncertainties related to predicting sales volume are usually much greater for distribution inventories than for manufacturing inventories, which are more predictable because needs arise from production schedules.

   EXAMPLE: *Consider the difference between purchasing paper to be used in the firm's office and purchasing paper to be sold in an office supply store. Purchasing paper for the office is largely predictable, but purchasing paper to be resold, no matter how effective the firm's inventory policies, still involves greater uncertainties.*

c.   *Inventory control systems:* Inventory management policies need to coincide with the kinds of inventories they are designed to control. To accommodate the differences, firms need to select those systems best suited to their goals. Several inventory management systems are available.

1.   *Fixed order–interval control system:* This system establishes periodic intervals, such as weekly or monthly, when the inventory is reviewed. The quantity ordered will be the amount needed to buy the inventory on hand, including any inventory on order, up to the minimum quantity level established. This system is also known as the *fixed order–period system.* The system's order point is frequently tied to a time period rather than a fixed quantity.

2.   *Fixed order–quantity control system:* This system relies on maintaining a perpetual (continuous) record of the amount of inventory on hand. A set amount is ordered when the stock on hand reaches that fixed quantity level. The system depends on the continuous monitoring of inventories.

   EXAMPLE: *At the grocery store, every transaction rings up the item sold and sends the information to the inventory system. When a certain level is reached, the system puts in an order.*

3. *Combined systems:* Inventory control systems that combine the features of both the fixed order–interval and the fixed order–quantity systems are also used.

4. *Just-in-time (JIT) inventory control system:* Some organizations have adopted the practice of keeping only enough inventory on hand to meet immediate needs. This system of inventory control is called just-in-time (JIT). Technology assists in making this system more feasible today. This system relies on forecasts and production or operations control reports.

d. *Computerized inventory control systems:* Computers are used by organizations today to control inventory. Barcodes and tracking information are widely used. Computers are not able to resolve inventory management problems, but they can provide management with data needed to make cost-effective inventory decisions.

Check Point—Section B

Directions: For each question, circle the correct answer.

B–1. The most widely used inventory management system is

A) CAM (computer-assisted manufacturing)

B) CIM (computer-integrated manufacturing)

C) EOQ (economic order quantity)

D) CAD (computer-assisted design)

B–2. Warehousing facilities are

A) reasonably available and full of inventory

B) used for distribution inventory only

C) not necessarily considered in inventory control

D) an extremely important materials management task

B–3. Make or buy decisions are

A) made during economic downturns

B) fitted to the strategic plan

C) made when it is off-season

D) made by fiscal year

C. Facilities

Successful firms recognize that facilities have strategic implications on the profit earned. If a firm is "overbuilt," it will face unnecessary overhead costs. If the facility is "underbuilt," the firm may miss opportunities for selling the product. When making decisions regarding the right facility, several questions need to be asked:

- Where should the plant be located?
- What will be the most optimal physical design for the facility?
- How much space needs to be allocated for each business function, that is, for administrative activities? for production space?
- What might be the most cost-effective layouts available for staff support functions?

1. *Plant Locations:* If a facility is built in the wrong place, operating costs can be extremely high. In addition, locating a facility in the wrong location might cause the firm to miss opportunities to sell its product or service. Determining the right location is complicated. The importance of selecting the right location is not uniformly impor-

tant for all kinds of businesses. Many factors may be employed for determining the proper location. Some of these include nearness to ultimate consumers, suppliers, raw materials, and major transportation facilities; and availability of a trained labor force. Room for growth and expansion of the company is another important consideration. Studies have shown that when some of the other factors are equal, the location selected is the one closest to the owner's or chief executive officer's home.

EXAMPLES:

Beer production is dependent on sufficient water supply.

Firms that ship goods must be near major ports, trains, highways, or other transportation facilities.

Firms that need highly skilled computer programmers or engineers tend to locate in centers where people with these skills live; supporting universities are often nearby.

L. L. Bean is still located in Maine where the founder grew up and started his business.

The Internet and World Wide Web are reducing some of the need for firms to be located in high-rent areas where they depend on consumers to pass by and shop.

EXAMPLE: *Amazon.com has a warehouse and office facility that is not decorated for consumers.*

2. *Facility Design:* The physical design of any facility should be consistent with the organization's purposes, functions, and customers. Factories have gone from being multistoried to only two or three floors; offices are being moved into new high-rise towers and former malls.

   a. *Common production facility layouts:* Production may be planned for a facility with a fixed layout or one that focuses on a specific process or the assembling of a finished product: fixed layout, process-focused layout, or product-focused layout.

   EXAMPLES:

   A large jetliner is assembled in a huge hanger with a fixed layout where the plane does not move.

   A paper mill produces paper by passing raw material through a sequence of machines where the product comes out at the end of the process, thus utilizing a process-focused layout.

   Automobile assembly-line plants have a product-focused layout where the product moves through the assembly line.

   b. *Operations facility layouts:* Some functions require specific layouts because of the events scheduled or the services provided: fixed layout or service-oriented layout.

   EXAMPLES:

   A sports arena for hockey and basketball competitions (fixed layout).

   A concert hall for operatic performances (fixed layout).

   A fenced-in area for a rodeo competition (fixed layout).

   A supermarket that groups similar items, but different brands, near each other to maximize sales and customer convenience (cereals, beverages, pet food) (service-oriented layout).

3. **Relation of Administrative and Production Space:** Once the decision has been made to organize facilities on a functional or a production or operations basis, the next question is where to locate each function or unit within the facility. In addition, the amount of space to be allocated to each function or unit needs to be decided.

   EXAMPLES:

   > *In a hospital, should the x-ray room be near the emergency room or adjacent to the intensive care unit? Should the intensive care unit be adjacent to the operating room? Or would a portable x-ray unit allow for using only one location to serve both the emergency room and the intensive care unit?*

   > *How much movement of patients, nurses, and x-ray technicians will occur if the facilities are adjacent? if the facilities are not adjacent?*

   > *Support functions, such as accounting in a hospital, would be assigned less space than the x-ray department.*

   > *The manager's office in a fast-food restaurant would probably be significantly smaller than the office of the communications support manager in a large financial institution.*

4. **Office Design:** Just like the production facilities have changed because of technology, new office designs are responding increasingly to the way in which technology has revolutionized the office. The office is a workplace with computer networks that permit communication of various kinds to be transmitted almost instantaneously around the country and the world. No longer are computers used only by information processing specialists. Computers are used by everyone—management at all levels, administrative and support staff, and production workers. Networking between the production facility and the office is essential today to keep up with rapid changes. Offices no longer have to be connected to production facilities. Real-time communication technologies can allow for looking for the most cost-effective and efficient use of office space.

   a. *Modern technology:* Technology has freed up distance and space considerations for managers and staff. Managers and workers may work from home or the office today.

      1. Offices for managers, administrators, and staff may be designed with open areas and enclosed offices. It is important to design enclosed spaces for offices that require privacy.

      2. Modular furniture, task lighting, and movable walls that comprise the open office are used frequently in settings that do not require closed offices.

      3. High-tech and ergonomic furniture has created more choices for design.

      4. Privacy is still a priority for managers to perform some responsibilities and walls are considered essential to ensure this.

   b. *Ergonomic advances:* Office furniture must be given attention as new office space is being designed or existing office areas are redesigned to accommodate new technology and functions. Successful firms recognize that ergonomically designed furniture and work areas take stress off employees, thus leading to greater productivity.

   c. *Environmental factors:* Other factors that impinge on human performance and must be considered in designing office space are temperature and ventilation. These conditions affect everyone.

The most important requirement in designing an efficient office is flexibility. Everything from walls to chairs must be adjustable and movable to respond to emphasis on *ergonomics* (the study of the work environment in relation to people and their individual needs and requirements).

Check Point—Section C

Directions: For each question, circle the correct answer.

C–1. One of the important concerns with office design today is

   A) type of computers purchased

   B) ergonomically designed work spaces

   C) a good price on office furniture

   D) that employees do not always work in offices

C–2. Plant location considerations

   A) are not uniformly important for all kinds of businesses

   B) need to be located where labor is cheapest

   C) must be close to providers of inventory

   D) must be close to inventory and customers

C–3. The methods for organizing facilities are

   A) functional, production, or operational

   B) technological, operational, or cost effective

   C) production, warehousing, or functional

   D) operational, technological, or production

D. Quality Control Systems

Planning and control are interrelated. An effective control system requires that plans and predetermined standards provide a basis for evaluating and controlling actual performance. Similarly, it is impossible to have an effective planning system without efficient controls to pinpoint discrepancies between planned performance and actual results. The aim in controlling the operations of a business enterprise is to ensure that all activities required are on a schedule and that preestablished quality and cost standards are met.

1. *Quality:* The term *quality* generally means "fitness for the intended purpose." Quality is a measure of how closely the firm's goods or services meet specified standards. Quality is a relative concept. The aim in a business context is to provide customers with a product at a level of quality that assures customer satisfaction while minimizing cost. To pursue a quality standard higher than customers reasonably expect, so-called gold plating, adds cost for the company but gives no economic advantage.

   a. *Managerial problems with quality:* The primary blame for poor quality lies with management.

      1. *Letting defective products go out:* Products are shipped out with defects with the expectation that customers will not complain. Many firms find it easier to ship out a defective product or provide a lesser-quality service and deal with occasional complaints than to make a high-quality product the first time.

      2. *Avoiding follow-up service:* When poor or defective products are allowed to enter the market, corrective services must be made available to the public.

Some managers are reluctant to provide adequate corrective services to remedy the initial defects. The customer is blamed for misuse when the real fault is with basic product quality. Follow-up service costs money, which bothers many managers who are trying to maximize every dollar of profit in the short run. Some countries require that products with defects are recalled and repaired or replaced.

3. *Lacking clear work or quality standards:* For workers to produce quality products or services, standards must be clear. Very often, standards are not shared with workers. Or, if they are, managers allow products that violate the standards to be shipped out, rendering ineffective any quality control process that is being used.

4. *Being unaware of the costs of poor quality:* People do not realize how much poor quality costs. Many organizations rework their products and services without any awareness of the costs involved. Quality could have been instilled at the very beginning of the process. One related problem with this approach is that many customers do not return their defective products for reworking. Instead, they complain to their peers and go elsewhere for new products. Most firms are unaware of all the direct and indirect costs of poor quality, both short- and long-term costs.

5. *Establishing the fault:* Management does not accept responsibility for poor quality. Managers tend to blame workers, competitors, and customers who want products to be made correctly the first time rather than to accept blame themselves for the poor quality. The manager's primary job is to achieve organizational goals through people and other resources. If the manager has quality products as an ongoing goal but then permits second-rate products or services to go to the customers, who is at fault? Too many managers are not held accountable for poor-quality work and receive their bonuses for short-term results, without factoring in the true costs of poor quality.

b. *Measures of quality:* All businesses, whether they sell products or services, need to be interested in quality control. The measures of quality will obviously differ among manufacturing and service systems.

1. *Manufacturing systems:* Measures of quality in manufacturing systems can be related to rather objective standards of dimension, chemical composition, and actual performance tests.

2. *Service systems:* In service-oriented firms, measures of quality are often not as objective. Such measures may relate to time standards (time required to handle a customer claim), output standards (the accuracy of the procedures used), and overall performance of individuals within the system.

EXAMPLE: *Consider the typical quality measures of output for a bank, a doll manufacturing firm, and an air-freight delivery company. The bank might measure the quality of output on such factors as the number and kinds of clerical errors and the customer waiting time to get to a teller's window. The doll manufacturer's quality control might be concerned with the dimension of the product, the surface finish, and the chemical composition. Yet, the air-freight firm might measure the quality of its service by reviewing its overall delivery time and errors in delivery.*

3. *Economic quality level:* For some people the term *quality* means the best or the most costly features. Successful enterprises know that this is a very limited and one-sided perception of quality. Competitive firms know that any product or service tends to have a most economical quality level. To determine this level, one starts by assessing what the customers consider to be an acceptable quality in relation to the price of the product or service.

EXAMPLES:

A ballpoint pen that runs out of ink after being used for three months will please the customer who expected the pen to last only two months.

A cartridge of copier toner that meets or exceeds the number of copies estimated by the manufacturer will meet the quality level expected by the customer.

The next step is to develop a consistent strategy for product or service quality control and to use a quality control system for implementing the strategy chosen.

Thus, the functions of quality are to:

a. Determine optimal quality standards

b. Monitor production so that goods and services of the specified quality are the outputs

Quality control involves measurement, feedback, comparison with established standards, and correction when necessary.

c. *Liability and quality:* In recent years the liability of firms for poor product quality has been well established. Some people believe that the number of product liability cases being heard in courtrooms throughout the nation has increased at an alarming rate. Consumer concerns about the quality of the products and services purchased has significantly affected the importance of quality control policies.

1. *Negligence:* Central to a manufacturer's liability for consumer injury is the concept of negligence. In the eyes of the law, negligence can include foreseeable use and misuse of the product. The question is: Could the manufacturer have reasonably foreseen the use and misuse of the product? If so, the manufacturer could be held liable for the consumer's injury.

2. *Product warranty:* Product warranty includes both that expressed by the manufacturer (written and oral) and the implied warranty that the product will be safe for consumer use. The uses by the consumer are not restricted to those included in the warranty but include those that may be foreseen. The concept of foreseeable usage is often interpreted to mean that if the product was misused by the consumer, such use was foreseeable. These legal concepts place a heavy burden on the quality control function.

Service businesses are certainly not exempt from quality control legal issues. As a general rule, no business—manufacturing or service—is ever exempt from being liable for the goods or services it sells.

EXAMPLE: *Increases in the number of medical malpractice cases shed some light on how important quality control issues have become in the health care field. In some medical areas, malpractice insurance premiums have skyrocketed.*

2. ***Quality Control Process:*** Every company has its own specific quality control problems. The actual quality control process implemented must be responsive to the firm's needs and reflect the firm's uniqueness. The firm's special qualities must be reflected either in the specified quality standards, in permissible tolerances from these standards, or in the way that quality inspection is carried out. **Quality control** generally consists of a series of planned measurements designed to verify compliance with all specified quality standards. It must be recognized that quality control cannot be limited to the final product or service but must include the materials and components that go into the final product or service. This suggests that quality control must be considered as an integral activity in the flow of operational events.

   a. *Quality control of products:* The quality control techniques selected by a firm need to be considered in terms of where the control process can be implemented most effectively and economically. Quality control can occur at any one or all three production phases: input, production, and/or output. The available techniques for controlling quality fall into three categories: mechanistic, statistical, and motivational techniques.

      1. *Mechanistic quality control techniques:* Automatic sensing and feedback devices are used to register whether the tested parts conform to established quality limits.

      2. *Statistical quality control techniques:* These techniques involve sampling and probability concepts, minimizing the number of inspections. By inspecting samples, a firm's inspection costs should be reduced while maintaining an acceptable quality level.

         EXAMPLE: *If 100 percent of 1,000 glass bottles manufactured must fall within established quality tolerances, every bottle must be inspected. On the other hand, if a 98 percent standard is acceptable, a statistically valid sampling scheme can be devised. Inspection of a sampling will probably be less expensive than inspecting every bottle.*

         The premise for using statistical techniques in quality control is that 100 percent inspection is often economically wasteful. Inspection of a selected sample can reduce inspection costs and, most importantly, attain an acceptable quality level.

      3. *Motivational quality control techniques:* This category of quality control techniques is based on the premise that quality defects are caused by human errors resulting either from a lack of knowledge or a lack of attention. In the early 1960s many aerospace firms developed what were called zero-defect systems. These programs were designed to motivate each employee to eliminate all quality defects in their assigned job tasks.

         EXAMPLE: *Zero-defect programs use posters, slogans, letters to the employees, and financial awards for outstanding performance as motivational incentives.*

   b. *Quality control of services:* Typically, quality control schemes have focused on production or manufacturing activities. Quality control activities have involved measuring the physical dimensions of a product, performance, and tolerances. Firms that sell services have often been reluctant to implement the quality control process because the inherent quality of services is often difficult to measure. As the service industries increase and more consumer dollars are being spent for services, businesses that sell services as their product need to consider adopting quality control strategies. Service industries are finding that there are controllable qualities for which standards can be set that represent acceptable and unacceptable performance.

EXAMPLE: *In the banking industry, the acceptable number of clerical errors and the acceptable length of time for a customer to stand in line waiting for an available teller can be determined.*

Various examples of quality control systems being implemented in service businesses indicate that setting standards for desired outcomes, monitoring performance with comparisons to the standards set, and taking corrective action may have valid use outside manufacturing.

c. *Quality circles:* Much attention has been given to comparing productivity rates in the United States to those in Japanese industry. U.S. firms began to ask why Japan was having such success with quality control. Did the Japanese have more effective quality control models?

Most economists agree that Japanese industries use concepts and models of statistical quality control that were exported to Japan in the 1950s. They have been able to not only learn the techniques of quality control well but also to train their workers in the techniques.

In the United States, quality control functions in most firms were developed and performed by technical staff, not by the workers doing the job. Since this was the case, U.S. workers often resisted the quantitative models and viewed quality control with suspicion. Japanese workers, on the other hand, were actively involved in arriving at solutions to quality problems rather than the technical specialist attempting to solve quality problems and convincing the workers of the merits of the program. This concept of **quality circles,** though popular in U.S. business and industry for 25 years or more, is on the wane today as more sophisticated total quality management processes develop.

3. ***Total Quality Management (TQM):*** Total quality control and management is not a new theory, but its application in management has caused business executives to examine strategic quality goals and the means being used to achieve these goals. The underlying principle of **total quality management (TQM)** is the same as the total marketing concept—that all activities and operations of any organization should be focused upon discovering and meeting the needs of the customers. The aim and focus of all programs should be based on meeting customers' needs on an ongoing basis, regardless of any short-term losses that may be involved.

a. *The quality control era (1980s to present):* During the period following World War II and continuing into the mid-1970s, American firms became very complacent. With little external competition, they were successful in meeting the public's needs though production and management practices were inefficient.

1. *Recognition of quality of Japanese products:* In the early 1980s American consultants and academicians became aware of the gain in market share and quality of Japanese products such as steel products, automobiles, television sets, clothing, and toys.

2. *Establishment of quality standards:* The quality of Japanese products became new standards for American-made consumer goods in the 1990s. Product quality, service, and competitive prices were major concerns in comparisons of Japanese and American products. Now India and China are beginning to have a similar quality impact.

Some organizations claim that they are following TQM concepts when, in reality, their operations do not really have a central focus on the customer. Traditional management exemplifies the use of the production or marketing era approaches. Enlightened organizations practice total quality control in all their activities.

b. *Deming's TQM system:* W. Edwards Deming (1898–1993) believed that total quality is a constant standard for industry and advocated the use of statistical measures to track quality. American business leaders did not accept his theories as readily as Japanese leaders did. He pushed for employee involvement in the quality control process. Under Deming's guidance, many changes were made to improve production processes and quality of output in Japanese industry. Deming and his Japanese counterparts were responsible for numerous improvements in Japanese production processes and the country's economy, leading to more prosperous lifestyles.

    1. *Deming's absolutes of quality:* The total quality management (TQM) movement has 14 rules.

        a. *Creating constancy of purpose:* A firm's rationale for existence must include the rationale to maintain high-quality products and services and to recognize that improvement should be a part of daily operations.

        b. *Adopting a new philosophy:* Management must embrace the total quality concept and eliminate counterproductive management methods.

        c. *Inspecting products or services continuously:* Workers should themselves be quality inspectors.

        d. *Awarding contracts for quality service:* Relying strictly on the lowest price often results in increased costs.

        e. *Improving the production of goods or services:* Organizations should be constantly seeking to improve their products and services, operating processes, and customer relations.

        f. *Providing training and retraining:* Training is an absolute necessity and must be maintained and continuously upgraded for success.

        g. *Instituting leadership:* Leadership must focus on learning and satisfying customer needs. In this regard, both the external client and the internal employee are essential for a quality product to be produced and received.

        h. *Eliminating fear of innovation:* Management must support innovation at every level to ensure quality.

        EXAMPLE: *Minnesota Mining and Manufacturing Company (3M) encourages and rewards employees who try new and innovative ways of doing things as well as developing new products or services.*

        i. *Fostering teamwork:* Barriers that stifle teamwork must be broken down. Corporations that foster team activities will experience success.

        j. *Eliminating useless slogans and targets:* Replace slogans with praise for good work on a regular basis and reward friendly, courteous salespeople.

        k. *Eliminating numerical performance quotas:* Meeting a numerical quota forces the employee to concentrate on the quantity rather than the quality of a product and may guarantee inefficiency.

l. *Developing pride of workmanship:* The manager's job should be to ensure that the workers are able to achieve their best by having good tools, supplies, and working conditions.

m. *Providing training in TQM approaches:* Organizations provide vigorous programs of education and retraining. Workers should be taught TQM tools, techniques, and team-building approaches.

EXAMPLE: *Organizations like QuadGraphics, Inc. and 3M know that informed employees are better employees and also that quality comes from increased knowledge, understanding, and effort.*

n. *Taking managerial action to make changes:* Top levels of management must make the necessary changes. TQM often involves a complete organizational transformation.

2. *Deming's "Deadly Sins of Quality":* Along with the basic rules for the TQM process, Deming identified seven major barriers to the effective implementation of the TQM process. A basic understanding of TQM is not complete without an examination of the major problems that Deming envisioned.

a. *Lack of constancy of purpose:* An organization without long-term direction has insecure employees and managers as well as a hesitancy to commit to an ongoing program that will not produce instantaneous results. Without constancy of purpose, TQM will fail.

b. *Emphasis on short-term profits:* One of the shortcomings of the American enterprise system is the pressure of owners on management to deliver short-term profits. TQM is a long-term approach. Looking just to improve the next quarter's dividends undermines quality.

c. *Evaluation through performance appraisal:* Deming had a bias against routine performance appraisals, arguing that they cause rivalries, build fears, and destroy teamwork. If performance has to be measured, the use of traditional individual appraisals on a periodic basis creates more problems than the approach solves.

d. *Mobility of management:* Another feature of the American system is the tendency of managers to switch firms every few years. This is in contrast to the Japanese system, which allows more readily for building and maintaining constancy of purpose and TQM. While many American employers have encouraged managerial mobility, this practice is counterproductive to the TQM movement.

e. *Operating a company on visible figures alone:* The short-term profit margin has very little to do with a firm's chances of being successful a few years later. There are better measures of organizational effectiveness than quarterly financial reports.

EXAMPLE: *The success of respected firms, such as Merck, RubberMaid, and General Electric, cannot be measured on financial statements alone. The quality of products, among other factors, must also be a determining factor.*

Unfortunately, such abstract and qualitative studies are not as simple to grasp as monthly income reports.

f. *Excess medical costs:* Deming suggested that high medical insurance costs interfere with corporate profits and the quest for quality. He encouraged the maintenance of sound, healthy working environments, as well as the establishment of fitness centers and preventive medical programs to help reduce insurance programs and money lost from absences due to illness.

g. *Excessive warranty costs:* When products are defective, eventually they need to be repaired. Many firms ignore the excess amounts that they have to spend on warranty maintenance costs and product liability lawsuits. Both are significant and detract from overall organization profits, productivity, and quality.

After noting the success of the TQM process in Japanese products, the Baldrige Award was established in 1987–1988 for U.S. companies that have achieved the highest in quality. The criteria are similar to the criteria for TQM.

4. ***ISO 9000 and ISO 14000:*** ISO 9000 is a set of standards created by the International Organization for Standardization. The ISO is a nongovernmental organization established in 1947 to promote the development of standardization throughout the world. ISO 9000 is very popular and serves as a foundation for almost all quality standards, whether an organization is following quality management, Deming's approach, management by objectives, or some other popular variation. Customers can count on products and services provided with ISO 9000 assurances. ISO 14000 is a set of policies to protect the environment internationally. It was developed by the same group. The standards set by this organization are becoming benchmarks for organizations that do business internationally.

a. *Developing standards:* Standards are developed through a process that begins with a panel that drafts a recommended standard, which can be a few pages long or can be hundreds of pages. The standards address intellectual, scientific, technological, and economic activity. The draft is then reviewed by any delegation that believes the standard will have an impact on its nation's economy. Feedback is examined, and the process is repeated. The entire organization votes on the proposed standard.

The majority of ISO standards are very specific and relate to documented agreements containing technical specifications or criteria used as rules, guidelines, or definitions of characteristics to ensure materials, products, and services are fit for their purposes.

1. *Generic management system standards:* The business community has become especially interested in two standards that have been developed as generic management system standards: ISO 9000 and ISO 14000.

a. *Generic:* The same standards can be applied to any organization, any size, whatever the product.

b. *Management system:* What the organization does to manage its processes relates to its management system. These may be written procedures or instructions.

b. *Defining ISO 9000 standards:* ISO 9000 is a set of technical standards first established in 1987 by the ISO, which is itself a network of standards institutes from 146 countries. Each country has one member. The organization is a blend of private and public entities, and governments do not necessarily control their respective delegation. Some governments do, however, incorporate their standards agencies into the network. The organization creates and publishes standards that are mostly technical in nature, but because of their uniformity, result in assurances that have broader impact than technical quality.

The ISO 9000 family of standards was the first generic management system standard (referred to earlier), and it is primarily concerned with quality management. Following the standards means that an organization is following an international consensus concerning what makes a product or service that meets customers' quality requirements.

c. *Defining ISO 14000 standards:* ISO 14000 standards address the environmental impact of products and services. The ISO environmental standards have two focal emphases:

   1. *Sampling and test methods.* To determine the environmental impact of a product, standards for testing must be followed.

   2. *Proactive approach to environmental issues:* The second emphasis is on standards that guide environmental management itself (not just product development and manufacture).

Check Point—Section D

Directions: For each question, circle the correct answer.

D–1. An effective quality control system requires that

    A) all employees do their best work
    B) all managers do their best work
    C) predetermined standards are set
    D) evaluations be done on every product

D–2. In America, the quality control era began

    A) in the 1800s
    B) in the 1940s

    C) after the 9/11 attacks
    D) in the 1980s

D–3. An international quality standard is

    A) MBA 2000
    B) ISO 9000
    C) CAD 20000
    D) CIM 12000

E. Human Resource Management

Human resource management (HRM) is a contemporary term for a field formerly called personnel management. This places more importance on the people part of the equation in management. An organization's resources equal people, capital, and natural resources. People are any organization's most vital asset. HRM describes the identification, selection, training, development, and retention of employees.

1. *Planning:* HRM planning requires that every aspect involving people in the organization is covered as a part of the strategic plan.

2. *Staffing:* The major purposes of HRM in any organization should be to attract, train, develop, and retain the most qualified employees in all positions. HRM includes many

separate functions. Staffing includes the identification and recruiting of qualified and skilled employees.

As stated above, people are any organization's most critical asset. Firms that encourage employees to grow personally on the job and promote job development activities find that their workers experience greater job satisfaction. Companies concerned with career development for employees benefit from the results of such programs as much as do the employees themselves.

3. *Compensation and Development:* This is the area of HRM where the most change is occurring. Typically the most important issue for employees is making a competitive salary. Compensation is a common source of complaint and causes some employees to want to change jobs.

   Wage and salary administration presents one of the most complex and difficult functions of HRM. Employee benefit programs have become an important component of a firm's wage and salary program. In particular, health insurance is an issue for many employees.

4. *Training and Development:* Training and development of employees is a key to productivity.

5. *Employee Safety, Health, and Stress:* Businesses in some countries face legal mandates to provide a safe environment. However, in other countries, the legal protection is nonexistent. HRM is the division in an organization that is concerned with providing the healthiest environment possible. Such an environment is not a motivator; it is a hygiene factor.

   Some types of work settings, by their very nature, require that people work under less than optimally safe or comfortable conditions. Employees still deserve to be treated with dignity and respect. They need managers who will constantly strive for healthier and safer working environments.

   EXAMPLES:

   > *Steel construction workers installing high-rise buildings have some safety rules and conditions in place. However, it is still a dangerous job.*
   >
   > *Health care workers face unknown illnesses and must deal with the most private part of being human.*

   Simultaneously, employees expect fringe benefits (indirect compensation), at minimal cost, to provide for undue hazards that may arise. Regular active-duty members of the U.S. Armed Services can purchase large amounts of life insurance for nominal sums. Officers are expected to avoid unduly dangerous working environments in providing suitable accommodations for troops, except during wartime or in battlefront conditions.

6. *Performance Appraisal:* One of the major responsibilities of HRM involves developing and retaining the best employees for the organization. An integral part of this responsibility requires that employees be evaluated on a regular basis to determine strengths, weaknesses, areas for additional training, possible promotions, and future career development within the organization. Evaluation needs to be done on a continuing basis, both formally and informally.

   Few areas of HRM are more important or more disliked than performance appraisal. Performance appraisals are protected or covered, directly and indirectly, by a number of laws.

In the evaluation process, a manager or supervisor points out an employee's strengths, weaknesses, and areas for possible future improvement. In many cases the employee gets an opportunity to respond to the evaluation and to sign the form, indicating understanding of the content. Many managers prefer to be in a position to praise subordinates. However, some are apprehensive about praising an employee for fear that the employee will ask for a raise. The task of delivering negative information, even for the sake of future career development, is often dreaded, both for the evaluator and for the employee. HRD departments need to have ongoing programs to provide the skills and education required. Performance appraisals should have a goal of motivating employees.

7. *Labor Relations:* Many managers feel uneasy about collective bargaining. The fact is that management and unions often have common goals. A competitive firm recognizes the importance of the management–union relationship and attempts to develop plans that allow both management and unions to have cooperative, positive interactions.

   Firms that establish a sincere relationship with unions will function within a friendly atmosphere rather than trying to maintain adversarial relationships.

8. *Grievance and Discipline:* Activities related to employee grievances involve far more time and attention than the resolution of the union contract.

   The United States has become a service-oriented society rather than a production-oriented, blue-collar environment. The probability of unions increasing their membership dramatically in manufacturing is low. Most union membership gain is in service industries.

   Considerable differences exist between grievance procedures and disciplinary process in unionized firms as opposed to those in nonunionized firms.

   Coaching and counseling also enter into grievance and discipline processes. Coaching involves helping employees develop the requisite skills to improve their on-the-job performance. If the situation exceeds the manager's area of responsibility, counseling is outsourced or a department is established to take care of the situations that arise.

9. *Employee Separation Process:* One of the most difficult tasks that most organizations confront involves the separation of people from their workforce, temporarily or on a permanent basis, voluntarily or involuntarily. While some people will leave voluntarily, others may have to be asked to depart, temporarily or permanently, for various reasons.

   The separation process needs to be included as part of the staffing policy of an organization. HRM has the responsibility to train managers in working with employees in all issues related to resignation, layoff, dismissal, or retirement.

Check Point—Section E

Directions: For each question, circle the correct answer.

E–1. Which one of the following functions of the organization is *not* a concern of HRM?

A) Manufacturing
B) Training and development
C) Staffing
D) Compensation

E–2. The major purpose of HRM in any organization is to attract, train, develop, and retain the most qualified employees in all positions. This function is called

A) performance appraisal
B) coaching and advancement
C) planning
D) staffing

E–3. Which one of the following HRM areas encompasses all aspects of collective bargaining?

A) Labor relations
B) Employee safety
C) Compensation
D) Appraisals

For Your Review

Directions: For each question, circle the correct answer.

Case 1: Tech, Incorporated

A large electronics firm, Tech, Inc., on the east coast of the United States does millions of dollars in business each year and employs thousands of workers. A new group of management trainees has just been hired. Smith, the HRM manager, hired the new management trainees personally. Smith led each of the new trainees through the HRM hiring process and made the final decisions as to employment.

The HRM group at headquarters includes the HRM manager, an office administrator, a benefits manager, a training manager, and support staff. The training manager, Sanchez, began work several months ago. Sanchez has a background as a trainer. The office administrator, Thompson, has a close working relationship with Sanchez. Sanchez has discovered since coming to work with Smith that Smith is focused on reducing the HRM budget. Smith discussed with Sanchez the plan to reduce training money for new employees. Sanchez feels that the budget for training has been cut to a level that is too low to complete an adequate job. Sanchez has to find resources to train the newly hired, incoming management trainees.

Sanchez has a work history of successfully conducting training activities. The staff in the HRM department is very supportive. Sanchez has made contacts with managers throughout the business.

1. The HRM department would be able to perform training better if it

   A) had not hired Sanchez
   B) uses internal staff for training
   C) focuses on the firm's goals
   D) replaces "long-term" employees

2. If Smith empowers Sanchez, training can be accomplished by

   A) allowing more money to be spent
   B) restricting the time to train to one day
   C) using other staff and managers to assist
   D) expecting new managers to learn on the job

3. Smith has demonstrated a/an

   A) understanding that the budget is important

   B) interest in reaching the goals of Tech, Inc.
   C) knowledge of employment safety
   D) understanding of the importance of staffing

4. Sanchez can provide an excellent training program for the new management trainees if

   A) the network inside and outside the HRM department is used
   B) the HRM department's dilemma can be solved with more money
   C) Smith becomes involved in the actual training itself
   D) the training program is limited to one day per week for a month

5. The issue of the reduced training budget is resolved when the HRM department realizes that

   A) performance appraisals will pinpoint weaknesses
   B) computers and technology are the solution
   C) hiring techniques can solve this problem
   D) proper training can actually save money

Case 2: Publishing Professionals

Chou is an executive at a major publishing company. The corporation has just finished recruiting for the next round of their management training program. They have hired the best and brightest graduates from top universities in the country. These new employees are under Chou's supervision during their six-month probationary training period. The new employees are working with managers in areas in which they were hired to work, such as marketing, copyediting, production, and so on. Each trainee will work with as many as six managers in his or her assigned area. Chou has been receiving calls from managers concerning the trainees almost since the day they started their employment. Chou is hearing similar complaints from many other staff members. Some of the complaints are that the trainees are not appropriately dressed for the position; that some walk into offices without knocking; several address others on a first-name basis in front of major clients; and there have been other numerous protocol errors.

6. The publishing company's problem is that the

   A) mission statement needs to be rewritten
   B) culture of the company needs to change
   C) quality control system needs to be reviewed
   D) training and development policies need to be modified

7. Chou could conduct management training more successfully if

   A) HRM is incorporated into staffing
   B) total quality management is used
   C) management is sensitized to good labor relations
   D) the employee appraisal process is clarified

8. If Chou were to utilize the total quality management approach advocated by Deming, which one of the following would address the trainee problem?

   A) Developing pride of workmanship
   B) Eliminating useless slogans
   C) Inspecting products or services continuously
   D) Eliminating fear of innovation

9. Chou should change the

   A) performance appraisal policy
   B) grievance procedures
   C) HRM policy statement
   D) hiring and training policy

10. The management trainees can ensure their job success by

   A) following job performance criteria
   B) paying attention in training class
   C) learning grievance procedures
   D) joining the union

Case 3: Belford's Department Stores

Belford's is a big retailer in the United States. Belford's uses a sales campaign that emphasizes that its products are made in the United States. News stories have accused some of the suppliers of making their products in foreign countries using child labor and where the working conditions are considered inhumane.

Since the news stories broke, Belford's stores have had a downturn in sales in the areas disclosed by the news stories. Immediate contact was made with suppliers to determine the country of origin and the labor conditions for each of the products.

Goods are still being shipped to company warehouses and stores. Authorization for buying these products is still occurring through the organization's automatic reordering inventory system. Manufacturing costs are rising, and negative news reports about Belford's suppliers are continuing. Management is meeting to consider how to control the situation. Belford's news releases are immediately sent to the major news media.

11. After managing the information released to the public, Belford's should next

A) purchase a new inventory management system

B) move facilities to areas where its products will sell

C) control inventory, warehousing, and supplier selection

D) change the inventory system to a just-in-time system

12. It would be beneficial for Belford's to review its

A) buy decisions

B) make decisions

C) costs of buying

D) inventory software

13. The kind of control that is needed immediately is

A) budgetary

B) cost

C) production

D) information

14. Which one of the following areas of control does Belford's have to consider at this time?

A) Inventory

B) Information

C) Accounting

D) ISO 14000

15. Review of controls is necessary in

A) compensation and development

B) quality of services

C) grievance procedures

D) materials procurement

Solutions

Solutions to Check Point—Section A

Answer:	Refer to:
A–1. (C)	[A]
A–2. (D)	[A]
A–3. (A)	[A-3]

Solutions to Check Point—Section B

Answer:	Refer to:
B–1. (C)	[B-4-a]
B–2. (D)	[B-3]
B–3. (B)	[B-1]

Solutions to Check Point—Section C

Answer:	Refer to:
C–1. (B)	[C-4-b]
C–2. (A)	[C-1]
C–3. (A)	[C-2]

Solutions to Check Point—Section D

Answer:	*Refer to:*
D–1. (C)	[D]
D–2. (D)	[D-3-a]
D–3. (B)	[D-4]

Solutions to Check Point—Section E

Answer:	*Refer to:*
E–1. (A)	[E]
E–2. (D)	[E-2]
E–3. (D)	[E-6]

Solutions to For Your Review

Answer:	*Refer to:*

Case 1:

1.	(B)	[A]
2.	(C)	[E]
3.	(D)	[E-2]
4.	(A)	[A & D]
5.	(D)	[E]

Case 2:

6.	(D)	[E]
7.	(A)	[E-2]
8.	(A)	[D-3-b-(l)]
9.	(D)	[E-2,4]
10.	(A)	[E-6]

Case 3:

11.	(C)	[A-1-d]
12.	(A)	[B-2-b]
13.	(D)	[A-1-d]
14.	(C)	[B]
15.	(D)	[B]

Chapter 4

Mentoring and Training

OVERVIEW

A few decades ago a person could stop formal learning activities after completing high school or college. This is no longer true. There have been more technological advances in the past 10 to 15 years than there have been in all prior history of civilization, and one can anticipate that changes in the next 5 years will have an even greater impact than those that have already occurred.

A central element of dealing with change that occurs in any successful corporation is an effective system focused on employee development and training. There are several dimensions involved in preparing the employee for on-the-job success. The very first is the initial employee orientation training. The employee must be oriented to work tasks, organizational procedures, and future opportunities involved in becoming an employee of the organization. A second dimension is an understanding of the different types of mentoring, coaching, developing, and training of employees. Both of these preparatory dimensions require a foundation in the theories of learning that provide the scaffold for creating effective training and development exercises and experiences. Every experience and training activity must be assessed in order to make necessary modifications for future improvement.

KEY TERMS

Affective domain, 78
Assessment, 104
Classical conditioning, 79
Coaching, 88
Cognitive domain, 78
Cognitive learning, 80
Development, 89
Distributed practice, 83

Evaluation, 104
Feedback, 82
Learning, 78
Learning curve, 80
Massed practice, 83
Mentoring, 87
On-the-job training, 98

Operant conditioning, 79
Orientation, 86
Overlearning, 83
Psychomotor domain, 79
Reinforcement, 82
Social learning, 80
Training, 95

A. Learning Basics

Learning is a lifelong process. Formally and informally, each person starts learning on the day of birth, and learning does not stop until life ends. Rapid changes over the last few decades have resulted in the need for continuous formalized learning to keep up with the many dynamic forces interacting within each person's individual life sphere and the surrounding external environment. The commitment to lifelong learning for the administrative professional cannot be stated strongly enough.

1. *Learning—A General Overview*

    a. *What learning is:* **Learning** can be defined as any relatively permanent change in behavior that occurs as a result of practice and experience. Learning involves only changes in the way a person behaves or acts that will last for a period of time. Learning is a continuous process utilizing practice and repetition to strengthen acquired behaviors. Finally, learning is different from the process of maturation, though maturation supports physical and mental changes that make most learning possible.

        EXAMPLE: *A youngster or a senior citizen may have difficulty throwing a discus because of normal physical limitations related to the aging process. Learning requires the change of behavior that results from experience and is not the result of maturation.*

    b. *Domains of learning:* Learning can occur in any of three general dimensions or domains. Learning a skill, knowledge, or behavior involves a combination of cognitive, affective, and psychomotor learning.

        1. *Cognitive domain:* The thinking and knowledge skills most associated with the learning process are in the **cognitive domain,** according to Bloom's taxonomy of learning objectives. A hierarchy of five learning outcomes is included in the cognitive domain, in rank order from basic knowledge to evaluation, the most advanced learning.

            a. *Basic knowledge:* Defining specific terms and principles, reciting specific facts and rules, and selecting and matching concepts with explanations.

            b. *Comprehension:* Explaining facts and principles, interpreting charts and graphs, and predicting future consequences implied in data.

            c. *Application:* Distinguishing between facts and inferences, explaining the relevance of data, and analyzing the major causes of a problem.

            d. *Synthesis:* Composing a musical score, designing a comprehensive plan to solve a problem, and revising sections of a chapter.

            e. *Evaluation:* Discriminating between the findings of two research studies, summarizing the highlights of a report, and judging the value of a work by using externally established standards of excellence.

        2. *Affective domain:* Learning indicated by emotions, feelings, or expressions is in the **affective domain.** The affective domain, as defined in Bloom's taxonomy, also includes interpersonal communication and the sharing of feelings and emotions with others. Trainers can and should devote more attention to the affective domain in various learning activities and techniques.

        3. *Psychomotor domain:* Learning is expressed by the actual performance of specific acts and the capability of operating equipment and technology by

moving and manipulating various levers and devices. This type of learning is in the **psychomotor domain.**

a. Many types of vocational and business education courses or programs include components designed to help an individual learn how to operate computers, lathes, drill presses, and vehicles.

b. Rapid changes in technology have led to the need for more psychomotor learning experiences to help people keep abreast of the changes in operating tools and technology.

EXAMPLE: *Dentists and surgeons have to be retrained in the latest procedures and tools related to their work. This involves changes in hand and body movements. "Painless" dentistry and arthroscopic surgery require training with the most current drills, lasers, and probes.*

Learning should start with a determination of which domains are to be emphasized and which learning outcomes need to be altered. However, many learning programs focus initially on the theories or techniques rather than the basic domains involved.

c. *Theories of learning:* The most common formal learning theories include classical conditioning, operant conditioning, cognitive learning, and social learning.

1. *Classical conditioning:* **Classical conditioning** theory refers to the learning that has occurred when a living organism responds to a stimulus that would normally not produce such a response. Learning a conditioned response involves acquiring an association between a conditioned stimulus and an unconditioned stimulus.

EXAMPLE: *Ivan Pavlov, a Russian psychologist, discovered classical conditioning by experiments involving dogs and meat. The meat was the unconditioned stimulus. He trained a dog to respond to the likelihood that meat was going to be given by ringing a bell every time the meat was about to be given. The dog would salivate at the very sight of the meat. After a while the dog began salivating at the mere sound of the bell. The bell was the conditioned stimulus, and the salivating was known as the conditioned response.*

2. *Operant conditioning:* The premise of **operant conditioning,** also known as the *law of effect,* is that behavior results from its consequences. B. F. Skinner is considered to be the founder of operant conditioning. Operant behavior usually modifies voluntary behavior. Reinforcement principles: The laws of effect, contingent reinforcement, and immediate reinforcement are basic principles of operant conditioning that govern how consequences influence behavior.

a. *The law of effect:* Behaviors that are rewarded tend to be repeated, while behaviors that are not reinforced tend to cease.

b. *The law of contingent reinforcement:* For a reward to have maximum reinforcing value, it must be delivered only if the desired behavior is exhibited. Rewards given indiscriminately or inconsistently do not serve as reinforcers and may adversely affect the entire reinforcement process.

c. *The law of immediate reinforcement:* For a reward to have maximum reinforcing value, it must be given as soon as possible after a desired behavior occurs. Delayed reinforcement has a less positive effect on the continuation of desired behaviors.

Operant conditioning is a very effective learning technique for managers to use because it provides excellent control of behavior.

EXAMPLE: *An administrative professional quickly learns that those who are rude and disrespectful toward clients or managers do not fare well, while those who are courteous toward their coworkers and superiors may be regarded more highly and given the benefit of the doubt, if required. The adage "Once burned—once learned" is the heart of operant conditioning.*

3. *Cognitive learning:* When thinking about the perceived relationship between events and individual goals and expectations, a person is utilizing **cognitive learning** theory. Cognitive learning focuses on examining how people pursue desired goals, interpret work tasks as opportunities to satisfy desires, and reduce perceived inequities.

4. *Social learning (observational learning):* The essence of **social learning** theory is that people can learn by observation and direct experience. Social learning theory involves role and behavioral modeling by observing and following the actions of others. Social learning theory recognizes the value and importance of learning through observation and perception. Models are an integral part of social learning theory. Four processes support the learner's response to the model: *attention, retention, reproduction,* and *motivation.* In brief, these processes involve the ability to pay attention to a behavior to be imitated; the ability to retain (remember and recall) the behavior; the ability to reproduce the behavior physically; and the desire that results in motivation to perform the behavior.

Social learning is popular but may be less effective because of the need for consistency in the actions of role models. This consistency is sometimes difficult to attain.

d. *The learning curve:* A graph can be used to depict the course of learning that most people tend to follow. The **learning curve** depicts how behavioral changes occur. The key point to remember is that changes in behavior occur only after repeated practice. On the graph of the learning curve, a gradual slope indicates a slow rate of acquiring new behavior, and a steep slope indicates rapid progress. The closer one gets to the maximum level of performance, even small improvements require more practice than at the beginning of the training process.

EXAMPLE: *In learning a basic skill like keyboarding, early practice results in rapid gains. Once an optimal speed is reached, additional improvements in speed require longer periods of drill and practice. Improving from 40 words per minute to 50 words per minute may require only a few weeks. A similar gain of 10 words per minute when improving from 90 words per minute to 100 may take several months.*

e. *Basic styles of learning:* All persons tend to use one of four basic learning styles. One might ask, "Which one of these styles best describes your primary learning style?" as a means of understanding the differences in these styles.

1. *Concrete experience:* This learning orientation focuses on direct involvement in experiences and dealing with human situations in a personalized manner.

2. *Reflective observation:* Individuals with this learning style focus on understanding the true meaning of ideas and situations through careful observation, reflection, and description.

3. *Abstract conceptualization:* People with this learning orientation focus on the use of logic, ideas, and concepts and are able to excel in systematic planning, quantitative analysis, and manipulation of abstract symbols while solving problems.

4. *Active experimentation:* Individuals who learn better through active experimentation are concerned primarily with influencing people and changing situations.

5. *Combination approaches:* Some people will see their primary learning orientation representing selected facets of two or more of these styles. However, one approach will tend to be dominant.

While other ways of describing learning styles can be presented, these four basic learning styles illustrate current thinking about typical learning orientations.

2. ***Principles of Learning in the Training Context:*** A review of some of the most pertinent principles of learning provides a foundation for learning. Specific training and development techniques can be utilized to foster learning within the organization designed to achieve certain goals and objectives.

a. *Preconditions for learning:* For learning to be effective, especially when training and development approaches are utilized, two preconditions must exist: learner readiness and learner motivation.

1. *Learner readiness:* The learners (trainees) must have the basic skills and knowledge necessary to understand and to grasp successfully the content that will be presented to them.

EXAMPLES:

> *If a student takes an advanced economics class and does not understand the principles of supply, demand, and elasticity, his or her learning efforts definitely will be hindered.*

> *The person who does not have basic computer literacy will have a difficult time participating in training sessions where knowledge of spreadsheet analysis and database management is required.*

2. *Learner motivation:* Motivation comes from within. If the learner does not want to learn and lacks sufficient motivation to get through difficult moments, the amount of retained knowledge will be minimal at best.

a. When people attend training sessions because their employer, their parents (spouses), or their peers require them to attend, the learning retention rate tends to be low.

b. Learning is much more effective and efficient when the learners have a high motivation to acquire new knowledge and skills before and during the learning process.

b. *Other prerequisites for learning:* Besides the two preconditions for successful learning (learner readiness and motivation), other prerequisites exist that will influence the effectiveness of learning in training activities.

1. *Career plans:* Students with definite career plans are more likely to learn than persons who are undecided about future directions.

2. *Realistic training preview:* Persons who have been given a realistic training preview learn more than those who enter a learning program with high expectations about the course outcomes and low expectations about the amount of effort required. Some form of advance information helps trainees develop realistic expectations.

3. *High expectations for learning:* High self-efficacy expectations breed success in learning. *Self-efficacy expectations* are an individual's beliefs about personal ability to perform a given task or learn a new skill successfully.

c. *General learning principles:* Trainers and instructors can apply many learning principles to ensure that learners master new knowledge, skills, or behaviors. Specific principles emphasize feedback, reinforcement, practice, transfer of learning, relevance of material, and conditions for learning.

1. *Feedback:* Learners need to be given frequent information about how they are performing. As Kenneth Blanchard and Spencer Johnson observe in *The One Minute Manager* (William Morrow, 1983), "Feedback is the breakfast of champions." **Feedback** is necessary for both learning and motivation.

   a. When learners are not given feedback promptly, they may repeat improper procedures or techniques.

   b. Feedback, positive or negative, is essential to maintain motivation for continued learning.

   c. Any improvements in performance should be positively rewarded and recognized.

   d. As learners' skills increase, the instructor's performance expectations should also be raised. Higher degrees of achievement should be required before additional positive feedback is provided.

   e. As learners begin to master the content, the instructor should help them learn how to provide self-generated feedback.

   EXAMPLE: *When a child first learns to read, teachers, parents, other relatives, and family friends usually provide much reinforcement. Without this feedback, the child may not try to improve his or her reading skills. Of course, as the child discovers the excitement reading brings, he or she will be intrinsically motivated to improve. Once the child has learned how to read well, continual reinforcement is typically no longer necessary or important to the child.*

2. *Reinforcement:* Directly related to feedback is the learning principle of **reinforcement.** Employed in operant conditioning, reinforcement involves providing incentive when the learner has attained a specified level of performance. Continuous and intermittent reinforcement are the primary types of reinforcement.

   a. *Continuous reinforcement:* Continuous reinforcement refers to reinforcing every time a desired behavior occurs. In initial learning trials, a desired response occurs more rapidly with continuous reinforcement than with any other type of reinforcement. However, continuous reinforcement is more costly, time consuming, and difficult to administer.

   b. *Intermittent reinforcement:* Some types of recognition are delivered only on a periodic basis. Reinforcement occurs on an intermittent basis, either predictably or unannounced. Behaviors rewarded by intermittent rein-forcement will remain in effect longer, even when all reinforcers are elim-inated, than do behaviors encouraged by continuous reinforcement.

EXAMPLE: *Hourly workers are intermittently observed by a supervisor for conformance to proper procedures and maintaining high quality. Not knowing when they will be observed, they maintain a steady work rate, conform to procedures, and maintain consistently high quality. Bonuses are given for consistent behavior.*

With random, intermittent reinforcement, learners do not know when they will be tested or observed and thus are more vigilant at all times. However, with fixed times or quantities, learners can be prepared at cer-tain times. Learners who review often, rather than just at test time, will retain more, especially in the long run.

3. *Practice:* For a person to learn effectively and adopt new behaviors perma-nently, practice is required.

   a. *Whole versus part learning:* The major issue to be resolved is whether learners should focus on practicing the entire task at once or on master-ing component parts of an assignment, one at a time. Integration of the parts would occur near the end of the learning experience. The progres-sive method of practice, whereby a person learns one part of a very com-plex task during the first session and works until it is mastered, goes on to the next, and eventually is able to perform all parts of an assignment well, is a recommended learning approach.

   b. *Simple versus complex learning:* Projects that are simple should be prac-ticed in their entirety. Tasks that are moderately complex should be di-vided into component parts that can be practiced separately and eventually integrated and performed in their entirety. Extremely complex assignments with closely related steps that are difficult to divide should be learned and practiced as a whole, working at a slow but steady pace so as not to burn out at the very beginning and also to ensure mastery and a high motivational level at the very end.

   c. *Cramming versus distributing:* The learner can attempt to learn everything in one session (cramming, or **massed practice**), or the learning episodes can be spread across several practice sessions (distributing or **distributed practice**). Cramming works well with simple tasks, while distributed prac-tice is a more successful technique with difficult or complex assignments.

   d. *Amount of practice for learning:* Sometimes people will try to reduce practice time, relying more on intuition, memory, and common sense. If knowledge or skill has yet to be mastered, the learner may not have a large enough base of familiarization for intuition to be effective. **Over-learning** involves repeated practice even after the task has been mas-tered. It is appropriately used when critical tasks are involved that are usually performed only a few times a year, if they are stressful tasks to perform, and if the initial responses must be 100 percent accurate.

   EXAMPLE: *Members of the U.S. military practice putting on, wearing, and working with nuclear, biological, and chemical warfare (NBC) suits frequently. Whenever a signal is given, soldiers are expected to cease their other actions immediately and properly don these suits instanta-neously. When U.S. forces were committed to the Gulf War and faced threats of chemical warfare, the troops were prepared.*

4. *Transfer of learning:* The entire purpose of learning is to change behaviors. The measurement of learning effectiveness is clearly seen in the ability of employees to apply newly acquired skills and behaviors to job performance. Instructional efforts are cost effective when the skills, knowledge, and behaviors acquired can be applied to present jobs and also transferred to others.

   a. *Guidelines for transfer of learning:* Guidelines such as the following help ensure successful transfer of learning through training and development activities.

      (i) Highly motivated persons transfer learning more readily than do individuals who are not motivated.

      (ii) Learning through positive reinforcement transfers more readily and effectively than learning directed by punishment and negative reinforcers.

      (iii) Active participation in the learning process leads to greater transferability than does passive involvement.

      (iv) Persons who set realistic learning goals acquire and transfer more knowledge to their jobs and lives than do those who set unrealistically high objectives, those whose objectives require little effort to achieve, or those who have not set formal learning targets.

   b. *Teaching–learning methods:* A number of methods may be used to enhance the transferability of learning:

      (i) Demonstrating similarities between learning episodes and actual on-the-job performance.

      (ii) Allowing the learners to have as much experience as possible with knowledge, skills, and behaviors being learned.

      (iii) Utilizing a variety of examples when teaching concepts or theories to add more concreteness and pragmatism to the learning experience.

      (iv) Designing learning experiences so that learners can readily identify the transferability features.

      (v) Ensuring that newly transferred behaviors, skills, and attitudes are recognized and rewarded.

      EXAMPLE: *Lewis finally learned how to process the payroll by using a personal computer with a payroll program. One day an employee came in seeking an advance because of a family emergency. Lewis was tempted to process this transaction manually. If the temptation to resort to manual bookkeeping is overcome, Lewis will be less likely to revert to old methods and will continue to use the computer effectively.*

5. *Relevance of material:* Students have higher levels of readiness and are more willing to learn if they can perceive that the instructional episodes can be of direct and immediate value (training) or have long-range personal applicability (development). When learners believe that the materials being covered

have little value, their motivational levels decrease and their readiness to adopt new behaviors also declines.

   a. Learners must be shown that the knowledge, abilities, and attitudes to which they are going to be subjected will be highly beneficial to their jobs and lives immediately or in the foreseeable future.

   b. Trainers should explain and reinforce the importance, relevance, and value of the knowledge, skills, and attitudes that they expect trainees to learn and to apply in their work.

   c. Instructional programs must be designed and integrated to coincide with the learners' needs and perceived as relevant. The situations where the newly acquired knowledge and skills will be used must be realistic, too.

6. *Conditions for learning:* Environmental factors can play a significant role in the learning process. Environmental factors can enhance, neutralize, or negate the positive effects and benefits of otherwise well-planned and well-implemented learning experiences.

   a. Workers who are allowed to learn in comfortable settings tend to acquire and retain more knowledge than do those who have to learn in uncomfortable settings.

   b. Persons who can learn without worries or impending job deadlines while they are receiving instruction will acquire and transfer more knowledge than will those who have to return to their workstations and make up for the time lost during the educational process.

   EXAMPLE: *From the mid-1940s to the early 1960s an educational institution just north of the downtown area in the city of Chicago was perceived to have a horrendous environment for learning—the Navy Pier Branch of the University of Illinois. The corridors were long, narrow, and dark; the ventilation system was grossly ineffective, the learning resource center (library) was inadequate, faculty offices were dismal, and classrooms offered unique challenges.*

Check Point—Section A

Directions: For each question, circle the correct answer.

A–1. Behaviors that are rewarded tend to be repeated. This phenomenon is called the law of

   A) exercise
   B) contingent reinforcement
   C) immediate reinforcement
   D) effect

A–2. In order to learn new skills or knowledge, the learner must have all the precursor skills and knowledge. This is known as

   A) learner readiness
   B) realistic training preview
   C) feedback
   D) whole versus part learning

A–3. The transfer of learning is more likely to occur when people

   A) establish high expectations with unreachable goals
   B) engage in massed practice
   C) set realistic learning goals
   D) train in challenging environments

B. Employee Development Through Mentoring and Coaching

Experienced managers can be very effective in coaching and mentoring junior managers and providing supervisory assistance. Mentors are senior-level persons who help new people (protégés) get accustomed to their jobs and provide guidance, direction, and support during the process. Other development processes can be used to prepare an employee in areas of professional development that do not focus on the more immediate acquisition of job skills. Job training programs are devoted to this more immediate need, whereas employee development focuses on more long-term improvement.

1. *Employee and Workforce Orientation:* All members of an organization, whether the organization is a corporation or a civil agency, whether it is for-profit or nonprofit, must become familiar with the rules and regulations that govern the organization. Employees must receive appropriate orientation to any activity, whether it be a mentor relationship, coaching, development activities, training, or just work procedures.

   a. *Orientation:* **Orientation** involves initial introduction of a new or transferred employee to work itself, the organization and its rules, other members of the organization, and the organization's goals in order to prepare the new employee for successful contribution to the organization.

      1. *New employee orientation:* More than 90 percent of companies have some form of new employee orientation. This focuses on introduction and preparation for the employee in a new setting.

      2. *Transferred or promoted employee:* Employees who have transferred between departments or who have been promoted to another level of the organization require orientation in their new setting. However, some of the basic concerns, such as introduction to the organization and completing forms for benefits, are unnecessary.

   b. *Types of orientation:* Whether or not orientation will be divided into types depends greatly on the size of the organization. Larger organizations will be able to provide segmented orientation sessions that focus on important details, but that always begin with general introductions and move to more specific concerns. These may include a facilities tour or a session on completing forms in a benefits package. Orientation can be one of two types:

      1. *Work unit orientation:* Typically, a supervisor or a human resource employee would introduce the employee to the work unit, its members, its rules and processes, and its role in the organization. The supervisor addresses specific job tasks.

      2. *Organization orientation:* A trainer from the human resource or personnel department addresses broad issues related to the organization's structure, its mission, and its expectations for the future. The session often involves completing employment forms and learning about pay periods, employee retirement and investment plans, and health benefits.

   c. *The goals of orientation for the employee:* There are several very important functions served by employee orientation. They include reduction of anxiety, realistic presentation of the work and its setting, education about the organization, and welcoming of the employee:

      1. *Anxiety and stress:* Orientation reduces stress and makes the employee feel welcome.

2. *Presenting a realistic picture of work:* The orientation program must present realistic expectations by emphasizing the pace of work, the high level of expectations that others will have, the supportiveness they can expect, and so on.

3. *Education about the organization:* Employees must learn about the organization through a formal process, though once in the job, employees will continue an informal education.

4. *Making the new employee feel welcome:* A new employee and even a transferred employee must be made to feel welcome to the unit and the organization. This helps the employee begin making important workplace affiliations and associations.

d. *The goals of orientation for the employer:* Orientation helps the employer in at least two ways:

1. *Reduce turnover:* Effective orientations reduce early turnover caused by mismatched employees and expectations. The more familiar the employee is with the expectations being made, the greater the chance that a smooth entry will be successfully accomplished.

2. *Save time:* Effective orientations reduce time required for mundane items like properly completing forms and understanding procedures, reduce confusion, and increase preparation for work.

2. *Mentoring:* **Mentoring** can serve several purposes in an organization. Mentors, who typically are experienced members of the organization, can serve as advocates, coaches, and sponsors. The greatest role they serve, though, is that they model successful skills for their charge. The role of a mentor is to build esteem and confidence, and to serve as a guide.

a. *The characteristics of mentors and mentorship:*

1. *Mentoring leads to success:* Most successful managers have one or more mentors along the way. The mentoring concept has proved to be a very effective training and development technique.

2. *Mentors build relationships:* At times personal relationships develop between the mentor and the protégé. These relationships can be the foundation for long-term associations and networks that last beyond the immediate developmental process.

3. *Mentors provide guidance:* Mentors must be watchful of their protégés' progress and provide positive as well as negative feedback and also champion the protégés' causes when appropriate.

EXAMPLE: *Becker, the new manager of the Retailing Division, was assigned a mentor—Lawrence, the vice president for marketing. The assignment was made by mutual assent. While the mentor and the mentee were in contact on a daily basis and Lawrence was in a position to provide negative feedback about any mistakes, the only type of reinforcement was positive. Later, Becker encountered some interpersonal problems with one of the other senior managers. The mentor failed to advise Becker ahead of time about the misunderstandings, did not give advice on how to resolve these difficulties, and also failed to "champion" the protégé to the other managers.*

b. *Mentoring programs:* Some programs are carefully designed and implemented, whereas others occur naturally as a consequence of work environments.

   1. *Designed mentoring programs:* In designed programs, the mentor is often, but not always, a person from upper-level management who meets with one or more designated employees on a regular basis to discuss problems, explore issues, and develop plans for professional enhancement.

      a. The mentor is a model for the trainee (sometimes called a *mentee* or *prot*égé).

      b. The mentor establishes a rapport and trust with the trainee.

      c. The mentoring program is carefully monitored and assessed regularly.

      d. Typically, the mentor uses activities and assignments that are common to all participants in the program.

   2. *Unstructured mentoring activities:* The most successful mentorships occur accidentally, without a corporate design. People are attracted by the qualities of a successful individual and will approach them for advice or coaching.

      a. The relationship develops naturally as a consequence of a work-based relationship.

      b. The mentor shows interest in the protégé without the need for a structured approach. Sometimes the mentor recruited the employee, sometimes the relationship may be one of grooming a replacement, and sometimes the mentor undertakes the role to be sure that organizational goals are accomplished.

      c. The protégé learns by observing and imitating the behavior of the mentor. Highly involved mentorships may also include advice on every aspect of work, including introduction to the social life of the company and the unstated social order and etiquette.

3. **Coaching:** In its simplest form, **coaching** requires that a trainer, most often a supervisor or manager, serve as coach in one-on-one situations with an employee being trained. The coach provides an explanation of what is expected, an evaluation of performance, and clear and constructive feedback. The coach may often model the desired skill for the employee.

   a. *Flexibility:* One of the advantages of coaching is its great flexibility.

   EXAMPLE: *Simpson has a problem with absenteeism. Jetson, the manager, should meet with Simpson and discuss the problem. The discussion should follow several simple steps: (1) Identify the problem. This means that Simpson and Jetson should agree on how to understand that a problem exists and what it is. In this case, the problem is absenteeism. (2) Discuss alternative solutions. Then Jetson asks questions of Simpson that help understand the cause of the problem and explore ways to solve it. Perhaps Simpson has difficulties with children and needs a different schedule while the Simpson family works through the other difficulties. (3) After identifying a course of action, both Jetson and Simpson agree that it is the action to be taken. (4) After the action is taken, Jetson must monitor Simpson to see that the solution is being tried and whether it is helping solve the problem. (5) Finally, when the problem is solved, Jetson should confirm this with Simpson and offer supportive or constructive feedback.*

b. *Intensity:* Coaching has an advantage of being able to be spread over a period longer than the short period allowed for most training.

   1. Coaching helps increase productivity and sales through the extended period of coaching intervention.

   2. A disadvantage is that coaching is not as widely used as would be expected considering how successful it is. The drawback is the substantial time commitment for the supervisor.

   3. While managers may not intentionally use the coaching approach, the activity that people recognize as coaching is used frequently. Any kind of interaction between a person who has a skill and one who does not regarding that skill is a form of coaching.

4. ***Employee Development:*** Development is more ability-based and future-oriented than training. Most development programs focus on preparing personnel (managers and nonmanagers) for increased responsibility at higher levels within the organization. However, some development programs focus on upgrading executive abilities and are designed for managers who currently hold top-level managerial positions, while others provide opportunities for people at lower hierarchical levels.

   a. *Development:* While *training* focuses on improving skills needed to perform one's present job, *development* is aimed toward improving an employee's competence for possible job opportunities in the future. In some organizations, the terms *training* and *development* are used synonymously.

      1. *Generally accepted definition:* A comprehensive definition of **development** relates to planned organizational activities that involve individual employees, teams, or the entire organization in expanding their capacities to meet future opportunities and challenges. Development requires a futuristic perspective and is concerned with how individuals and groups will deal with unanticipated, but expected, changes in the work environment. Development helps individuals prepare to meet future challenges, not necessarily those they are currently experiencing.

      2. *Difference between training and development:* While training specifically refers to the upgrading of on-the-job performance of nonmanagerial employees, development is broader in nature, directed mainly toward preparing present and potential managers to deal with future events.

   b. *Management development needs:* Many difficulties exist in trying to identify specific needs of managers to initiate proper experience, knowledge, and behavioral change for the improvement of managerial and leadership effectiveness. Here are some of the primary reasons for difficulty in determining management development needs.

      1. *Managerial competence at different levels:* Required management competence varies with different levels of the managerial hierarchy.

         a. First-line (operational) managers must have strong technical and interpersonal skills and abilities as well as basic knowledge of administrative functions. These managers must be excellent communicators, relate well with others, and understand the technical details of the jobs and tasks they are expected to oversee.

b. Persons holding middle-level management positions are expected simultaneously to satisfy the optimistic demands of top-level managers and to balance the realistic world in which first-line managers' function. These two groups can be far apart in their expectations and capacities to perform. Middle managers must possess enough conceptual knowledge to understand where the organization is heading and how middle-level operations affect the overall organization's objectives and mission.

    (i) Superb communications and interpersonal skills are needed in facing pressures through both downward and upward communication.

    (ii) In addition, some technical ability helps middle managers understand problems confronted by first-line managers.

    (iii) Organizing and planning skills are needed to help in the structuring and goal setting required for basic work units to function effectively.

    (iv) Middle managers should possess sufficient administrative and computer literacy skills and abilities to handle the large amounts of detail confronting them and the capacity to analyze data even while facing myriad other deadlines.

    (v) Middle managers must be able to tolerate a high degree of ambiguity, not be afraid to take some risks, and have the self-confidence to continue while downsizing and structural changes are taking place within the organization.

EXAMPLE: *Both top- and lower-management levels are constantly squeezing middle-level managers. Having to satisfy two sets of opposing forces simultaneously is difficult enough under normal circumstances. However, recent trends toward elimination of middle-management layers, increased use of computerized controls by top-level management, and the greater empowerment of first-line managers have created some chaos. A number of organizations have reinstated some middle-management positions as a result.*

c. Top-level managers face the need to show positive results in short periods despite environmental factors that might not permit them to do so. They confront enormous external pressures to keep stock prices rising, costs decreasing, market share and profits growing, and workers more efficient and effective, all at the same time.

    (i) Top-level managers must have superb conceptual abilities and be consummate planners and organizers.

    (ii) Contemporary top-level managers require strong interpersonal and communication skills to inspire their employees and satisfy their diverse stakeholders.

    (iii) Enormous amounts of energy are required to be able to work long hours; deal with many different issues at the same time; and constantly make minor, intermediate, and major decisions.

    (iv) Top-level managers must be able to function effectively despite constant criticism and media attention.

Trying to meet the diverse management development needs for individuals at all managerial levels, while avoiding duplication and maximizing the use of every moment in the day, is very difficult.

2. *Programs to meet management needs:* Some organizations view training and development programs as a frill, with the end results difficult to show. Those in charge of designing and implementing management development programs generally lead exciting but stressful lives. Management development specialists have difficulty in devising programs to meet appropriately the needs of all managers everywhere. Management development specialists must utilize diverse skills and knowledge to design and to implement effective management development programs.

c. *Effective development programs:* Organizations must first establish the purpose and objectives of the management development program.

1. *Major purpose:* The major purpose of management development is to provide continuing education opportunities to update managers' competence in dealing with future needs.

2. *Goals and objectives:* Management development programs are designed to improve the effectiveness of the manager's job performance, especially in terms of competence in:

a. Coping with change in the organization

b. Conflict resolution

c. Interpersonal and teambuilding skills

d. Written and oral communication skills

e. New developments in technology, international business, consumer trends and demands, and competition (direct and indirect)

f. Environmental issues relating to the sociocultural environment, legal and political forces, and the domestic and international economy

A critical objective of management development programs is to help managers understand and appreciate their individual strengths, weaknesses, interests, and core values.

d. *General development approaches:* Management development specialists focus on the needs of different constituencies or address the instructional media being used while identifying specific techniques to satisfy the organization's basic objectives for development.

1. *Designing programs for managerial levels:* Management development approaches may focus on different hierarchical levels. Programs can be designed and presented to meet the specific needs of first-line, middle, and top-level managers.

a. First-line managers need to develop or refine interpersonal skills, communication skills, problem-solving abilities, time management skills, supervisory skills, empowerment, and latent leadership capabilities.

b. Middle managers require assistance in learning to become more assertive, dealing with conflict, improving interpersonal and communication skills, and balancing multiple demands simultaneously. Delegation, empowerment, time management, and leading are other important aspects of the middle manager's position.

    c.   Top-level managers need special assistance in improving their leadership skills, interpersonal skills, visionary skills, planning and organizing skills, conceptual and analytical capacities, abilities to handle multiple constituencies at the same time, crisis handling, and managing stress.

  2. *Designing appropriate development programs:* Management development specialists can study the various techniques available for varied developmental needs of managers. After utilizing research instrumentation to identify the learning preferences of individuals, they need to design and to implement appropriate programs to meet the needs of the managers.

e. *On-the-job development methods:* Some of the most widely used on-the-job or on-site management development techniques include understudy assignments, junior boards, job rotation, and on-site off-job training techniques.

  1. *Understudy assignments:* Lower- and middle-level managers are assigned to assist top-level executives.

  2. *Junior boards:* Creating special boards of directors comprised of middle managers, and giving the members the right to study any facet of an organization's operations, is a unique management development technique. Such a junior board can also make recommendations to the corporate board of directors.

  3. *Job rotation:* New managers can be assigned to various departments on a systematic basis to gain more experience. This technique is also used for training purposes.

  4. *On-site off-job training techniques:* Many of the on-site off-job training techniques are also used for management development purposes.

    a.   Video technology (videotapes, videodisks) is used in development programs. One specific technique is to require the participants to provide critiques of taped sequences and to solve assigned problems.

    b.   Teleconferences and audio conferences are frequently used to enhance the development and training process.

    c.   Programmed instruction and interactive video training are effective techniques when problem-solving exercises are utilized.

f. *Off-the-job development methods:* Many management development techniques can be employed off the job but on-site. A number of these techniques are recommended for use with management development programs.

  1. *Role-playing and simulation:* Techniques such as role-playing, use of in-basket exercises, and simulation are used for training and development purposes.

    EXAMPLE: *One of the most commonly used in-basket exercises includes several memorandums describing tasks to be performed. The participants are asked to prioritize these memos, within a specified time limit, in the order in which the tasks would be performed: first, second, and so on. No ties are allowed. The rankings are discussed after all have completed the assignment individually.*

  2. *Seminars and courses:* Seminars and courses are offered through training firms and educational institutions for academic credit or continuing educa-

tion units (CEUs). Some seminars and courses are offered through formal classroom instruction, and others are offered as independent or self-study courses.

EXAMPLE: *Often, one-day seminars are scheduled on an ongoing basis by training and development firms or consultants. Seminars with titles like "Effective Communication Skills for Women in Business" or "How to Supervise People in Your Organization" are included in brochures or flyers sent to managers who might want to participate. Group discounts may be available when several people from the same organization attend.*

3. *Management and business games:* When management and business games are used as development strategies, teams of players are required to make a number of major decisions in typical business settings.

   a. Participants (players) may be asked to make production, marketing, and financial decisions about a new product or service that a major firm is considering.

   b. The players may be required to develop detailed information, such as specific prices, production schedules, types of funding sources, and quantities of inventory ordered initially.

   c. To make the simulation more like the real world, the teams proceed without all of the information that may be desired and gradually receive information through the game.

   d. The problems may be fictitious or represent cases based on actual events.

   These games may be used for training purposes as well as management development. They foster team building, interpersonal relations, and communication skills as well as improvement in decision-making techniques.

4. *Behavioral modeling (interaction management or imitating models):* Participants in behavioral modeling learn new behaviors through role-playing and practice. The key to behavioral modeling is the process of learning through observation and vicarious participation.

   a. Team members might begin with an assignment of interpersonal problems that managers often confront. Sometimes videotapes are used to present these problem situations.

   b. The team members are required to solve the problems, primarily through the application of role-playing and interactive behaviors.

5. *Organizational development (OD) techniques:* Such techniques as team building are very effective management development methods.

6. *Case studies:* Individuals or groups are presented with written descriptions of organizational situations and then are asked to respond to specific questions or make overall operating decisions.

   a. Case studies add realism to training and development programs, especially when they involve corporations that the participants are familiar with (IBM, General Motors, Dell Computer, and Ben & Jerry's).

   b. The case studies help participants learn to apply principles and theories presented in professional books and literature, with a high level of learning transferability.

    c. The case studies also afford the participants the opportunity to improve analytical, written, and oral communication skills. They force participants to think, not just memorize, what is in a standard reference book or manual.

    7. *The incident process:* When the incident process is used, participants individually read a specific scenario and then work as a group to identify the problem and develop appropriate solutions. The incident process is a variation of the case study method. As a management development tool, the incident process enhances interpersonal relations and team-building abilities.

    EXAMPLE: *In a commonly used incident process, individuals are given lists of items. They are told to picture themselves being stranded on an ice floe in the waters around Antarctica. The individuals are first asked to prioritize the items on their own. Then they are told to gather in small groups and again rank these items in terms of their importance.*

    The exercise usually involves strangers required to work together as members of a team in solving a problem in which some members may have strong differences of opinion concerning alternative solutions. This exercise typically generates excitement and provides for a high degree of learning transferability.

  g. *Other management development and training approaches:* In making decisions about applicants for higher-level managerial positions, many techniques are used to screen candidates for interviews. Other techniques are especially useful for career development purposes, in assisting employees who aspire to higher-level positions. Here are some techniques that might be considered:

    1. *Assessment centers:* The application of management games and simulation to the process of selecting managers and identifying future training needs.

    2. *Organizational development exercises:* Situational problem-solving analyses based on the Leadership and Managerial Grids® developed by Blake, Mouton, and McCanse.

    3. *Decision-making exercises:* The application of Vroom and Yetton's model decision flowchart to move through a decision-making process by responding to diagnostic questions at each decision point.

    4. *Leadership matches:* The determination of the effectiveness of a leader based on matches between personality characteristics of the leader and the favorableness of the situation to the leader (Fiedler's contingency theory of leadership effectiveness).

    5. *Behavior modification:* An application of Thorndike's law of effect that emphasizes the reinforcement of behaviors that reduce the possibilities of errors being made or accidents occurring during the process.

Check Point—Section B

Directions: For each question, circle the correct answer.

B–1. Which one of the following is a goal of orientation for the employer?

  A) Reduce stress
  B) Save time
  C) Learn the job
  D) Complete paperwork

B–2. The relationship in which one person trains, guides, and supports the development of another employee is called

A) coaching
B) mentoring
C) training
D) consulting

B–3. The method of training in which the trainees engage in role-play and practice is called

A) case study
B) seminars
C) business games
D) behavior modeling

C. Training Design and Implementation for Improved Work Performance

Training is concerned with improving the ability and capacity of employees to perform their specific jobs and tasks. It is oriented to the present time and takes place as soon as it can be scheduled. Training is specifically geared toward overcoming deficiencies in job performance or preparing for modifications in work procedures, methods, or technology. The administrative professional should be a strong advocate for high-quality training programs.

1. *Training Defined:* **Training** is the process of providing the opportunity for individuals to acquire knowledge, skills, and attitudes required in their present jobs. Training should be viewed as systematic, continuous, and ongoing. Training generally refers to the job-related educational activities of nonmanagerial employees, the bulk of any organization's workforce.

   a. *General definition of training:* In general terms, *training* is defined as the systematic process of altering the behavior of employees in a direction to increase or to improve the achievement of organizational goals.

   b. *Specific definition of training:* More specifically, *training* is defined as activities intended to improve an employee's job-related work skills.

   c. *Focus of both definitions:* Both definitions focus on (1) providing formal activities; (2) changing the behavior of employees; (3) improving individual performance on the job; and (4) enhancing the achievement of organizational goals.

2. *Benefits of Training:* When training is treated as an important organizational function, benefits are derived for the entire organization.

   a. *Increased performance on the job:* Training helps employees raise their current skill levels and correct deficiencies in present performance. Training gives employees new skills to perform their present jobs in response to changes in technology, work processes, procedures, and other related factors.

   b. *Coping with change:* As a job changes or an employee demonstrates the need for additional skills to perform the present job, the organization may offer additional training.

3. *Assessment of Training Needs and Objectives:* The first step in designing a training program involves an assessment of training needs. Training programs should not be

instituted unless formal needs can be clearly identified. Needs assessment determines the training requirements of the organization.

a. *Needs analysis:* The first step in a needs assessment process involves a review and analysis of overall organizational needs.

   1. First, a strategic plan must establish the organization's short-term plans and long-term objectives, external threats affecting these plans and objectives, and the overall mission.

   2. Second, training programs must be linked to the strategic plan. Thus, the overall organizational needs assessment should include preparation of a human resources inventory and development plan, and an accurate, quantifiable assessment of the present and projected needs for human resources.

b. *Study of present and future job needs:* The next step in the needs assessment should involve a study of present and projected job needs.

   1. A job analysis includes a job description and job specifications.

   2. The job analysis process identifies specific skills needed to perform jobs and the minimum acceptable standards of job performance.

c. *Employee needs analysis:* The next step involves conducting an employee needs analysis which includes:

   1. A review of how present employees are performing their jobs according to the minimum acceptable standards identified during the job analysis process

   2. A comparison of the skills possessed by each employee, compared with the skills required to perform every job

d. *Self-assessment of training needs:* Once the foregoing analyses are completed, a self-assessment of training needs should be undertaken. The self-assessment is based on the premise that workers know their job performance deficiencies better than anyone else. Therefore, employees are in the best position to help design their own training programs. Many workers are hesitant to reveal their deficiencies because of fear that they might be writing their own resignations. This hesitancy reduces the effectiveness of the self-assessment process.

e. *Task–person analyses:* Finally, the organization may utilize a process involving task–person analyses to learn the needs and deficiencies specifically revealed during the self-assessment process. Trained personnel are used specifically to evaluate:

   1. The knowledge, skills, and abilities required to perform specific tasks and jobs

   2. The strengths and weaknesses of individual workers in terms of skills, abilities, and knowledge required to perform their specific tasks and jobs

As a result of this process, specific deficiencies can be identified and a formal program designed to meet training needs.

4. ***Training Program Design:*** The training program focuses on identifying and removing performance deficiencies in worker skills, abilities, and knowledge that are discovered in comprehensive needs assessment. The program design is based on responses to such questions as:

• What types of skills need to be taught and reinforced?

• Who will provide the training?

- Where and when will the training sessions occur?
- Which specific training techniques will be utilized to help overcome the workers' skill, knowledge, and ability deficiencies?

5. ***Purposes of Training Programs:*** Most training programs are oriented toward modifying or improving workers' skills in one of four primary categories: technical skills, interpersonal skills, problem-solving skills, or basic literacy skills. Preparation for professional certification examinations is another reason for office professionals and other specialized personnel to enroll in specially designed training programs.

   a. *Technical skills:* Most training focuses on upgrading and modifying workers' specific on-the-job technical skills for both blue- and white-collar positions. Technical skills training focuses on these purposes:

      1. Helping employees respond to changes in technology and equipment

      2. Assisting employees in adjusting to new and revised work methods

      EXAMPLE: *Virtually all employees in office settings, auto repair shops, assembly lines, and retail establishments have witnessed the advent of computers and robots. Some employees have also had to work in restructured organizations, partly due to decentralization, corporate mergers, and downsizing.*

   b. *Interpersonal skills:* Emphasis has been placed on the need for employees to interact more frequently and effectively with individuals from diverse departments. Managerial recognition of the costs and effects of on-the-job work conflicts has also resulted in the need for improved employee interpersonal communication skills. Types of programs to improve interpersonal relations include sessions in active listening, written and oral communication techniques, and conflict resolution methods.

   c. *Problem-solving skills:* With downsizing, job enlargement, job enrichment, and more participative management techniques, virtually all employees are being asked to devote more attention to problem solving. Problem solving and responsive thinking have become requisite skills for successful job performance. Types of programs aimed at improving problem solving include:

      1. Systematic decision making

      2. Brainstorming to generate new ideas

      3. Evaluation of problems and collective generation of optimal solutions

      4. Problem-solving workshops and analytical skill-building seminars

   d. *Basic literacy skills:* A new dimension in training programs receiving more attention relates to instruction in basic literacy skills designed to correct workers' deficiencies in reading, writing, mathematics, listening, and public speaking. Indications are that more basic literacy skill instruction will be included in U.S. organizational training programs in coming decades.

   e. *Professional certification:* Some individuals choose to participate in a training program designed to help them review for a certification examination in a specialized area of study related to their present or future employment. Such a training program is based on the structure of the exam and the study outline or bibliographic references provided by the professional association sponsoring the examination. The training program is most effective if offered during the weeks immediately preceding the scheduling of the exam.

EXAMPLE: *The accountancy department of a midwestern university offers a review course for the Certified Public Accountant (CPA) Examination twice a year to accommodate individuals who wish to prepare for the exam.*

6. ***Instructional Staff for Training Programs:*** Training specialists who come from within or outside the organization typically conduct organizational training programs. Interactive technology enables training personnel to participate in networked meetings, conferences, and seminars.

   a. *Use of trainers:* Training may be provided by in-house trainers or by training specialists from outside the organization.

      1. *Trainers within the organization:* Trainers may come from the same department, line or staff departments, specific departments (the human resource management department, the training and development department), or matrix structures with in-house educational specialists. Some of the larger corporations, such as General Motors, Ford Motor Company, IBM, McDonald's, and Motorola, have their own educational institutions. Trainers from within are particularly capable of providing job-specific training programs.

      2. *Trainers outside the organization:* Trainers from outside the organization may be individual entrepreneurs, consulting firms, and public or private educational institutions. These outside trainers provide broad and unbiased perspectives to accommodate the specific training needs of the organization.

   b. *Use of interactive educational strategies:* The use of interactive educational techniques and electronic media has permitted firms to tie into audiovisual networks for teleconferences, seminars, and skill-focused training sessions. However, presentations with electronic media may be more suitable for broad developmental purposes than for specific individualized training needs.

   The utilization of resources for training is efficient and effective while serving to increase morale as employees recognize new opportunities for challenge and personal growth.

7. ***On-the-Job Training (OJT) Programs:*** **On-the-job training (OJT)** is the most common type of training provided by organizations. It is defined as the use of the actual work site as the setting for instructing workers while also engaging in productive work.

   a. *Types of OJT programs:* Job instruction training (JIT), apprenticeship training, internships, field study programs, and supervisory assistance are specific types of OJT programs. Job rotation, enlargement, and enrichment programs are also beneficial to employees.

      1. *Job instruction training:* JIT, one of the more recently popularized OJT techniques, involves "train-the-trainer" practice. A professional trainer trains the supervisor who, in turn, trains the employee(s).

         a. Feedback sessions between the trainer and trainee permit discussion of performance in relation to the job requirements.

         b. Transfer of learning is facilitated because of direct application of the training to the job.

      2. *Apprenticeship training:* An apprenticeship program specifies performance guidelines and time requirements that apprentices must follow to receive certification and be allowed entry into chosen lines of work.

a. *Apprenticeships:* Many skilled trades have mandatory apprenticeship programs. There are many different forms of apprenticeship, but the term typically refers to a period of training in a skilled trade.

b. *Training time:* Most apprenticeships allow for extensive training over time while not interfering with specific job performance.

c. *Certification:* When apprenticeships lead to journeyman certification, they may be difficult to qualify for and can be very expensive in the short run until the apprentice becomes a certified journeyman.

3. *Internships and field study programs:* Agreements between schools (public and private) and employers provide students with realistic on-the-job learning experiences.

   a. The interns and field study assistants are usually paid but at a lower rate. They may also be earning academic credit. Sometimes, students/learners accept internship positions strictly for the experience, without receiving any monetary rewards.

   b. Employers are encouraging participation in internships and field study programs. Such learning experiences provide an opportunity to identify potential new hires.

4. *Supervisory assistance:* The most widely used informal type of on-the-job training is supervisory assistance, which is a regular part of both the supervisor's and the worker's activities. Coaching, counseling, and monitoring workers' performance enhance transfer of learning.

   a. Feedback and reinforcement are provided on a regular basis, especially during the beginning stages of any assignment.

   b. The only disadvantage of this type of training is that some supervisors do not like to coach, counsel, and train as a part of the normal routine.

5. *Job rotation, enlargement, and enrichment programs:* Exposure to organizational operations and job assignments is provided through job rotation, job enlargement, and job enrichment programs. These on-the-job experiences give employees the opportunity to learn more about their own jobs in relation to tasks performed by others in their work groups as well as the way the entire organization functions. However, especially with job rotation, the workers are not in any task long enough to really learn it. Participants in such a program often lack a complete sense of the responsibility needed to perform all tasks required in the job.

b. *Advantages of OJT:* There are a number of advantages of on-the-job training.

   1. OJT programs are cost effective and efficient to operate.

   2. During the program the opportunity exists to observe results of the training and gain immediate feedback.

   3. The transfer of training is maximized by direct and immediate on-the-job applications and abundant opportunities for practice.

c. *Problems related to OJT:* On-the-job training programs are not without problems, however.

   1. Costs associated with equipment and machinery reserved for training purposes rather than continued production does pose a problem.

2. The costs involved with using employees' and supervisors' work time for training purposes instead of production is another consideration.

3. The training is concentrated in the hands of the supervisor or a senior worker who may lack teaching abilities and the necessary learner sensitivity that is required in a training situation.

8. ***On-Site Off-Job Training Programs:*** Many training programs are conducted at the work site but away from the job while learning within a hybrid form of training program. Even though the training is conducted on a voluntary basis, firms often "urge" attendance at these programs; but participants are still expected to fulfill the requirements of their job assignments. Sometimes this can have a negative effect on employee morale.

   a. *Types of on-site/off-job training programs:* Some of the types of training programs that are conducted more efficiently on-site but off the job include training in specialized content (telecommunications), training involving specialized media (programmed and computer-assisted instruction, videotapes, videodiscs, interactive video training), and training utilizing specific methodology (vestibule training). The training is often conducted on a voluntary basis.

      1. *Telecommunications training:* Technological areas such as telecommunications require special training for employees so that communications within organizations will be greatly enhanced. Large and geographically dispersed organizations need to be able to communicate at a low per-unit cost.

         EXAMPLE: *One version of the teleconference is the audio conference. Using a simple conference call arrangement, people within an organization can learn and share from an outside expert at a basic cost that depends primarily on the time in use once the initial equipment is installed. While lacking the video dimension, audio conferences are still a highly effective training technique for small and medium-sized groups, especially if the participants have been provided background information about the speaker(s) ahead of time. Trainees' questions are encouraged, either in advance or during the session.*

      2. *Programmed and computer-assisted instruction:* Some people prefer to learn new content on an individualized basis. Personalized instruction, programmed or computer-assisted, enables the learner to work at his or her own pace, using a distributive approach to learning.

      3. *Video equipment systems:* Now that many firms have video equipment to use with training, videocassette or videodisc recorders or players have become very popular media for training. The portability of the media is the primary feature that enhances their use in a training setting.

      4. *Interactive televideo training (ITV):* Many of the most desirable features of videotaping and programmed instruction are incorporated into interactive televideo training (ITV).

      5. *Vestibule training:* With vestibule training, an off-job environment is created similar to an actual work setting. Work processes are simulated. Very often firms set aside on-site space (thus the "vestibule" where vestibule training is conducted.

b. *Advantages and disadvantages of on-site off-job training:* Sometimes training conducted on-site within the organization but away from the job site during the training period has some unique advantages.

1. Training programs are conducted on-site after normal work hours.

2. Technology and equipment can be utilized for learning purposes only during the specified training periods.

3. The scheduling of this type of training permits workers to have access to technology and equipment after hours.

4. A major disadvantage of on-site training of any kind is the nearby location of a work station to which the trainee may be called in an emergency. Off-site training usually eliminates this distraction.

9. **Off-the-Job Site (OFS) Training Programs:** Various types of training programs located off the job site are used widely by organizations of all sizes. These programs are relatively inexpensive to attend and cover virtually any topic desired. They are also suitable to development programs as well as training programs.

a. *Types of off-the-job site training and development programs:* OFS programs include formal classroom instruction, seminars, conferences, simulation approaches, and other types of training and development approaches.

1. *Formal classroom instruction:* The formal lecture–discussion format for instruction is the most widely used off-site instructional technique for training, development, and general education. Some organizations use the lecture method, supplemented by in-class discussion and participation, to promote sharing, interaction, and learning. The lecture–discussion method is more popular but cannot be used readily with mass audiences.

2. *Seminars and conferences sponsored by training firms:* Specialized training firms sponsor regular schedules of seminars and conferences for particular industries or firms or for general use with personnel from a variety of organizations. Many of these seminars and conferences are based on a lecture-type format, while others integrate audiovisual media or computer technology into the presentations.

3. *Distance education:* College credit may be earned or specific skills may be mastered through instruction provided on the Internet and the World Wide Web. The number of schools offering distance education for academic credit at the undergraduate and graduate levels or for continuing education units (CEUs) is increasing rapidly. Persons in Antarctic conditions or in very sparsely populated or isolated settings can learn and earn credits or CEUs if the appropriate technology is available. Many people in remote settings advance their education, taking full advantage of time gaps and the latest technology.

4. *Simulation:* As a training approach, simulation presents trainees with problems similar to those found in actual job situations. The trainees are expected to solve problems within a specified time period.

a. Some simulations are presented in computerized formats, and the trainees are expected to solve the simulated problems using a personal computer.

EXAMPLE: *Hewlett-Packard once featured advertisements that presented situations with many challenging scenarios and a person trying out various options on a personal computer to see "what if."*

    b. Simulations are often viewed as a form of vestibule training. They can be conducted on-site and off the job easily.

    c. Simulation can offer trainees realistic situations and provide transferable learning experiences. As trainees work through the simulation, they begin to see themselves in a real job situation rather than a fictitious one.

5. *In-basket exercises:* The use of in-basket exercises is an individualized simulation that gives individual trainees experience in resolving typical work problems or tasks associated with their jobs. Most often, the problems presented require the prioritization of tasks and making decisions related to task situations within a limited period. In-basket exercises present a high degree of realism, and transfer of learning can be achieved.

    a. Trainees find that the use of in-basket exercises creates situations where their motivational levels increase. Many trainees enjoy working on in-basket exercises and find them to be challenging.

    b. The only problem identified with in-basket exercises is stress, which some trainees experience when they have difficulty making decisions or completing the work within the time allotted.

6. *Role-playing:* Realistic situations may be presented in the form of role-playing. A trainee is cast in a specific position—for example, a manager—and must play the role of that individual. Role-playing is most effective in small or moderate-sized groups. In larger groups, multiple role-playing teams may be utilized.

EXAMPLE: *A supervisor is asked to take the role of a subordinate in dealing with a specific problem and may be required to respond to a subordinate who is cast in a supervisory position.*

Role-playing is especially helpful in gaining insights into the positions held by others or improving interpersonal skills even when the situations cannot be exactly replicated. A favorable amount of transfer takes place when role-playing is utilized.

7. *Corporate visits, committees, and meetings:* Sometimes visits and meetings with employees of other corporations are used to create increased awareness of needs and to develop improved interpersonal skills. Suppliers and customers are also excellent sources of information about business operations, functions, or problems encountered. Attendance, observation, and participation in committee meetings can provide realistic insights into group dynamics as organizational members work to solve specific problems. Committee assignments and observations can be valuable learning tools.

These visits and meetings focus on activities related to all three learning domains: improvement of interpersonal communication skills, awareness of the needs of others, and use of higher-level analytical skills to arrive at solutions.

b. *Benefits of off-the-job site training:* Numerous benefits may be derived from participation in an OFS training program.

1. OFS provides flexibility in meeting training needs.

2. Many individuals become highly motivated by attending OFS sessions.

3. Off-site training sessions usually provide a better climate and environment for learning.

4. Off-site sessions afford the trainees an opportunity to meet and discuss work-related concerns with people from other organizations, thus developing a localized support group.

5. Off-site sessions allow for much more flexibility and diversity in terms of the trainers being utilized.

6. Often, special facilities exist where off-site training sessions can be provided. These are more specific and job related than those that can be provided on-site.

7. When an organization permits employees (trainees) to attend off-site sessions, this provides them with some excitement, often resulting in a heightened commitment to the organization.

c. *Major disadvantages of off-the-job site training:* As with any other type of training program, there are some disadvantages associated with off-site training.

1. Participants incur travel and related instructional costs.

2. Training programs and trainers can become too generalized.

3. Some attendees are more reluctant to ask specific questions in sessions with participants from other organizations. In large groups attendees may have difficulty in asking questions.

4. Opportunities sometimes exist that permit attendees to focus more on meeting their personal needs than the training needs of their organization.

5. The transfer of knowledge and training is often not as high in off-site training sessions.

Check Point—Section C

Directions: For each question, circle the correct answer.

C–1. Activities undertaken to improve an employee's job-related skills are called
A) mentoring
B) coaching
C) training
D) development

C–2. The type of skills training used to help employees reduce conflict with other employees and supervisors is called
A) interpersonal
B) problem-solving

C) basic literacy
D) technical

C–3. River Technology International uses computer-assisted instruction at each of its assembly plants to train employees on new equipment and software. This is called
A) on-the-job training
B) off-the-job training
C) off-site on-job training
D) on-site off-job training

D. Assessment and Evaluation of Training and Development

The effective manager realizes that the implementation of any plan or program does not mean that his or her work is completed. The effectiveness (or lack thereof) must be evaluated to determine if the desired goals were attained and, if not, where and what types of program modifications might be required. **Assessment** refers to the collection of data and relevant information about a particular program, while **evaluation** combines assessment with a judgment about the effectiveness of the program.

1. ***Evaluating Training Program Effectiveness:*** To be effective, training must be evaluated systematically. The evaluation process involves documenting the end results of training:

    a. The behavior of trainees on the job after the training is compared with their performance before the learning began

    b. The relevance of the training in changing or modifying trainees' behaviors toward accomplishment of desired organizational objectives is determined

2. ***The Training Evaluation Process:*** The evaluation process requires a determination of whether a training program has fulfilled its objectives and, if so, to what extent. Questions such as the following need to be considered in evaluating a training program:

    - What are the strengths of the training program?
    - What are the weaknesses of the training program?
    - What is the cost-to-benefit ratio for the program?
    - Who has benefited the most from the training? Why?
    - Who has benefited the least from the training? Why?
    - How can the program be improved before it is presented again?

3. ***Kirkpatrick's Method of Evaluating Training Programs:*** Various approaches can be used in evaluating training programs. Perhaps the most widely accepted approach was developed by D. L. Kirkpatrick in 1977 and utilizes four distinct and related hierarchical levels of evaluation: reaction, learning, behavior, and results. Reaction and learning are considered to be *internal criteria* since they are concerned with the direct outcomes of the training activities. Behavior and results are viewed as *external criteria;* they indicate the impact of training on the job environment.

    a. *Reaction:* The first and most important criterion of training effectiveness is the participants' reaction to (feelings about) a training program.

        1. Adverse reactions to a training program indicate that subsequent activities should be redesigned, remarketed, or canceled.

        2. Positive feelings toward a training program reveal that others also would like to attend.

        3. The reactions themselves do not assess the usefulness of a training program to the trainees or the organization, but they do point out the strengths and weaknesses as perceived by the end users.

        4. The reactions usually include suggestions for improving the training so as to have greater positive impact on the trainees.

        5. Reactions are usually obtained by the learners' responses to questions presented before sessions begin and after training programs end.

b. *Learning:* The extent to which the trainees have learned the content represents the second training evaluation level.

   1. The learning criterion assesses the degree to which trainees mastered the concepts, information, and skills that were taught.

   2. Learning is typically measured during and after a training program by administering performance tests, simulation exercises, and examinations.

   3. Reactions and learning reveal the most direct outcomes of training programs and are most directly related to the specific jobs and tasks the trainees perform.

c. *Behavior:* The third level in training evaluation focuses on changes in worker performance and attitudes after the instructional programs have been completed.

   1. Comparing on-the-job behaviors before and after the training has occurred indicates whether the trainees have adopted any of the specific knowledge and skills imparted during the instructional sessions.

   2. Evaluations of changes in trainees' on-the-job behaviors can be secured from supervisors, subordinates, peers, and interested others (clients, vendors).

d. *Results:* A determination of the improvement of the person, unit, or organization because of the training represents the ultimate measure of training effectiveness.

   1. The results of training activities have an impact on individuals, work group(s), and the organization as a whole.

   2. The specific evaluatory measures depend on the objectives and techniques used during the training sessions.

   3. Typical criteria used to evaluate training program results include changes in:

      a. Quality and quantity of goods and services provided

      b. Turnover rates of workers who participated in the training sessions

      c. Costs incurred and profits realized

      d. Levels of employee morale

      e. Accident incidence rates

While the use of all four criteria (reaction, learning, behavior, and results) for assessing training effectiveness is highly recommended, a majority of the firms use only one or two criteria and focus especially on employees' reactions to the training. Therefore, in many instances the short- and long-run effects and results of training programs are never fully understood. Training programs are one of the first items to be curtailed by many firms when economic conditions tighten because of the lack of tangible and clearly understood results.

4. ***Designing Effective Training Evaluation Programs:*** Thorough design of training evaluation programs has had greater individual impact and has resulted in improved organizational operations. In comparison, programs with poorly or after-the-fact designed evaluation methods prove to be less satisfactory.

   a. *Multiple evaluative measures:* Effective evaluation program designs use multiple measures that are prepared before the training begins.

      1. These measures include pretraining and posttraining test data.

2. Trainers can examine the results objectively while the training is still going on or immediately after the training has been completed.

3. The immediate feedback allows for quicker, more effective changes in training approaches or methods used even while the sessions are being conducted.

b. *Ineffective evaluation programs:* Ineffective evaluation programs focus on only one or two criteria and are usually devised after the training has begun.

1. They usually include only posttraining results.

2. The data that are obtained are of limited value (if any) because of the lack of pretest measures or other methods of comparison.

3. Even when comparative data can be identified, opportunities for making changes in the training presentations are limited because of delays in receiving feedback. Circumstances may arise that also alter the trainees' behaviors and knowledge.

5. *Training Evaluation Program Designs:* When designing an appropriate training evaluation program, specific features of the program must be considered.

a. *Effective program features:* The strongest, most effective training evaluation designs have comparative measures built in, often using control groups as well as the actual training groups.

1. Pretest, posttest, and control group factors:

- Pretest . . training . . reevaluation
- Pretest . . no training . . reevaluation

2. Multiple measures over time to identify trends:

- Measure . . measure . . train . . remeasure . . remeasure

The most effective training evaluation designs use multiple measures (pretests, posttests) and allow for changes in trainees' attitudes, behaviors, and skills that may be caused by unanticipated or unknown environmental occurrences or events in trainees' lives.

b. *Ineffective program features:* Ineffective training evaluation designs have been prepared either spontaneously or after training has begun. Ineffective design schemes would include:

1. A one-shot design with only a posttest:

- Train . . measure

2. A pretest–posttest procedure only:

- Pretest . . train . . posttest

The most ineffective training designs are one-dimensional, with posttest only, and contain major lags between the time of the posttests and the time when the results are reported and evaluated.

EXAMPLE: *In some training courses, participants answer pretest and posttest questions before and after the sessions, while still on the premises. Although news received during lunch breaks may somewhat influence their behaviors, the basic and immediate effects of training activities are evaluated while they are fresh in the trainees' minds. The same rules apply to pretest and posttest role-playing episodes and problem-solving exercises.*

In other sessions, trainees are given survey forms to complete only after the training has ended. They may be given postage-return envelopes for mailing their responses. Some of these trainees may wait a week or two before responding, during which time they may have learned other information that affects the answers on their forms. The effectiveness of these training evaluations is questionable.

Check Point—Section D

Directions: For each question, circle the correct answer.

D–1. Which one of the following is a question that needs to be addressed in the evaluation of a training program?

A) Does learning transfer?
B) Who has benefited most from the program?
C) Were proper reinforcements used?
D) Was a proper job analysis conducted?

D–2. Kirkpatrick's method of evaluating training programs distinguishes internal criteria from external criteria. Which one of the following represents the set of external criteria he identified?

A) Reaction and learning
B) Learning and behavior
C) Behavior and results
D) Results and reaction

D–3. Thorough design of an effective evaluation program involves

A) multiple evaluative measures
B) posttest training data after an interval for maturation
C) measurement only after all the training is complete
D) one-dimensional measures

For Your Review

Directions: For each question, circle the correct answer.

Case 1: The Training Manager
Jaspers has just been placed in charge of the training division of the human resources department at a large manufacturer of household appliances. Jaspers will be responsible for about 12 trainers. The trainer position is considered entry level in the human resources department, and most of the current trainers have been hired within the last six months because the training division was recently reorganized.

The challenge for Jaspers is the need to train the training staff to perform their jobs even as they learn to train others for a variety of training responsibilities. Trainers will be involved in job skill training for new employees, interpersonal skill training, and information technology use. Most of the trainers have the skill base but have not been instructed in how to train others.

Jaspers accepts the challenge of the new position and plans to approach the task systematically. The first major task for Jaspers is to instill in the trainers a clear and uniform understanding of how learning occurs in the workplace.

1. Trainers need to know how a skill or new behavior is acquired. Jaspers should emphasize the
   A) psychomotor domain
   B) cognitive domain
   C) affective domain
   D) sensory domain

2. To encourage new learners to repeat a desired action or behavior, Jaspers instructs the trainers to
   A) condition the stimulus for action
   B) model the behavior repeatedly
   C) help the learners understand the behavior
   D) offer rewards

3. Before starting an individual in any training program, even the training for trainers, Jaspers must determine
   A) types of reinforcement
   B) conditioned responses
   C) learner readiness
   D) feedback protocols

4. Which one of the following represents the most effective learning circumstance for complicated information technology tasks that Jaspers should recommend to the training staff?
   A) Massed practice
   B) Intermittent reinforcement
   C) Distributed practice
   D) Continuous reinforcement

5. If Jaspers expects to be able to depend on the trainers and not be required to be involved in the development of every new training circumstance, then Jaspers must achieve in the trainers the effect called
   A) intermittent reinforcement
   B) transfer of learning
   C) massed practice
   D) material relevance

Case 2: The New Junior Manager

After several years of working as a claims adjuster for Plains Insurance, a multinational insurance company, Montoya has finally been promoted to the first level of management. The company always moves its managers from regional office to regional office as part of a long-term training and managerial development program. Montoya will begin as a manager of a group of claims adjusters, but eventually will be moved to manage another type of office.

Montoya was promoted because of excellent work and additional education acquired over the past few years. Because of the promotion from an adjuster position, Montoya already possessed the skills that would be overseen. However, there are many aspects of the corporate culture in the company and many administrative tasks that must be learned. The company has a mentor program, and Montoya's mentor is Davis, a senior executive at the regional office. Davis will probably send Montoya to many training and development exercises.

6. The method of management promotion at Plains Insurance is properly considered employee development because it
   A) hires from within the company rather than externally
   B) focuses on current skills needed for the job
   C) involves little or no orientation to the new workplace
   D) targets skills that will be important in the employee's future

7. Davis's role as mentor will help Montoya because
   A) mentors help establish crucial relationships
   B) mentors can locate needed specialized training
   C) protégés have less pressure to succeed
   D) protégés learn best through continuous reinforcement

8. The administrative duties and tasks will be best learned in programs that focus on
   A) technical skills
   B) interpersonal skills
   C) problem-solving skills
   D) basic literacy skills

9. The long-term management development program at Plains Insurance resembles
   A) junior boards
   B) job rotation
   C) the on-site off-job method
   D) business games

10. Davis sends Montoya to an activity that involves a business simulation designed to determine areas of training Montoya will need in the future. This activity is called a/an
    A) leadership match
    B) assessment center
    C) teleconference
    D) decision-making exercise

Case 3: Training Consultants

Executives at Trans-State Airlines have decided that its poor employee training programs hamper prospects for future growth. The consulting firm of Meier, Hong, and LeMoyne has received the contract to review, evaluate, and assess both the training needs and the current programs. The firm will then recommend a comprehensive overhaul of the training programs at Trans-State Airlines.

The process begins with Meier, Hong, and LeMoyne sending associates to observe both training and actual operations. They examine areas of customer service, baggage handling, aircraft maintenance, flight crews, sales, and the central office.

11. Meier, Hong, and LeMoyne have been contracted to improve the training processes at Trans-State Airlines. Which one of the following reasons accounts for why they would observe actual operations? Observation of operations will

    A) interpret training reinforcement methods
    B) examine training evaluation methods
    C) make known future training needs
    D) reveal actual training needs

12. For dealing with customers, flight attendants, sales representatives, and customer service staff especially need training in

    A) technical skills
    B) basic literacy skill
    C) interpersonal skills
    D) certification skills

13. The airline maintenance crews have a distinct hierarchy that includes younger employees who must work under the supervision of a senior maintenance chief. This kind of job training is called

    A) field study
    B) internship
    C) apprenticeship
    D) job instruction

14. A key method of training evaluation that Meier, Hong, and LeMoyne should utilize compares the behavior of trainees on the job after training with their performance

    A) prior to the training
    B) during the training
    C) prior to being hired
    D) after training for other jobs

15. Meier, Hong, and LeMoyne propose a training program that uses regular, ongoing evaluation to be certain that the program is working. The firm suggests pretesting all employees, posttesting after training, asking for employee feedback, and making other assessments. This evaluation will be effective because it utilizes

    A) pretesting participants' reactions
    B) multiple evaluative measures
    C) documentation
    D) one-shot design

Solutions

Solutions to Check Point—Section A

Answer:	Refer to:
A–1. (D)	[A-1-c(2)(b)]
A–2. (A)	[A-2-a(1)]
A–3. (C)	[A-2-c(4)(a)(iv)]

Solutions to Check Point—Section B

Answer:	Refer to:
B–1. (B)	[B-1-d(2)]
B–2. (B)	[B-2-a–b]
B–3. (D)	[B-4-f(4)]

Solutions to Check Point—Section C

Answer:	Refer to:
C–1. (C)	[C-1-b]
C–2. (A)	[C-5-b]
C–3. (D)	[C-8-a(2)]

Solutions to Check Point—Section D

	Answer:	*Refer to:*
D–1.	(B)	[D-2]
D–2.	(C)	[D-3-a–d]
D–3.	(A)	[D-4-a]

Solutions to For Your Review

	Answer:	*Refer to:*
Case 1:		
1.	(A)	[A-1-b(3)]
2.	(D)	[A-1-c(b)(i)]
3.	(C)	[A-2-a(1)]
4.	(C)	[A-2-c(3)(c)]
5.	(B)	[A-2-c(4)]
Case 2:		
6.	(D)	[B-4-a]
7.	(A)	[B-2-a]
8.	(A)	[C-5]
9.	(B)	[B-4-e(3)]
10.	(B)	[B-4-g(1)]
Case 3:		
11.	(D)	[C-3]
12.	(C)	[C-5-b]
13.	(C)	[C-7-a(2)]
14.	(A)	[D-1-a]
15.	(B)	[D-4 & D-5]

Chapter 5
Conducting Research

OVERVIEW

Effective action requires clear understanding of purpose. Clarity of understanding can be achieved best through careful research, collection of data, and analysis of both data and other types of information. In this chapter we examine the role of research in developing and then guiding plans of action toward a fruitful conclusion. Research comes in many forms. It can include the discovery and analysis of both quantitative data and qualitative information. Strategic planning processes require supportive data that leads toward reasoned conclusions.

Data can be drawn from a variety of places. Most commonly, corporate and public records include data, some of which can be found in libraries, on the Internet, in private archives, and so on. Research also involves collecting data from new sources. This data collection can include survey and observation of current work practices, as well as careful data collection about the performance of markets and the behavior of consumers.

A variety of research methods, including surveys, observations, and controlled studies, are employed throughout the professional world. Job analysis and evaluation provides another form of research. Similarly, basic data collection in the course of performing routine work is a form of research that will be invaluable to business success.

KEY TERMS

Correlation, 129
Data, 114
Data set, 114
Interjudge reliability, 116
Interval scale, 115
Job analysis, 123

Market analysis, 120
Mean, 127
Median, 127
Measures of central
   tendency, 127
Measures of variability, 127

Mode, 127
Nominal scale, 115
Objective data, 114
Ordinal scale, 115
Probability, 132
Range, 127

A. The Purpose of Research

All kinds of information can be collected, summarized, and used to justify changes or to make predictions about the future. Information can be collected on how people feel about work, how customers respond to product changes or services, and other factors such as costs, time, quality, or waste. Research is the means of collecting this critical information, and is important in every aspect of work.

1. ***Information and Analysis for Effective Decision Making:*** The reason for collecting information is to make decisions in a manner that produces desired results. Information can be used for comparison of choices and potential outcomes during a process of decision making. The goal is to make decisions that reflect the best option among those considered. Decisions should be guided by reasoned and well-documented choices, not by guesses and personal preferences.

2. ***Types of Information:*** Information can be divided into two broad types, subjective and objective.

   a. *Subjective:* *Subjective* refers to the perception and experience of events of information from an individual's point of view. The attitudes and feelings of customers about quality are considered **subjective data.** When subjective data are collected, care must be taken to ensure that the data represent the opinions and attitudes of all the customers being asked.

      EXAMPLE: *Quality, for instance, measured in this way depends upon the customer's own standards and expectations. These standards and expectations may be different for each customer.*

   b. *Objective:* When rejects and mistakes are counted, the measurement does not depend upon expectations or attitudes, but instead, they can be counted by anyone. **Objective data** include factors such as the number of events; measures of time and money; descriptive qualities like color, size, and shape; and many others.

3. ***Types of Data:*** Data can be divided into type broad types, quantitative and qualitative. Subjective and objective data can be represented as quantitative data, and qualitative data can be subjective or objective in turn.

   a. *Quantitative data:* Both objective and subjective measures can be *quantified*, or recorded as numbers. Once information is gathered, it is often called **data;** groups of similar data are called **data sets.** Collecting data is the important first step in analyzing and solving problems. However, the meaningfulness of the numerical data depends upon how they were gathered and how they were quantified.

      EXAMPLE: *If Simms, a CEO, asks only favorite customers what they think of quality, Simms may miss important input from other customers. In fact, if the favorite customers like Simms, they may be less candid when asked. It may be too costly or too time consuming to ask all the customers what they think.*

      A selection of customers that somehow represents all the customers should be made. This select group, called a *sample*, should then be asked for their opinions.

When people collect data about the procedures, costs, and attitudes concerning quality, they can give the data one of four forms. Most data can be placed on one of four kinds of scales called nominal scale, ordinal scale, interval scale, and ratio scale. Scaling shows the relative importance of each item on the scale. These scales give the data their form. Each form also limits the ways in which the data can be analyzed. These scales are defined below:

1. *Nominal scale:* A **nominal scale** puts each piece of information into a category or class. The nominal scale cannot be used to organize data into a hierarchy or ranked sequence. Data placed on these kinds of scales are called nominal data. Nominal refers to "naming" and thus to types of data that are simply named, like "states" or "brown-eyed subjects." Being classified as a state does not automatically create a hierarchy.

   EXAMPLE: *If Advantage Printing categorizes each customer according to the state and then a region, then the scale is considered a nominal scale. A customer in Kentucky is in the Southeast region. Advantage's state code for Kentucky is 17, because Kentucky is the 17th state on an alphabetical listing of states. The regional code for the Southeast is 2. The state codes or the regional codes cannot be averaged.*

2. *Ordinal scale:* **Ordinal scales** use a single dimension like "most to least sales" to rank the data on the scales. Ordinal scales can be used best to show the relative quality based upon the individual customer's perception. Ratings of job satisfaction ("like" versus "dislike," etc.), other worker attitudes, and evaluations based on judgment rather than actual behavior are examples of ordinal scales. While nominal scales only place items in classes, like "states," ordinal scales may arrange the states according to "population size" or "geographic area," thus creating an "order." However, the rank in population does not say anything about the difference from the first to the second, and then the second to the third, and so on. The differences could be several million for the difference between the first and the second, or ir could be several thousand. The ranking does not indicate a value for the position on the scale.

   EXAMPLE: *When the amount of sales for customers in Kentucky is placed on this scale, Kentucky ranks 31st. The Southeast region is number 3 among the five regions in total volume of sales. Ordinal scales cannot show the difference between the 31st and the 32nd state. A five-point ordinal scale is used to ask customers about the view of the quality of the work done by Advantage for them. The scale uses the following ratings: 1 = very high; 2 = high; 3 = good; 4 = poor; and 5 = very poor. On three occasions, one customer rates the service as very high and then on the fourth, the rating is good. The ordinal scale cannot tell the difference between very high quality and good quality. It is not the difference between 1 and 3, except on the scale. Furthermore, one customer's rating of "good" may be different from another customer's rating of "good."*

3. *Interval scale:* An **interval scale** measures the intervals or differences between data. Behavioral evaluations, IQ test scores, frequency of on-time mailings (for example, three in four mailings are on time), and similar data can be placed on interval scales. In an interval scale, unlike an ordinal or nominal scale, the difference between each step in the scale is clearly defined. The number of complaints for each week would form a scale based strictly on the

count: the interval between 10 complaints per week and 8 complaints per week is 2 complaints. The example explores this in more detail.

EXAMPLE: *What if Advantage rephrased its quality scale and asked: "How many complaints per thousand units do you receive for each mailing?" With the question it provides the scale: 1 = less than 5 complaints; 2 = 6 to 15 complaints; 3 = 16 to 25 complaints; 4 = 26 to 35 complaints; 5 = more than 35 complaints. Now the scale uses the number of complaints as a measure of quality and each choice, 1 through 5, has a clear interval. More interesting and useful to Advantage is that the ratings can be compared between customers. A rating of 2 made by one customer will mean the same as a rating of 2 given by another customer.*

4. *Ratio scales:* A **ratio scale** is a special form of an interval scale that has zero as a starting point. The number of performance errors per hour is a ratio scale. The lowest measure is "zero errors per hour." It is impossible to have a negative number of errors per hour.

EXAMPLE: *The Fahrenheit temperature scale can, on the other hand, have a negative temperature, like −10 degrees. It is an interval scale, but not a ratio scale. Because the temperature can be below zero, we cannot say that +10 degrees is ten times warmer than zero. A ratio requires zero as a starting point.*

A common error is to misinterpret ordinal scales as if they were interval or ratio scales. Is the quality rating of 1 twice as good as the quality rating of 2? No, because the customer with two complaints will rate a 1, and the customer with 12 complaints would rate quality as 2. The difference is six times in this case. Similarly, in the ordinal scale,"very high" (a 1 rating) is not three times better than "good" (a 3 rating).

b. *Qualitative data:* Qualitative data refers to nonnumerical information. Qualitative information includes descriptions of events, time lines or chronologies, customer comments, emotional responses, and similar material. These items can be ranked on nominal or ordinal scales, but not directly on interval or ratio scales.

1. *Observational qualitative data:* An observer can watch an event or series of events and record observations by preparing a script of the event, tallying how many occurrences of a particular behavior are observed, or by using electronic recordings of the events.

2. *Interjudge reliability:* Observational data must be checked by having more than one trained observer collect observations. With **interjudge reliability** often the observers are trained and in turn regularly check each other by observing the same event and comparing how they rate the events.

EXAMPLE: *Job performance evaluation based on actual work performance uses several observers to judge the performance. Typically, agreement between the observations will be high, but if a disparity exists, a third "judge" will be used to break the tie.*

4. ***Validity and Reliability:*** In any setting, the outcome of research must be considered valid and the methods of collecting and analyzing data must be reliable. These two critical concepts are often confused and considered interchangeable. However, they have distinct meanings, and they are critical for achieving research goals successfully.

a. *Validity:* In scientific measurements, **validity** is defined as the extent to which a measure actually measures what it is intended to measure. A measure of productivity must actually describe the relationship between worker time and the output of products. A quality measure must actually describe the quality of the finished product or the service provided. Validity is also applied to the conclusions drawn from research.

1. *Empirical validity:* This form of validity refers to an outcome, result, or conclusion actually being derived from evidence gathered from observation or other empirical means.

2. *Face validity:* This is the simplest form of validity, in which the question is whether the claims actually follow from common sense. An accountant's skill should be measured by whether or not the accountant was able to complete accounting problems and answer questions about accounting practices. The accountant's skill as a marathon runner would not have face validity for proof of the ability as an accountant.

3. *Criterion validity:* The action being measured can be called a criterion, such as completing 15 assemblies in an hour. If a test is found that predicts the ability to complete 15 assemblies in an hour, it is said to have criterion validity. A criterion may not even appear to be related. Perhaps running a marathon predicts assembly speed. Then running would be a valid predictor of assembling.

4. *Construct validity:* A construct is something that is thought to represent a particular concept, but that concept may have no agreed-upon definition. Leadership traits like ambition and charisma are constructs. A test that measures these traits would be depending upon construct validity. If someone tests high in these traits and then is separately recognized as a leader or accomplishes significant leadership results, then the test is said to have construct validity. The construct must be compared to some other measure that supports the construct.

b. *Reliability:* **Reliability** refers to the consistency and precision of a measure, test, instrument, performance, or other behavior. The methods of a research approach are said to be reliable if they consistently report the same outcome when given the same circumstance or data. If a meteorologist records a set of weather conditions on five different days, then the forecast of rain should be the same for each day. If each day the meteorologist gives a different forecast, then the meteorologist is considered unreliable—even if the forecast turns out to be correct. In this case, the meteorologist is using something other than weather forecast theory to make the predictions. There are several ways to establish reliability.

1. *Interjudge reliability:* This is described above as a means of cross-checking qualitative data. Sometimes, very sensitive instruments are checked against each other to be sure that both are reliable.

2. *Test–retest:* When measuring a worker's performance, repeated observations establish through "retesting" that the measures are reliable.

3. *Split halves:* Sometimes it is easier to measure half a group of participants at the beginning and then the other half at another time. For a test or instrument with several items, the test can be split and then measurements of all the participants can be taken in a test–retest format, only with a different version of the test being given each time.

5. **Research Methods:** The next step is to decide on the research method to be used. Naturally, if all the needed information is obtainable from secondary sources, no decision on research methods is required. If primary sources must be used, a decision is required as to the research method to be used: the interview method, the survey method, the experimental method, or the observational method. If secondary sources are adequate, then a review of published and archived reports (literature) may be adequate.

a. *Literature and archive search:* Reviewing written reports of studies is a common method of research, and it involves searching secondary sources as just described. In some cases, evidence is reported that makes further study unnecessary. This may include such things as chemical procedures or processes, manufacturing techniques, marketing methods, and so on. The report in the literature may be complete enough to provide the needed analysis and conclusions.

b. *Interview methods:* Interviews involve an in-depth questioning process in which involved participants, such as customers, workers, managers, and so on, are asked specific questions regarding the topic of interest. A questionnaire may be used and follow-up questions asked. Sometimes subjects in a survey, experiment, or an observation may be asked additional questions. In cases that involve only a few subjects, a detailed interview provides the best research avenue.

c. *Survey method:* In the survey method, information is obtained from individual respondents, either through personal interviews or by using such techniques as mailed questionnaires and telephone interviews. Questionnaires (personally administered, mailed, or telephoned) are used either to obtain specific responses to direct questions or to secure more general responses to "open-ended" questions. The survey method has three principal applications:

1. Gathering facts from respondents

2. Reporting their opinions

3. Probing the interpretations that individuals give to various matters

d. *Experimental method:* In scientific research, this method involves carrying out a trial solution to a problem on a small scale while attempting to control all factors relevant to the problem except the one being studied.

EXAMPLE: *An advertiser may run two versions of a proposed advertisement, ad A and ad B, in a city newspaper, with half of the copies of the issue carrying ad A and the other half ad B. This experiment, called a "split-run" test, might well have the purpose of determining the most effective advertisement, which after being determined in one market area, might be placed in newspapers in other markets or in national advertising media.*

e. *Observational method:* In the observational method, marketing research data are gathered, not through direct questioning of respondents, but by observing and recording their actions in a marketing situation.

EXAMPLE: *In studying the impact of a department store's mass display of shelving paper, observers are stationed in unobtrusive locations and instructed to record the total number of people passing by the display, the number stopping at the display, the number who pick up and examine the product, and the number who make purchases.*

The main advantage of the observational method is that it results in quantitative measurements of respondents' expressed actions and behavior patterns. Its principal shortcoming is that it is of limited usefulness in detecting buying motives and other psychological factors. In its pure form, the observational method involves simply watching or listening or both, with no attempt to probe for the reasons behind actions and behavior patterns.

6. ***Research Supporting Strategic and Tactical Planning:*** When research is used to support planning, it must be formulated in such a way as to allow comparisons as well as predict outcomes. For strategic planning, data must be collected on the current climate, the opportunities as well as the potential for responding to opportunities.

   a. *Understanding the current situation:* These data include both external and internal information. The data should be collected in a comprehensive fashion, covering all the influential aspects of the external environment as well as a description of how and where the organization is productive and unproductive. This analysis is sometimes called SWOT—strengths, weaknesses, opportunities, and threats, as discussed in Chapter 2.

   b. *Examining options:* Options can be examined only in light of how feasible they are and how likely they are to help the organization achieve its goals. Strategic planning includes a phase of goal setting, but planning for implementing a strategic plan (that is, tactical planning) will identify only objectives derived from goals.

   c. *Setting measurable objectives:* Objectives set by or derived from a strategic plan must be in measurable terms. That is, they must specify some quantity that will result from the action required to meet the objective. Collecting data related to an objective is research just as would be the preliminary steps of reaching an understanding of a situation. Collecting data for ongoing objectives and goals is a central research task that supports and then validates (or invalidates, as the case may be) the selection of an objective and the creation of a target for performance to reach.

Check Point—Section A

Directions: For each question, circle the correct answer.

A–1. Numbers of events, time, money, color, size, and shape refer to

   A) subjective data
   B) objective data
   C) quantifying data
   D) interval data

A–2. Haverty enters a room and grabs attention almost immediately and always takes the initiative. If these are seen as leadership traits, then the fact that Haverty is recognized as a leader means that the traits have

   A) construct validity
   B) interjudge reliability

   C) criterion validity
   D) split halves reliability

A–3. An assembly plant decides to test a new assembly procedure by having one line use the new procedure while another line uses the old procedure. This method of researching the new procedure is called the

   A) survey method
   B) observational method
   C) test–retest method
   D) experimental method

B. Types of Research

There are many types of research methods or means of collecting data or information, and the collected information can be in any format. Interpreting or analyzing data is limited by the type and quality of the data, but interpretation and analysis cannot occur without data. The quality of the analysis is directly linked to the quality of the data.

1. *Corporate Records and Internal Sources:* Corporate records include everything from personnel records to financial statements to reports of growth and expansion. Press releases and board minutes provide a record of important events for the company. All these items are held in archives for the purpose of maintaining an official, sometimes legally mandated record, and in some cases providing a historical archive of the company.

   EXAMPLE: *Companies with high public visibility will have a historian on staff to create a historical archive. Many maintain a museum with examples of early products. The Coca-Cola Museum in Atlanta is a public showcase for customers of all ages. Though the interactive displays have a strong commercial quality, the museum has a professional staff and an archive.*

2. *Open Information Sources and External Sources:* A variety of public institutions exist to preserve historical record and provide public access to information. These include:

   a. *Libraries and archives:* Local libraries and archives at universities and other government agencies are open to the public for research. These facilities have specialists who help patrons locate information and reference materials.

   b. *Internet:* The Internet and the World Wide Web provide an excellent research resource. One can locate scientific articles, opinion essays, academic journals, news archives, newspapers, corporate annual reports, and many other kinds of critical information. Unfortunately, the Internet is also a source of much uncritical information, entirely fabricated data, and "quack" theories about everything from the origin of the universe to the sexual activity of presidential candidates. One must use this medium with great caution.

   c. *News media:* News media retain a complete record of the publication or broadcast. Some can be used without charge, whereas in other cases a small fee may be required. Tapes of broadcasts can be purchased, and services exist that will transcribe the tape.

   d. *Research services and consultants:* Companies without resources to maintain a staff of researchers can also hire or contract research services. Strategic planning consultants, technology transfer consultants, and consultants specializing in focused sectors all conduct a form of research as part of their consultation. These firms can be contracted to complete a research task.

3. *Market Analysis:* As part of a complex network including economic and societal forces, the marketing function must continually adapt to change. Since people make up markets and their needs and wants are subject to continuous change, marketing activities are always in need of being analyzed to determine if they are reflecting these "people" changes. **Market analysis,** or *market research* as it is more commonly called, is the systematic gathering, recording, and analyzing of data about marketing problems toward the goal of providing information useful in marketing decision making.

   a. *Sources of data:* Putting information to use in marketing decision making typically requires the tapping of both internal and external sources of data.

1. *Internal data sources:* Internal studies focus on resources and activities within the company. However, the marketing decision maker must consider internal data in light of information obtained from external sources.

2. *External data sources:* External studies are concerned with the relations of the firm to its environment and, particularly, to its markets. Information revealed by external studies must be considered in relation to data obtained from internal sources.

Internal and external marketing studies, therefore, are necessary complements of each other. Both types of sources are essential elements in forming the informational groundwork for marketing decision making. In fact, the art of management takes into account the inner workings of the firm and its interaction with external forces simultaneously.

b. *Areas of market analysis:* Market research activities are primarily involved with finding facts in three areas: consumer, competition, and internal operations.

1. *The consumer:* A successful business knows its customers. Many firms do not have the capacity to conduct sophisticated market research studies on consumer preferences and tastes. These firms rely on the consumer research studies conducted by trade associations and business or consumer advocacy groups that are reported in trade journals and marketing publications.

2. *The competition:* Information about competition is important. Being aware of what competition is doing in the marketplace gives a business the opportunity to respond by evaluating appropriate marketing strategies.

3. *Internal operations:* The firm's records are an important source of information. They can be analyzed, for example, to determine which products sold best and in what price ranges.

c. *Market research projects:* Basically, a market research project is a planned search for information. Time spent in project planning should not only reduce the time required to conduct the project but also should ultimately result in securing more reliable and meaningful information. Developing any project plan for marketing research involves making four important decisions: establishing research objectives, identifying specific information needed to achieve the objectives, selecting the sources to tap in seeking information, and deciding on the research methods to employ in collecting the information.

1. *Research objectives:* The statement of research objectives should, whenever possible, take the form of a list of a small number of hypotheses to test. Alternatively, they can be stated as a small number of questions to be answered. The number must be kept small, for no research project can be expected to produce timely and reliable information for managerial decisions if the project is directed toward finding out too much information. In pruning the list of possible hypotheses that might be tested, the researcher should consider the value of testing each hypothesis by answering two questions:

   a. If the information is obtained, how useful will it be to the decision maker?

   b. If the information is of possible usefulness to the decision maker, is it useful enough to justify the cost of obtaining it?

2. *Specific information needed to achieve objectives:* The second key project planning decision is the determination of specific information needed to achieve the research objectives. When the research objectives have been clearly stated, the researcher proceeds to consider different types of information pertinent to achieving the objectives. The effectiveness of a market research study is directly related to the issue of how vital and relevant the information used is in finding answers to the research questions.

3. *Information sources:* The next step in project planning is to decide on the information sources. The sources from which different items of information are obtainable must be identified. For this purpose, it is convenient to identify sources as being either primary or secondary.

   a. *Primary data sources:* A primary data source is one from which the desired items of information must be obtained directly, such as through questionnaires and interviews. Primary data sources include consumers and buyers, middlepersons, salespersons, and trade associations.

   b. *Secondary data sources:* Secondary data sources are mostly published sources, such as government census publications. Secondary data sources are repositories not of items of information gathered specifically to achieve the objectives of the research project being planned, but rather of materials assembled for some other purpose or use. The researcher should always look to the secondary sources first. If the needed information is already available, the time and expense of gathering it from primary sources can be saved. The usual situation, however, is that some information can be obtained from secondary sources (for example, statistics on population and income), but the more crucial data (for example, the disposition of consumers to buy a given product under certain marketing conditions) have to be obtained from primary sources.

4. *Sales Analysis:* **Sales analysis** consists of a thorough and detailed study of the company's sales records with the purpose of detecting marketing strengths and weaknesses. Although sales records are, of course, regularly summarized in the sales section of the operating statement, such summaries reveal next to nothing about strong or weak features of the company's marketing efforts. Through sales analyses made at periodic intervals, management seeks to gain insights into the marketing efforts of the company.

EXAMPLES:

Information about the sales territories where the marketing effort is particularly strong and those where it is weak

Identification of the products responsible for the largest sales volume and those products with the least sales volume

The types of customers who provide the most satisfactory sales volume as well as those who provide the least satisfactory sales volume

Sales analysis, then, is used by management to uncover significant details that would otherwise remain hidden in the sales records. It provides pertinent information needed by management to allocate future marketing efforts along lines that will bring greater return.

EXAMPLE: *A manufacturer of office supplies and stationery made a detailed analysis of the firm's past sales records and discovered that of 150 distributors handling the*

company's products, 27 (18 percent) accounted for 79 percent of sales and the re-
maining 123 (82 percent) produced only 21 percent of the firm's sales.

Similar situations are to be found in many companies: a large percentage of the customers accounting for a small percentage of the total sales and, conversely, a small
percentage of customers accounting for a high percentage of total sales. Comparable
situations are found wherever a large percentage of the sales territories, products, and
orders bring in only a small percentage of total sales.

a. *Need for sales analysis:* Such sales patterns as those just described do not always
   result in unprofitable operations, but operations are often less profitable than they
   might be because marketing efforts and marketing costs all too frequently are divided on the basis of numbers of customers, territories, products, and orders rather
   than on the basis of actual or potential dollar sales.

   EXAMPLE: *Maintaining a salesperson in a strong territory usually costs just as*
   much as maintaining one in a weaker territory. It usually costs almost as much to
   promote a product that sells in large volume as one that sells slowly or not at all.
   Similarly, it costs almost the same to have a salesperson call on and service a cus-
   tomer who gives the company large orders as to have the salesperson call on an-
   other who orders in small quantities.

   It is not at all uncommon for a large proportion of the total spending for marketing efforts to result in only a very small proportion of the total sales and profits.
   The first step that management can take to improve such situations is to learn of
   their existence. That is the important task assigned to sales analysis.

b. *Primary types of sales analysis:* Each of the primary types of sales analysis is
   used to enlighten management on various aspects of marketing strengths and
   weaknesses.

   1. *Analysis of sales by territories:* The questions of how much is being sold and
      where are answered through this type of analysis.

   2. *Analysis of sales by products:* This type of sales analysis answers the ques-
      tions of what is being sold and how much.

   3. *Analysis of sales by customers:* Such an analysis responds to the questions of
      who is buying and how much.

   Notice that all types of sales analysis relate to the question of how much is being
   sold but that each answers this question in a different way. Although sales analysis can identify different aspects of marketing strength and weakness, it cannot
   explain why these differences exist. The "why" question is the province and responsibility of the marketing manager; but at least with the information cited
   above, sales analysis can assist in "putting the finger on" specific strengths and
   weaknesses. This is a necessary preliminary step to any explanation of the reasons
   for these strengths and weaknesses to exist.

5. ***Research on Jobs and Tasks:*** Basic to developing sound personnel policies is the
   completion of various human resource management functions and tasks. Conducting
   job analyses, writing job descriptions and job specifications, and performing job evaluations are tasks inherent in developing effective human resource policies.

   a. *Job analysis:* A **job analysis** is a detailed study of the job to determine the exact na-
      ture of the work, the quantity and quality of output that is expected, organizational

aspects of the job, and necessary personal qualities such as leadership, judgment, tact, and the ability to cope with emergencies.

1. *Nature of the job:* A detailed job analysis will give accurate information about the nature of the work. The job study will identify the tasks that an employee must perform to complete the work, the conditions under which the job is performed, and the equipment or technology used in getting the job done.

2. *Job analysis formula:* Every job analysis consists of two parts: a job description and job specifications. Therefore, the job analysis formula is:

$$\text{job analysis} = \text{job description} + \text{job specifications}$$

3. *Basis for job descriptions and job specifications:* Job analyses need to be part of a continuing process. As products change, new equipment and technology are installed and work methods change. Job analyses then need to be updated. A thorough job analysis is the basis for preparing accurate job descriptions, meaningful job specifications, and a sound job evaluation program.

b. *Task analysis:* **Task analysis** is an integral part of the job analysis process. A task is an element of a total work process that can be performed separately from other elements in that same work process. Task analysis is the process of breaking work down into its constituent elements.

EXAMPLES:

In preparing a copy machine to run, individual tasks might be checking toner level, loading paper, changing number of copies desired, and selecting the appropriate paper tray.

The tasks of a one-person office, administrative professional, and bookkeeper might be stated as opening and closing the office, making bank deposits, posting transactions, and preparing documents.

The "tasks" in the first example refer to one specific type of operation, whereas each task in the second example obviously consists of a number of individual actions, steps, or motions. The term *task*, then, can be defined more or less broadly.

1. *Time-and-motion-study approach:* The basic methodology related to task analysis was established around 1900. Generally discussed as part of the scientific management approach, task analysis was largely developed around an industrial engineering framework.

   a. *Sequencing steps:* Optimum sequencing of steps in the work process were first determined.

   b. *Determining required motions:* Necessary motions required of a human to accomplish the action were analyzed.

   c. *Determining time required:* The amount of time necessary for an average person to perform the motion was then determined.

   d. *Measuring time for work process:* The amount of time required for the entire work process, including work flow, was calculated by accumulating all the individual time-and-motion estimates.

   e. *Using methods-time measurement (MTM):* Methods-time measurement is a term applied to the process of task analysis. This method is still in use and is frequently applied to clerical operations as well as the more usual manufacturing operation.

2. *Worker estimate methods:* Less formal methods of task analysis are frequently used when jobs have obviously changed or have never been clearly specified. The importance of the task analysis to the individual worker is that a better understanding of the requirements of the job should develop. Many employees who perform routine tasks every day really do not have the opportunity to analyze these tasks. Task analyses are usually conducted under the direction of the supervisor as a part of a departmentwide or a companywide research project. Here are some ways that task analyses may be conducted:

   a. *Interviewing employees:* Usually, an employee is asked to respond to the analysis because she or he is actively involved in the day-to-day performance of these tasks. One method often used by supervisors in obtaining this information is a direct interview, sometimes conducted by an outside consultant. Typical questions asked during the task analysis are:

      (i) What tasks are routinely performed in this position?

      (ii) What specific skills, knowledge, and behaviors are an essential part of the duties and responsibilities of someone in this position?

      (iii) How frequently is each task performed: daily, weekly, monthly, longer?

      (iv) What is the relative importance of each task performed: very important, important, nonessential?

      (v) What work conditions are necessary for completion of these tasks (e.g., special tools, ergonomic needs, acceptable noise level)?

      (vi) What criteria are used to measure the quality of the work performed?

   b. *Interviewing employers:* Supervisors or managers may be interviewed as well so that a comparison might be made of what the supervisor or manager thinks is done in a particular position and what the employee says is actually done.

   c. *Using a questionnaire:* Another way to gather information is through the use of a survey instrument or a questionnaire. If this method is used, care must be taken to develop specific questions so that the respondent will be able to provide the information easily.

   d. *Observing performance:* After reviewing specific job duties as perceived by the worker and the supervisor, managers should observe actual job performance. These types of observations are a very effective, although time-consuming, way of identifying job duties accurately.

   e. *Using computer measures:* Many positions today require the use of the computer or other technical devices. Actual output can be measured and quantified on a regular basis.

      EXAMPLE: *The time spent answering each telephone or online inquiry, operating the cash register, and stocking shelves can be tracked easily using computerized devices. Telephone recordings often state that messages and employees' responses are being taped for quality assurance purposes.*

Computers have enhanced the process of job evaluation, although some people complain that privacy has been compromised, both for workers and customers. Through the use of task analysis, jobs may be redesigned or restructured to avoid duplication of job tasks among employees in a given department or to centralize the performance of certain tasks.

EXAMPLE: *In the accounting department, form letters for different purposes have been written by individuals in purchasing, accounts payable, and accounts receivable. Now the work of preparing these letters can be channeled to a communications support center that does all word processing needed by the accounting department as well as other departments within the organization.*

Check Point—Section B

Directions: For each question, circle the correct answer.

B–1. Which one of the following will have the greatest chance of giving fabricated data during research?

A) Library
B) Internet
C) News media
D) Research service

B–2. A local ice cream maker cannot afford sophisticated research studies to determine popular flavors. The ice cream maker would be best helped by

A) competitors' studies of the market
B) news media reports

C) studies conducted by trade associations
D) secondary data sources

B–3. A ceramic cup maker who specializes in putting customer logos on cups and other items wants to find the best technique with the fewest steps to preparing and firing the cups. The cup maker should conduct a/an

A) time-and-motion study
B) market analysis
C) job analysis
D) employee interview

C. Statistical Analysis

The basic statistical methods most commonly used are divided into several classes of tools: descriptive statistics, correlation, and probability.

1. *Descriptive Statistics:* The branch of statistics that focuses on how to organize a set of data so that tendencies within the data become clear is called *descriptive statistics.* Descriptive statistics includes the average (also called the mean), the most commonly repeated score or response (called the mode), and the middle point (called the median). These three measures are called measures of central tendency. Descriptive statistics also includes measures that show how much the data vary. These include measures called the range and standard deviation. Before any of these measures can be made, the information must be collected into a numerical form.

   a. *Measures of central tendency:* Once the data have been collected through research, they can be analyzed using statistical procedures. The most common measures show the way in which the data are distributed between lows and highs. These measures are called measures of central tendency and measures of variance. **Measures of central tendency** show the average, the most common number, and the middle data. These are called the mean, median, and mode.

1. *Mean:* The **mean** is the average. It is determined by totaling all the data and then dividing by the number of pieces of data. A mean can be the average number of hours worked each week by each employee, the average hourly pay, the average cost of each item of mail, and the average of the daily production runs.

2. *Mode:* The **mode** is the most common score. Often the most commonly reported total or score will be near the middle. In the daily production totals, the number 10,000 occurs twice. The mode then is 10,000.

3. *Median:* The **median** is the middle score in a set of scores or middle data in a set of data. The median is often reported when the high or low of the data is extreme and would make the data have a high average. Housing prices, for instance, are usually reported with the median. The mean would reflect the costs of multimillion-dollar houses, making the average cost of a house not reflect what an average house would cost. Incomes are often reported with emphasis on the median incomes. Extremely high incomes distort the average. The presence of a day with no production suggests that the mean may not be very representative. The median is probably a better figure.

   Figure 5–1 represents 21 daily production totals arranged from lowest to highest. The median of the daily production runs is 9,700. Each day's production is counted as one piece of data, so if all the production runs were arranged from most to least, the production run in the middle, number 11 (the 11th run is the middle of the 21 runs). The 11th daily total is highlighted.

Mean, median, and mode are very useful for planners who want to establish patterns of typical performance. If supplies must be purchased a month in advance, then the mean would show how much should be purchased. The median and the mode are useful because they can show the more common, or typical, totals. These become more important if the data include a wide range of totals. Range is one of the measures of variability.

b. *Measures of variability:* Mean, median, and mode help show the typical patterns of performance and production. However, the daily totals in the chart in Figure 5–1 include one day with no production and one day of very high production. The extent to which production varies from one day to another is analyzed using **measures of variability.** The common measures of variability are the range and standard deviation.

   1. *Range:* The **range** of a set of data is the difference between the highest and the lowest pieces of data. The range can show the difference between lowest hourly wage and the highest hourly wage. It may show difference between the smallest mailing and the largest. For daily production totals in Figure 5–1, the range is the difference between 0 and 13,200, or 13,200.

   2. *Standard deviation:* Statisticians have devised an index of variation that is sensitive to differences found in sets of data. This is called the **standard deviation.** The standard deviation is one of the more complex procedures that is commonly used. It is also preferred because it produces a number that is

FIGURE 5–1   Production Data Arranged from Highest to Lowest *Source:* Mark Garrison and Margaret Anne Bly-Turner, *Human Relations: Productive Approaches for the Workplace* (Boston: Allyn & Bacon Publishers, 1997), 581.

Rank	Day	Production
1	18	13,200
2	9	12,100
3	13	11,000
4	3	10,500
5	15	10,300
6	14	10,200
7	6	10,100
8	2	10,000
9	9	10,000
10	4	9,800
11	**1**	**9,700**
12	17	9,200
13	8	9,000
14	21	8,800
15	16	8,700
16	7	8,500
17	5	8,400
18	11	7,300
19	12	5,200
20	20	4,100
21	19	0

Note: The median is the middle data. In this set, the middle is the 11th day counted from either direction.

similar to numbers within the range of the data. Standard deviation is most useful when comparing two different data sets, for example, the production totals for two different months. If both have similar averages, the month with the higher standard deviation has a greater amount of variation among the daily totals. In Figure 5–1, for the 21 days, the standard deviation is 2,792. This means that most of the production runs would fall within 2,792 units of the mean of 8,861. That is, most of the daily production totals would be between 6,100 and 11,600. Those outside this range would be considered unusual.

EXAMPLE: *The importance of measures of variability can be illustrated in another way. If Advantage were planning to hire a typesetter to prepare the copy for printed brochures, it would want to hire a fast but consistent typist. If two applicants have the highest typing speed of 92 words per minute, which would you hire? Consistency would be the one with the lowest amount of variation during the typing test. In other words, the applicant with the lowest*

FIGURE 5–2 Typing Tests *Source:* Mark Garrison and Margaret Anne Bly-Turner, *Human Relations: Productive Approaches for the Workplace* (Boston: Allyn & Bacon Publishers, 1997), 583.

Minute #	Applicant 1*	Applicant 2†
1	85	74
2	92	67
3	46	79
4	82	81
5	85	72
6	76	77
7	71	78
8	89	81
9	99	69
10	101	74
11	52	81
12	83	77
13	89	80
14	32	78
15	79	77
Average Rate	77.40	76.33

Note: The speed of each typist was calculated by a computer every minute for 15 minutes. If consistency was important, which one would you hire? The smaller standard deviation for applicant 2 suggests more consistency and less variability in typing speed—even though the mean rates are almost the same.

*Applicant 1 standard deviation: 18.997.

†Applicant 2 standard deviation: 4.189.

> *standard deviation would be preferred. Figure 5–2 compares the two typists during their 15-minute test.*

2. ***Correlations:*** **Correlations** show the extent to which the change in one factor relates to the change in another factor. A positive correlation occurs when an increase in one factor occurs with the increase in another factor. A negative correlation occurs when the increase in one factor occurs with the decrease in another factor. A *positive correlation* is a relationship between two items in which one factor increases while the other factor also increases, and vice versa. A *negative correlation* is a relationship between two items in which one factor increases while the other factor decreases.

EXAMPLE: *If an envelope insertion machine develops a problem that requires the operator to stop the machine and make a correction, then the number of insertions should drop. The relationship between the number of times the machine stops and the decrease in the output of the machine is called a correlation. There are several simple ways to represent this relationship. The amount of time the machine runs in a shift is correlated to amount of production. An increase in the running time leads to an increase in the production. This is a positive correlation. But what if the machine is having errors because the operator is trying to run the machine too fast for the number of pieces being inserted into the envelope? The speed of the machine is then positively correlated to the number of shutdowns. The faster the machine runs, the more time it loses. As the machine speeds up, the production falls off. This is considered a negative correlation. One factor increases while the other factor decreases.*

a. *Correlation coefficient:* A correlation coefficient is a simple index that illustrates the direction and strength of a correlation; written as a number between -1 and $+1$. This correlation can be depicted using a scatterplot, a graph on which each point represents the measures of two factors for that particular individual or item; for example, a growth chart (plots the height and weight of an individual).

b. *Pearson correlation:* A method called the Pearson correlation is used to develop a simple index that illustrates the direction and strength of a correlation. The outcome, called a *correlation coefficient,* is represented with *r* and written as a number between -1 and $+1$. A correlation of $+1$ says that shutdown and lower productivity are always correlated. A correlation between machine speed and lower productivity of -1 says that for every unit of speed that the machine increases, a comparable measure of productivity decreases. Perfect -1 and $+1$ correlations are never seen, and they suggest the existence of a cause-and-effect relationship. Unrelated factors will have correlations of 0.

   EXAMPLE: *If a team is trying to account for the drop in productivity, several factors should be correlated. The factor with the best correlation could be considered the primary factor related to the drop in production. However, it does not suggest that the factor is the cause. There may be a combination of factors that cause the drop. In fact, the actual cause is that the machine does not fill envelopes when it is idle. Since everyone knows this, what is important are the conditions under which the machine works best and the conditions under which it works worst. Correlation does not show cause, but it does show influencing or interacting factors. At best, a correlation will be moderate: Sometimes the speed of the machine is related to the lower production; sometimes it is not. A moderate correlation would be represented in the .30 to .60 range (can be positive or negative).*

   After discovering this connection, the investigating team might then want to explore the possibility that certain operators are more effective than others. Some simply run the machine as fast as they can. Others know how and when to run the machine fast. Some production teams may do better on certain projects and worse on others. With these ideas suggested by the initial data, the investigating team can suggest further analysis and possibly some tests that can be undertaken. For instance, they may suggest that different combinations of employees on production teams may improve overall production.

c. *Scatterplots:* The analysis would begin by plotting the number of hours a project takes and the final output. The plots are made on what is called a *scatterplot.* This graph uses one axis for the total hours required and another for the production totals. Other relationships can be represented on scatterplots as well: the number of shutdowns and the machine speed; the actual time the machine runs, and the output. Figure 5–3 shows scatterplots that combine different factors. Any two factors can be correlated and analyzed for each team combination as well. In the end, the

FIGURE 5–3   Scatterplots   *Source:* Mark Garrison and Margaret Anne Bly-Turner, *Human Relations: Productive Approaches for the Workplace* (Boston: Allyn & Bacon Publishers, 1997), 587.

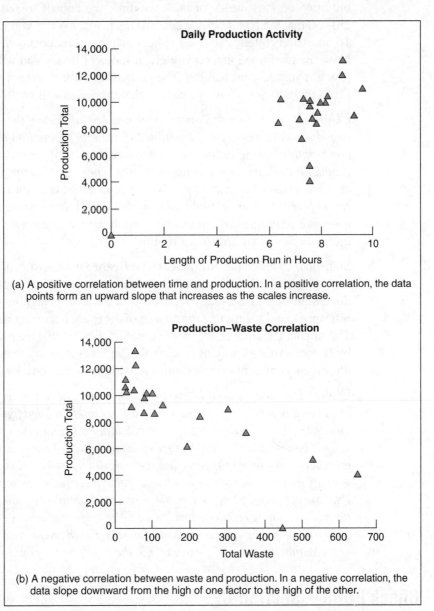

(a) A positive correlation between time and production. In a positive correlation, the data points form an upward slope that increases as the scales increase.

(b) A negative correlation between waste and production. In a negative correlation, the data slope downward from the high of one factor to the high of the other.

Note: These scatterplots show different sets of data that have been tested for possible correlations.

best combinations of teams will be those that distribute the employees so that each team achieves the highest correlations between total hours worked and output.

3. ***Inferential Statistics:*** *Inferential statistics* is a field of statistics that makes generalizations about events.

EXAMPLE: *If only 20 percent of the customers were surveyed for their attitudes about quality at Advantage Printing, then inferential statistics is used to generalize the response of the smaller sample to the rest of the customers. It may be too time consuming to monitor every single day's production, so a sample of work is taken, and the results generalized to the rest of the work.*

a. *Probability and chance:* The judgment called **probability** is the likelihood, or chance, of a certain event occurring. Simple events like the toss of a coin have only two options, heads or tails. Anytime the coin is tossed, the probability is .50–.50 that the result will be heads. This is true even if you have tossed the coin 10 times and gotten heads each time. Each toss is independent of the other tosses. Now, the likelihood that on any given series of tosses you will get 10 heads in a row is a very low probability. The probability is .001, meaning that out of 1,000 series of 10 tosses, there is 1 chance that the series will be all heads.

EXAMPLE: *How does this apply to the problem of finding the best combination of employee work teams for Advantage? If a single production test is run with each combination, an important question to be asked is "What are the chances that the production results were a random consequence of unknown factors?" The same could be asked of a series of production tests. However, how many tests should be run before the investigation team can be reasonably certain that the results are not a matter of random chance? These concerns are answered by the use of probability to determine statistical significance.*

b. *Statistical significance:* **Statistical significance** is a measure of the confidence that researchers have in their results. A result may have a 1 in 100 chance of being random. Significance is usually referred to as the level of significance. A level of significance of .05 means that the chance of the event occurring randomly is 5 in 100. The smaller the number, the more confident they are that the results did not happen by chance. Another way of reading the .05 level is to say that the researchers are 95 percent confident in their results. A .01 level would be a 99 percent confidence.

EXAMPLE: *You have heard reports of surveys that have a margin of error of "plus or minus 3 points." This margin of error is a closely related figure to statistical significance (though a different type of calculation is made). In both cases, the surveyor's or investigator's confidence in the accuracy of analysis is being reported. A margin of error of ±3 suggests that the range of the population from which the survey was taken could vary as much as 3 percentage points from the survey's results. If the survey found 52 percent of the population sample intending to vote Democratic in an upcoming election, then the ±3 margin of error means that as few as 49 percent of the total population may vote that way. For the Republicans, this is important news. Within the margin of error of ±3, the Republicans could win the election.*

Check Point—Section C

Directions: For each question, circle the correct answer.

C–1. An auto manufacturer has data showing how much time is required for each step in the assembly process. Which one of the following statistical methods would show the typical length of time for each assembly?

A) Inferential statistics
B) Correlational statistics
C) Descriptive statistics
D) Probability statistics

C–2. The relationship between customer satisfaction and how often the customer comes back to purchase another product would be shown in a

A) median score
B) standard deviation
C) test for significance
D) correlation coefficient

C–3. A major manufacturer of computers cannot survey all of the company's hundreds of thousands of customers to determine the level of customer satisfaction. The statistical technique used to take a small sample and determine the most likely view held by most customers is called

A) descriptive statistics
B) inferential statistics
C) analysis of correlation
D) standard deviation

For Your Review

Directions: For each question, circle the correct answer.

Case 1: Planning and Transition, Incorporated

Miko, an administrative professional, works for Planning and Transition, Incorporated. The company assists other businesses in developing strategic plans, business plans, and transition plans. Miko's supervisor, Patel, is chief of research, so in addition to supporting Patel's diverse staff of research professionals, most of whom have advanced degrees, Miko often aids Patel in research duties.

Every project requires a project plan and is assigned a project manager. Each project has its own special needs and often its own particular type of research. Furthermore, each project involves a unique team of staff members from Planning and Transition, Incorporated and occasionally an outside consultant.

1. In a project designed to help a client convert all reporting to an electronic system, Miko orders types of reports into categories by placing them in a/an

   A) nominal scale
   B) ordinal scale
   C) interval scale
   D) ratio scale

2. Transition planning includes transitions caused by mergers. Recently, Miko has had to collect data for clients' human resource departments relating to employee reactions to mergers. Which one of the following methods will produce the in-depth response data?

   A) Observational qualitative
   B) Split halves
   C) Interview
   D) Experimental

3. In establishing a goal of "improve quality" in a strategic plan, the client wants to measure the quality as a reduction in customer complaints. Miko notices that through the year, complaint rates fluctuate. To be sure the measure will be consistent, Miko must determine whether or not the measure is

   A) reliable
   B) valid
   C) subjective
   D) qualitative

4. A client wants to upgrade technology in the main office, but the exact technology needs of the staff are unclear. Miko will be able to identify those needs using a/an

   A) literature search
   B) survey
   C) experiment
   D) observational study

5. The reason Planning and Transition, Incorporated relies on systematic research is that

   A) qualitative data can be made useful
   B) information and analysis guide effective decisions
   C) reliability will ensure satisfied clients
   D) only experiments can prove cause and effect

Case 2: Barton and Associates, Market Research Specialists

Directors of an international conglomerate are considering making a major investment and entering the cable market. To keep the exploratory option out of the press, they have hired a market research team through a third party. Barton and Associates has been contracted to research the business opportunity and prepare a comprehensive initial report in 90 days for delivery to the client.

Simmons, a senior administrative staff member, has been assigned as team leader for the project. The challenges are exciting, particularly since the project seems fairly wide open, and the charge is to conduct a thorough analysis of the market and business opportunities.

Simmons chooses a team composed of individuals who have demonstrated their skills in the past. Each brings a special area of expertise to the team.

6. Simmons determines that a preliminary examination of information about current businesses in the cable industry will be the best place to begin. Simmons would find the most reliable sources by directing the team to research

    A) the Internet
    B) cable company records
    C) at libraries and archives
    D) using consultants

7. Since the project calls for an analysis of the entire market, which one of the following would be a useful external source about cable customers?

    A) Records of the clients international conglomerate
    B) Team member opinions
    C) Analysis of sales by products
    D) The cable trade association

8. During one phase of the project, Simmons and the team administer questionnaires to a broad selection of people, including customers and potential subcontractors, to determine what kinds of obstacles the client may need to overcome. This research is based on

    A) sales analysis
    B) secondary data sources
    C) job analysis
    D) primary data sources

9. Simmons must determine the consumers' acceptance of the client as a new entry into the cable industry. This phase of the research is called

    A) market analysis
    B) sales analysis
    C) task analysis
    D) statistical analysis

10. In order to make appropriate project assignments within the team and match skills to work, Simmons should conduct a

    A) time-and-motion study
    B) sales analysis
    C) performance observation
    D) task analysis

Case 3: Productivity Reporting

Nelson, the plant general manager, has asked Gassett to compile a special report on recent changes in productivity and the outlook for the next year. Gassett is neither a statistician nor a production manager. Gassett has been asked because Nelson believes a neutral person will make a more objective report. Nelson assigns several other staff to provide support, and these include an accountant and a data manager (who has the skills to conduct statistical analysis).

The accountant is known for presenting excruciating details when a bigger picture would do. The data manager enjoys "crunching the numbers" using every statistical process available. Gassett must ask the accountant to reduce the numbers to a manageable size and the data manager not to run every statistical test. Fortunately, they are both cooperative and will do an excellent job if Gassett can keep them focused.

11. Which one of the following measures should Gassett use to determine the consistency of each production line over a given period?

A) Mean
B) Standard deviation
C) Mode
D) Pearson correlation

12. Part of productivity is the number of defects that must be subtracted from the total unit produced. Which one of the following measures would be recommended to show the tendency toward rejects?

A) Median
B) Range
C) Mean
D) Statistical significance

13. It is impossible to time every assembly action continuously, but Gassett decides that the average time for each assembly step should be determined. So, times for each step are taken throughout the day, and the data manager estimates the average times using

A) mode
B) standard deviation

C) range
D) probability

14. Gassett thinks that running the assembly line slightly slower will decrease the reject rates and thus increase the overall productivity. This relationship is called a

A) median
B) chance event
C) probability
D) correlation

15. In several lines in the assembly area, Gassett discovers tiny differences in production from one day to another. Which one of the following would determine whether these differences were important or merely a result of chance variation?

A) Range
B) Standard deviation
C) Level of significance
D) Probability

Solutions

Solutions to Check Point—Section A

Answer:	Refer to:
A–1. (B)	[A-2-b]
A–2. (A)	[A-4-a-(4)]
A–3. (D)	[A-5-d]

Solutions to Check Point—Section B

Answer:	Refer to:
B–1. (B)	[B-2-b]
B–2. (C)	[B-3-b-(1)]
B–3. (A)	[B-5-b-(1)]

Solutions to Check Point—Section C

Answer:	Refer to:
C–1. (C)	[C-1]
C–2. (D)	[C-2-a]
C–3. (B)	[C-3]

Solutions to For Your Review

Answer:	*Refer to:*
Case 1:	
1. (A)	[A-3-a-(1)]
2. (C)	[A-5-b]
3. (A)	[A-4-b]
4. (B)	[A-5-c]
5. (B)	[A-1]
Case 2:	
6. (C)	[B-2-a]
7. (D)	[B-3-b-(1)]
8. (D)	[B-3-c-(3)-(a)]
9. (A)	[B-3]
10. (D)	[B-5-b]
Case 3:	
11. (B)	[C-1-b-(2)]
12. (A)	[C-1-a-(3)]
13. (D)	[C-3-a]
14. (D)	[C-2]
15. (C)	[C-3-b]

Chapter 6

Organizational Leadership

OVERVIEW

Managers have been necessary because humans perform work: *managers lead people.* Though people share a great number of similar features, each of us is unique. People experience situations differently. One way of imagining what organizations must do is to realize that organizations must constrain the variety of human behavior in such a way as to produce a consistent product or service. The more different we are the greater chance we have of behaving differently. Because participatory management requires that people with differing views work together to find common solutions, it actually offers a better means of governance of behavior than does a single manager with his or her own, individual understanding of people. Delegation of authority and the use of employee empowerment are two means by which organizational goals are met in today's competitive atmosphere.

Essentially, *leadership* is the act of influencing others to work toward a desired goal. Leaders direct people and coordinate the projects that lead to the achievement of goals. The act of leadership can range from commanding others to inspiring others to take the initiative. Since the origination of the scientific study of management, each effort to describe and understand organizational processes has included a definition and model of leadership. The result has been a wide range of definitions. Perhaps the single best definition is that there are two interrelated traits necessary for leadership: expertise and empathy. These two traits of knowledge of tasks and of understanding of people must be exhibited through actions. Today, most researchers agree that there is no common set of personality traits found in every leader. At best, there are a number of common traits typically found in leaders and a number that usually exclude people from leadership.

KEY TERMS

A. Defining the Leadership Role

Leadership not only implies the act of leading but also the importance of following. A leader must have followers or the leadership function will cease to exist. The follower role is very often as important as the leader role. These roles must complement one another in order to achieve personal and organizational goals.

1. *Leadership and Leaders:* **Leadership** is the exercise of influence by one person (a leader) over another in such a way that the follower behaves as the leader directs. Generally, the follower accepts the leader's direction because she or he believes it is right or appropriate for the leader to have dominant influence in that particular situation. The leadership process in organizations includes guiding, directing, and influencing individual and group behavior and activity toward setting and achieving the organization's goals. Thus, leadership is the dynamic element of a manager's day-to-day performance.

   a. *Leadership and management:* The terms *leader* and *manager* are often used synonymously. *Management* refers to the process of achieving organizational results through people and other resources. There are usually four management functions: organizing, planning, influencing (directing), and controlling. While managers must focus on all four functions, leaders are concerned with influencing people to achieve organizational results. All managers perform the leading (influencing) function. However, all leaders do not have to perform the organizing, planning, or controlling functions.

      1. *Formal leaders:* Those leaders who rely on organizational authority or status to influence people are known as **formal leaders.** Formal authority can establish and help maintain leadership, but it alone does not guarantee leadership effectiveness. Leaders rely on personal power attributes, not just formal authority.

      2. *Informal leaders:* **Informal leaders** must rely on their own abilities to influence others; they lack the official support of the formal structure. Often unofficial, unsanctioned leaders will emerge from within organizations and be more credible, effective influencers than those holding formal leadership positions.

In reality, therefore, all managers are not true leaders. Managers may lack influencing skills or abilities, and all leaders do not have to hold positions as managers to succeed in leading. Furthermore, leaders rely on personal power rather than the vestiges associated with organizationally bestowed authority.

b. *Leadership and authority:* Leadership differs from authority. *Authority* is the formal right to command, set group goals, and direct people's efforts to achieve group goals. Authority relies largely on two concepts, delegation and legal rights.

  1. *Formal and informal authority:* Leaders rely on various types of influence to get others to achieve specific goals. Formal authority is only one of the types of influence, as mentioned, that leaders have at their disposal. To the extent that leaders can utilize other types of influence, they can be less bound to the formal structure. Informal leaders cannot rely on formal authority to succeed.

  2. *Legal rights:* All legal rights given to an organization are specifically assigned to one person or a group of persons. These rights provide the authorization, or authority, to appoint managers and delegate authority to them. This authority includes the right to command or direct employees' activities within the business. Rights do not guarantee leadership.

     EXAMPLE: *The owners of a business have the rights to decide, to set goals, and to do what they think is best in running the business as long as they operate within the law.*

     There is no guarantee that people chosen to lead by their organizations and granted the rights to do so will be able to use their formal leadership rights effectively.

  3. *The acceptance of authority:* Originated by Chester Barnard, the acceptance view of authority is based on the premise that managers get their authority from subordinates. Unless managers can get their subordinates to accept their authority, it doesn't matter how much formal authority managers are given. The right to command, however, does not itself guarantee that employees will comply. Compliance depends very much on employees' attitudes and beliefs about the fitness of the person in authority or the appropriateness of the order. Thus, leadership becomes the factor that vitalizes authority—the ability to influence followers to comply with orders, develop commitment to organizational goals, and contribute their efforts at more than minimum performance level.

c. *Leadership and motivation:* Effective leaders recognize that their ability to influence largely rests with their skill in recognizing values, interests, personalities, perceptions, and motivational factors that lead others to act in given ways in specific situations. Therefore, leaders should know about the concept of self, values, beliefs, attitudes, perception, and motivation theories, especially if they want to influence others effectively.

2. *Leadership and Power:* **Power** is the motivational factor, or force, that provides the leader with the ability to influence others to change their behaviors as the leader desires. People are influenced to respond to a leader's direction to the extent that they perceive the leader to possess power. Merely being perceived as a person with power

is to be recognized as having the potential to influence others. Individual leaders, simply because of differences among people, will possess and use power differently in their organizational roles.

a. *Types of power:* Leaders have five primary types of power at their disposal. When each type is used, the typical response by subordinates may be resistance, compliance, or commitment.

  1. *Legitimate power:* Power that comes from holding a formal management position in an organization is called **legitimate power.** Legitimate power is often refered to as *traditional power.* Most subordinates realize that they must follow the directives of leaders who have legitimate power, with respect to work activities, even though they may not agree with the commands given.

  2. *Reward power:* Power that emanates from the leader's authority to bestow formal rewards (tangible or intangible) or favors on others is called **reward power.**

    a. *Tangible rewards:* Pay increases, promotions, days off, and special prerequisites such as a company car

    b. *Intangible rewards:* Recognition, praise, and attention

    Leaders frequently use rewards to influence others to act. The use of reward power generally results in long-term compliance, although in the short term, a sense of commitment to the leader may be noted.

  3. *Coercive power:* Power may arise from a leader's ability to mete out negative consequences or remove positive consequences for not performing desired behaviors. The effectiveness of one's individual **coercive** (punishment) **power** is really found in the perception of its existence in the minds of those who may be punished. The use of coercive power inevitably results in a sense of resentment by the followers toward the leader.

    EXAMPLE: *It is not sufficient that the leader has the power to make deductions from an employee's wages for tardiness. If this power is to influence employees to be on time, they must recognize that the leader has this power and believe that it will be used. The means available to leaders who wish to punish or coerce followers include threats of withholding wages, promotion, recognition, or approval.*

  4. *Expert power:* Informational power resulting from a leader's special knowledge or skills associated with the tasks being performed by subordinates or the possession of special information which is considered to be very important is called **expert power.** A leader possessing special expertise or information usually finds followers because of that superior knowledge or database.

    EXAMPLE: *Gutierrez received training on a new software application and is expected to train the other eight members of the office staff. Being the only one who knows how to operate this software application, Gutierrez is able to develop unilaterally the time schedule for the training sessions. If showing sensitivity to power issues, Gutierrez may be tempted to exaggerate time spent in training to avoid other work.*

  5. *Referent power:* A leader may possess personal characteristics and personality traits that command subordinates' respect, admiration, and commitment, making them want to copy or follow the leader. When workers admire a supervisor or manager because of the way she or he deals with them, this influ-

ence is known as **referent,** or charismatic, **power.** Subordinates do what these leaders desire because of a sense of liking, respect, or wanting to be held in high favor. Personal magnetism is a form of referent power.

EXAMPLES:

Leaders who possessed referent power include wartime leaders (Adolph Hitler, President Franklin D. Roosevelt, and General Omar Bradley) as well as President John F. Kennedy and Dr. Martin Luther King, Jr., who were known for their charismatic power.

Perhaps the most successful business leader who combined referent and expertise power was the founder of Wal-Mart, Sam Walton.

b. *Position power and personal power:* The five types of power—legitimate power, reward power, coercive power, expert power, and referent power—may be placed into two general categories: position power and personal power.

$$\text{leadership power} = \text{position power} + \text{personal power}$$

Leaders who are most effective possess and know how to use both types. Figure 6–1 identifies some sources of position power and personal power and typical long-term responses.

1. *Position power:* Power that is available to someone holding a position by virtue of its legitimacy as well as the rewards and punishments that can be meted out is known as **position power.** For people who are moderate or low in readiness, position power—which includes power based on status, reward, connection, and coercion—is more effective.

2. *Personal power:* Power available to any leader through the use of his or her personal resources, including on-the-job expertise and charisma, is known as **personal power.** The use of personal power generally results in subordinates demonstrating a commitment to the organization's goals and tasks. For people who were high in their level of readiness, personal power—which includes power based on expertise, information, or association (called referent power)—is more effective.

FIGURE 6–1 Sources and Responses to Power Types

Sources of Power	Typical Long-Term Responses		
	Compliance	Resistance	Commitment
Position			
Rank/title	X		
Rewards	X		*
Coercion	*	X	
Personal			
Expertise/information			X
Charisma			X

Rewards may result in short-term commitment, and coercion may lead to short-term compliance. But, in the long run, the response to rewards will be compliance and the response to coercion will be resistance.

3. *Knowledge-based versus status-based power:* Knowledge-based power comes through training and experience. Status-based power can be acquired through the hierarchy of authority or through the informal, collective recognition given by coworkers. *Knowledge and status* correspond to Hersey and Blanchard's two broad categories of power: personal power and position power.

c. *Responses to the use of power:* Followers will generally respond in one of three typical ways to the application of each type of power.

1. *Resistance:* Followers will resent the influence being applied and will deliberately seek to avoid carrying out the leader's directives as well as often openly thwarting the leader. The use of coercive power leads most often to resistance because punishment is deeply resented.

2. *Compliance:* Followers will obey the leader's orders and carry them out, although they may not be committed to the directives. In addition, they may exhibit unenthusiastic work efforts in many instances. The use of legitimate power and reward power most often leads to compliance by subordinates.

3. *Commitment:* Followers will share their leader's viewpoint and enthusiastically carry out his or her requests. They are willing to give more than 100 percent to fulfill the leader's suggestions. Expert power and referent power most often bring the commitment response from followers.

Responses to the three types of position power sometimes lead to resistance and often to compliance. Position power, in this respect, can be regarded as a *hygiene* factor. Personal power brings forth a highly committed and motivated response; thus personal power can be regarded as a *motivational factor.*

d. *The zone of indifference:* Sometimes leadership directives are regarded as consistent with the followers' basic employment of psychological contracts with the organization. In such cases where followers will accept and follow directives almost automatically—referred to as the **zone of indifference**—the use of the three types of position power is effective because the directives fall within the followers' indifference zone.

At other times, leadership requests fall outside the automatic zone of indifference, meet resistance, and tend to be rejected. In such instances the leader may be able to get a positive response only by applying a considerable amount of his or her personal power to get the desired action. The *acid test of power* is when a leader recognizes the limits of position power and uses personal power to gain a worker's compliance and commitment. The refusal to use personal power indicates leadership weakness.

EXAMPLE: *Sommers the supervisor asked Keiko to work overtime this Friday evening and all day Saturday to complete a project. Keiko is tired, has made other tentative plans for Friday evening, and does not want the extra pay or recognition for working overtime. Because this request falls outside Keiko's zone of indifference, Keiko rebels and indicates a preference to have the time off. Sommers, the supervisor, might be able to get Keiko to agree to work by using charisma or expert power or by making a trade-off.*

e. *The abuses of power and leadership:* By just viewing some of the most successful leaders, abuses of power can be seen readily. Power can be used for the good of the people or for the personal gains of the leaders. These two goals may be presented such that they are perceived as being equal, which is an inaccurate perception. If power is over- or underutilized, it can become ineffective because of the perception the overuse or underuse creates in the followers. Failure to give a reward or to use a sanction when others see it as appropriate undermines later attempts to use the power.

As long as there is greed and people seek an advantage over others, abuses of power will exist. However, abuses of power can be controlled. When there is diligence, vigilance, respect for individuality, and respect for the leaders, abuses of power can be minimized.

When leaders are respected, they are not offered bribes. When individuality is respected, abuses of individual rights, such as through sexual harassment, are not tolerated by society. Ethical leadership should be openly encouraged. Abuses of public or private trust should be dealt with promptly, openly, and severely.

3. ***Leadership Ability:*** Specific leadership training takes place within the context of the workplace. It makes more sense in that context because it draws on the specifics of work. Two important facets of leadership can be learned in virtually every situation: expertise and empathy. The technical expertise comes from technical schooling and specific applied experiences. The expertise in dealing with humans originates with the human relations and continues throughout one's career with the variety of interactions each person experiences. The human relations experience forms the basis of empathy. Specifically, empathy means that you are able to put yourself in another person's place.

   a. *Developing leadership ability:* The following items are meant to provide a lifelong strategy for acquiring and sustaining leadership skills. Style and the appropriateness of particular leadership behaviors will depend upon actual experiences. However, to make sense of these experiences, one needs to develop a personal strategy for understanding them.

   b. *Gaining knowledge and experience:* Gaining leadership knowledge and experience happens in a number of ways and in a variety of settings. Leadership knowledge requires learning the technical and human relations skills needed. Experience comes with opportunities to practice skills and utilize knowledge. The knowledge important for leadership falls into four categories—political, bureaucratic, technical, and professional.

   c. *Defining the types of leadership are:*

      1. *Political knowledge.* **Political knowledge** includes knowing the specific interests of others and how to balance competing interests. Political knowledge may involve assigning vacations, assigning work stations, distributing budgets, and even hiring or firing people. These tasks are very important to the people involved. The leader must treat employees as fairly as possible within budgetary limitations. Also, how a leader hires and fires reflects on his or her leadership skills.

      2. *Bureaucratic knowledge:* Knowing how to file reports and knowing the procedures and policies for all manner of managerial activities—called **bureaucratic knowledge**—requires more than just meeting a few guidelines. While companies may be trying to streamline policies, the government continues to create new guidelines for the treatment of employees and others, for safety and health, and for environmental concerns. The more one attends to these

mandates, whether they originate with the company or with the government, the better prepared one will be when the opportunity to lead arises. For example, in the area of safety, the simple act of reporting a safety violation can be critical to the safety of other employees. In this way, such a report made by even the newest employee exhibits leadership.

3. *Technical knowledge:* **Technical knowledge** refers to the skills required to complete work tasks. These skills can include using all the tools required for the task. These tools can be computers or screwdrivers. The core of a person's work knowledge will be technical in nature. Mastery of the technical knowledge requires practice and continued learning.

   EXAMPLES: *Southwest Airline founder Herb Kelleher's law degree provided useful technical knowledge in the first five years of his venture at Southwest. He spent much of that time in court fighting other airlines for the right to fly passengers.*

   The general who directed the logistics operation during a military operation must know the capabilities of certain transport vehicles that may not have been used by the general for decades. Technical knowledge can retain its usefulness in unexpected ways and for long periods of time.

4. *Professional knowledge:* **Professional knowledge** refers to how people interact with others who have the same skills and capabilities. A machinist union operates on the basis of professional knowledge. The technical skills form the common ground for discussions about issues that concern the machinist trade. Professional knowledge is the primary basis for collaborative and participatory leadership.

   EXAMPLE: *After being fired by Handy Dan, Bernie Marcus and Arthur Blank formed Home Depot. They made sure that no one would be humiliated by being fired as they had been. Their experiences, in turn, shaped the people-oriented management approach they established at Home Depot.*

   The expansion of knowledge depends greatly on experience. Practice of technical skills strengthens self-confidence. However, negative experiences can be very important as well.

d. *Gaining power and using it effectively:* Effective leadership depends on the ability to acquire and use power from both personal and position sources. Leaders may follow some of these general guidelines to enhance their power and influence. Power and influence result in the effective coordination of both people and projects in the course of achieving goals.

   1. *Accepting formal authority as given:* Position power sources are usually needed and should not be ignored.

   2. *Creating a sense of obligation:* Doing little things for others creates a sense of obligation on their part. It is better to be owed favors than to owe them. Obligations owed to a leader expand that leader's power base.

   3. *Creating dependency feelings:* The more reliant the followers are on the leader, the greater the leader's power. Finding and acquiring needed resources and giving help when requested, rather than training others to help themselves, create dependency and expand one's power base.

4. *Building expertise and confidence:* A leader can expand his or her power base by acquiring more technical, job-related expertise and building a reputation of having more skills and capabilities. Leaders who are afraid to "blow their own horn" cannot expect others to follow them. Expertise is one of the two sources of personal power.

5. *Accepting the leader as a person:* When followers know and respect leaders as people rather than just as images, they tend to act more in accord with the leaders' wishes.

   EXAMPLES:

   > *One of the reasons that General Dwight D. Eisenhower became such a great leader was that he allowed his troops to meet with him and to share his dreams, goals, and fears.*

   > *Dr. Martin Luther King, Jr., President Ronald Reagan, and Sam Walton of Wal-Mart also used this strategy.*

6. *Understanding the necessity of power:* Leaders require power to influence others. Those who cannot view power as good and necessary will never become effective leaders.

7. *Recognizing costs, risks, and benefits:* Each of the primary sources of power has costs, risks, and benefits associated with it. Leaders must learn to use appropriate power sources at the right times.

8. *Taking control of power:* Effective leaders are mature, have self-control, and recognize their need for power to be effective in their roles. Such leaders must learn to use the power sources with which they are most comfortable and do not try to abuse others with the power they possess or may be able to acquire. They use their power wisely!

e. *Developing affiliation and support:* Affiliation and support come from subordinates, peers, and supervisors. Leadership requires close attention to those people who are already leaders and who have acquired the authority to delegate authority to others. In a democratic group, the *group* affirms leadership. However, the leader must have recognizable skills or useful associations to be granted authority by a group. To gain the group's support, the leader must gain support from as many of the individual members as possible. This may require supporting others first, and then gaining through the alliance established by helping others. It may require asserting oneself and defending the rights of the group or several members of a group. It could also be achieved by demonstrating competence and mastery of the skills and knowledge needed for the group's work.

f. *Supporting supervisors:* In a system that has a hierarchy of authority and power, the affiliations that will succeed depend upon the individual knowing and accepting the lines of authority, identifying with the organization's goals, and learning how to communicate within the organization. One of the most important alliances, and the most important supporter one can have, is the immediate supervisor.

   1. *Identify performance expectations:* Discovering and meeting the needs that he or she has for performance establishes the possibility of later reciprocal support.

      a. Supervisors are far more dependent on their subordinates than the subordinates may realize. The supervisor is the link to the rest of the organization. Both the boss and the subordinate must recognize their mutual dependence.

b. First, an understanding must be developed of the needs, strengths, weaknesses, and personal style of both the boss and the subordinate.

c. Second, that understanding must be used to manage a healthy and productive relationship.

EXAMPLE: *If your supervisor prefers to read information and then discuss it, you should oblige by sending the information before a meeting. If your supervisor prefers to listen to an input and then read about it in a follow-up memorandum, then follow this pattern.*

2. *Identify mutual objectives:* The most critical step in beginning to understand the supervisor (and oneself) is to identify all the objectives that the supervisor has. He or she may define a specific objective for the worker. If the worker is expected to improve worker morale, then the worker should be certain that the time lost in the short-term does not create productivity or other problems. Be aware of as many of the boss's objectives as possible. It is important that the supervisor recognize the worker's objectives as well. If the employee is intent upon moving up in the organization, he or she should be certain that the boss understands and accepts their ambition. Several more specific aspects of this relationship include:

- *Compatible work style:* Identify the personal work style and the boss's style. One should adapt to a style that does not generate conflict. Absolute conformity is not necessary. Rather, one should define a style of interaction that works for both.

- *Mutual expectations:* The boss does not necessarily make every objective and expectation clear. Either ask or investigate.

- *A flow of information:* Keep the flow of information moving upward. Even if the boss does not like to hear bad news, the subordinate still must communicate it.

- *Dependability and honesty:* Do not make promises that are difficult to keep, and do not make a habit of breaking promises.

- *Good use of time and resources:* Bosses usually have little time and need to have information presented to them in a concise and useful manner.

g. *Coordinating projects:* The coordination of projects is a major task of management. It involves planning, organizing, and directing people and resources to complete the project in a timely manner.

1. *The production and operations process:* The task of production and operations management is to manage the efforts and activities of people, capital, and equipment resources in changing raw materials into finished goods and services. The actual production and operations conversion process should be easy to understand. The process involves three primary components: inputs, conversion, and output.

a. *Inputs:* People and organizations begin with inputs that include raw materials, ideas, requests for information, capital, energy, and equipment resources.

b. *Conversion or production:* The inputs need to be changed (converted) into other items to meet the requirements of the process. Some of the conversion activities might involve keying data and information into the computer system. This is also called *production*.

EXAMPLES:

> *Mixing ingredients*
> *Assembling parts*
> *Performing computations and calculations*
> *Creating illustrations for parts of the process*
> *Reviewing reports*

c. *Output:* The end product is the result in the form of finished products or services.

EXAMPLES:

> *A final report*
> *A new automobile*
> *A decorated cake*
> *Catered meals*
> *Plans for business travel*
> *The awarding of a mortgage*
> *Preparations for a wedding*

The production and operations process utilizes inputs that are transformed into outputs as finished goods or services.

2. *Classification of production and operations methods:* Production and operations processes may be classified in two primary ways: the time employed in a single day and the method used (analytic or synthetic).

a. *Time-based methods:* The process may be carried on intermittently (a few hours at a time) or continuously (around the clock).

(i) *Intermittent processes:* Those production and operations processes that run for a given period of time and then stop are known as intermittent processes. They do not operate continuously 24 hours a day, but typically for a shorter period of time.

EXAMPLE: *Retail stores and boutiques as well as podiatrists and veterinarians generally provide services during certain hours of the day. While these hours may be extended, in most cases they do not go around the clock, except in emergency situations.*

(ii) *Continuous processes:* Some organizations function 24 hours a day, all through the year, maintaining continuous services.

EXAMPLE: *Hospital emergency rooms and city police departments provide continuous service 24 hours a day.*

b. *Production method used:* Production and operations processes require the use of either an analytic method or a synthetic method. Some organizations are involved in both types, but most use only one primary method.

(i) *Analytic method:* Analytic-type firms break down things into components and usable parts that can be used for new purposes.

EXAMPLES:

> *A meatpacker slaughters animals and divides the carcasses into meat products, glue, soap, and leather.*
>
> *Petroleum refineries break crude oil down into gasoline, wax, fuel, and kerosene.*
>
> *Laboratory technicians may draw blood and then break a sample down into several parts to be tested and studied.*

(ii) *Synthetic-type firms:* These firms collect parts and then put them together into new, finished products.

EXAMPLES:

> *A baker purchases supplies of raw ingredients and, through transformation processes, creates cakes and other delicacies.*
>
> *A ship builder takes many different parts and pieces of equipment from all over the world and makes them into floating vessels.*

(iii) *Combination operations:* Some firms are involved in both analytic and synthetic processes.

EXAMPLES:

> *The military takes "pliable" individuals and brings them together as part of a large cohesive organization aimed at protecting the nation.*
>
> *Some firms not only break down iron ore into component materials but then put them together as finished cars and appliances.*

Understanding the basic classifications of production and operations is one of the essential steps in starting to study this area.

Check Point—Section A

Directions: For each question, circle the correct answer.

A–1. The process of achieving organizational results through people and other resources is

A) management
B) leadership
C) informal authority
D) empowerment

A–2. A leader's special knowledge or skills associated with the tasks being performed by subordinates defines

A) referent power
B) reward power
C) coercive power
D) expert power

A–3. A leader must know the interests of others and be able to balance the competing interests. This type of leadership knowledge is known as

A) professional
B) technical
C) bureaucratic
D) political

B. Organizing People, Delegating Authority, and Directing Others

A leader cannot for long manage an entire organization without the help of trusted subordinates. The ability to organize and manage others is crucial to leadership effectiveness. One of the key means of extending one's presence and power is through delegation of authority so that others may act in the organization's best interests. Past the small group of immediate subordinates, an effective leader will direct others through others.

1. *Types of Organizations:* Each of the views about organizational structures examined below has different ways of addressing these five factors. These different views are very important because they reflect views that continue to drive organizations. The three main views are classical, neoclassical, and contemporary.

   a. *Classical organizational theory:* The **classical organizational theory** developed along with the strict military and governmental bureaucratic structures. The classical theory divides organizations according to functions. It has a pyramidlike chain of command, a span of control, and a distinction between line and staff workers. The division by function is based on the kinds of specialized tasks that must be performed.

      1. The pyramid-shaped chain of command is typically a steplike structure within each functional unit.

      2. Each unit has a designated leader. That leader is in charge of a specified set of functions and processes.

      3. *Advantages and disadvantages:* The advantages and disadvantages of the classical organizational theory are as follows:

         a. *Advantages:* When used effectively, the classical organization operates along the well-defined lines of authority and functional control. Its officers and management team maintain control and manage workflow smoothly. Employees do their assigned jobs efficiently and productively. Productivity is motivated by merit and seniority, which help individuals move up the hierarchy.

         b. *Disadvantages:* While this view may seem out-of-date, many corporations continue to abide by its structural definitions. Often supervisors will take the view that they are in charge and that they have the authority, so what they say goes. This kind of attitude reflects the classical theory. Usually the supervisor maintains the view because it continues to be part of the organization's culture. When organizations follow this view, the distinctions in function and the importance of line of authority become very rigid.

   b. *Neoclassical organizational theory:* **Neoclassical organizational theory** began as a criticism of classical theory. People who studied organizations realized that the classical approach did not reflect what really happened in organizations. Organizations were changing and were no longer following guidelines dictated by the classical view.

      1. It represents an attempt to humanize the rigid classical structure by adding components that counteract the depersonalization that occurs in the rigid structure.

      2. The effective organization follows the workflow and productivity of the classical organization. However, it also meets the employees' needs as they appear in the informal networks and social components of the workplace.

c. *Contemporary organizational theory:* **Contemporary organizational theory** looks at the organization as a system composed of people, formal structures, small (sometimes informal) groups, roles, and physical environment.

1. In this view, the actual organizational structure—the formal structure—is only one of several parts.

2. Contemporary organizational structures recognize the informal communication patterns and depend on them for innovation and for encouraging commitment and participation.

3. Rather than try to make the people, who are now much more diverse, fit the formal system, many corporations are fitting the system to the people and to their informal communication and interaction styles.

The effective contemporary organization realigns work according to its products and services rather than work functions. The organization reflects the goals of productivity and employee satisfaction rather than goals of sustaining command processes and the control of information. Structure depends upon the organization's culture. Transformations occur as a result of trying to meet challenges of the market and changes in expectations of employees.

2. *Approaches to Managing People:* Views of human nature influence theories about what is required to motivate and direct the work activity of people. These views influence the degree of trust that managers have in their subordinates, and thus the degree to which authority and responsibility will be shared between supervisor and worker. The classic theories are *Theory X, Theory Y,* and *Theory Z.* Theory X and Y were made famous by Douglas McGregor, and Theory Z was introduced by William Ouchi. These views underscore the power and popularity of *participatory management,* especially as it influences teamwork.

a. *Theory X:* From the point of view of a manager who accepts **Theory X,** the employee is lazy and requires constant monitoring to ensure that performance remains at the expected standards. The following assumptions would be typical of a manager influenced by Theory X:

1. In Theory X, people avoid work by their very nature.

   a. People have no ambition to take responsibility and thus prefer direction.

   b. People are motivated most by the need Maslow identified as security.

   c. People will work toward corporate goals only through coercion and threat of punishment.

2. McGregor argued that people exhibited these characteristics because they were managed in a way that made them do so. If management would change, then people would change their exhibited characteristics. In effect, the manager's views had created self-fulfilling prophecy. If McGregor was right, then a company could change its people by changing its management style. The style element may even be no more than an attitude about workers.

b. *Theory Y:* The **Theory Y** view of management takes a much more optimistic view. Based more on needs of affiliation, self-esteem, and self-actualization, the typical assumptions of a manager influenced by Theory Y would be:

1. Work is natural.

2. If people are committed to the organizational goals, self-control will be exercised.

5. *The exception principle:* Problems should be solved at the lowest level of the organization that has the necessary authority. In other words, only exceptional matters (those beyond a person's authority) should be referred to a higher level manager. This principle asks that each subordinate perform work functions with full responsibility and that a higher level manager's time is protected from routine matters.

Basic principles of organization are established to yield guidelines that are derived from experience, yet practical to implement within an organization.

b. *The organization process:* The process of organizing establishes a systematic grouping of persons with needed equipment and materials, in a fashion that will facilitate achieving the objectives of the organization. This involves a consideration of different skill and knowledge specializations; different types and amounts of authority; and coordination of departments, divisions, or work groups. Every organization must deal with five factors: (1) design of jobs and specialized tasks, (2) coordination of separate tasks, (3) location of decisions and authority, (4) the chain of command, and (5) the flow of information. The specifics of these factors help one understand how different organizational structures approach each of them.

1. *Design of jobs and specialized tasks:* Organizations exist to distribute specialized tasks among group members. A detailed analysis of all the tasks to be performed within a particular organizational grouping—an organizational unit—is essential to ensure that everything needed is planned for to achieve the objective. These tasks are then grouped by similarity and divided into individual jobs. A job is a set of tasks or authority assigned to one individual who is responsible for the completion of those tasks.

a. *Taylor's scientific management:* More than a century ago, Taylor's scientific management was focused on making the process of specializing tasks more effective and completely routine. The fundamentals include:

(i) The more repetitive and routine, the less chance of error. As tasks become more specialized, the workers become more efficient.

(ii) Tasks may be redefined and regrouped, but they are still specialized in some manner.

EXAMPLE: *In computer assembly, an assembler may no longer be putting only one chip in a board, but instead may be assembling complete boards. However, the assembly of the board is still a specialized task.*

(iii) Even though managers have abandoned Taylor's original approach, the notion of task specialization remains critical. In fact, as industries move toward task groups, the training of an employee who can do all the required tasks may require even greater specialization.

EXAMPLE: *The Shoe Company plans to advertise nationally and to share local advertising equally with local shoe retailers. Thus the advertising unit, headed by the advertising manager, will include at least two different tasks: (1) national advertising and (2) local advertising. One job with the responsibility for everything connected with national advertising will be assigned to one person. If the volume of work is too heavy for that person to perform, further subdivision is necessary to create additional subordinate jobs.*

2. *Task coordination:* These specialized tasks must also be coordinated, or the flow of work will become inefficient. Coordination of tasks can be quite complex.

   EXAMPLES:

   > *The computer board assembler's work must be coordinated with other assemblers who may be configuring the power supply, the various data drives and connections, and other whole components.*

   > *In automobile assembly, delivery of parts and components assembled in other plants and the flow of supplies from one plant to another require careful and thorough planning. This planning is itself a specialized task.*

   a. *Division of major activities into horizontal groupings:* Primary activities need to be established into horizontal groupings.

   > EXAMPLE: *A firm's mission is the manufacture and distribution of shoes through wholesalers. Major activities will include manufacturing, marketing, finance, research and development, and personnel.*

   b. *Vertical division into horizontal groupings:* Each horizontal grouping, noted in the example above, will include many different specialized activities. Each set of specialized activities should be grouped together.

   > EXAMPLE: *The marketing activity will include sequenced activities related to sales, advertising, market research, and credit and collections functions.*

3. *Location of decisions and authority:* The power to make decisions is usually located in an identified place. Authority resides in the legal owner of a business or in the legally appointed director of a nonprofit organization. The need to group and to divide activities requires delegation since the owner or director cannot effectively exercise all authority over large numbers of people or wide ranges of specializations. Even fully participatory management has the location of decision-making power clearly defined.

   a. The decisions can be localized in centralized structures that have a single individual or a small group at the top of the organization hierarchy. These individuals at the top have the power to make decisions.

   b. The opposite structure decentralized structures that distribute authority to make decisions throughout the organization.

4. *Chain of command:* The **chain of command** is a military concept that can be defined as the organizational design for the flow of communications and decision making. The right to command, to exercise authority, should be delegated in a continuous chain, or line, from the top to the bottom of the organization.

   a. Not all command structures need to be shaped like the military pyramid that rises to a single individual in charge.

   b. The chain of command also has levels of responsibility and specific goals at each level.

   c. The chain of command can go through a number of layers or through only a few. Organizations with many layers are called tall organizations.

   > EXAMPLE: *At one point, GM had as many as 32 layers of management. At the same time, Toyota had only 8.*

5. *Flow of information:* The control and flow of information is very important because information is one of the forms of power in an organization. As the information flows up through a hierarchical structure, managers and directors who receive the information gain more ability to control the organizational processes. One key to empowerment is to give employees access to information.

c. *Line and staff authority:* A distinction is made between authority that is widespread and covers the primary mission and objectives of the organization and authority that is permitted in areas where specialists provide advisory support. *Line authority* is direct authority that carries with it the right to give orders and have decisions implemented. *Staff authority* is advisory and supportive in nature; it does not give the right to command. Instead, individuals with staff authority assist, recommend, advise, and facilitate activities related to the organization's objectives. *Functional authority* is the right granted by top management for specialists to have their expertise followed in specific areas such as equal employment opportunity legislation and workplace violence. Line managers must heed functional managers only within their designated areas of expertise.

1. *Line activities:* Those activities directly associated with the primary product or service of the organization are called line activities and represent such areas as production, marketing, and finance. These activities follow the chain of command that exists from top to bottom within an organization.

   EXAMPLE: *In a hospital, nurses, doctors, and other direct health-care providers represent some of the primary (line) activities within the organization. Usually the doctor in charge has the overall authority in decision making.*

2. *Functional activities:* Functional activities tend to represent specific areas of support guiding the primary activities within the organization. However, specific components of functional authority may be necessary to follow for organizational survival, such as meeting Equal Employment Opportunity (EEO) guidelines and Consumer Product Safety Commission rules.

   EXAMPLE: *In a large retail firm, an information system specialist may be given specific authority to direct product managers in certain areas related to computers and decision support systems.*

3. *Staff activities:* Staff activities are those specialized activities that facilitate the performance of the primary activities but are less directly related to it.

   EXAMPLE: *Accounting, human resources, and labor relations activities are examples of staff units.*

   Staff units provide advice to the line units. Obviously, if there is more than one person in the staff unit, the superior will exercise staff authority over the subordinates within the staff unit. This preserves unity of command.

d. *Authority and responsibility:* Both of these terms have already been used and partially defined. Because they refer to the attempt to regulate people within organizations, the different shades or degrees of authority delegation become quite complex.

1. *Authority:* The term *authority* is defined simply as the right to command—the right to exercise the legitimate powers vested in the organization by society. As discussed, the three types of formal authority are line, staff, and functional authority.

2. *Responsibility:* The complementary side of authority is responsibility. It is the duty or obligation to exercise the authority to achieve the purpose for which the authority was delegated.

e. *Effective delegation of authority and responsibility:* Delegating authority to a subordinate requires the supervisor to engage in typical duties related to controlling and directing work and workers. The supervisor achieves objectives primarily through the cooperative work efforts of others. Directing and leading people through various business processes requires effective **delegation,** the process by which authority is distributed downward in an organization. Sufficient authority must be granted so that the work can be completed. Delegation is one of the most difficult jobs supervisors have to learn. Assignment of a task should carry with it sufficient authority to perform the needed operations. Effective delegation requires attention to several key actions.

1. *Clearly defined assignments:* The basic supervisory duties must be completed in a manner that has resulted in clearly identified assignments, tasks, and related duties. Work assignment must be clear, the specific task must be understood, output goals must be stated, and adequate resources must be provided. With these elements in place, the assignment of the authority to act will provide an opportunity for successful action.

   a. *Determination of necessary work functions:* The supervisor must decide exactly which tasks need to be performed, usually on a short-term basis (daily, weekly). In addition, tasks must be prioritized so that those items with the highest priority will be completed first. The supervisor needs to establish work procedures that will accommodate the differing priorities of work assignments.

   b. *Assignment of tasks:* Each specific task must be assigned to the personnel who will perform the required operations. Assignment of a task means that an individual is delegated the responsibility of completing that task. When the task is assigned, it is particularly important that the supervisor provide a complete set of instructions and details for completion.

2. *Clearly specified limits of authority:* The act of delegation must include any limitations of authority as well as grants of power to act. Failure to identify those limits may result in accidental abuses of power and authority.

   a. *Accountability for actions and results:* A supervisor needs to expect employees to be accountable for work results obtained through the enforcement of standard criteria for acceptability. If a supervisor has given complete directions and assigned adequate time to perform, no less than acceptable performance by the individual should be expected. In turn, higher level management will expect the supervisor to be accountable for employees' work. This accountability involves the supervisor in checking and approving completed tasks and taking responsibility for them.

3. *Employee participation:* Employees must be ready to assume the power and responsibility being conferred by the delegation. One means of testing this

readiness is to have the employee participate in constructing the delegation. The employee will be more comfortable with rules and regulations, expectations for feedback, and so on that he or she has helped formulate.

4. *Established feedback and other administrative controls:* Successful delegation must have clearly defined schedules for feedback and regular progress reports. The supervisor and employee must maintain adequate but not stifling communication. Preparing a schedule in advance can alleviate any sense of potential supervisory interference with the delegated action.

   a. *Provision for adequate supervision:* Some people require more supervision than others. The effective supervisor will permit some individuals the autonomy to perform tasks on their own to achieve objectives, knowing that they can perform them with minimum supervision. Others may need more supervision because of the complexity of tasks or incomplete knowledge of the task.

   b. *Criteria for production output:* Standards for production output are becoming more common in office systems. People working with data processing or other types of office systems need to know the criteria established for output so that they can meet productivity standards.

   c. *Allocation of resources:* Supervisors must ensure that workers have adequate resources, supplies, and equipment to perform assigned tasks and utilize those resources effectively and efficiently.

   d. *Employee safety:* The workplace must be maintained to ensure that employees will be safe and working in healthful conditions. The supervisor has the responsibility to correct any conditions that prove to be unsafe or unhealthy.

5. *Notification of the delegation:* Others with the organization must know and accept the delegation that has occurred. Failure to notify others can jeopardize the willingness of others to cooperate or to share information.

Delegation is an important tool for supervisors. No supervisor can conduct all the functions required for the unit, so delegation is a necessity for efficient management. Delegation is not participative management in that decisions made through delegation are ultimately the responsibility of the supervisor. Participative management involves shared decision making while delegation may result from the supervisor's decision alone.

Check Point—Section B

Directions: For each question, circle the correct answer.

B–1. Collective decision making, slow evaluation and promotion, and informal control linked to formalized procedures are hallmarks of Theory

A) X
B) Y
C) Z
D) P

B–2. The restricted time and ability of an individual manager means that the number of people reporting to a manager should be limited. This is called

A) unity of command
B) span of control
C) departmentalization
D) commensurate authority

B–3. When a supervisor exercises effective control and direction of others, responsibilities must be assigned and power given to others to carry out the assignments. The act of giving others this authority is called

A) delegation of authority
B) chain of command
C) span of control
D) Theory Z

C. Empowering Employees

The changes being made in many major corporations today embrace the concepts of empowerment and teamwork. Empowerment requires self-leadership and grants individuals the power to lead others. Teamwork requires leaders that arise from within the team. Leadership will be an important skill for every employee, regardless of long-term goals.

1. *Empowerment Defined:* **Empowerment** is an extension of delegation in which the power and responsibility for relevant decision making is extended to the employee without supervisory direction or oversight. The employee must have knowledge, power, and resources necessary for success.

    EXAMPLE: *A motorcycle manufacturer assigns the decision for selecting costly equipment to the employees who will be using the equipment. Managers have difficulty relinquishing the power and authority, but the act of decision making means that the employees will have a sense of pride and ownership in their participation in major corporate goals. The pride is also a motivating factor, resulting in increased quality and productivity.*

    a. *Sharing of responsibility:* Many methods of sharing responsibility for achieving goals in the workplace have been explored. These range from single-task assignments in the context of a highly centralized organization in which each task is assigned in detail and then monitored for completion, to a highly decentralized organization in which independent teams form for each goal. Independent teams in these "matrix" structures are called self-leading teams. Teams represent the extreme form of group and individual empowerment. Empowerment can be represented on a continuum from the most restrictive assignment to the most entrepreneurial independence.

    b. *Motivation through empowerment:* Empowerment has motivational qualities that arise through internal rewards more often than external rewards.

        1. **Self-management**—managing one's own behavior so that less external management control is needed—provides a sense of individual success and individual self-direction that traditionally supervised work does not. The employee understands how his or her actions are linked to the desired outcomes of work whenever he or she has been made responsible for those outcomes.

        2. *Initiative* enhances ownership and pride and responds well to all kinds of work-related rewards.

        3. *Workers are more effective* when they perceive that they have more than a cursory role in decision-making, planning, problem solving, and quality improvements.

4. *Empowered employees* are typically more responsive and quicker to solve problems and adapt to changes than employees with little power or opportunity for initiative.

c. *Participation and involvement:* Empowerment results in job enrichment because it causes power, knowledge, information, and rewards to move lower into the organizational structure. Thus, empowerment tends to increase the skills and expectations of employees, resulting from acquisition of skills that lead to responsibility for self-control, for product completion, and for product quality. These responsibilities also empower the employee with potential skills for self-management or participatory management.

1. *Traditional job enrichment programs:* The programs have been aimed at enriching the individual's skills and improving characteristics of specific job tasks. They have not been aimed at increasing the employees' role in management.

2. *Empowerment leading to involvement:* As the employee becomes more enriched, he or she becomes more involved in the organization. The organization must be ready to accept and utilize the increased commitment created through enrichment.

3. *Expectations from participation:* If greater responsibility and collaborative management do not accompany the increase in knowledge, then both satisfaction and productivity may suffer. If skills are acquired, yet opportunities to exercise them do not exist for the employee, then the chances for dissatisfaction increase.

2. ***TQM as an Empowerment Technique:*** W. Edwards Deming (1898–1993) believed in total quality as a constant standard for industry and advocated the use of statistical measures to track quality. During the late 1960s and 1970s, American business leaders did not accept his theories as readily as Japanese management did. He pushed for production-line employee involvement in the quality control process. Deming was in great demand throughout Japan, and scores of changes were made to improve production processes and quality of output there under his guidance. Deming and his Japanese counterparts became the saviors of Japanese industry and the country's economy, leading to more prosperous lifestyles.

a. *Basic premises of TQM:* **Total quality management (TQM)** relies on the satisfaction of multiple customers with products or services, employee empowerment, and the use of statistical tools for problem solving.

1. *Satisfaction of multiple customers:* The main focus of TQM must be on the end consumer. However, some departments must provide assistance and support to other units within the organization. In this case, their primary customers are internal to the firm, not external. Managers must recognize that unless their employees are "satisfied customers," quality will not be realized. Suppliers are customers. Competitors are customers. All internal departments are potential customers. Outside organizations with whom a firm comes in contact are also customers. Awareness of the need to satisfy multiple constituencies is one of the problems that managers must deal with in designing and implementing effective TQM programs.

2. *Employee empowerment:* The most important and neglected part of the TQM process involves employee empowerment. The basic premise of TQM is that

employees on the line are the persons who can find the problems that are the cause of quality issues and solve them. Unfortunately, many managers and organizations recognize this but do not allow the employees the right to act. Empowerment involves trusting people. Many managers are still of the Theory X mindset and do not recognize the contributions that their employees will make, if given authority as well as responsibility. Unless workers are knowledgeable about TQM, including statistical tools and teamwork techniques, and then entrusted (empowered) with the responsibility of implementing quality improvements on their work sites, TQM will always fail!

3. *Statistical tools for problem solving:* One of the basic premises of TQM is that problems are not known until they have been identified and evaluated properly. The entire TQM process involves the use of various statistical tools, charts, and graphs to identify, measure, and evaluate the extent of problems and then to help determine the most effective approaches to improve quality. While a detailed presentation of total quality tools is beyond the scope of this section, some of the devices used include fishbone diagrams (cause-and-effect diagrams), flowcharts, run charts, scatter diagrams, and histograms. These tools are easy to use and become very helpful in the TQM process.

b. *Deming's absolutes of quality:* Deming established a series of 14 rules regarding the achievement and maintenance of quality within any organization. These rules are the very essence of the total quality management (TQM) movement. (See Chapter 3 for a list of the 14 rules.)

In both types of participatory management, the employees must accept a view of management that governs the whole of their work lives. Total quality management requires an attitude about quality as a guiding force in work life. In self-directed teams, employees must accept a level of responsibility not available to them before. Both of these forms have partial variations. In most variations, however, the employee is empowered to achieve quality or to engage in self-management.

3. **The Success of Empowerment in the Workplace:** Empowerment has many advantages and a few disadvantages. To be successful, however, careful steps must be taken to ensure that all the elements presented come together. Empowerment requires clear definitions of authority, task, resources, limits, and even rewards. Several steps will ensure successful employee empowerment.

a. *Advantages of employee empowerment:* Corporations may utilize empowerment for one or more of the following reasons:

1. *Improve productivity:* Empowered employees have a better understanding of the link between their performance and company success.

2. *Improve quality:* Empowered employees are focused on quality, take pride in their work, and have a strong sense of affiliation with the company. Consequently, a greater focus on quality occurs.

3. *Improve job satisfaction:* Empowered workers report greater job satisfaction.

4. *Improve responsiveness and problem solving:* Empowered employees are able to react quicker to changes and solve problems at the place they occur. This can increase efficiency as well as conserve resources.

b. *Disadvantages of employee empowerment:* Corporations that do not fully empower employees, yet expect partially empowered employee to behave as if they are fully expected to exercise authority and take responsibility, can suffer significant setbacks.

   1. *Poor training can have significant costs:* Poorly trained employees may misuse their opportunities to be self-managed and make errors that are extremely costly to the company.

      EXAMPLE: *An upscale fashion retailer allowed its employees to misrepresent how many hours were worked to achieve high sales figures. These underreported hours caused the company's productivity to appear artificially high, in turn artificially increasing stock values. Severe penalties were charged against the firm.*

      Employees cannot be unethical in order to enhance their own rewards and bonuses.

   2. *Pressure to achieve corporate goals cannot be disguised as empowerment:* Empowerment is a means of improving many facets of organizational success, like productivity, efficiency, expansion, market leadership, and quality. It is not a means of scapegoating, pushing employees to do illegal acts, or improve numbers through substandard work.

   3. *Empowerment is not a shortcut:* Proper empowerment cannot be accomplished overnight. It requires extended cooperative work to establish a foundation that all members of the organization accept. Efforts to shortcut the process frequently result in failure.

c. *Steps to empowerment:* The following are some of the more common steps required to achieve and sustain successful empowerment.

   1. *Identify the starting point:* Who will be involved and to what extent?

   2. *Train and learn:* Employees must learn about procedures, issues, resources, and other aspects of the business beyond their current work responsibilities. The employee must understand his or her role in the bigger picture.

   3. *Share information and be honest:* Trust can be achieved only through full disclosure of all relevant information.

   4. *Assess, track, and report:* Employees must know the relevant details of the situation at all times (for instance, productivity rates, waste percentages, market trends).

   5. *Maintain a consistent operation:* Standards are a key to guiding work, even if frequent changes are proposed and accepted. Once a standard is used, all employees must abide by it.

   6. *Be methodical about exploring alternatives:* Teams, groups, and individuals have ideas for improvement, and these must undergo a rigorous evaluation before implementation.

   7. *Demonstrate loyalty:* Through praise, constructive criticism, financial reward, and a supportive atmosphere, demonstrate how valuable each participating and empowered employee is of the organization.

Check Point—Section C

Directions: For each question, circle the correct answer.

C–1. The sense of individual success and individual self-direction that accompanies empowerment results from

A) job enrichment
B) total quality management
C) delegation of authority
D) self-management

C–2. Total quality management is closely associated with employee empowerment because employees

A) have high expectations
B) solve quality problems
C) are committed to quality
D) experience pressure to achieve

C–3. Which one of the following is a serious disadvantage of employee empowerment?

A) Employees come to understand the link between productivity and work
B) Job satisfaction increases making employee less committed
C) It is a shortcut to corporate success
D) Problems are solved through employee initiative

For Your Review

Directions: For each question, circle the correct answer.

Case 1: Leaders Lead at Halls, Incorporated

McNally has been chief executive officer of Halls, Incorporated for about five years. Prior to becoming CEO, McNally served in progressively more important positions in almost every division of the company. As a shift supervisor, McNally worked directly with about 75 employees, and then as a plant manager worked with 7 shift and staff supervisors with a total of about 500 employees overall. McNally moved to the headquarters after a period of time as a regional manager and then held several key senior executive positions.

McNally has always been known as a person who had worked up through the ranks and not only understood the workers but also had actually worked with them. The series of positions educated McNally about the inner workings and culture of Halls, Incorporated.

1. The employees at Halls like McNally and trust that McNally knows the company and its work. McNally's apparent fitness as a leader indicates

   A) reward power
   B) acceptance of authority
   C) coercive power
   D) zone of indifference

2. Through a long presence at Halls, McNally has knowledge that allows careful balance between all the competing interests within the company. This knowledge of the interests of others is called

   A) political knowledge
   B) bureaucratic knowledge
   C) technical knowledge
   D) professional knowledge

3. Rotation through jobs and plants at Halls and the systematic increase in responsibility with each new job means that McNally has built personal power based on

   A) creating a sense of obligation
   B) developing expertise and confidence
   C) recognizing costs, risks, and benefits
   D) taking control of power

4. In the years leading to being appointed chief executive officer, McNally formed many friendships and collaborated with many other Halls employees. This contributed to the development of leadership ability through

   A) gaining technical knowledge
   B) learning production and operations processes
   C) finding compatible work style
   D) acquiring affiliation and support

5. McNally depends on subordinates working together to solve problems and engage in planning. Which one of the following would be identified as the organizational style used by McNally?

   A) Theory Y
   B) Unity of command
   C) Participatory management
   D) Informal leadership

Case 2: Project Manager

Krystal oversees dozens of projects each month. Most of the projects involve customized proposals dealing with the logistics of design, customization, assembly, and delivery of products and services provided by a multifaceted company. Each project has an assigned team and a team leader. Krystal must manage each team and ensure the timely completion of the project. Team members are drawn from more than a dozen divisions of the company.

Surprisingly, each team seems to thrive under a different organizational style. Some teams are completely self-managed, whereas others require clear directives from the start to be successful. Krystal knows the people fairly well and can anticipate what structure they will need, what guidance is required, and what kinds of resources they will request.

6. In selecting a team leader, Krystal knows that the team leader should be from the division to which the team will submit its completed project. Team leaders should report to their regular supervisors. This principle is known as

A) the span of control
B) commensurate authority
C) the unity of command
D) departmentalization

7. Krystal selects team members according to the notion that the team needs only one specialist for each type of task that the team will need to accomplish. This allows the team to coordinate tasks by

A) division of major activities into horizontal groupings
B) span of control
C) vertical division of groupings
D) chain of command

8. The charge to any team must be clear and describe the outcome that is expected. To accomplish this, Krystal must

A) create a proper chain of command
B) establish harsh penalties for failure to meet deadlines

C) follow the exception principle
D) delegate both authority and responsibility

9. For most teams, Krystal establishes criteria for production output, allocates resources, sets timetables, and creates communication links. These are all aspects of

A) clarifying the limits of authority
B) establishing feedback and administrative controls
C) empowering the team to be self-governing
D) distinguishing between line and staff authority

10. Which one of the following best describes the organization in which Krystal works?

A) Theory X
B) Theory Y
C) Theory Z
D) Participatory management

Case 3: Reinventing Customer Service

Directors of the New Flanders Bank believe that they can attract customers away from established banks in town by offering the best customer service to be found in any bank. They have even imitated a major international discount store by introducing a "greeter." They do not stop there. Over time, every employee who interacts with customers, even the bank president, must be able to perform the basics of every other customer-related job in the bank. Specialists still do the detailed processing of loan applications and trust investments. However, if tellers need help, any employee can step in and help. If the greeter is helping one customer and another customer walks in, then anyone can step in to be the greeter. When problems are discovered, the employee is expected to find a satisfactory solution or take the problem to someone with the ability to solve it. Applications for loans are processed promptly, and customers get answers more quickly than at neighboring banks. Customers feel welcome, and the bank is among the fastest growing banks in the region.

11. The greeter's role at New Flanders Bank includes taking responsibility for customer needs and trying to satisfy them. This responsibility is called

   A) employee empowerment
   B) delegation
   C) political knowledge
   D) informal leadership

12. Having employees take responsibility for their work and for the success of the bank should result in

   A) increased technical knowledge
   B) greater efficiency
   C) more delegation
   D) improved job satisfaction

13. The approach at New Flanders Bank includes employees stepping in and assisting other employees as the need arises. This aspect of empowerment is based on the view that

   A) bonuses must be based on willingness to help
   B) everyone is a potential customer

   C) productivity will increase if expectations are kept high
   D) participation must be clearly defined

14. Which one of the following might cause the efforts of empowerment to fail?

   A) Excessive loyalty that results in blindness to problems
   B) Poor training that results in misuse of opportunities
   C) Use of statistical procedures to track employees
   D) Overly eager employees who make it seem that the bank is trying too hard

15. New Flanders Bank has borrowed the greeter concept from a highly successful model. Which one of the following aspects of empowerment does this idea resemble?

   A) Improved productivity
   B) Increased self-management
   C) Increased organizational involvement
   D) Improved problem solving

Solutions

Solutions to Check Point—Section A

Answer:	Refer to:
A–1. (A)	[A-1-a]
A–2. (D)	[A2-a-(4)]
A–3. (D)	[A-3-b-(1)]

Solutions to Check Point—Section B

Answer:	Refer to:
B–1. (C)	[B-2-c]
B–1. (B)	[B-3-a-(2)]
B–1. (A)	[B-3-e]

Solutions to Check Point—Section C

Answer:	Refer to:
C–1. (D)	[C-1-b-(1)]
C–1. (B)	[C-2-a-(2)]
C–1. (C)	[C-3-b-(3)]

Solutions to For Your Review

	Answer:	*Refer to:*

Case 1:

1.	(B)	[A-1-b-(3)]
2.	(A)	[A-3-b-(1)]
3.	(B)	[A-3-c-(4)]
4.	(D)	[A-3-d]
5.	(C)	[B-2-d]

Case 2:

6.	(C)	[B-3-a-(1)]
7.	(A)	[B-3-b-(2)-(a)]
8.	(D)	[B-3-e]
9.	(B)	[B-3-e-(4)]
10.	(D)	[B-2-d]

Case 3:

11.	(A)	[C-1-a]
12.	(D)	[C-3-a-(3)]
13.	(B)	[C-2-a-(1)]
14.	(B)	[C-3-b-(1)]
15.	(C)	[C-1-c-(2)]

Chapter 7

Team Building
and Team Leading

OVERVIEW

Groups are fundamental to human behavior—without them individuals would have great difficulty surviving. People thrive on the interdependent relationships they find in groups. Affiliation is an important need. Groups are also critical to the success of governmental and corporate organizations because productivity requires cooperative effort toward common goals. Groups are as essential to work as they are to life.

Industry recognizes the value of groups that are formed separately from the traditional structure. Eight out of 10 U.S. organizations with 100 or more employees use some form of work team as part of the organization. This concept reflects the contemporary organizational structure. Nine out of 10 (90 percent) companies with more than 10,000 employees use teams. More than half of the employees in these organizations work in some form of team groupings.

This chapter examines the various types of groups, especially teams, and group membership as well as the kinds of interaction that occur in groups and how to improve participation in the groups. Also examined are group processes, or the ways groups can achieve their goals. Other topics include how to maintain group effectiveness in the face of several potential dangers of group behavior.

KEY TERMS

Circle, 172
Cohesiveness, 183
Command group, 173
Committee, 175
Cross-functional team, 174
Distinctiveness, 183

Formal group, 173
Group, 172
Group dynamics, 181
Homogeneity, 183
Horizontal team, 174
Informal group, 175

Interest group, 176
Norms, 179
Proximity, 182
Quality circle, 174
Role, 180
Self-managing team, 174

A. Groups

A **group** is any collection of two or more people who share a common goal or purpose, who work together, and who share an awareness of the common goals and work.

1. *General Types of Groups:* Groups can be formally or informally composed, large or small, permanent or temporary, and focused on any aspect of life. A common classification distinguishes groups by membership: community, family, friends, and work.

   a. *Community:* Throughout your community you will find a number of church, civic, and volunteer groups. The community itself is a kind of group. These groups serve a range of needs and purposes shared by the members of the community. The community groups define and strengthen individual and group attitudes. They also have a formal identity within the community. Their purposes may be religious or social. They may focus on members of the community that have special needs, like people who are homeless or economically disadvantaged. Civic, social, and religious groups satisfy the needs of individuals. They also give the community its strength and identity.

   EXAMPLE: *The Girl Scouts, the Boy Scouts, the YMCA, and similar organizations have as part of their express goals the development of "community values" in their membership.*

   b. *Family:* In order to survive, humans had to form cooperative groups that would share the responsibilities of childrearing and the collection of food. The type of group that evolved for this endeavor is called the family. Though the typical family is thought to be composed of a father, a mother, and children, the family is actually quite a flexible unit.

   c. *Friends:* Everyone has a close group of friends and acquaintances. Sociologist Kurt Back calls this group "the circle." The **circle** is comprised of a loosely formed and highly informal collection of individuals. The role of this group is important for the individual. In fact, this collection of people may arise from other community and work groups.

   d. *Work:* By definition, any corporate organization constitutes a grouping. The group has a very specifically defined goal—that of making profit through some form of enterprise. Within large organizations there are many smaller subunits that form groups, each having their specific objectives. At work, people may become members of several different groups. The groups are usually formed to maximize the energy of a number of people working on a common task. This task can be organized in different ways. Workers may work on the basis of the direct production of goods. They may form groups to support roles that are intended to increase productivity. Those roles may be intended to improve job satisfaction and motivation. Because of the desire to reap a common and tangible benefit (usually money), the processes of the work group are different from those of the other groups. Other kinds of work groups, like charity or civic groups, will be organized to make the most of the efforts of the members of the groups. Profit is not the only purpose of work groups. In fact, a more universal purpose of the work group is to achieve the greatest productivity through collaboration and efficient use of human labor.

Another common classification of groups deals with how they are formed as formal groups or informal groups. The following section addresses this distinction.

2. *Formal Groups:* Groups created by management and charged with carrying out specific tasks to help the organization fulfill its objectives are **formal groups.** Formal groups function as smaller subsystems within the structure of the overall organization. These groups are assigned appropriate authority and responsibility from management.

EXAMPLES:

> *Accounts receivable department*
>
> *Communications services*
>
> *Copy services*
>
> *Human resources department*

a. *Components of the formal group:* The formal group has at least one leader who works with and supervises the members of the group (subordinates) in accomplishing its goals and objectives through specific work arrangements.

1. *The leader:* The head of the formal group is a person who is appointed by managers in the formal structure to accomplish the group's goals and objectives through subordinates and within the official work structure.

2. *Members or subordinates:* The members of the group are those individuals who are appointed by management or supervisors to carry out the specified goals and objectives under the group manager's direction and within the official work structure.

3. *Goals and objectives:* The particular mission and specific measurable tasks or projects that management expects the formal group to accomplish are known as goals and objectives of the formal group.

4. *Work arrangement:* The work arrangement is the way in which management officially assigns tasks among the group members to ensure efficient and effective goal accomplishment.

Individuals enjoy the prestige of belonging to high-status groups, successful groups, and groups where goals are compatible. Obviously, in formal groups, access to pay, position, and "perks" controlled by the organization are primary reasons for joining the group or accepting employment.

b. *Types of formal groups:* Primary types of formal groups include command groups, teams, and task forces. Other types of formal groups within organizations include committees and quality circles.

1. *Command group:* A formal group created by the organization, consisting of a manager and his or her subordinates, is known as a **command group.** Such a group often represents a specific department or work unit, has permanence, and is usually shown on the formal organization chart.

EXAMPLES:

> *Quality control department*
>
> *Accounting department*
>
> *A second-shift nursing department at a local hospital, under the direction of a nursing supervisor*

Managers often belong to more than one command group. In fact, the formal structure of an organization often consists of a series of overlapping command groups.

2. *Team:* One of the most successful methods utilized by some organizations to become more competitive is the use of teams. A **team** is a group of two or more people who interact and coordinate their work with each other in order to accomplish a common objective. Formal teams are created by the organization as part of its hierarchical structure. Some managers still are fearful of the very thought of their employees working formally together. Teams represent a form of power that is harder to manipulate than individual workers standing alone. Teams may be classified by *level* (vertical and horizontal) or by *purpose* (work team, special-purpose team, and self-managing team).

   a. *Vertical team:* A group of employees at different hierarchical levels and their manager who function within the organization's formal chain of command is known as a **vertical team.**

   b. *Horizontal team:* A group of employees brought together from the same hierarchical level but representing different areas of expertise is called a **horizontal team.**

   c. *Work team:* A **work team** is a form of task force or group formed primarily to help organizations deal with problems involving rapid growth or the need for increased organizational flexibility.

   d. *Special-purpose team or problem-solving team:* Special-purpose teams, which usually consist of organizational members from all hierarchical levels, are established primarily to help resolve problems of strategic importance or those requiring a great deal of innovation and creativity. A **quality circle** is a special form of a problem-solving team.

       • Special-purpose teams are often referred to as work teams, and the terms tend to be used synonymously in various organizations and the professional literature.

       • Special-purpose teams often exist away from the formal organizational structure because of the autonomy needed to succeed.

       • Special-purpose teams can have their own reporting and control entities but are ultimately responsible to the parent organization.

       • Special-purpose teams may be used to create new products or to deal with significant issues involving both labor and management.

   e. *Cross-functional team:* The **cross-functional team**—a version of the special-purpose team—usually consists of members of different departments from the same hierarchical levels working together to ensure that widespread views are shared and more diversity is included in the decision making and acceptance and implementation processes.

       • Cross-functional teams need autonomy to succeed in their objectives.

       • Cross-functional teams may be used to create or to critique new products or to deal with important issues facing labor and management.

   f. *Self-managing team:* **Self-managing teams** consist of groups of employees who work together on a day-to-day basis to produce an entire product (or a major identifiable component) and carry out various managerial tasks related to their jobs.

- Self-managing teams have full responsibility for the products, components, or services on which they are working.

- Self-managing teams are empowered to direct their own operations and manage themselves.

EXAMPLE: *One of the firms using self-managing teams most successfully today is Johnsonville Foods, Inc., of Wisconsin, a meat supplier for companies like McDonald's. Johnsonville's self-managing teams even have the power to hire, evaluate, promote, or terminate their members. The use of self-managing teams in this firm enables top-level managers to devote more attention to planning and strategic direction, knowing that the workers, with very limited direction, are giving full commitment and providing high-quality outputs for their organization.*

There is no optimal size for a team. Some teams consist of 80 members, while others have only 3 or 4 members. Members of a team have regular interaction with each other. Persons who meet casually or on an irregular basis do not serve as members of a team. Team members share a common objective in addition to each team member's personal objectives. The common objective keeps them working together. The terms *team* and *group* are sometimes used synonymously.

3. *Task force and committee:* A **task force** is a temporary formal group created by management to solve a particular problem within a limited time period. A **committee** is a group of people who are brought together from the organization to deal most often with problems that arise on a regular basis.

3. *Informal Groups:* Informal groups also thrive within any formal organizational setting. Groups that are created by the employees themselves rather than by the organization are referred to as **informal groups.** Whenever people associate on a fairly regular basis, an informal group is formed. Informal groups often cut across formal organization lines and serve primarily to satisfy the mutual needs of the members. Membership in an informal group transcends hierarchical levels. The members rather than the hierarchy usually pick from informal group chairpersons within the groups.

a. *Components of the informal group:* The informal group consists of at least one leader who works with the members to accomplish certain goals and objectives established by the group.

1. *The leader:* The informal group leader is elected or appointed by the informal group's members to guide goal accomplishment.

2. *Members:* The members of the informal group are persons who join a group or are invited by other group members to participate in carrying out the specified goals and objectives as determined by the membership and leader(s).

3. *Goals and objectives:* Particular missions and specific tasks (as determined by the members of the group) that need to be accomplished to fulfill the purposes of the group, become the goals and objectives of the group.

4. *Work arrangement:* Work tasks and assignments are allocated to the membership in an informal manner by the group's leader(s) to be carried out by the members to achieve mutual goals and objectives.

b. *Types of informal groups:* Interest groups and friendship groups are the two primary types of informal groups.

   1. *Interest groups:* An informal association of people formed because of common concerns or needs is recognized as an **interest group.** This type of group occurs in work settings quite frequently. Once the concerns have been resolved, the interest groups either disband or find other areas of mutual preference to resolve. Companies like Southwest Airlines and Home Depot encourage employee community service. Such service groups typically evolve from interest groups.

       EXAMPLE: *Interest groups would include after-work social groups, company-sponsored community athletic teams, bowling leagues, service groups, gourmet dining clubs, and travel groups. Community service groups would include Big Brothers and Big Sisters, Optimist clubs, United Way, and others.*

   2. *Circles or friendship groups:* An informal group that is created because of the personal factors that members have in common with each other (job, religion, race, gender, or hobbies) is seen as a *circle* (like "circle of friends") or *friendship group.* Some groups come together because the members enjoy interacting with each other, possibly because of commonalities in age, ethnic background, political sentiment, or family structure. Members of friendship groups can simultaneously be members of interest groups. These groups are commonly found as part of the informal social order in the workplace.

       EXAMPLES:

       Crafts club

       Church fellowship group

       Local senior citizens group

       The membership of informal groups changes over time because of shifts in interests, affiliations, or friendship; however, the groups themselves usually remain viable.

c. *Reasons for formation of informal groups:* Many reasons exist for developing informal groups. Some of the primary reasons or motivations are described briefly here.

   1. *Affiliation:* Humans are social creatures who have very strong needs to belong, to join, and to share common experiences with others. Work situations are designed to provide only those social interactions necessary to complete the assigned work. Typically, the work-required interactions fail to satisfy *all* human needs for interaction and belonging. Thus, conditions for creating informal groups are almost always present.

   2. *Mutual aid:* In a typical work situation, people are often reluctant to ask their immediate supervisor how a job or task should be performed. Instead, they might contact another person in the organization for help or information. The person who gives assistance often feels important because someone is asking for help. This pattern of mutual aid or assistance is a common occurrence in organizations. Such actions on a regular basis may bring about the formation of a larger informal group.

3. *Protection:* The idea here is "strength in unity." Often, individuals are motivated to defend themselves against the organization, or they wish to have support for behavior that may violate organization policy.

4. *Communication:* For the sake of economy, formal communications provided by the organization are deliberately designed to minimize interaction and information flows. Humans generally desire to know more than this task-oriented communication system will provide. A common way to satisfy this informational need is to form groups of persons in strategic positions in the organization who have critical information. This type of informal group is commonly known as *the grapevine*.

5. *Proximity:* Since most people are physically confined to a narrow work location, it is natural that friendships and informal relationships develop most readily among persons in the same or contiguous work areas.

6. *Attraction:* A basic motivation is the desire to be liked and accepted. The normal expectation is that people who are similar to us are most likely to like and accept us; this creates a directing force for alliance with an informal group that seems to hold opinions similar to our own (like attracts like).

7. *Sharing of norms and values:* Perhaps most important, informal groups maintain and reinforce the norms and values that their members share in common. If the members want to limit production toward the end of the day, for example, they can do so. Those who go against the informal group's norms are dealt with very effectively and learn how to get along within the organization or else they are forced out.

4. **Goals of Groups:** Groups exist for a variety of purposes. Most organizations have regular work groups that are defined by the organizational structure. Each part or division of the organization's structure may be an office. It may represent a unit headed by a manager, or may be a collection of such units.

a. *Goals define the group:* The goals of the group determine characteristics for the group by defining it as temporary or permanent, purpose-oriented or support-oriented, and formal or informal. The kinds of information needed and the nature of the specific goal contributes to the character and function of the group.

b. *Goals are shared:* Groups have goals that are shared by the members.

c. *Goals vary:* Different goals require different kinds of group activity.

   EXAMPLE: *If a group exists to examine production problems in a manufacturing plant, then several things will be necessary for the group to function properly. Such a group must first have a clearly stated and defined purpose. It must have a method of governing the group behavior. The form of the group's contribution must be clearly understood—whether it is a report, a recommendation, or even putting a corrective action in place.*

d. *Some groups have special goals:* A quality control group, merger task force, even a family group will have specific needs of its members that it must fulfill. Each member has a set of roles that must be performed.

Check Point—Section A

Directions: For each question, circle the correct answer.

A–1. Which one of the following is a type of group focused on a common tangible benefit, usually money?

A) Work
B) Circle
C) Leadership
D) Task force

A–2. Informal groups

A) do not have leaders
B) share a common tangible benefit
C) do not occur in the workplace
D) share common goals

A–3. A group of employees at different levels of the hierarchy including the person who manages them is called a

A) horizontal team
B) self-managed team
C) problem-solving team
D) vertical team

B. Dynamics of Group Membership and Participation

Most believe that a group of people can accomplish more than the same number of people working separately. Organizations exist primarily to channel the efforts of people toward the organization's goals (like profits). When a group forms to achieve a common goal, the characteristics of the group's goal and the appropriateness of the group's structure greatly determine the success that the group will have.

1. *Group Characteristics:* While characteristics of formal groups are determined by the official organization, informal groups are created freely to meet the needs, desires, and norms of their members. Among the major characteristics of groups are size, norms, roles, and status.

    a. *Size:* Group size obviously affects ease of communication, potential for influence, and member satisfaction. The appropriate number of people to be assigned to a formal group is a function of many factors, such as volume of work, commonality of tasks to be performed, technology in use, homogeneity among the members (especially in terms of education, prior experience, attitudes, and aptitudes), supervision desired, competition from other groups, and importance of tasks to be carried out.

        No magic number of members will make a group function effectively. Ideal formal groups range in size from 5 to 15, and the maximum recommended group size is often stated at 12. Groups smaller in size than 5 are too reliant upon the continuing contributions of each member. Groups larger than 12 to 15 start to lose the intimacy of shared interactions among members, become harder to manage, and are confronted with less active individual member participation. Groups with more than 10 members tend to form subgroups within the overall structure. Here are some general rules about the size of groups.

        1. *Group agreement and opinions:* Smaller groups show more agreement, ask more questions, and share more opinions. They report a higher degree of satisfaction and tend to be more informal and more participative with lower absenteeism and turnover. Larger groups tend to have more disagreement and

differences of opinion, more turnover and absenteeism, are more formal and less friendly, have more centralized decision making, and tend toward a lower degree of satisfaction with the tasks under consideration.

2. *Formation of subgroups:* Larger groups tend to form subgroups, each with its own members and subgoals, to allow for more individual participation and satisfaction. When groups exceed 20 members, the leaders should form subgroups to permit more individual member participation and satisfaction.

3. *Size of informal groups:* The size of informal groups is less critical because the members form the group for themselves. The "freedom of choice" factor in becoming a member of an informal group leads to more initial satisfaction and commitment. As long as the informal members are satisfying their needs, group size can be more flexible.

4. *Group efficiency:* In general, smaller groups are more efficient, meet members' needs better, and accomplish their specific tasks more effectively with a higher degree of individual satisfaction.

b. *Norms:* **Norms** are standards of behavior that apply in specific situations. They define the boundaries of acceptable behaviors. Norms of formal groups are usually embodied in official policies, procedures, and work rules *authoritatively established.* The norms of informal groups are established informally as a result of member agreements and are usually unwritten. Norms may be positive or negative. Once norms are well established and accepted by the group, the group as a whole expects each member to comply with the norms.

EXAMPLES OF POSITIVE NORMS:

> *Producing washing machines with zero defects*
>
> *Maintaining very high attendance and punctuality levels*

EXAMPLES OF NEGATIVE NORMS:

> *Working just hard enough to get by*
>
> *Encouraging pilferage*
>
> *Occasionally slowing down the production line*

1. *Teaching norms to newcomers:* Members of an ongoing group use direct and indirect methods to indoctrinate potential new members concerning the norms of the group. The pressure may be subtle, with an indirect statement such as:

> *"Our group believes everybody should take the full coffee break and not be time-clocked into going back to work."*

Or the lesson may be given very directly:

> *"Sit down! Our group doesn't rush back from coffee break!"*

2. *Complying with norms:* For the individual, compliance with the norms of the group becomes the price of belonging. Higher status group members find compliance easy, since they have been able to influence strongly the group adoption of norms they personally hold.

3. *Enforcing norms:* The desire of individuals to continue to belong gives power to the group to enforce its norms. The group has numerous ways it can pressure a member who violates its norms. The group may criticize the member; directly

hinder individual work performance; or use threats, ridicule, or the ultimate enforcing weapon of "eliminating" the deviating person(s) from the group.

c. *Roles:* For any group or team to be successful, it must be structured so that each member exhibits certain required sets of specific behaviors. The **role** is the task each member is expected to perform. Individuals do *not* define roles; the group, the community, or the society establishes role expectations.

EXAMPLES:

"Teachers should be role models (examples) for their students."

"Children should not talk back to their parents."

1. *Group problems with roles:* Roles are so important that failure to specify and clarify them usually leads to two major group problems, role ambiguity and role conflict.

    a. *Role ambiguity:* Role ambiguity results when job roles are vaguely defined and the persons who are supposed to perform specific functions are uncertain about what they are expected to do and the norms they are to follow. Both formal and informal groups must take steps to ensure that roles are clearly defined and understood. Members' roles are officially specified by the organization in formal groups. In contrast, in informal groups the determination of roles is usually decided upon by mutual agreement.

    b. *Role conflict:* When people interpret their determined roles differently, role conflict results. In such cases conflicts often arise due to differences in perceptions about job descriptions, leading to confusion about the job or task to be performed.

    c. *Problem consequences:* Role ambiguity and role conflict can be serious problems that affect group efficiency and effectiveness or result in dissatisfied members. While formal groups may use their legitimate authority to ensure that persons at least fill their assigned roles, those experiencing role ambiguity or role conflict in informal groups can easily become less active or leave the group.

2. *Critical roles within groups:* Successful formal and informal groups often exhibit two critical roles: task specialist and socioemotional support role.

    a. *Task specialist:* The task specialist role involves one or more persons within a group focusing personal energies and free time to help the team accomplish its objectives.

    b. *Socioemotional support role:* The socioemotional support role involves focusing attention on individual group members' emotional needs and helping to strengthen the team's social structure.

    In some groups one person plays both roles, although the common practice calls for different people fulfilling each role. When teams do not have members working to fill both roles, difficulties in maintaining harmony and achieving organizational goals may develop.

d. *Status:* **Status** refers to the relative importance of individuals within a group. It is the *position* in which others in the group place each member. Status is an inevitable component of human relationships in family, friendships, work, and play. General social attitudes, personal factors, and group specific factors are all sources of group attitudes that determine an individual's status. A person's status may be high, low, or equal in the eyes of the group. Confusion can arise when a person has different status levels based on different factors.

EXAMPLE: *Diehl's advanced degree gives high status in the group, but Diehl is not strongly committed to the group's goal. Diehl's personality is pleasant, but a tendency to have a different moral standard regarding social life than most group members places Diehl in an uncomfortable position. It is difficult for the group to "place" Diehl; thus, free communication and interaction will likely be inhibited.*

Status is a factor to consider in evaluating both formal and informal groups. In formal organizations, groups are usually ranked in a hierarchy depending on how important they are viewed. Informal groups are also rated on the importance of their mission and objectives to the members and society. Also, with both types of groups there are differences in the importance of members according to positions or roles.

1. *Status in formal groups:* One's assigned organizational position largely determines that person's status in the formal group. Status is most easily recognized by the existence of *status symbols* (privileges awarded by the organization). Job titles are the formal marks of status from the point of view of the organization. Members of the organization, however, look as much or more to the surrounding symbols.

   EXAMPLE: *People take for granted that a department head has the plushest office or the best parking space. A separate executive dining room or health club privileges are other status symbols.*

2. *Status in informal groups:* The group's consensus of one individual's worth within the group indicates individual status in the informal group. Usually, the highest status is awarded to the member who personifies the group's values, attitudes, and goals. Depending upon the group's goals, other factors give status: seniority, expertise, personality, age. The most significant symbols of status in informal groups are intangible. The person to whom other members defer or toward whom most conversation is directed is generally the one who holds highest status.

2. *Group Dynamics:* Goals, functions, and membership differ from group to group. Other factors play a role in the differences among groups. The term **group dynamics** refers to the interactions within a group that characterize the group. Factors of size, membership, personality, and conflict influence this interaction. For the dynamics of the group to lead to effective action, the group must minimize conflict without stifling productivity. Factors that help minimize conflict are proximity, homogeneity, distinctness, and cohesion.

   a. *Stages of development:* The stage of group development greatly affects the productivity, degree of participation, and amount of member satisfaction. Those stages generally agreed upon include the following:

      1. *Forming:* This stage involves the initial entry of members into the group. The period is one of becoming oriented, breaking the ice, testing for friendship, and learning about the specific objectives that the group is expected to achieve. Productivity and member satisfaction are usually not very high at the onset.

      2. *Storming:* During this stage of development, members become more assertive in clarifying their roles and learning what is expected of them. There may be stormy periods as tension often arises over the group's mission or

interpersonal conflicts. Successful leadership, direction, and active participation will help the group through this difficult stage.

3. *Norming:* During this stage, conflict is resolved and group harmony emerges. Members come to accept each other and their various roles. Members develop a sense of group cohesiveness, and productivity and effectiveness begin to increase. This stage is usually short in duration.

4. *Performing:* During this stage, the primary focus of the group members is on problem solving and goal accomplishment. Frequent harmonious interaction aims at fulfilling the group's objectives. Productivity, efficiency, effectiveness, and member satisfaction is at its highest level. Many successful groups remain in the performing stage.

5. *Adjourning:* Sometimes the group is disbanded. This is especially true with temporary groups. Once the assigned tasks have been completed and no further work remains, the members have a feeling of satisfaction from their achievements. Successful leaders will try to recapture this spirit by rewarding the members and trying to assign them to other goals where their new relationships and effectiveness can be retained.

6. *Setbacks:* Often a group will regress from a higher stage of development to a lower one for many reasons (changes in membership, goals to be achieved, timetables). Setbacks are common, and the members must work out their difficulties, often with guidance. Focusing on accomplishing group goals can be a successful rejuvenation strategy.

b. *Proximity:* **Proximity** refers to the physical closeness of people to each other in any particular setting.

1. *Familylike strengths:* The strength of a work group with familylike qualities results in part from the tendency of members to work in the same offices (as family members would share a home) and come onto contact frequently through each day. The bonds formed in close contact help the members cope with conflict. Work groups with this kind of closeness will respond well to stress.

2. *Work and community groups:* In work and community groups, proximity refers more to how often and how long people share the same work or social space. In this case, proximity refers to working in the same office and seeing each other throughout the day.

3. *Telecommunication and proximity:* Telecommunication capabilities have increased the range of proximity to include people with whom you have regular contact. The degree of comfort one has with being around others helps reduce conflict.

EXAMPLE: *Miller works day in and day out with Cho who needs a wheelchair to get around. Miller has become comfortable with the unique challenges that Cho faces throughout the day. Working in proximity with Cho gives Miller the opportunity to become familiar with Cho's expectations, concerns, distractions, and affections—the special challenges everyone faces.*

In fact, by becoming aware and sensitive to members' needs, a group can minimize conflict.

EXAMPLE: *The importance of proximity has other applications as well. At Titeflex, the Genesis teams have the desks placed in a circle, so members can simply pass information back and forth. The configuration allows them to see each other and to see when problems are developing.*

c. *Homogeneity:* **Homogeneity** refers to the sameness of individuals. In our diverse culture we can expect to find people of various backgrounds and interests working together.

　　1. *Common purpose:* When a common purpose is shared, individuals tend to adopt the attitude of the workplace. In a homogeneous group, the members recognize a common purpose.

　　2. *Heterogeneity:* Heterogeneity, or the extent of individual differences, is becoming the norm.

　　3. *Diversity:* Diversity can be a serious challenge to group function, or it can be used to the group's advantage. People of different backgrounds, upbringings, and cultural identities can have different ideas and thus contribute to the diversity of thought needed to solve complex problems.

d. *Distinctiveness:* Unity can be fostered in a group by giving it something unique. Examples of **distinctiveness** are: its own special location; its own support staff; a special uniform; or some other characteristic that gives it a visible and distinctive identity.

　　1. Having the special location is not always possible, and it is not a necessity.

　　2. Other ways of achieving distinctiveness can occur through:

　　　　a. project identification

　　　　b. status in a hierarchy

　　　　c. functional relationship (like marketing, shipping, etc.)

　　3. Some of these identities can produce subcultures that divert attention from the corporate goals and produce tension.

　　4. To prevent the negative effects of this kind of grouping, some companies will issue uniforms that identify the individual with the company.

e. *Cohesiveness:* Group cohesion refers to the degree to which members are willing to join with each other and work with the group. Cohesion is a concept that applies to *voluntary action* in informal groups and is crucial for effective formal groups. **Cohesiveness** refers to the desire of the members of the group to remain part of a group. A member who is attracted to the group will want to remain a part of the group. The group offers either tangible rewards or it supports the individual's self-concept. Cohesion of the group, however, depends on the group having this kind of appeal to all its members. Cohesion is an important characteristic of job involvement and organizational commitment. When these two attitudes about the company are strong, the cohesion of the group will be strong as well.

　　1. *Group factors affecting cohesiveness:* Cohesion or degree of commitment is the result of many different forces within the group.

　　　　a. *Size of group:* In general, cohesiveness is higher in smaller groups because opportunities for frequent interactions exist. Deeper friendships and clearer understanding of group purposes and norms result from increased communication.

b. *Member dependence:* Members will remain with the group to the degree to which they depend upon the group for satisfaction of personal needs.

c. *Goal achievement:* Since group goals also become the individual goals of members, success in achieving goals is a powerful motivation for continued membership.

d. *Group status:* Members are far more likely to remain in a group that is seen by outsiders as powerful or important. Conflict is much easier to handle in highly cohesive groups because of this feature.

e. *Outside pressure:* To the degree that members perceive themselves to be pressured by management, they will feel the necessity to "hang together" to express their resistance.

2. *Relationships among group factors:* Specific relationships have been found among various group factors.

a. *Cohesiveness and satisfaction:* Cohesiveness and member satisfaction enhance each other in the group process. As members find satisfaction in the group's activities, cohesion increases. Highly cohesive groups achieve their goals more effectively and thereby provide more satisfaction to group members.

b. *Cohesiveness and morale:* Cohesiveness describes the *quality of commitment* among the membership of a group. *Morale* refers to the way the group cohesiveness is expressed in action in the organization. Generally, the more cohesive the group, the higher the morale.

The exception to this rule occurs in those groups formed for the specific purpose of resisting organizational pressure. Such groups are frequently highly cohesive; members are committed to each other and to the group's goal of resistance. At the same time, they deliberately present an antagonistic "face" to the rest of the organization.

c. *Cohesiveness and status:* Differences in group cohesiveness are often the result of differences in status. Generally, the higher a group ranks in status, the greater the cohesiveness among its members. Furthermore, groups with high status and rigid norms are often more cohesive.

EXAMPLE: *Alumni of Notre Dame, students at West Point, and members of the Metropolitan Opera have more status and cohesiveness than graduates from the local branch of a state university or participants in a bowling league.*

d. *Satisfaction and productivity:* There is no direct relationship between satisfaction and productivity. In groups where group goals are compatible with the goals of the organization, high satisfaction or cohesiveness leads to high productivity. As high productivity accomplishes the group's goal, satisfaction of members increases, leading to another cycle of productivity. In those groups where the group goals are *not* compatible with the organizational goals, high satisfaction with the group may result in either high or low productivity. The exact outcome in this case depends upon factors completely outside the situation.

EXAMPLE: *Poor economic conditions or few job opportunities in an area are conditions that may bring about high productivity from very dissatisfied groups.*

e. *Cohesiveness and productivity:* The greater the cohesiveness of the groups' members, the greater the chances for high productivity, efficiency, and accomplishment of the organization's objectives. Members of groups with a low degree of cohesion cannot be expected to work together very effectively or to achieve the organizational objectives.

Both members and leaders of groups can work toward achieving these factors in their group.

EXAMPLE: *When corporate leadership sponsors a softball team, leadership is in effect working toward increased proximity, homogeneity, distinctiveness, and cohesiveness. Supporting the team or being a member of it increases time spent with other members of the group. Having the common purpose of winning a game, cheering each other on, and sharing social interactions increases homogeneity of the group members. Team membership provides a distinctiveness by adding the identity of the team to the group identity. Finally, the team can add to the appeal that membership in the group carries.*

While this example might seem trivial, it is not. Many recognize the power of extending the identity with the corporation beyond the workplace and thus actively encouraging a community spirit among the corporate employees. Community spirit reduces conflict and increases loyalty to the corporation.

3. *Participation—Being a Good Group Member:* Membership in a work group will require several types of interaction.

a. *Frequent contact:* The most frequent will be the interaction throughout the workday with other members of the group. Sometimes this interaction will be on an individual basis; other times it will be with several people.

1. *Frequent informal contact:* Some of the interaction will be informal.

2. *Frequent work-oriented contact:* Sometimes it will focus on work tasks.

b. *Formal meetings:* On occasion, you will find yourself in a formal meeting of the entire group.

1. At that time certain rules of conduct will be required. Some of these circumstances require participation from the group members as well as the leader.

2. A good leader will keep the members informed as to the nature of the meeting so the membership will know when they are being asked for their responses, ideas, concerns, and suggestions.

c. *Meeting dynamics:* During an open and collaborative meeting, a good member will be involved in the following ways:

1. *Accepting others:* Members must work with the other members of the group. An attitude of acceptance and tolerance is crucial for the smooth flow of work and for securing the cohesiveness of the group.

a. *Acceptance and respect:* While this should be an ongoing aspect of membership, acceptance and positive regard should be maintained in meetings as well.

b. *Protocol:* Using proper business protocol will assist people in working with others that they do not know or who may not be their favorite coworker.

2. *Supporting others:* Good membership requires that members recognize the motivation, interests, and expectations of others in the group or team. Though members are not required to agree with others, mutual understanding will strengthen the group. To do so means being aware of the concerns of the other members.

   a. *Daily contacts increase mutual understanding:* One learns of the concerns of others through interactions throughout the day and in other settings.

   b. *Mutual support:* Supporting others also means that, if appropriate, supporting the ideas of others with additional evidence or reasoning.

3. *Asking questions:* The best route to creating understanding is through asking questions.

   EXAMPLE: *If a suggestion is made that shortens one process, you may be concerned about how it affects other related processes.*

   a. Using good protocol will assist in understanding the difference between questions that put the listener on the defensive and opening up the channels of communication to jointly searching for a solution.

   EXAMPLE: *For instance, rather than asserting that you do not know what will happen, you should ask if these other processes have been considered and what conclusion was reached.*

   b. Asking questions should inform everyone about changes and procedures, and it will also inform everyone about the thinking that produced the changes.

4. *Responding to requests:* Sometimes, people just do not seem to understand what has been said.

   EXAMPLE: *If it is something that you said, their lack of understanding can be quite painful to you. If someone asks for a clarification, your response should be honest, straightforward, and patient. You should not be afraid to say, "I never thought about that." Never say "You idiot, this is the fifth time I have had to explain myself."*

   Requests help others understand an individual's ideas, but they also help improve the idea.

5. *Making suggestions and other contributions:* The role of a member in most situations usually means that personal experience and skill is respected enough that the member's thoughts would be welcome.

   a. *Suggestions are not a requirement:* However, this does not mean that members must make a suggestion. Contribution to the group by recommending compromises can be helpful.

   b. *Build on others' ideas:* Members can help by building on the ideas of others. Offer specific ways to implement the idea; identify a time frame; or identify obstacles that will arise if a suggestion is followed.

As one can see, simply being critical of the contributions of others is not sufficient to make a good member. As a good member, one should be aware of the problems that undue conflict can bring. If group cohesion begins to fade, so too will its efficiency.

4. ***Leadership—Facilitating Membership:*** Leaders and managers should be aware of the importance of cohesion in appointing members to formal groups. The amount of cohesion that will exist in informal groups is a result of the decisions and actions of the leaders and individual members. If the needs of the groups' members and the goals of the organization can be more closely related, a higher degree of cohesion will exist among group members.

   a. *Strategies for increasing group cohesion:* Many specific strategies may be used to increase the cohesion of members in groups. Four of the most commonly recommended strategies include:

      1. *Introducing competition:* Conflict with outside groups or individuals tends to improve team competitiveness and cohesion.

      2. *Increasing interpersonal attraction:* Forming groups consisting of members who share key values and interests and have mutual respect improves team cohesiveness.

      3. *Increasing interactions:* Allowing the members more time to work and share together increases the cohesion and feelings of the members for each other.

      4. *Creating common goals and common fates:* In both formal and informal groups, success in achieving common goals and mutual interdependence are keys to increasing cohesiveness. "Birds of a feather flock, stay, and share together" is an adage that reflects this notion.

   b. *Responsibilities of leaders:* Responsibilities of leaders differ in formal and informal groups. An informal group voluntarily sets its own goals and norms and then selects a leader who is the group member most likely to lead them in achieving these goals. In a formal group, leadership is expected to be exercised by the group supervisor or manager appointed by the organization to serve in this capacity.

      1. *Responsibilities of informal group leaders:* Informal group leaders assume responsibilities for upholding group norms and representing the group's point of view.

         a. *Complying with group norms:* The leader is expected to act, teach, and influence others to comply with the group's norms. This has tremendous importance for the day-to-day maintenance of group identity and cohesion.

         b. *Representing the group:* As the spokesperson for the group, the leader represents the group's point of view to managers in the work situation, to the public through interviews or appearances before governmental bodies in civic affairs, and to any outside person or group who must be involved in achieving the group's goal. Since the leader is generally chosen because he or she is perceived to be the person most committed to the group's goals, actions taken by the leader are likely to be acceptable to the group even when the outsider's response is not favorable to the group's desired action.

2. *Responsibilities of formal group leaders:* Leader-managers must be ready to assume such responsibilities as leading the group toward achievement of organizational goals and representing the work group to the organization and to other work groups within the organization.

   a. *Leading to achieve organizational goals:* The leader-manager is appointed by the organization to exercise the formal, delegated authority of the organization to achieve the organization's goals. The leader-manager's salary is justified on the grounds of efficiency, management's belief that the work of the group will not be performed efficiently without having a representative of the organization in charge. The leader-manager is first expected to represent the organization's point of view, needs, and requirements to the work group.

   b. *Representing the work group to the organization:* The leader-manager is expected to be knowledgeable about the special problems of the work group in performing organizationally directed tasks. The work group and superiors expect him or her to provide information and suggestions about changes needed so that work assignments can be completed more efficiently and problem free.

   c. *Representing the work group to other work groups:* Rarely does one work group perform all the work functions of the organization. Generally, the total task is divided among many groups, each performing different functions and each dependent upon other groups' outputs to perform subsequent work effectively. Interdependency between groups can give rise to many real or potential conflicts. The leader-manager's responsibility is to discuss and negotiate the best possible arrangement for his or her group with leader-managers of other interdependent work groups.

Check Point—Section B

Directions: For each question, circle the correct answer.

B–1.   Which one of the following lists the four major characteristics of groups?

   A) Norms, roles, status, and proximity
   B) Status, proximity, size, and roles
   C) Size, norms, roles, and status
   D) Roles, norms, proximity, and size

B–2.   Having a special location, special uniform, or special identity specifically contributes to a group's

   A) goal achievement
   B) distinctiveness

   C) proximity
   D) diversity

B–3.   During a group meeting, qualities of good membership result in participation that includes

   A) asking questions
   B) enforcing group norms
   C) agreeing with others
   D) placing productivity over cohesiveness

C. Team Building

The value of people working together is not merely the bonus over and above the value of individual efforts combined. Instead, the concept of teamwork has become an economic necessity, a way of maximizing effort. The human relations movement recognizes that the right number and mixture of skills, while important and necessary, is not sufficient to make an effective team. Concerns of the team members must be considered. Such motivational concerns include opportunities for growth and realization of personal objectives. They may focus on the rewards that come with productivity. Members also are concerned about themselves and their relation to the group. The team needs to contribute to the quality of life of each of its members. Not only should the team work productively and with a common sense of purpose, but a delicate balance between personal achievement and team achievement must be sustained. **Team building** refers to the processes intentionally undertaken by management to strengthen the members of a work unit so that they work together toward a common goal.

1. *The Work Team—A Building Block for Efficiency:* No single individual ever wins a football, basketball, or baseball game alone. Winning requires teamwork. Sports and the military have traditionally used teams. However, industry has had an interest in teamwork since the Hawthorne studies introduced the idea that people work better when they have a shared sense of purpose. About half of all employees work in some form of team. For those employees, 45 percent are involved in permanent work teams and about 30 percent in temporary project teams. As stated earlier, a work team is a special group within the workplace organization. It consists of individuals depending upon each other as they work toward completing a common task.

2. *Types of Team Tasks:* There are four basic types of tasks that a work team can undertake.

    a. *Providing advice and increasing involvement:* Some teams have the goal of enhancing the work environment and the involvement of the employees in the life of the company. These kinds of teams are found in every type of industry and at every degree of participation.

       EXAMPLE: *Quality of work life (QWL) programs, employee involvement teams (EIT), quality circles (QC), total quality management (TQM) teams, and many other unique names have been assigned to this type of team.*

    b. *Providing production and service:* Some units form around a specific business model that produces a product or service. In the most innovative versions, each business unit has autonomy. Consulting firms often use autonomous units to provide highly specialized services.

       EXAMPLE: *Electronic Data Systems, or EDS, one of the largest software applications support companies in the world, uses project teams that fit the autonomous pattern as well. Most work teams fall into this group. This type of team does not need to be self-managed, but more and more are being formed to be self-managing or self-directing. The genesis teams, business development teams, and final assembly teams at Titeflex are examples of this kind of team.*

    c. *Completing one-of-a-kind projects:* In highly innovative work settings, teams form just for a specific project; they create their own leadership and follow the work through until it is complete. Most members are on several teams at the same time.

EXAMPLE: *IDEO, a small West Coast design company, uses teams to produce one-of-a-kind designs. Each new project leads to the formation of a new team to solve design problems.*

d. *Implementing actions:* After a task force creates a proposal, implementation teams can be formed to complete the various components of the proposal.

EXAMPLE: *At Sola Ophthalmic, a maker of contact and eyeglass lenses, the next step after creating a problem identification task force was to complete a job analysis of the entire production process. A team of managers, quality control personnel, and engineers rated each job so that it could be placed in the pay-for-skills plan with a value or rating that reflected its worth. Once their tasks were completed, the team was no longer needed.*

3. ***Special Techniques for Team Building:*** Often corporations will hire consultants to help foster the sense of teamwork. The consultant can help in at least two ways. First, the consultant is a specialist and knows special techniques that will encourage development of the five characteristics just described. Second, and equally important, is the fact that a consultant is outside the corporation and can offer an independent, fresh view of problems and issues. This allows open and frank communication to occur early in the process of building a team. In general, there are four possible types of activity that can occur:

a. *Activities that build cohesion by examining interpersonal processes:* Group interventions may use various techniques to break down areas of conflict and to build the confidence of team members. Some common techniques are assertiveness training, Transactional Analysis, and sensitivity training—or a combination of training methods.

b. *Activities that help set and clarify goals:* Sometimes, teams can help communicate goals and objectives more effectively than can top managers and executives. Activities can be used to help teams focus on the goals.

EXAMPLE: *The Chicago Tribune used an intervention that set goals. Members of production units worked together to set specific performance goals and to make recommendations for performance bonuses. The result was increased production and cost savings.*

c. *Activities that clarify roles within the team:* By examining expectations, behavior, and how responsibility is shared among the members (and leaders), the team can begin to establish its own direction and self-management.

d. *Activities that take a task-oriented approach to solving problems or making decisions:* The techniques discussed in the next chapter outline the more traditional and more common approaches to using teams to make decisions and solve problems. These techniques include the Nominal Group Technique and the Quality Circle, these techniques are still quite active in their original form. Task forces also are oriented to identifying and solving problems.

As teams have become a popular solution to the challenges of employee satisfaction, involvement, and productivity, the work of building teams has become an industry in itself.

4. ***Ways to Build and Maintain Team Effectiveness:*** In building a team, both the leader and the members need to make an active effort to make the team successful. Qualities of good group membership must be at work at all times. The functions of leadership have to be shared without jealousy or insecurity getting in the way. In the team con-

cept, the formal leader actually encourages these leadership processes to be shared. In building a team, five characteristics must be developed and nurtured:

a. *Group participation in problem solving and decision making:* Commitment to a decision or a solution appears to be highest when the group members have accepted the decision or solution as their own. Also, in many cases, the group can formulate a better solution than can an individual working alone. The sharing of responsibility among the group members can also increase creativity. Even at the individual level, a sense of control over a decision improves the physical and mental well being of the worker.

b. *Mutual trust and respect for other team members:* Trust is necessary for good cohesiveness and cooperative communication. Without mutual trust, individuals are likely to lose their desire to collaborate, to begin to focus only on their own needs, and to depend less on other team members.

c. *Communication and mutual understanding:* Trust establishes the groundwork for developing mutual understanding through open communication. Teams cannot collaborate effectively in an atmosphere of suspicion and restrained communication. The first thought in anyone's mind when told only "what you need to know" is suspicion. The second is that of being excluded. These feelings will work against the building of a successful team.

d. *Minimization of destructive conflict:* When conflict spreads beyond a difference of opinion and loses its place in the process of negotiating solutions, it becomes destructive. Conflict can be managed in problem-solving processes if trust and open communications exist, and if team members follow responsible guidelines for participation. Also, group cohesion and a shared, common goal should mean that once a decision to act a certain way has been made, all members accept and support the decision. If members fail to conform to the decision, team effectiveness will be imperiled.

e. *Individual responsibility for actions:* While the team shares the credit and reward for collective actions, individuals must also be recognized for individual initiatives. The more responsible a team member feels for his or her contribution to the team, the more positive will be the results for both team and individual. The individual gains a sense of self-efficacy and self-esteem. As a result, he or she increases the cohesion of the team through increased loyalty and identification with team goals and purpose.

Check Point—Section C

Directions: For each question, circle the correct answer.

C–1. Providing advice and increasing involvement, completing one-of-a-kind projects, providing production and service, and implementing actions are types of tasks undertaken by

    A) task forces
    B) work teams
    C) informal groups
    D) committees

C–2. To make a team become more cohesive and have less internal conflict, which one of the following types of activities would be most helpful? Activities that

    A) take a task-oriented approach to problem solving
    B) clarify roles within the team

C) set goals of the team
D) examine interpersonal processes

C–3. In the context of teamwork, the individual must

A) avoid building self-efficacy
B) sacrifice personal rewards

C) be recognized for individual initiatives
D) accept whatever role is assigned

D. Team Leading

Many strategies and techniques can be used to create and maintain operating teams and groups effectively and efficiently. The opportunity for people from diverse or similar backgrounds to work together closely toward achieving common objectives improves the synergy that should exist within any organization. Using the adage that "two (or more) heads are better than one," work teams and task forces can help an organization realize the full contributions of its members and achieve new levels of creativity and entrepreneurial success.

1. ***Strategies for Improving Effectiveness of Formal Groups and Teams:*** Addressing members' concerns, clarifying the group's purposes, establishing group or team goals, and assigning responsibility and authority improve the effectiveness of groups and teams. As managers become aware of a group's strengths and deficiencies, they can make specific adjustments as needed.

    a. *Members' concerns:* The first step should be to learn all about the actions and areas of concern of the group members. Areas to study include:

    - Who actually does what within the group
    - The group's norms
    - The status order among the group members
    - The present amount of group cohesion
    - How well the members understand their overall objectives and individual assignments
    - The degree of commitment of individual members to meeting organizational objectives
    - The effectiveness of the group's official leaders

    b. *Purposes and expectations of teams:* The team's purposes, parameters, and expected results need to be specified before the team is organized. When teams or committees are established, the purposes and expectations must be defined ahead of time. If the leaders do not know what the group is expected to accomplish, how will the members know what needs to be done?

    c. *Establishment of goals:* Establishment, dissemination, and insistence on adhering to clearly written goals are absolute requirements for teams to be successful. Loss of sight or focus on the reasons why the team exists is the easiest way to fail.

        1. When there is strict attention focused on adhering to the team's mission or goals, the chances for hidden agendas being adopted are greatly reduced.

        2. When the team adheres strictly to the established goals, individual members will be less likely to "showcase" their skills at the expense of others.

3. A clear focus on the group's super ordinate (overriding) goals leads to a greater possibility of goal attainment and the resulting feelings of satisfaction, achievement, and recognition in all the team members.

d. *Group responsibility and authority:* The group's responsibility and authority need to be clearly identified. Teams normally will not play in arenas in which they do not belong. Similarly, teams and groups will focus on the areas in which they have responsibility and are expected to perform. Conflicts resulting from over-stepping boundaries are much less likely to arise if the amount of authority that team members have in trying to accomplish goals is clearly understood. Most workers like the responsibility and social interaction involved in participating in work teams that can have an active voice in the organization's operations, products, and services.

1. Some authority and responsibility conflicts may be attributable to

    a. Simple misunderstandings without any questionable motives

    b. Open attempts by some members to achieve greater results

    c. Members' seeking to acquire more individual prominence and recognition

2. When authority–responsibility conflicts arise, they can be curtailed by reference to the original mandates either on the part of other team members or by those in higher authority levels.

e. *Boundaries of group activity:* Parameters, timetables, and restrictions should be stated clearly and in writing at the beginning of the group process.

1. Often teams lose their direction because of a lack of knowledge about the parameters within which they are expected to perform, the restrictions they face, and the timetables they are expected to meet.

2. When the timetables and parameters are made clear at the onset, followed up with reminders, teams tend to adhere to them. By the same token, when teams are not advised of these parameters until they are "halfway through the game," confusion and chaos can be the inevitable results.

f. *Leadership by team leaders:* Team leaders must lead, not mandate. Teams often fail because of dictatorial leadership. However, *Roberts' Rules of Order* and other sources of parliamentary procedure clearly define the rules for conducting meetings in virtually every type of situation. Moreover, the organization can determine the roles, rules, responsibilities, and authorities of its group leaders ahead of time.

1. Leaders are expected to guide and facilitate.

2. Leaders are expected to influence group members by providing guidance and a sense of direction.

3. Leaders are not expected to rule, dictate, and mandate.

4. Leaders are successful when they serve as facilitators and get the team players actively involved.

5. Successful leaders learn that the key to being effective results in sharing power and information with the members. A person gains influence by sharing what he or she has with others, not by keeping information that could be shared a secret.

g. *Training for cooperative working:* Team members should learn how to work together. Too often groups are established without any formal briefings or training by higher authorities.

1. Often the presumption is made that "everyone knows how to serve as a team member."

2. Management may not provide any type of orientation for the team members.

Even experienced team and committee members learn from training and briefing programs. At all stages of the team's operations, the rules and benefits of effective teamwork should be presented and reinforced.

h. *Plans, rules, and agendas:* Work rules, game plans, and agendas should be prepared in advance. The team that goes into battle without a sense of strategy or direction will usually spend countless hours figuring out how to compete and accomplish the mission.

1. The plans, rules, and agendas should be standardized but still specific enough to respond to specific situational factors.

2. Agendas, game plans, and supporting materials should be presented in advance and time allowed for their review ahead of time.

3. While "secrecy" may seem to indicate the need for surprise agendas, team members should be briefed ahead of time. The obsession with secrecy can become a thoroughfare to failure.

i. *Equal treatment of team members:* Rules and game plans should not be deviated from for certain participants. All players should be treated equally.

1. In reality, there is a tendency to give star performers preferential treatment.

2. One exception leads to another, and that exception leads to still another.

3. Rules and plans that are fairly made should be enforced fairly. Any exceptions allowed should apply to all the team members.

j. *Required participation by team members:* All team members should be required to participate. No team member should be allowed to be a free rider.

1. Some members may take a more vocal role than others.

2. Active attempts should be made to get the views of the less vocal members.

3. The highly vocal members should be reinforced for encouraging their more subdued peers to actively participate, not for trying to play a solo act.

k. *Fostering of synergy:* Dissent and diversity should be encouraged and fostered. The whole purpose for using team efforts is to achieve **synergy,** a state that exists only when $1 + 1 = 2 +$ (that is, more than the sum). If the collective results of all the players' activities do not exceed those of all the individual members working alone, attempts should be made to get more active participation and greater contributions by all team members. Here are some adjustments that can be made:

1. The team members may be shifted to different assignments.

2. The goals and parameters of the team may need to be redefined.

3. The group activities could be disbanded.

Enlightened managers and organizations revel in the accomplishments of workers who achieve much greater synergy when interacting and sharing for the common good.

l. *Acceptability of dissent:* Team members should be taught that dissent is desirable. Often, members are afraid to speak out because of fear of offending or being viewed as being contrary.

   1. Members should be shown the pitfalls associated with blind conformity and domination by self-appointed individuals.

   2. The organization should place a premium on new ideas and challenges to the status quo, rather than minor variations of the present approach.

   3. Team training may be needed in the process of creating and resolving conflict.

   4. Team members should be shown the synergy that results from full participation of each and every member, and the loss of synergy that occurs when some prefer silence, even in the face of impending disaster.

2. ***Strategies for Working with Informal Groups:*** Working with members of informal groups is usually a greater challenge because these groups have been established by and for the members. Informal group leaders are selected by the membership and typically are not part of the formal management structure of the organization. Informal groups serve as a helpful source of satisfaction and support for their members. Informal organization can sustain or destroy formal structure. Of great significance is the fact that *informal groups cannot be controlled or eliminated by management.*

EXAMPLE: *After the terror attacks of September 11, 2001, people spontaneously formed groups to help each other look for missing loved ones. These support groups quickly evolved in many cases into formal groups with voices in the government efforts to help.*

Successful administrators have learned how to work effectively with informal groups to benefit the entire organization. Here are some strategies often used in working cooperatively with informal groups:

a. *Acknowledging the existence and importance of informal groups:* This is the first step that any manager or leader must take in order to understand the informal structure. Understanding precedes action.

b. *Creating a positive environment for informal groups:* The second step is to create an environment within the formal organization where the informal groups can flourish. The manager who tries to nurture informal groups finds that this strategy eventually leads to the realization of formal objectives.

c. *Using power and politics to advantage:* Successful managers will try to attract the support of informal groups. They focus efforts on making accommodations to satisfy members of informal groups through their use of official power. This conscious use of official power is often referred to as *organizational politics,* interpersonal interactions that establish, transfer, and exercise power. While some people view the use of power as evil and politics as something to be shunned, both are part of organizational life and are necessary for groups to exist.

d. *Recognizing the existence of informal groups:* The final strategy used in dealing with informal groups is to recognize that they indeed exist and can be beneficial to the formal structure. This recognition leads to acceptance and respect of the roles of informal groups. Managers who show respect for informal groups will be reciprocally repaid and relations with formal groups will be enhanced.

Some administrators work under the basic premise that informal groups can be manipulated or destroyed. Managers who function with this belief will find that they can be "broken," professionally and personally. Ignoring an informal group is a better managerial procedure than trying to control or to eliminate the group. The best approach is to work positively with informal groups for the betterment of all.

Check Point—Section D

Directions: For each question, circle the correct answer.

D–1. Teams are susceptible to failure when the leader of the team

   A) serves only as a facilitator
   B) offers guidance and only a sense of direction
   C) rules only by mandate and dictates
   D) shares power only with team members

D–2. Dissent and diversity should be

   A) encouraged and fostered
   B) redirected toward homogeneity

   C) required for participation
   D) accepted as a last resort

D–3. In a work-oriented organization, informal groups

   A) should be completely discouraged
   B) provide useful political advantage
   C) will distract employees from their core tasks
   D) are an excellent source for synergy

For Your Review

Directions: For each question, circle the correct answer.

Case 1: Groups at Smith and Associates

As part of the role of human resource trainer, Noki has taken on the task of describing all the various types of formal and informal interactions in the office of Smith and Associates, the public relations and advertising firm where Noki works. Not only must the association and affiliations be charted, but also a description of the relationships that are the foundation of the groups needs to be written. The goal is to be able to inform new associates about group interactions that are so critical to Smith and Associates' success. The company is highly successful because its many groups and teams have made it flexible and responsive. As the company grows, however, new associates need to be indoctrinated into the almost latticelike structure.

To accomplish the task Noki has, in the tradition of the company, assembled a team to help identify and describe this fluid process.

1. Noki recognizes that most teams are composed of members who are at the same level in the company. This describes a/an

   A) special-purpose team
   B) horizontal team
   C) vertical team
   D) cross-functional team

2. A few of the groups are permanent, with specific leaders who do not change. These groups perform regular, routine, and repeating functions like accounting and payroll. The groups would be called

   A) special-purpose teams
   B) command groups
   C) task forces
   D) horizontal teams

3. Some groups and teams are formed for special projects, whereas others form as resources for support. These informal groups reflect a basic human need for

   A) affiliation
   B) work arrangement

   C) common goals
   D) unit of command

4. Which one of the following types of groups best describes the group Noki assembled to help define the team structure at Smith and Associates?

   A) Vertical team
   B) Quality circle
   C) Informal group
   D) Task force

5. Another feature of the groups and teams at Smith and Associates is that the team members often form relationships that extend beyond work. These groups are called

   A) interest groups
   B) mutual aid groups
   C) friendship groups
   D) cross-functional teams

Case 2: Procurement Department

Bates has been a member of the procurement department for almost six years. The department has a director, Carver, who likes Bates very much. Carver has gradually converted Bates's position from assistant to the director to assistant director. The department includes about a dozen staff members and a half-dozen "couriers." The couriers have a wide array of tasks, primarily overseeing arriving materials in the plant, checking on whether or not the departments are satisfied with the delivery, and confirming order and delivery schedules. The staff members generally work on locating materials, matching inventory to projected needs, securing long-term vendor contracts of all kinds, and other activities related to procurement of materials and supplies needed for production.

The department has a conventional hierarchy of its members, and Carver is the department head. Carver has always encouraged activity that makes the department function more effectively as a group. Sometimes that may mean following the rules strictly, sometimes that may mean responding creatively. Bates plays an important part as an informal leader, which is why Carver appointed Bates as a true second in command. Bates and Carver are held in the highest regard by the members of the department.

6. Carver changed Bates's job from assistant to the director to assistant director to reflect the work Bates was actually doing. This change recognized the relative importance within a group and is called

   A) dynamics
   B) norm
   C) role
   D) status

7. The couriers perform a number of different tasks. If their duties and tasks are not clearly assigned, they may experience

   A) role ambiguity
   B) role conflict
   C) storming
   D) setbacks

8. Since members of the department have been together so long and worked in close proximity, Bates would be able to expect the group to have

   A) familylike strengths
   B) high levels of heterogeneity
   C) many subgroups
   D) a small group size

9. Carver heads a group that has high respect among other divisions of the company. The use of couriers to check shipments and whether the internal "customers" are satisfied is a source of pride and uniqueness that results in

   A) role conflict
   B) distinctiveness
   C) member dependence
   D) formal contact

10. During the regular contact of work and informal interaction, the division runs smoothly. Participation is reflected because staff and couriers support each other, accept views of others, and ask questions for understanding. These behaviors are signs of

    A) homogeneity
    B) groupthink
    C) good membership
    D) proximity

Case 3: Teams at Glade Printers, Incorporated

The executive leadership at Glade Printers, Incorporated has decided to improve quality and productivity by modeling all aspects of the business after the team approach used so successfully by one of the world's leading automobile manufacturers. The print maker will use teams in all divisions, including design, production, sales, and research.

The company has followed a traditional hierarchical, classical organization. The transition to teams will be easy for some divisions and difficult for others. The plan calls for careful transition rather than giving a mandate that all changes be made at once. The idea is to work from the ground up, basically beginning at the lowest level of the organization. The next step is for the senior executive in each division to make specific plans for the development of the team approach.

11. Which one of the following describes the type of team tasks that Glade is planning to utilize as its regular organization of work?

A) Providing advice and increasing involvement
B) Completing one-of-a-kind projects
C) Implementing actions
D) Providing production and service

12. Glade plans to build the team approach beginning with the lowest level of the company. As these workers already know their job tasks, on which one of the following types of activities should team building focus? Activities that

A) take a task-oriented approach to solving problems
B) clarify roles in the team
C) build cohesion by examining interpersonal processes
D) help set and clarify goals

13. A few of the line workers believe that the move to a team approach is being made because they are not trusted as individuals. This problem may become a serious impediment to

A) team effectiveness
B) homogeneity

C) increasing destructive conflict
D) individual responsibility

14. Some of the teams that will be formed may have members of different status participating. In order to lead such a team effectively, the team must be directed to

A) establish proximity by having team members work together
B) recognize that higher status means more authority
C) give lower ranked members special access
D) treat each team member equally

15. Which one of the following steps will provide Glade with the means of reducing the possibility of hidden agendas taking control of a team?

A) Avoid any conflict over misunderstandings
B) Allow members to showcase their skills
C) Pay strict attention to the team's goals
D) Have only one leader, whether formal or informal

Solutions

Solutions to Check Point—Section A

Answer:	Refer to:
A–1. (A)	[A-1-d]
A–2. (D)	[A-3-a-(3)]
A–3. (D)	[A-2-b-(2)-(a)]

Solutions to Check Point—Section B

Answer:	Refer to:
B–1. (C)	[B-1]
B–2. (B)	[B-2-d]
B–3. (A)	[B-3-c-(3)]

Solutions to Check Point—Section C

Answer:	Refer to:
C–1. (B)	[C-2]
C–2. (D)	[C-3-a]
C–3. (C)	[C-4-e]

Solutions to Check Point—Section D

Answer:	*Refer to:*
D–1. (C)	[D-1-f]
D–2. (A)	[D-1-k]
D–3. (B)	[D-2-c]

Solutions to For Your Review

Answer:	*Refer to:*

Case 1:

1. (B)	[A-2-b-(2)-(b)]
2. (B)	[A-2-b-(1)]
3. (A)	[A-3-c-(1)]
4. (D)	[A-2-b-(3)]
5. (C)	[A-3-b-(2)]

Case 2:

6. (D)	[B-1-d]
7. (A)	[B-1-c-(1)-(a)]
8. (A)	[B-2-b-(1)]
9. (B)	[B-2-d]
10. (C)	[B-3-c]

Case 3:

11. (D)	[C-2-b]
12. (C)	[C-3-a]
13. (A)	[C-4-c]
14. (D)	[D-1-i]
15. (C)	[D-1-c-(1)]

Chapter 8

Solving Problems and Resolving Conflict

OVERVIEW

Few organizations today would depend upon a single individual to solve corporate problems, no matter what the scale of the organization or the problem. For most, teams or groups of all kinds solve problems. Teams may include external experts as well as representatives from all components of the workforce. There are both formal and informal techniques for problem solving that utilize groups. There are also many advantages as well as disadvantages associated with depending upon groups to solve problems.

Groups share resources and can have a wide range of expertise not held by one person, yet, because there will be several people involved, sometimes the differing views can cause deadlock or an inability to move forward in a timely manner.

Some problems arise from procedures and processes that need to be reformed, updated, modified, or discarded. Other problems arise from one of the many forms of conflict: intrapersonal, interpersonal, and organizational. Conflict is a key factor in the interactions within the group. The way the group copes with conflict largely determines its effectiveness. Conflict can have negative effects on the health of the group. Such effects need to be kept to a minimum. Conflict can also serve positive ends by providing alternative points of view.

KEY TERMS

Adventure training, 227

Approach-approach
conflict, 215

Approach-avoidance
conflict, 215

Assertiveness training, 222

Avoidance-avoidance
conflict, 215

Brainstorming, 213

Cognitive dissonance, 216

Conflict, 214

Delphi technique, 210

Double approach-avoidance
conflict, 215

Groupthink, 206

A. Advantages and Disadvantages of Groups and Teams

The synergy that often results from bringing people together to assist in solving problems may be very advantageous. At the same time, group or team involvement may have the disadvantage of taking a great deal of time away from other assigned tasks. Here are some of the primary advantages and disadvantages of using groups or teams.

1. ***Advantages of Using Groups or Teams for Problem Solving:*** Group problem solving is often advantageous over reliance on individuals only. One must be cognizant that "two heads are better than one." Some of the major advantages include:

   a. *Identification of alternative solutions:* A major advantage of using groups for solving problems is that with several people working together, more alternatives will be identified for solving specific problems. As a general rule, the wider and larger the number of alternatives identified, the greater the chances are of developing successful solutions that meet the needs of the many groups and individuals who will be affected directly and indirectly.

   b. *Knowledge sharing by cross-functional teams:* Another advantage that groups bring to the problem-solving process is the increased amount of knowledge sharing that is possible. This is especially true when teams involve people with diverse backgrounds who bring varied perspectives to bear in addressing and solving specific problems.

      EXAMPLE: *When an engineer, an administrative assistant, an accountant, a production machine operator, a salesperson, a maintenance specialist, and a researcher get together, a wealth of ideas will be shared from different points of view.*

      The use of cross-functional teams is becoming more important. A group of market research people dealing with a marketing problem relies on their own education, work experience, analytical style, personal likes and dislikes, and frame of reference in sharing ideas with other group members. If the group is of workable size and cohesive, with good leadership, there is great value to the diversity of opinions that will be shared.

   c. *Implementation effectiveness:* Another advantage of employing groups for problem solving is the implementation of feasible solutions. When people participate in determining the proper causes of a problem and then develop the best method for solving it, the chances for effective implementation of the solution are greatly increased. When people are owners, they take better care of something than when they are just tenants. Involvement of people to solve a problem results in their ownership of the solution; they have more at stake to ensure that the solution works.

   d. *More acceptance of decisions:* Top-down problem solving by managers taking a unilateral approach may meet with more resistance than that experienced when people at lower operational levels are involved in helping with the solution. Greater acceptance results when people participate in decision making and problem solving. Furthermore, involving groups in the decision-making process reduces the risk of inaccurate communication because the people involved have played key roles in the formulation of an acceptable solution.

e. *Increased energy level:* When groups are directly involved in problem solving, the energy level expended increases. Committees and task forces often generate enormous energy and creativity from employees who want to be involved and use their knowledge and power effectively.

f. *Improvement of personal decision-making skills:* An indirect benefit of using groups for solving problems is that the group members involved improve their own decision-making skills and knowledge. They grow personally by being involved as active participants in decision making. The opportunity for personal growth and the chance to achieve are very powerful motivators.

g. *Increased ability to solve problems:* When employees become involved in solving diverse problems through a group decision-making process, the organization is helping to create a workforce that will be able to compete in turbulent times. Expecting employees to help solve a variety of problems, with interaction among different groups of individuals, leads to a flexible, competitive, well-trained, and well-satisfied workforce. Many companies are using cross-functional teams to help solve problems with outstanding results.

   EXAMPLES:

   The Macintosh was created by Apple Computer using a task-force approach.

   Toyota uses quality circles extensively to help in retaining its competitive edge as new and improved high-quality products are introduced.

h. *Creation of interactive environments:* In the past, organizations like 3M and Chaparral Steel have openly encouraged their employees to work together and create mechanisms, such as wide hallways and "open" cafeterias rather than executive dining rooms, where people can have the chance to interact with others from different departments and levels of the hierarchy. The leaders in these firms recognized that while team efforts may take more time, the end results far outweigh the costs involved.

   EXAMPLE: *Volvo is known for its Kalmar, Sweden, plant where workers serve on teams while manufacturing automobiles. Each team is responsible for all phases of the assembly of complete vehicles. The workers divide responsibilities among themselves on their own, without any interference from higher level management. The results, in terms of quality, efficiency, and effectiveness, are easy to see.*

2. ***Disadvantages of Group and Team Activities:*** Advantages of using groups or teams for solving problems must be tempered by disadvantages that often arise. Where there is shared responsibility, there is often no direct accountability. Some of the major disadvantages of using groups for problem solving include:

a. *Resistance to new approaches:* One major disadvantage, which is often overlooked, is that while groups can develop a virtually unlimited number of alternative problem-solving approaches, in reality many times this does not occur. Instead, group members may focus only on traditional solutions or those that are presented most skillfully. Resistance to new ideas and approaches is a common trait of groups as well as entire organizations. Unless management strongly encourages and supports creative thinking, chances are that few new or unique solutions will be offered or adopted. Therefore, solutions adopted may be only variations of present approaches while more innovative and exciting solutions may be shelved.

b. *Lack of group participation:* Despite all attempts by the leaders, sometimes a lack of cohesiveness among group members prevails. When this happens, chances are that the group will fail in its attempts to develop and to implement viable solutions to problems it has been charged with solving.

c. *High cost related to group problem solving:* Excessive costs may be incurred in group decision making: funds required for coordination, difficulties involved in scheduling meetings for people from diverse projects, and slowness that sometimes seems to symbolize group members working together.

d. *Free riders:* Many groups are affected by free riders. A *free rider* is a team member who gains benefit from being a member, but contributes very little to the group's work. A group of five almost always has one free rider, and often only two or three of the members really do the work. Dealing with free riders is one of the challenges that group members and managers too often must confront without success.

   EXAMPLE: *Many colleges are using more team assignments for decision-making practice. Virtually anyone who has served as a member of a group knows the frustrations involved when all members are expected to participate. Yet there is typically one person who cannot come to all the meetings, is hardly ever prepared, and seems reluctant to take responsibility for any part of the work.*

e. *Barriers imposed by managers:* Another overlooked disadvantage of group decision making is the reluctance of managers to surrender their traditional problem-solving duties to their subordinates. Managers fear that they are being bypassed and will eventually lose their jobs, and sometimes they even block subordinates from serving on problem-solving teams.

f. *Domination by team members:* A common disadvantage of group decision making lies with the ability of a few to dominate the problem-solving process.

   1. Sometimes highly extroverted and socially assertive people or those with vested interests dominate group decisions. Less dynamic, introverted people may get frustrated and "tune out."

   2. The group may divide into competing coalitions and stalemates may result because of internal power plays.

   3. Some individuals use the group decision-making process as a way of getting management to notice their leadership tactics, with promotion as a goal.

   Very often groups become unknown tools for advancing hidden agendas of the dominating individual(s). These ploys violate the basic premises of group problem solving.

3. *Potential for Conflict and Ineffectiveness:* All groups suffer the possibility of engaging in unproductive conflict. Some of the conflicts arise from disagreements about actions to take, whereas others stem from interpersonal conflicts unrelated to the problem at hand. One of the most unproductive approaches occurs when no one will challenge or question group decision. This problem is known as "groupthink." Other problems include resistance facilitation and interpersonal conflict.

a. *Groupthink:* A major disadvantage of the group problem-solving process involves **groupthink,** the tendency to conform automatically and uncritically to group judgments even when those judgments have clear dangers. Groupthink may lead to a situation where group members become so committed to the group, and to not disturbing the group, that they become reluctant to express contrary opinions even when they recognize that solutions being proposed may have disastrous impacts. Irving Janis, a communication consultant, introduced the concept of groupthink to explain how seemingly brilliant, knowledgeable people can make what turn out to be serious errors.

1. *Factors causing groupthink:* Groupthink occurs when members of a group desire to achieve consensus to such an extent that they lose the ability to be critical in their assessment of alternatives.

    a. *High group cohesion:* The more cohesive the group, the greater the chances of groupthink occurring.

    b. *Five aspects:* In the process of decision making, groupthink is marked by five aspects.

        (i)   Few solutions are discussed.

        (ii) Negative consequences of a chosen plan are ignored.

        (iii) Alternatives that appear unsatisfactory are not developed at all.

        (iv) Experts are not contacted.

        (v)   No contingencies are made in case the first plan fails.

    c. *Invulnerability, morality, and pressure:* Often groups that are subject to groupthink have an illusion that they are invulnerable, believe they are morally correct, and have high pressure to conform.

2. *Combating groupthink:* The way to combat these tendencies might include assigning one of the group members to be a critical evaluator who asks each person for input (like the NGT, below). Group members are then requested to check the plan with others outside the group. Someone plays the "devil's advocate" to explore problems with expressed ideas. The group meets later to evaluate the decision that is made.

    EXAMPLES:

    > *One of the most disastrous examples of groupthink occurred when President John F. Kennedy was dealing with the Bay of Pigs crisis early in his term. Some members of the group acquiesced, even though they knew the plan would be a disaster. To prevent this phenomenon from occurring again, President Kennedy used a different approach to handle the Cuban missile crisis, including requiring members to be mandated devil's advocates.*

    > *President Nixon's ill-fated Watergate resulted from groupthink.*

    > *The* Challenger *space shuttle's demise on a cold day in Florida when even subcontracting engineers knew the O-rings might freeze up has been attributed to groupthink.*

3. *Resistance facilitation:* **Resistance facilitation** occurs when members of the group support a position resisting change. Resistance may be voiced by only one person, but the tendency to resist change and innovation, as discussed earlier, offers a path of low involvement and low stress.

4. *Interpersonal conflict and ineffectiveness:* Unfortunately, conflict over ideas and interests can either lead to interpersonal conflict or be caused by it. The goals and objectives of one group may conflict with the goals and objectives

of another. In an era when cooperation has become a mainstay of corporate culture, unmanaged interpersonal conflict can be devastating. Types of interpersonal conflict and means of coping with it are discussed below.

b. *Group decision making—weighing the evidence:* The involvement of too many people may spoil the outcome of group work. Skillful leaders and seasoned group members can make collective problem solving an asset or a liability.

1. *Development of creative solutions:* While a clash of ideas may occur among group members, a large number of creative solutions can be identified. By appealing to the need of individual members to share in successful solutions, problems are solved and implemented successfully by many, whereas one or two people working alone might have failed.

2. *Conflicts among group members:* Clashes among members representing different functional areas or points of view may also arise. Without skillful handling by group leaders, problems may not be solved properly. Conflicts may not be resolvable.

3. *Risk involved in group decisions:* Often groups make decisions that require more risk than those decisions made only by individuals. Members of the group can accept responsibility collectively. Many times riskier decisions are better solutions.

4. *Group ownership of decisions:* Group decisions take longer to make and can be more costly than those of the same number of individuals working alone because of high coordination costs. Final solutions, however, are sounder and receive better acceptance because of the ownership concept. Groups should not be involved in routine problems; they should be used only when new, more difficult problems arise with no precedents already established.

5. *Differences in members' opinions:* At the beginning of almost any group problem-solving assignment, individual members of the group will hold very different opinions. If some people refuse to suspend their judgment and review additional evidence, chances are that the group will fail in its attempts to solve the problem.

Check Point—Section A

Directions: For each question, circle the correct answer.

A–1. Which one of the following is a major advantage of group problem solving?

A) More participation that overcomes resistance to new approaches

B) Greater involvement leading to acceptance of decisions

C) Increased savings of time and money

D) Less interference by managers who are not part of the group

A–2. Team members who gain benefits, but who contribute very little to the group's work, are known as

A) free riders

B) groupthinkers

C) resistance facilitators

D) loafers

A–3.   Which one of the following is a recommended approach to combating groupthink?

    A)   Assign a devil's advocate

    B)   Encourage resistance facilitation

    C)   Support members who are free riders

    D)   Discuss fewer solutions

B. Group Problem-Solving Techniques

T-group, Delphi technique, nominal group technique, and quality circle are just four of the more well-known of the intervention techniques used for problem solving and decision making. These techniques are often used in both industry and public organizations. A better understanding of them is important for future managers and employees as well.

1. *T-group:* **T-group** intervention is the grandfather of intervention techniques. Few companies use the technique in its original form anymore, but it still embodies the spirit of human relations in the workplace. This technique was introduced in 1947. **T-group** refers to "Training Group" in which a trainer leads a group of individuals in an open-ended discussion of problems and concerns focused on improved mutual understanding among the members. Where most contemporary approaches have very specific instructions to help initiate participation, the T-group has none. The T-group technique works as follows:

    a.   *No agenda:* Participants meet without an agenda and cope with their anxieties of having no agenda.

    b.   *Goal:* The goal is to get members to give nonevaluative feedback to each other. The "T" stands for *training*. Participants are being "trained" to be sensitive to the thoughts and feelings of others in the group.

    c.   *Size:* T-groups usually consist of 10 to 15 participants and one or two trainers. The trainer serves to facilitate participation rather than provide specific activities.

    d.   *Similarity to sensitivity training:* A form of the T-group is the sensitivity group. The use of sensitivity training continues to increase as the need to accept people of diverse backgrounds increases. Sensitivity training, however, tends to follow more structured approaches than the open-ended approach first used by T-group training.

    e.   *Advantages and disadvantages of the T-group:* The T-group has both advantages and disadvantages.

        1.   *Advantages:*

            a.   Participants have an opportunity to express themselves.

            b.   Emotional energies can be easily dissipated once the process has begun.

            c.   Rule-free discussion can lead to interesting ideas and solutions.

        2.   *Disadvantages:*

            a.   Once participants can be at all levels of an organization, some fear of later retribution may persist.

            b.   Once the session has ended, most return to a previous state.

2. *Delphi Technique:* The **Delphi technique** is often a valuable approach to use in predicting future human resource demands. It was developed in 1950 at the RAND Corporation. The Delphi technique involves surveying outsiders as well to learn their views and trying to develop consensus among these experts as to the most appropriate course to follow.

 a. *Basic procedure:* The Delphi technique requires that participants provide their opinions independently, working alone. The technique requires two groups: (1) a monitor or staff group and (2) a respondent or participant group.

  1. *Data gathering:* The monitor group prepares and sends questionnaires to the respondent group. The respondent group is a selected group of individuals, usually people with specific expertise. Individuals return their questionnaires. Then, another set of questionnaires is prepared using the first responses. Respondents can give opinions and develop ideas without being influenced by the ideas of others.

  2. *Surveying of experts:* Sometimes outside experts are asked to provide their opinions regarding future directions. These experts may be part of the continuing participant group.

  3. *Providing input:* Participants provide their inputs to a staff coordinator who compiles data, tries to combine and summarize like views, and submits data back to the participants for refinement and selection of preferred directions.

  4. *Responding:* The Delphi technique may involve a number of rounds of responses. The computer and electronic mail and modems have made responses quicker to receive and information faster to synthesize and disseminate back to participants. This cycle can occur many times.

  5. *Prioritizing:* The responding group members evaluate the feedback they receive as they answer each new set of questions. At some point they may be asked to give a prioritized ranking of issues, problems, and solutions. These priorities help produce a final report, a set of recommended actions, or a specific plan of action that will be given to whomever established the group and will be making the decisions.

 b. *Advantages and disadvantages of the Delphi technique:* One of the great advantages of this technique is that respondents are independent of one another.

  1. *Advantages:*

   a. Participants have an opportunity to express themselves.

   b. Each person gets to contribute until all have said everything they can.

   c. Each idea is given equal footing at the beginning and discussed fully.

  2. *Disadvantages:*

   a. It can be time consuming and result in strange solutions.

   b. Because of the voting technique, some ideas may be completely left out, reflecting only popular opinions.

 c. *Electronic Delphi techniques:* When first developed, Delphi was a time-consuming technique. Now, computer conferences can complete the summary and feedback loop in a matter of hours, making the process take no more than several days. "Electronic meeting" refers to a meeting that occurs using electronic links. With new communication links like the Interactive Tele-video and Internet meetings, this and similar techniques can also be combined with discussion and interaction.

3. *Nominal Group Technique (NGT):* The **nominal group technique (NGT)** was introduced in 1968. In this technique, the group first generates a list of ideas about a given problem, discusses each idea in turn, and then the group ranks the ideas.

   a. *Process of NGT:*

      1. It is a structured meeting of about 7 to 10 people and a facilitator.

      2. At the beginning of the meeting, each individual records ideas about a single question on a pad of paper.

      3. The facilitator asks each participant to share one idea in turn, until all ideas have been presented. The facilitator usually records these ideas on a flipchart or chalkboard.

      4. Each idea on the master list is then discussed again, one idea at a time.

      5. At the end of the process, the group votes to develop a rank-order (picking the best, second best, and so on) of the ideas.

   b. *For larger groups:* If more people are to be involved, the larger group is divided into smaller groups. The smaller groups conduct the NGT process. They then reassemble to share the findings of each smaller group, again with a rank for each idea to be produced at the end.

   c. *Advantages and disadvantages of NGT:* The nominal group technique has several advantages and disadvantages.

      1. *Advantages:*

         a. Anyone can participate, not just experts.

         b. The facilitator should not be an expert, though training in how to conduct the technique is important.

         c. Strangers can work together easily because the structure controls the interaction.

      2. *Disadvantages:*

         a. Participation may be uneven.

         b. Conclusions may not represent what any single person would develop, so acceptance may be difficult.

NGT continues to be fairly popular for complex problems. An interactive videodisc program based on the NGT, called the Group Decision Program, has been designed to make group decision processes move more quickly and be more flexible.

4. *Quality Circles:* Quality circles were discussed briefly in Chapter 3. One estimate is that up to 700,000 workers have been involved in quality circles or a variation.

   a. *Basic structure:* Members of the group are usually line workers, that is, the people actually doing the job that they are reviewing. The processes that the group uses will differ from one corporation to another, and usually the corporation sets the rules.

      1. *Establishing group goals:* Their role may be to find improvements in production or assembly techniques and then to make recommendations for the

changes. A major goal of the group is to engage employees in problem solving and decision making.

2. *Finding problems, developing solutions:* The circle may be presented with a problem to solve, or its members may initiate a recommendation. After collecting information, developing solutions, discussing alternatives, and in some cases testing the solution, the group will make a recommendation to management in the form of a report.

3. *Testing the ideas:* In some settings, these employees will test the recommendation and suggest broader implementation.

The method is used extensively in Japan. Its success has been mixed in the United States, probably because it may conflict with existing management styles.

b. *Basic steps:* The quality circle process requires, essentially, five steps:

1. *Identify the problem:* Quality circle members can identify a problem on which they have been asked to work. Other employees may suggest a problem to be dealt with by the circle. A member of the circle may recommend a problem.

2. *Analyze the problem:* The circle then conducts a thorough analysis of the problem. They may observe the activity that contains the problem, conduct formal or informal surveys, and even go to other places that have experienced a similar problem.

3. *Develop a solution:* The circle next considers a range of alternatives and develops a solution that they believe will work. Often, the circle may collect evidence to support their solution.

4. *Propose the solution to management:* The circle makes a formal presentation of the solution to management.

5. *Management accepts or rejects:* Implementation will follow if management accepts the solution. Often, the circle will participate in implementation as well. If management rejects the idea, clear rationale must be given, and the circle returns to the solution stage and develops another solution.

EXAMPLE: *Some companies have the quality circle integrated into their organization. Toyota Motor Company Plants have hierarchies of quality circles to increase integration. Figure 8–1 illustrates Toyota's system. Note the levels of leader circles and leader councils.*

c. *Advantages and disadvantages of quality circles:* The quality circle technique has several advantages and disadvantages.

1. *Advantages:*

   a. Problems are thoroughly analyzed using objective techniques and careful observation.

   b. Solutions are devised and tested as part of the process.

   c. Problems and solutions are identified by those actually working in the setting where the problem occurred, or solutions will be tried.

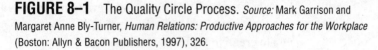

FIGURE 8–1   The Quality Circle Process. *Source:* Mark Garrison and Margaret Anne Bly-Turner, *Human Relations: Productive Approaches for the Workplace* (Boston: Allyn & Bacon Publishers, 1997), 326.

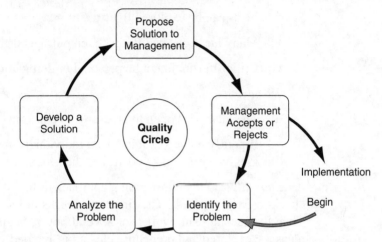

2. *Disadvantages:* According to research in the United States, several factors have hindered the effective implementation of quality circles in some organizations. Those factors include:

   a.   Failure of management to be committed to the quality circle process.

   b.   Adversarial relationship between union and management that interferes with the cooperation necessary for quality circles.

   c.   Weak implementation process, such as using inadequate training or choosing individuals to serve on the circle who are not committed to the process.

   d.   The quality circle had to begin before it was ready.

   e.   Objectives and roles are not well defined.

   f.   Feedback to the quality circle is inadequate to serve as a guide for improving the next round of recommendations.

5. ***Brainstorming:*** Anytime several people meet in an unstructured setting they are likely to engage in some form of brainstorming. An idea is presented, and everyone offers a solution or two. Some of them are fairly outrageous—like meeting everyone's desire for a corner office by designing a building that has only four offices per floor. But this idea might turn into a round building, where no one has corner offices, or a cross-shaped plan that at least has eight corners. The concept of **brainstorming** began in the 1930s as a technique that would bring a group of decision makers together to address a specific problem with as many ideas as possible. When used in a formal, structured manner, ideas are encouraged, evaluation is minimized, and active modification of ideas is encouraged. Brainstorming allows people to generate a number of ideas and to participate freely.

   a.   *Brainstorming as a natural process:* Brainstorming does reflect what we normally do, and it does help people begin to think creatively.

   b.   *Advantages and disadvantages of brainstorming:* Research suggests that, generally, ideas that appear in brainstorming sessions are not as well developed as those created by individuals.

1. *Advantages:* Used in an appropriate manner, with clear statement of what is and is not allowed in the session, brainstorming is a good technique to initiate creative problem solving.

   a. Ideas can be explored freely.

   b. Many ideas can be offered, even outrageous ideas.

   c. Criticism should not be personal or derogatory.

2. *Disadvantages:*

   a. The method is open to pressures to conform, like groupthink.

   b. If poorly managed, it can lead individuals of higher status or greater aggressiveness to take control of the group.

c. *An alternative:* One brainstorming approach utilizes two teams to brainstorm in a "back-to-back" process. The first team works at the problem for several hours. Then the second team works for several hours, beginning entirely fresh. Many ideas are explored and premature closure is avoided.

Check Point—Section B

Directions: For each question, circle the correct answer.

B–1. In this group problem-solving technique, group members identify and analyze a problem, develop a solution, and propose the solution to management. This technique is called

A) T-group
B) Delphi technique
C) nominal group technique
D) quality circles

B–2. In this group problem-solving technique, members of the group first generate a list of ideas about a problem, discuss each idea in turn, and then rank the ideas. This technique is called

A) T-group
B) Delphi technique

C) nominal group technique
D) quality circles

B–3. In this group problem-solving technique, members of the group first provide their opinions while working alone. Opinions are collected and summarized, and then another round of responses occurs. This technique is called

A) T-group
B) Delphi technique
C) nominal group technique
D) quality circles

C. Conflict

Conflict is a natural part of human interaction, and management of conflict is part of human relations. Conflict occurs whenever there is disagreement, competing interests, different expectations, or incompatible styles between two or more individuals or groups. Conflict occurs between friends and between enemies, between children and parents, and between spouses or partners. Coworkers and supervisors experience conflict as well. Recognizing that conflict has different forms is an important step toward understanding and dealing with the conflict one experiences. Conflict, too, can be managed. Managing various types of conflict is important for effective interaction and requires knowledge of the types and causes of conflict.

1. *Types of Conflict:* **Intrapersonal conflict** refers to conflict within an individual. Intrapersonal conflict can be in the form of approach-approach, approach-avoidance, avoidance-avoidance, and double approach-avoidance conflict. **Interpersonal** conflict refers to conflict between individuals. **Organizational conflict** refers to conflict with the units of an organization. Conflict can occur when people disagree about the topics being discussed, when people genuinely dislike each other, or when both of these situations are present.

   a. *Intrapersonal conflict:* Conflict that occurs within the individual is called intrapersonal conflict. For the most part, individuals are aware of ideas and desires that are incompatible. They try to find ways to satisfy their needs and desires without creating too much internal conflict.

   EXAMPLE: *You cannot both eat all the cake and ice cream you want and go on a low-calorie diet. The desire to eat high-calorie foods conflicts with the desire to be healthy or lose weight. Similarly, you cannot stay single and get married—even though both alternatives have their advantages.*

   Kurt Lewin, a social psychologist and founder of the study of group dynamics, described these types of conflict in the following way:

   1. *Approach-avoidance conflict:* **Approach-avoidance conflict** refers to a decision that has both positive and negative consequences, and the conflict arises in the competing desirability and undesirability of the action. An office affair illustrates this type of conflict very well. Lovers will have common interests at work and be able to see each other often (approach), but the negative consequences of ending the affair or being found out can be devastating (avoidance). Forming strong friendships in a work situation may have a similar impact if one of the friends gets promoted and has to manage former coworkers.

   2. *Approach-approach conflict:* **Approach-approach conflict** refers to two alternatives, one of which must be chosen, and both have positive consequences. Thus, an individual would prefer to have both, but cannot since a choice must be made. The "get married versus stay single" choice may be one of these kinds of choices. Selecting which position to accept from several is another form. Another choice is reflected in the decision to accept a relocation offer or stay in the same location. Relocating brings new opportunities, but may create hardships for family and friends. Staying put may limit opportunities, but it appears very safe.

   3. *Avoidance-avoidance conflict:* **Avoidance-avoidance conflict** refers to a set of choices that have few redeeming qualities and mostly negative consequences, thus making them choices that one wants to avoid; however, one of the choices must be taken. For the individual unemployed as a result of downsizing, the choice may eventually be accepting a menial or low-paying job or losing a home to foreclosure.

   4. *Double approach-avoidance conflict:* With **double approach-avoidance conflict** both choices have good and bad aspects. The decision will require identifying and weighing all the factors.

   EXAMPLE: *You may be offered an attractive new position with another company that requires you to relocate. In comparison, you are comfortable in*

your current job, but would like to make more money and accept new chal-
lenges. Furthermore, the move will disrupt family life and require leaving a
comfortable setting and friends.

5. *Cognitive dissonance:* Another form of intrapersonal conflict occurs when an individual has conflicting attitudes or behaviors. This conflict is what gives rise to **cognitive dissonance.** Conflicting attitudes and behaviors cause distress and discomfort that motivates the individual to change some aspect of the conflicting elements.

6. *Intrapersonal conflict is normal and common:* Everyone encounters these forms of conflict daily. Usually, we employ sets of priorities and criteria for decisions that relate directly to our desires, needs, and goals. Typically, the conflicts do not persist long. On occasion a difficult decision may come from one of these conflicts.

b. *Topic conflict:* Two people like each other, but they disagree on the topic being discussed. This form of conflict has the potential to challenge the friendship if it is not resolved satisfactorily for both.

c. *Interpersonal conflict:* Two people dislike each other, but they agree about the topic being discussed. Interpersonal conflict can arise from incompatible goals, ineffective communication, or incompatible personal styles. As a result, conflict may appear in the interactions between people that reflect efforts to block the goals of others, failures to communicate effectively, and outright personality conflicts.

d. *Combination or multilevel conflict:* Two people dislike each other, and they disagree about the topic being discussed.

EXAMPLE: *Two coworkers are assigned to lead a team project that involves several months of collecting information, exploring alternatives, and incorporating new expectations from upper management as the situation changes. Masouk is very informal—calling a quick meeting to share new information within a few hours of it becoming available. Jenkins is quite formal—preferring to prepare a memorandum that summarizes the new information and offers initial estimates of the impact it will have on the project. This approach will prove incompatible if Masouk and Jenkins do not work out a compromise. Otherwise, Masouk's information will seem more urgent and be incorporated more quickly than will Jenkins's. Jenkins's approach, on the other hand, will provide a better chance to think through the information before jumping to conclusions. Their conflict is a result of a matter of style.*

If Masouk and Jenkins did not like each other (personality conflict), or if Jenkins felt that Masouk was trying to steal the show (goal conflict), then the style difference could become part of a broader conflict. A failure to communicate the existence of the style differences could lead to assumptions by either of hidden agenda's and self-interest.

e. *Organizational conflict:* The more groups that exist within an organization, the more likely conflicts will develop between the different units. These conflicts can take several forms.

1. *Horizontal conflict:* Horizontal conflict refers to conflict between different units within the organization that are at about the same level of organization. Turf battles over who is responsible for recent successes or failures, who gets new equipment, and even who gets which parking place reflect vertical con-

flict. Conflict can also exist between support staff and line workers. Differences in function between office staff and factory workers are sufficient to create division between them. With division, conflict is likely.

2. *Vertical conflict:* This is as common as conflict can get. The lower echelon believes that the upper echelon does not understand its needs and the conditions in which it works. The upper echelon thinks that employees are simply out to get what they can and do not embrace organizational goals. This conflict may be over the location of power, distribution of profit, recognition of authority, and many more aspects of the hierarchy of the organization. This is the basic form of manager–employee conflict.

3. *Role confusion:* Whose job is it anyway? A poorly defined task or role can cause conflict. In an approach that depends upon employee involvement and creative decision processes, the definition of a job can quickly become unclear. Lack of clarity can cause intrapersonal and interpersonal conflict— leaving the individual uncertain about whether to take an initiative or leaving two people arguing over who should act.

2. ***Sources of Conflict in the Workplace:*** The three types of organizational conflict just described are present in the workplace. When one of these types of conflict occurs, specific characteristics of the people involved and the situation will be useful in determining the cause and the appropriate course of action to resolve conflict. There are some general tendencies that contribute to conflict in the workplace. Recognizing these forces is important as well, since they may be behind either the motivations of the individuals or the characteristics of the situation. The sources of conflict in the workplace include diversity, competition, territorial turf building, and scapegoating.

a. *Diversity:* Diversity contributes to conflict through prejudice, discrimination, and anxiety about differences.

b. *Competition:* People compete for promotions and raises. Competition for limited rewards, recognition, the best offices, the best accounts, sales routes, and the most desirable jobs fuels a competitive spirit. This competitive spirit is an effective way of keeping the organization thriving.

    EXAMPLE: *If three people are vying for a promotion, only one will get the promotion and the other two will be disappointed.*

c. *Turf:* Units within an organization compete with one another, striving to establish territory, gain recognition, and wield power. Establishing turf is only one way to shore up cohesiveness of the group. Needless to say, turf battles that result are a major source of conflict.

d. *Scapegoating:* Just as prejudice can result in blaming a group of people with causing the ills of society, a unit of a company can be used as a scapegoat for failure. **Scapegoating** refers to the diversion of blame from a larger group to a few or even one individual. Sometimes out-groups, especially defenseless or minority out-groups, are blamed in order to protect the in-group.

    EXAMPLE: *"Inventory control was responsible for our not being able to meet demand during last month's rush of orders." Suppose accounting had told the warehouse to trim the inventory? They can blame accounting, who in turn will probably blame upper management, who in turn could blame the increase in interest rates for causing a cash shortage.*

Typically, the scapegoat will be the group with the least power. Another variation in this cycle is the conflict between union and management.

3. **Conflicting Management Styles:** A starting point for conflict management is to take steps to minimize prejudice and harassment. Even if the environment could be completely free of these two factors, conflict would exist in the form of competing goals, diverse interests, and different values. When conflict arises, individuals can assert their positions through their actions and communications. How conflict is managed is also affected by the extent to which the conflicting individuals (or groups) take a cooperative attitude.

   a. *Assertiveness and cooperation:* Assertiveness and cooperativeness define two dimensions of interaction that can be used to describe different styles of conflict management. The degree of assertiveness and the degree of cooperativeness are two dimensions that Robert Blake and Jane Mouton, developers of the Leadership Grid, used to identify styles of conflict management. The concept has been popularized and further developed by several authors, but the basic idea has remained the same since Blake and Mouton introduced it in the early 1960s. These two dimensions produce five styles of conflict management: forcing, withdrawing, smoothing, problem solving, and compromising.

      1. *Forcing:* High assertiveness/low cooperativeness. Forcing has been described as a win-or-else kind of approach. It is useful in situations where actions must be taken and conflict resolved quickly. By "forcing" the issue, though, coercion and power must be used, making employees and coworkers uncomfortable.

      2. *Withdrawing:* Low assertiveness/low cooperativeness. Withdrawal is also considered avoidance. This style can be seen in people who avoid arguments and disagreement, or remain neutral. While it can serve to keep conflict from increasing, it does little to resolve it.

      3. *Smoothing:* Low assertiveness/high cooperativeness. Smoothing is a style that involves accommodating others by going along with their points of view and being unselfish. The person who uses this style consistently is likely to be seen as submissive and not very strong.

      4. *Problem solving:* High assertiveness/high cooperativeness. The problem-solving style is also seen as a collaborative style. It involves people who recognize that conflict is healthy and can be productive, and they are unafraid of asserting their position. To be effective, individuals utilizing this style must trust one another and must recognize that the process will result in an outcome to which they can make a commitment.

      5. *Compromising:* Moderate assertiveness/moderate cooperativeness. This type represents a middle ground. It requires that the involved parties be willing to negotiate and to compromise.

   The problem-solving and compromising styles together are the two styles most appropriate to management based on employee involvement. Each requires significant willingness to work together to solve conflicts and develop good solutions.

4. **Resolution of Group Conflict:** Steps that force the individual to take a calm approach, think through conflict or confrontation, describe conflict constructively, and give the other person a way out will help most people deal with conflict effectively.

   a. *Effects of group conflict:* At times people will disagree in a meeting situation. Disagreement can have a positive effect, resulting in some needed change; or disagreement can lead to conflict, with the result being very negative. Conflict can cause communication to deteriorate and people to become openly hostile toward each other. The goals of a meeting in which conflict occurs cannot be achieved effectively.

b. *Steps to resolve group conflicts:* Business to be conducted during a meeting can be stalled as a result of conflict; therefore, conflict must be resolved. Here are some basic steps used to resolve conflict:

1. *Fact-finding:* Do the people in conflict disagree with the topic, or do they dislike each other, or both?

2. *Isolating factors creating the conflict:* It may be necessary to move to the next agenda topic rather than trying to solve conflict at this time. This action depends upon how heated the argument might be. A compromise might be discussed to bring out elements that are important to each individual.

3. *Defusing the causes:* The presiding officer (or leader) must take steps to ensure that a similar conflict will not occur again. More information about the particular topics can be gathered and disseminated to participants so that they will understand the topic better. Interpersonal differences will take a little longer to resolve.

c. *Steps to resolve personal conflicts:* Dealing with personal conflict is a critical first step in becoming a better manager of conflict in general. Corwin King, a specialist in communications, suggests a very simple and direct approach that involves four steps:

1. *Allow time to cool off:* If you respond to someone while in a fight-or-flight mode, then you are likely to get a similar response from the other person. You should cool off. Calming down emotionally will make rational thought more likely and will lead to a win/win outcome.

2. *Analyze the situation:* Once removed from an emotional outburst, you can analyze the situation. You must put yourself in the other person's place and try to understand the reasons for his or her actions or words. With this perspective in mind, a more reasonable solution to the conflict becomes possible. When you understand what the other person needs to win, there will be better control over the options.

3. *State the problem to the other person:* After time has passed that allows cooling off and thoughtful reflection, a description of how the confrontation is understood can initiate interaction that can lead to resolution. Direct and calm communication with the other person has the best chance of demonstrating a professional and responsible attitude. You must not focus on personality or character of the individual or on your own personality. The description of events and the problem in terms of actual, observable behaviors must be realized. Questions that ask for motivation can put the other person on the defensive, making a resolution less likely.

4. *Leave the other person a way "out":* If you understand the other person's objectives and have a sense of their motivation, then a wise step would be to make sure that the other person always has a way to escape the situation without losing face. Otherwise, attempts will appear to be another effort to win at the other person's expense. If you seek a win/win outcome, then an option that would be considered a win must remain viable.

No technique has a guarantee of success. However, avoiding emotional reactions and maintaining a professional attitude is the best approach. Even if efforts fail, you will know that they tried in a responsible manner that was respectful of others.

   d. *Outcomes of conflict:* Conflict must be resolved for the business at hand to move forward. Causes of the conflict must be determined for final resolution to take place. Outcomes of conflicts can reflect one of three resolutions: win/win strategies, win/lose strategies, and lose/lose strategies.

      1. *Preferred results:* The most desirable result of any conflict should be that both parties win. Whether achieved through negotiation, collaboration, or friendly dispute, everyone involved is better off in the "win/win" situation.

      2. *Three main strategies:* Whatever style an individual uses in managing conflict, there are three possible strategies: win/win, win/lose, and lose/lose. Sometimes people purposefully select these strategies; sometimes they result from the necessity of very difficult situations.

         a. *Win/win strategy:* In the win/win strategy, individuals on both sides of an issue recognize the need to compromise, or at least to trust that each party has genuine interests in a positive outcome. A win/win strategy may involve two employees working through a conflict over schedules by each compromising. One employee may accept the need to work late to cover the other employee. In return, the other employee works late on another day. This kind of negotiation places the opportunity to succeed with each individual. Conflicts like these can occur when scarce resources or additional personnel are needed, and the negotiation of a compromise is just one way to work the problem through.

         b. *Win/lose strategy:* The coercive use of power leads to a situation in which one person will win and the other will lose. Energies expended can be damaging to productivity and morale. The choice of one candidate over others in a promotion decision will initially look like a win/lose event, but losers in the selection process do not have to view their failure to be promoted as the end of the line. Opportunities should continue to arise if individuals have the qualifications. In a fight for a job in a downsizing situation, however, there will be clear winners and clear losers. Some losses are inevitable.

         c. *Lose/lose strategy:* Sometimes, conflicts present irreconcilable differences that must nevertheless be resolved. Conflict between labor and management often results in strikes, one of the clearest forms of lose/lose events. What makes this a strategy is that the union and the company actually are willing to allow the strike to show their resolve against demands of the opposite party. In a strike, both sides suffer (thus the lose/lose situation).

      3. *Personal coping style:* Although it seems reasonable that everyone wants a win/win result, this assumption can be misleading. Sometimes, interpersonal dislike and a history of personal or intergroup conflict can lead people to seek revenge, or to undermine efforts of the other person at every juncture. While not very polite or very respectful, people are motivated by their emotions, prejudices, and dislikes. To avoid falling into these kinds of behaviors, a personal coping style that is thought through and deliberate will help people manage conflict more effectively.

Check Point—Section C

Directions: For each question, circle the correct answer.

C–1. When a decision has both positive and negative consequences and conflict arises because of them, this refers to a/an

A) win/lose strategy
B) cognitive dissonance
C) approach-avoidance conflict
D) interpersonal conflict

C–2. Which one of the following is a form of intrapersonal conflict in which conflicting thoughts result in feelings of anxiety?

A) Scapegoating
B) Role confusion

C) Cognitive dissonance
D) Turf building

C–3. The style that involves accommodating others by supporting their views and being unselfish is called

A) compromising
B) withdrawing
C) forcing
D) smoothing

D. Group Techniques for Reducing Interpersonal Conflict

Learning effective interpersonal skills can reduce most interpersonal conflict. Interpersonal skills can be learned in many different ways. Popular programs include sensitivity training, assertiveness training, transactional analysis, motivation training, quality management, and many others. Knowledge of these types of training and methods used is critical for the administrative professional to be prepared for demands for continued learning in the future workplace. Training centers have been developed in many corporations, and organizations continue to depend upon specialized consultants as trainers.

1. *Sensitivity Training:* **Sensitivity training** is perhaps the oldest specific type of human relations training program. It started in 1946 with a group that soon became known as the National Training Laboratories. This type of training focuses on being sensitive to and aware of the attitudes and feelings of others.

    a. *Methods:* Sensitivity training includes encounter groups, T-groups, and cultural awareness seminars. In the traditional encounter or T-group, people meet without an agenda and talk about topics that arise.

        1. *Encourage free expression:* Free expression is encouraged. Usually several levels of management attend. People must be assured that reprisals for comments they make will not occur at any time.

        2. *Focus on interpersonal tension and anxiety:* Usually, sensitivity groups focus on an anxiety-provoking issue or statement like the one just described (this is especially true of T-groups).

    b. *Training goals:* These goals suggest how the process trains one to be sensitive to the feelings and viewpoints of others.

        1. Helping the participant understand how others view the participant's actions.

        2. Providing insights to members of the group about themselves.

3. Learning patterns of behavior of the group.

4. Teaching participants to listen.

5. Increasing tolerance of each other.

c. *Effectiveness and consequences:* The effectiveness of sensitivity training has been questioned. It is unclear that the assurance of protection is enough to keep people from having negative reactions to the process once they return to work. Nevertheless, it remains fairly popular.

2. *Assertiveness Training:* **Assertiveness training** is a means of self-improvement through learning to express one's feelings and act with confidence. Assertiveness became popular in the 1960s through the work of assertiveness trainer, Arnold Lazarus. The topic has had fairly wide popularity. A number of self-help books have appeared since. As might be expected, the promoters of the concept believe that assertiveness is usually the best approach to interaction with others. Assertiveness requires that people hold firmly to their own position or stand up for their rights without infringing on others.

EXAMPLE: *Corporations like Ford Motor Company have depended on assertiveness training to teach managers and employees to cope with difficult situations effectively.*

a. *Assertive behavior:* Assertive behavior requires a distinction between getting one's way and standing one's ground. The aggressive focus on succeeding at all costs helps hide insecurity about failure. Assertive people have a sense of confidence that allows them to compromise their position without compromising their sense of self or integrity. The interpersonal skills at stake include:

1. Being able to cope with coercive, aggressive, as well as, passive behavior of others.

2. Presenting one's views in an honest and direct manner.

3. Being able to work cooperatively and to resolve conflicts without resorting to aggressiveness or passiveness.

b. *Assertiveness versus aggressiveness and passiveness:*

1. *Aggressive behavior:* Aggressive behavior appears in people who insist on having their own way. Aggressive people will ignore the rights and concerns of others in order to achieve their own personal interests. Aggressive people also have complaints about everything and everyone.

2. *Passive behavior:* Passive behavior is marked by an individual who consistently attempts to accommodate others, even when his or her own interests are not served. Passiveness leads to denial of self, a poor self-concept, avoidance of conflict, and anxiety about rejection and failure. Passive people are frequently exploited.

3. *Passive-aggressive behavior:* Passive-aggressive behavior is a combination of these two styles. This particular form of behavior is found in a person who uses passive behaviors to express hostility toward others (there is more to the clinical problem than these expressions).

EXAMPLE: *Harry, a man with traditional expectations about his spouse's role in the family, gives in to her desire to work; but he makes a comment like,*

"Go ahead, Martha, and get a job. I'm sure the children will not miss you while they are in day-care." Hostility is expressed in the barbed implications of desertion carefully aimed at the wife's potential sense of guilt about leaving her children in the care of others. At work, Harry tells his subordinates, "Don't worry about tomorrow's early deadline. Go on home for the evening. I can stay all night to finish the report if I have to. At least you can get some rest for tomorrow." (Note that this reference to gender is here only because it reflects a very common pattern. There is no intention to imply that more than a small minority of males engage in this behavior.)

Usually, passive-aggressive behavior like this will stifle employees' tendency to protest against the unreasonable behavior on the part of the supervisor—and they will go home. Typically, a passive-aggressive behavior pattern involves alternation between passive and aggressive behavior. Which behavior is expressed depends on whether the individual is in a subordinate or a superior position.

    c. *Benefits of assertiveness training:* Assertive behavior requires a distinction between getting one's way and standing one's ground.

        1. While assertiveness training begins with learning to distinguish aggressive, passive, and assertive behaviors, the way to train people to behave assertively usually involves role-play and *modeling*. Modeling is a very powerful technique for demonstrating almost any human interaction, and it is the key to the powerful learning theory called observational learning.

        2. In role-play, situations are contrived where individuals are given passive, aggressive, or assertive roles. In role-play, a film or live models enact examples of different kinds of behavior in different situations.

        3. Assertiveness training may also use reverse role-play.

  3. *Transactional Analysis:* **Transactional analysis (TA)** provides a means of conceptualizing the types of interactions between people by using a simple formula of identifying behavior toward others as parent, child, or adult. Transactions between people are governed by whether one person interacts with another as a parent to child, parent to parent, parent to adult, adult to child, and so on. The other person does not necessarily interact on the same basis.

EXAMPLE: *One person, such as a supervisor, may approach a subordinate as a parent interacts with a child. The subordinate may respond on the basis of an adult-to-adult relationship. This imbalance creates problems in the relationship.*

From the point of view of transactional analysis, the goal in an organization would be for everyone to engage in adult-to-adult transactions while transacting business. By examining cases and examples that may resemble the work situations of a particular organization, and then through role-play, individuals become aware of the kinds of transactions that occur in their many relations with others.

    a. *Three personality states:* These three ego states form the basis for analyzing interactions between people. These interactions are called *transactions* because they involve specifically an action on one person's part and a reaction by another person. To emphasize the exchange, behaviors are considered transactions rather than simply interactions. Eric Berne, the founder of transactional analysis, defines parent, child, and adult roles as three ego, or personality, states:

1. *Parent-ego state:* The *parent-ego state* invokes nurturing, prejudicial, and critical behaviors that reflect how a person's parents behaved.

2. *Adult-ego state:* The *adult-ego state* is oriented to reality and objectivity; it is adaptive, rational, and organized.

3. *Child-ego state:* The *child-ego state* is impulsive and infantile and composed predominantly of feelings and patterns of behavior individuals originally exhibited toward their parents.

b. *Transactions:* To emphasize the exchange, behaviors are considered transactions rather than simply interactions. The popularity of transactional analysis probably rests in the ease with which almost anyone can analyze these transactions. Transactions can be complementary, crossed, or ulterior.

1. *Complementary transactions: Complementary transactions* are those in which two people are behaving in ego states that match. One person behaves as a parent and the other as a child; both can be parents; both can be adults; or both can be children. Figure 8–2 illustrates complementary transactions.

2. *Crossed transactions: Crossed transactions* involve one person behaving as parent and the other as an adult, or both being in parent states and treating the other as a child. Figure 8–2 illustrates crossed transactions.

3. *Ulterior transactions: Ulterior transactions* occur when an individual uses language that appears to be from one state but the message is from another, hidden state. The term *ulterior* refers to the hidden transactions.

EXAMPLE: *A subordinate, Yudice, prepares a report with a recommendation to be put into effect. Yudice knows, however, that the supervisor, Morello, will not consider anyone's ideas. So, Yudice includes some key errors in the report for Morello to find. This puts Morello in the parent role of correcting Yudice. By correcting, Morello takes charge and nurtures; by taking charge, Morello also possesses the ideas. The ideas become Morello's and, once corrections are made, they are supported. The ulterior transaction had a payoff for Yudice. Yudice was able to control and manipulate the supervisor by taking on a hidden parent role.*

c. *Scripts and strokes:* Training can teach people communication rules that support desired ego states. A person can also learn about scripts and strokes.

1. *Scripts: Scripts* are preprogrammed transactions, usually from parent or child roles. They may lead to procrastination, manipulating others, and being a loser. According to TA, recognizing scripts is an important step in becoming "OK." Being OK represents one of the patterns of attitudes people have toward themselves and toward other people. Figure 8–3 illustrates the four possible configurations of attitudes one can have: (1) I'm not OK. You're OK; (2) I'm OK. You're OK; (3) I'm not OK. You're not OK; (4) I'm OK. You're not OK.

2. *Strokes: Strokes* are behaviors that recognize others and can be as simple as saying "good morning" to people in the office or telling your children "goodby" as they head toward school. Strokes are a form of reinforcement and support (or nonsupport, if strokes are negative) we give one another.

FIGURE 8–2   Types of Transactions.

Source: Mark Garrison and Margaret Anne Bly-Turner, *Human Relations: Productive Approaches for the Workplace* (Boston: Allyn & Bacon Publishers, 1997), 178–180.

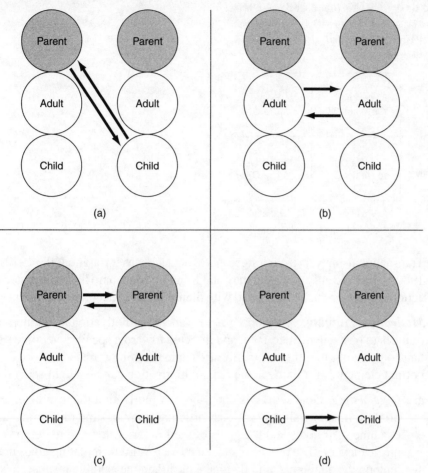

In (a): The parent says, "Clean your work area." The child says, "Yes, sir." In (b): The adult asks, "Is the report ready?" The adult answers, "Yes, we just finished." In (c): The parent says, "Those assembly workers . . ." The parent says "I know what you mean." In (d): The child says, "They just don't give me the support I need." The child says, "They don't seem to care at all about us."

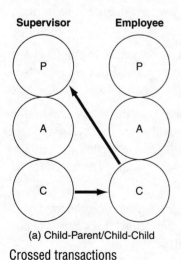

(a) Child-Parent/Child-Child

Crossed transactions

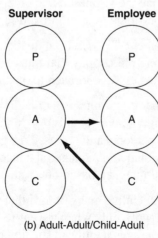

(b) Adult-Adult/Child-Adult

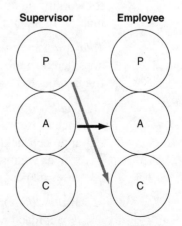

Superficially the supervisor is treating the employee as an adult, but the ulterior transaction is a parent-to-child transaction.

FIGURE 8–3 I'm OK, You're OK. *Source:* Mark
Garrison and Margaret Anne Bly-Turner, *Human Relations:
Productive Approaches for the Workplace* (Boston: Allyn &
Bacon Publishers, 1997), 181.

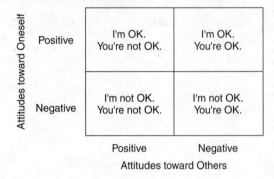

Transactional analysis is no longer in vogue, as it was throughout the 1970s and early
1980s. More recently, Paul Hershey and Kenneth Blanchard have suggested that transactional analysis can be integrated with their popular concept of situational leadership.

4. ***Motivation Training:*** All training is in some way motivational. Trainers want their
   trainees to be excited, energized, and directed toward a specific outcome. It is important to point out that the motivation to achieve can be trained, and some of the important elements of training achievement motivation can be taught separately.

   a. *Goal setting:* Goal setting is one aspect of motivation that can be examined in a
      brief seminar or training session. Participants in this kind of seminar are asked to
      examine their goals and the goals of their organization and to determine how re-
      alistic they are. The process can then move toward formulating goals that are chal-
      lenging yet attainable, and that have clear and measurable results.

   b. *Self-concept:* A critical component of motivation, and especially of achievement
      motivation, is how one views one's self. Self-concept can also be examined in a
      training seminar with techniques taught to enhance self-concept and self-esteem.
      Transactional analysis and assertiveness training are but two means among many
      for working on how one views oneself and others. Any new interpersonal or tech-
      nical skills should contribute to an improved sense of self and self-confidence.

   c. *Total quality management (TQM):* Total quality management (Chapter 3) is also
      considered an all-round philosophy that must be incorporated into all aspects of
      life in order to be a successful approach to quality in organizations.

      1. *Quality:* Often the term *management* is dropped from the phrase, and refer-
         ence is made simply to the "quality" or "total quality" approach. As such, the
         approach tackles personal and professional growth and interpersonal skills, as
         well as organizational and managerial concerns for quality. The approach fo-
         cuses on personal integrity based on a value system.

      2. *Major differences:* Unlike many of the other training programs, the total qual-
         ity approach will work only when the entire organization "buys into" the phi-
         losophy and encourages it enthusiastically at all levels.

         a. *Organizational change:* This requires a transformation of the organiza-
            tional culture and identification of ways to reward those who participate
            in the quality concept.

b. *Individual change:* Individual training programs then focus on a full range of training topics guided by the quality approach. Quality itself is intended as a motivating factor.

EXAMPLE: *A participant may learn statistics in order to interpret quality measures. He or she may learn about leadership styles in order to take initiatives and to guide others toward the quality concept, and so on.*

5. *Adventure Training:* **Adventure training,** which is sometimes called outdoor training, wilderness training, or survival training, follows a popular youth training program known as Outward Bound. Participants go into a wilderness area and must work together and build mutual trust in order to achieve a common goal. Often management teams are sent to experience the training as a group.

a. *Challenge:* Adventure training requires emotional and physical challenge.

b. *Teamwork:* Adventure training challenges require teamwork and mutual trust. Trusting relationships are necessary in work as well as during the training.

c. *Success as a team member:* Participants learn how to accept roles in teams and to take pride in team successes and the success of other team members.

d. *Transfer to the workplace:* A major assumption of this training is that by overcoming challenges offered by nature, these same collaborative skills will appear in the workplace.

Check Point—Section D

Directions: For each question, circle the correct answer.

D–1. In this group technique for reducing interpersonal conflict people first learn to identify passive, aggressive, and assertive roles; then they engage in role-play to practice. This technique is called

A) sensitivity training
B) assertiveness training
C) transactional analysis
D) adventure training

D–2. In this group technique for reducing interpersonal conflict, people meet without an agenda and discuss anxiety-provoking issues. This technique is called

A) sensitivity training
B) assertiveness training

C) transactional analysis
D) adventure training

D–3. In this group technique for reducing interpersonal conflict, people go into a wilderness area and learn to depend on each other to meet specific physical challenges. This technique is called

A) sensitivity training
B) assertiveness training
C) transactional analysis
D) adventure training

For Your Review

Directions: For each question, circle the correct answer.

Case 1: Disastrous Decision Making

Mook is a headstrong and willful person who acts with self-assurance. Mook always appears to have all the answers. As division manager for HA Appliances, a major manufacturer of home appliances, Mook has responsibility for design, development, manufacturing, and assembly of refrigerators. The professional support staff for the division includes electrical and chemical engineers, design specialists, and market analysts. The market for energy efficient refrigerators has become competitive, so HA Appliances must compete by introducing a new energy efficient refrigerator in the next business cycle.

The engineering problems have been difficult to solve, and there are at least three possible approaches. Mook knows which one is best. Because Mook is such a forceful character, none of the decision-making group members are willing to challenge. In fact, the decision turns out to be the wrong one, and the target date for developing a new refrigerator is not met.

1. The fact that Mook dominates the group and forces a decision on the group suggests that the group suffered from

   A) misidentification of alternatives
   B) implementation ineffectiveness
   C) brainstorming
   D) groupthink

2. Which one of the following is an advantage of group decision making that Mook could have expected if the approach used had been successful?

   A) More balanced level of energy
   B) An increase in sharing of knowledge
   C) Detection of free riders
   D) Avoiding the high cost of decision making

3. Managers like Mook may create barriers to allowing subordinates to have more say because

   A) group problem solving results in high costs
   B) knowledge would be shared by cross-functional teams

   C) they are reluctant to surrender traditional problem-solving duties
   D) groupthink can be resolved only using resistance facilitation

4. HA Appliances employs a variety of professionals who have specialized in the engineering needed to develop a new refrigerator. A team composed of these specialists would be called a/an

   A) vertical team
   B) interest group
   C) cross-functional
   D) quality circle

5. If the group suffered from groupthink, which one of the following would be evidence?

   A) High pressure to conform
   B) Resistance to new approaches
   C) Lack of group participation
   D) Improvement in personal decision making

Case 2: Office Politics at Lifeline Health Insurance Company

In the competitive atmosphere of Lifeline Health Insurance Company, Crotty and Kym are at constant odds. Their jobs are very similar, though they each handle slightly different types of accounts. Crotty manages corporate accounts for several agents who specialize in small businesses, and Kym manages government accounts for agents who work with counties and small cities and towns. They frequently turn to the same resource people for contributions to health insurance plans that they must customize for agents. Consequently, they frequently find themselves in competition.

Conflicts between them have begun to spread to the resource people they depend upon. Each has made what appear to be alliances and encouraged favoritism. The office is nearing a point of jeopardy that may undermine the company's effectiveness.

6. Which one of the following group problem-solving techniques would help Crotty and Kym work through the problem that they have created?

    A) T-group
    B) Delphi technique
    C) Nominal group technique
    D) Quality circle

7. The source of the conflict between Crotty and Kym, as it is described, is

    A) diversity
    B) scapegoating
    C) approach-avoidance conflict
    D) competition

8. As the conflict spreads from being one between Crotty and Kym to involving many of their coworkers, the conflict would be called

    A) horizontal organizational conflict
    B) intrapersonal conflict
    C) topic conflict
    D) double approach-avoidance conflict

9. Managers who supervise Crotty and Kym could work toward resolving the conflict between them by first

    A) leaving each person a means of escaping the conflict
    B) engaging in fact-finding about the problem
    C) defusing the causes
    D) isolating factors causing the conflict

10. Which one of the following strategies would be best for Crotty, Kym, and Lifeline Health?

    A) Approach-approach
    B) Win/win
    C) Double approach-avoidance
    D) Win/lose

Case 3: In-Balance Tire, International

In-Balance Tire, International is out of balance. Quality is suffering, productivity is dropping, and factory and office workers have lost their motivation. In-Balance has contracted with Life Harmony to develop and to conduct a series of workshops to help restore the company to its former glory. Some of the workshops will focus on improving motivation, and some will become part of the continuing effort to improve quality and productivity.

Several major problems may be at the core of In-Balance's recent woes. More of the workforce is now composed of recent immigrants, increasing material costs have lead to manufacturing and assembly shortcuts, and a stagnant economy has meant fewer wage increases and higher benefit costs. Trainers at Harmony believe that the place to start is with the people.

11. For In-Balance to deal with increasing conflict between new immigrants and long-standing members of the workforce, trainers from Life Harmony should use

    A) assertiveness training
    B) quality circles
    C) sensitivity training
    D) adventure training

12. To identify root causes of the problems being encountered by In-Balance, Life Harmony wants to undertake a process that includes both internal staff and external experts called

    A) Sensitivity training
    B) Quality circles
    C) Nominal group technique
    D) Delphi technique

13. To encourage the workforce and staff at In-Balance to feel like they have ownership of the solutions to be used to turn the company around, Life Harmony recommends

    A) allowing managers to make the first proposals
    B) adventure training

C) using group and team problem solving
D) encouraging groupthink

14. Life Harmony discovers that few managers trust each other and most complain of sabotage of efforts by other managers. To rebuild trust among managers, Life Harmony plans to use

    A) adventure training
    B) nominal group techniques
    C) assertiveness training
    D) quality circles

15. Upper-level management at In-Balance has little respect for line workers, and one executive was even heard referring to them as "babies" after a complaint about safety was made. Which one of the following approaches is most suited for reversing this type of thinking among executives?

    A) Assertiveness training
    B) Transactional analysis
    C) Adventure training
    D) Delphi technique

Solutions

Solutions to Check Point—Section A

Answer: *Refer to:*

A–1. (B)   [A-1-d]

A–2. (A)   [A-2-d]

A–3. (A)   [A-3-a-(2)]

Solutions to Check Point—Section B

Answer: *Refer to:*

B–1. (D)   [B-4]

B–2. (C)   [B-3]

B–3. (B)   [B-2]

Solutions to Check Point—Section C

Answer: *Refer to:*

C–1. (C)   [C-1-a-(1)]

C–2. (C)   [C-1-a-(5)]

C–3. (D)   [C-3-a-(3)]

Solutions to Check Point—Section D _____

Answer:	*Refer to:*
D–1. (B)	[D-2]
D–2. (A)	[D-1]
D–3. (D)	[D-5]

Solutions to For Your Review _____

Answer:	*Refer to:*
Case 1:	
1. (D)	[A-3-a]
2. (B)	[A-1-b]
3. (C)	[A-2-e]
4. (C)	[A-1-b]
5. (A)	[A-3-a-(1)-(c)]
Case 2:	
6. (A)	[B-1]
7. (D)	[C-2-b]
8. (A)	[C-1-e-(1)]
9. (B)	[C-4-b-(1)]
10. (B)	[C-4-d-(2)-(a)]
Case 3:	
11. (C)	[D-1]
12. (D)	[B-2]
13. (C)	[A-1-d]
14. (A)	[D-5]
15. (B)	[D-3]

Chapter 9
Conducting Meetings

OVERVIEW

Meetings are at the core of corporate communications. In meetings, members of organizations share information, solve problems, develop plans of actions, review and evaluate prior plans, and generally oversee the conduct of business. In addition, face-to-face meetings provide opportunities for personal contact and increased esprit de corps. Meetings can involve as few as two people and as many as the entire organization. They may be restricted to members of the group or be inclusive. Inclusive meetings may involve shareholders, the press, and the general public.

Administrative professionals must know how to manage a meeting, whether it be preparing only the details of the practical elements of setting a meeting, inviting the participants, and securing the physical space (or the electronic remote and virtual places), or whether it be participating in the meeting as a contributor or even the convener and chair. All aspects of group and team work (discussed in Chapters 7 and 8) require well-prepared and properly managed meetings. Details are critical to the success of a meeting as a process that controls the interaction of participants and the effective achievement of goals being addressed by the meeting.

KEY TERMS

A. Types of Meetings

Traditionally, a meeting is defined by the interaction of two or more people in an actual physical location. Recent advances in telecommunications, including interactive videoconferencing and Internet-based meetings, have expanded the traditional definition to include linked, distance communications where people can conduct real-time, synchronous interaction. That is, people may not be in the same physical location, but technology allows them to carry on two-way discussions. The primary distinction for meetings is formal and informal. All forms of meetings can be conducted in either formal or informal formats. A **formal meeting** is a meeting that proceeded under the control of a chair, following an agenda, and typically utilizing rules of conduct that specify how action will be taken. The special form of a conference as a formal meeting of an association of professionals or experts is sometimes separated from this distinction.

1. *Formal Meetings:* One of the most prominent strategies used to communicate information is the *meeting.* Managers tend to spend at least one-third of their time in meetings each week, and many organizations spend up to 15 percent of the personnel budgets directly on meetings. With changes brought about by technology and globalization organization, it has become even more imperative that people communicate effectively with each other in groups to ensure that the objectives of the organization are met. People must be brought together within the firm (by person-to-person contact or electronic means) to consider topics of mutual concern. Changes in technology have revolutionized the ways that meetings can be held.

   EXAMPLE: *Wal-Mart conducts informational and training sessions with its many stores spread over vast geographic distances from corporate and division headquarters by way of interactive technology and large screens.*

   Local area networks, the Internet, and the World Wide Web (WWW) allow meetings to be held more readily. New sets of rules called netiquette guidelines are being defined so that participants know acceptable behavior to follow.

   a. *Types of formal meetings:* A formal meeting would definitely have to be planned in advance so that the participants in the meeting would be aware of the agenda items to be covered during the meeting. In-house meetings will generally fall into one of these categories: general meetings, departmental meetings, or committee meetings.

      1. *General meeting:* The **general meeting** is scheduled for all people within the organization, including all managers and supervisors. As a rule, meetings of this nature are scheduled very seldom because only a few topics are relevant to *all* employees in the organization. Most general information is passed along from top management to lower levels of supervision in departmental meetings. The head of the organization presides at all general meetings. There are two additional forms of general meetings, annual and external annual meetings.

         a. *Annual general meeting:* Annual general meetings are often held off-site and include most managers. If the company has a sales force that is distributed geographically, then this is often the time the sales representatives are brought together. New products may be announced, annual recognition awards given, retirements recognized, and general information about corporate goals presented.

         b. *External annual general meeting:* The external annual general meeting includes shareholders and the interested public. Sometimes a company might have a new product that involves vendors, both for production and sales, who would be invited for the product announcement. In this case, the meeting may be more or less frequent than an annual meeting.

2. *Departmental meeting:* **Departmental meetings** involve departments, divisions, or other work groups and may be scheduled on a more regular basis. Depending on the organization, weekly, biweekly, or monthly meetings may be scheduled. The department manager or work group supervisor generally presides at these meetings. The efficient operation of the department, division, or work group is the primary concern of the people involved in the meeting.

3. *Committee meeting:* A **committee meeting** is when a group of people meet for the purpose of discussing problems, tasks, or responsibilities. Usually, committee assignments are performed in addition to regularly assigned duties.

   a. *Standing committee:* Members of a **standing committee** are appointed for a definite term such as one or two years. The standing committee has definite objectives assigned for which it is responsible during the term.

   b. *Ad hoc committee:* An **ad hoc committee** is usually charged with a single task. The task may be to investigate a problem or develop new procedures or policies. When the task is done, the committee is dissolved. Sometimes new duties require a permanent committee to be formed. At the end of the assignment, the committee may produce a final report.

4. *Board meeting:* Board meetings occur on a regular schedule, often every quarter or every six months. Boards include board of directors, board of governors, board of trustees, board of regents, and board of overseers (this one is now fairly uncommon). At a typical board meeting, the president or CEO makes a report to the board about progress toward initiatives set by the board. Often, delegates of the CEO, such as the chief financial officer or a vice president, will make a presentation to the board. A board meeting will always be managed with a formal agenda following Roberts' Rules of Order or a similar parliamentary procedure.

   a. Public institutions must follow the open meeting laws in the state where they take place, with closed sessions occurring typically when personnel issues are discussed.

   b. Private companies and nonprofit organizations vary, some having open meetings, or at least parts of their meetings open, while some conduct their business entirely in closed sessions.

   c. Most board meetings end with public announcements, press conferences, or press releases. These methods of announcement provide the official stance of the board and help create a public record that will be reported in the press.

   d. Board meetings may precede annual general meetings and external general meetings, and they may even be considered part of the annual meeting. Annual stockholder and shareholder meetings are usually held in this context, though the shareholders have votes in the official shareholder meeting, which is not part of the board meeting. There are several types of structures that govern the process and the meetings themselves.

5. *Public meeting:* **Public meetings** occur in a variety of formats. They can be public shareholder or stockholder meetings; the news conference or public

portion of a board meeting; or the public hearing of local, state, or federal commission, committee, or legislative session. The public has various levels of interaction opportunities, from full interaction with the governing body to mere observation of official proceedings. The following describes several general types:

a. *Public hearing:* Boards, commissions, legislative committees, task forces, and so on may hold a public hearing to present and receive feedback from interested citizens and stakeholders prior to taking an action or as a means of informing the public of an action or soon-to-be-implemented regulation. Many boards and commissions, especially publicly elected or officially appointed commissions, are required to hold a series of public meetings prior to making a decision or voting on an issue.

b. *Public forum:* One step short of a mandated hearing, and often without the requirement of making anything public, organizations—including private companies and public boards—use a public forum to serve as both an informative session and as a means of collecting citizen responses. Whenever an action will affect a group of people who have no control over the action, like people who live next to a power station, a landfill, or a prison facility, the entity taking the action will hold public forums to help reduce anxiety and respond to questions.

EXAMPLE: *A local citizens' group petitions for a ballot to merge local and county governments, and law requires that a "merger commission" be formed. Guidelines then require a series of public hearings and forums, to inform the public and to get public feedback. Since the merger will affect businesses, governments, and private citizens, the commission is itself composed of representatives from across the spectrum. The commission then holds formal and informal sessions to collect as much input as possible. Once the merger plan is developed, more hearings are conducted, and, finally, the plan goes to a vote for all county and city citizens to decide.*

c. *Public debate:* Another form of meeting includes political campaign debates. Over the past several elections cycles, the length of campaigns has increased, and the involvement of all segments of society has grown. Now companies find themselves cosponsors of debates and public forums with private organizations. This change reflects the view that companies have a social responsibility to local citizenry. Administrative professionals find themselves working with organizers and sometimes themselves becoming the organizer of such activities.

d. *Public rally:* Public expression of opinions and support have become commonplace. Surprisingly, an industry has also formed that organizes and promotes public rallies to support everything from a local football team to a candidate for office. While these may appear informal and spontaneous, they often require careful planning, well-managed human and financial resources, as well as proper advance preparation.

2. ***Conferences:*** A conference is a special type of formal meeting, and it deserves a separate section here to clarify the differences. Conferences require focused planning and special efforts for facility location and preparation. Participants typically come from widely dispersed geographical locations. International conferences have needs for

language and cultural concerns. Conferences are also called *conventions,* and these two terms are interchangeable.

a. *Conference defined:* A **conference** is a formal meeting of people with a common purpose. Typically, these people are professionals assembled to share information and research. Participants may be defined by the jobs they perform, such as human resource personnel or accountants, just as much as they are identified by their professional vocation. The major activity at a conference or convention is that of sessions that address topics of special interest to the participants as well as displays of equipment, information, and vendors. There may be several topical sessions occurring simultaneously. Some conferences are as large as 20,000–25,000 participants.

b. *Types of conferences:* A company, an association of companies, a professional association, or a community association can sponsor conferences. Government agencies will sponsor conferences that involve recipients of grants and contracts from special departments of the agency.

EXAMPLE: *The U.S. Department of Agriculture (USDA) holds conferences of extension agents and representatives of the public it serves.*

1. *Company-sponsored conference:* Companies may sponsor conferences that occur at the same time as their annual general meeting or for special presentation of new products and services.

    a. *Location:* The location for the conference may be near company headquarters or at a desirable location.

    b. *Leadership:* The company conference will be lead by a designated officer within the company. The company may contract for convention services to cover all the basic meeting details.

    c. *Participation:* Company employees will travel to the designated location, and this travel needs to be carefully coordinated. Usually, for such a large travel event, the company will utilize a travel service unless the organization is large enough to have its own travel department. Also, participants will include travel expenses to conferences in their yearly budget.

2. *Business association conference:* Many organizations and their employees are members of professional business associations that address issues and events of concern to their particular type of business. Marketing companies will be members of a national marketing association; accounting firms will be members of statewide and national accounting associations; manufacturers will belong to associations in their manufacturing area (auto, appliance, electronics, etc.), and so on. In most cases, the association not only convenes and discusses business issues, but also has legislative activists that promote legislation supportive of the business association's goals.

    a. *Location:* Business association meetings are typically held in preferred locations like major cities or attractive geographical locales. A facility that can adequately support conference needs for meeting space and lodging is a major consideration as well as the appeal of the conference location's area attractions to the attendees.

    b. *Leadership:* The business association has officers and often an entire independent staff with an executive director. The association president may be a member who is a high-ranking individual employed by an outside business member, but the executive director and association staff are employed by the association. They oversee the daily work of the association.

c. *Participation:* Participation varies from association to association, but it can include a wide range of administrative professionals, from entry level to top management. Most membership is based on the profession involved, rather than status in an organization. In some cases, there may be an organization of chief executive officers, or comptrollers, and so forth.

EXAMPLE: *A marketing association would potentially include all the marketing professionals in a company.*

3. *Professional association conference:* A professional is typically defined by the education and work experience required for membership. Originally, "professional" referred to a person who made a living at a specific task, such as someone who practiced law, medicine, dentistry, or someone who earned a living with a sport (as distinguished from amateur), such as golf, basketball, football, soccer, hockey, and so on. Today, professionals include anyone who is identified by a specialized vocation. This includes administrative professionals, teachers, college professors, writers, actuarial accountants, and so on. Now, most professions have distinct associations with rules for membership regular regional, national, and international conferences.

a. *Location:* Local, regional, national, and international meetings usually rotate location assignments for the major annual convention of the professional association. Particularly large associations in the United States, like the American Psychological Association, the American Medical Association, and the National Teachers Association, for instance, are so large that they must meet in large cities that can handle tens of thousands of participants.

EXAMPLE: *The International Association of Administrative Professionals is an international organization that brings its membership together at all levels, from local to the international.*

b. *Leadership:* Professional associations have a well-structured and often extensive leadership group. There may be a president, president-elect, and past president. There may also be several vice presidents. Like business associations, even small to medium professional associations may have year-round employed staff dedicated to one of the functions of the organization, such as running the convention, managing membership, monitoring legal issues, and supporting lobbying efforts. Similarly, an executive director may be in charge of this staff.

c. *Participation:* The association governs membership. There may be different levels, including regular members, associate members, student members, and retired members. All members of an association are typically invited to participate in the conference and work to be included in the governance of the association. Officers are formally elected at the conventions. Some organizations vote on or approve new members at their annual meetings. A roster of new members may be presented to the current members present at the business-meeting portion of the convention and elected in a pro-forma (merely a formality) vote.

4. *Community association conference:* Community associations are usually community service associations like the Rotary International, Jaycees, and the Optimist Club International, but service and support organizations like the Business and Professional Women's Association are service groups drawn from a specific sector of the workplace (like professional women). Each community organization has clearly stated missions and goals, and seeks members who share its service and support goals.

   a. *Location:* Community associations hold regular meetings, often weekly, at the level of the local organization. Regional, national, and international conventions are usually held annually, and the locations vary according to organizational preferences.

   b. *Leadership:* The local groups do all their own work, with duties assigned to officers like treasurers, program chairs, and the organization's president. These associations may be divided into local, district, regional, state or province, national, and international levels. All the major groups have permanent staff though the leadership is elected from members at the different levels. Professional staff typically manages the conventions.

   EXAMPLE: *Optimist International holds an annual convention in one of the major countries of the world, while each state and province in North America holds an annual meeting as well.*

   c. *Participation:* Some organizations require a predetermined level of participation in club activities throughout the year in order to qualify to attend a regional meeting. Others open their regional meetings to all levels.

   d. *Activities:* Different from the research presentations of professional conferences and the business trends and information of company sessions, the conventions of community service groups are focused on the mission of the service organization. They may include planning and training sessions for club-level activities, including membership drives, youth outreach, college scholarships, fund-raising drives, and so on.

3. *Informal Meetings:* An **informal meeting** can occur anywhere and at any time. Many meetings of this nature begin in the employee snack room during breaks and over lunch. Others occur in the hallway or in an office where a coworker has dropped by to "chat." Informal meetings are recognized as very crucial to individual and team creativity and innovation. Sometimes informal meetings are actually planned and occur on a regular basis. A work team may meet informally at the beginning or end of each work week to discuss progress toward the common goal.

   a. *Types of informal meetings:* There are several types of informal meetings. An informal meeting typically involves discussion of issues and may include a decision to act based on consensus.

      1. *Impromptu meeting:* Important but difficult to depend upon, the casual meeting that starts as a chance encounter in the break room may result in a good idea. It cannot be counted on to provide regular progress, however, and the productivity enhancements it may contribute are difficult to verify.

      2. *Committee meeting:* Many committees have a set time and agenda for meeting regularly, but they often provide a fertile ground for sharing all manner of information. A meeting can be informal even if it follows the agenda. It is the

responsibility of the chair to keep the meeting manageable. One danger is the tendency to drift to social concerns and issues, and sometimes even politics.

3. *Office meeting:* An employee evaluation may be delivered to an employee in an informal **office meeting.** An office meeting is a meeting that can be by appointment or unscheduled and involves two or more people in an office conferring on a particular task. It can be a private meeting between a supervisor and subordinate. The evaluation may be discussed and future expectations articulated, but the only official action is the transmittal of the written evaluation. Another office meeting may include several team members working on a specific problem, such as the finalization of a report. In this case, the team members may have already completed most of the project, and the meeting involves only a review and minor correction process. A third type of office meeting might be to discuss, in private, the conduct of an employee and make suggestions for improved performance. These types of meetings require privacy and confidentiality.

4. *Lunch or dinner meeting:* The informal meeting can occur anywhere, and often do occur over meals. The dining experience allows for informal discussion that can stray to social issues and concerns of personal interest. The evolving comfort allows people to be more candid and forthcoming, often leading to more productive outcomes. Each person in the group develops a clearer understanding of the work interests of the others, and can thereby address these issues. Problems that arise have more cordial resolutions when explored in an informal setting of entertainment.

b. *Actions of informal meetings:* A few activities can occur in informal meetings that make these meetings very efficient.

1. *Sharing ideas:* Informal meetings are an excellent place to share ideas without concern for whether or not they will be rejected. People will be more open in small group settings that proceed without formal actions, but instead involve discussion and brainstorming.

2. *Resolving issues:* Informal group meetings provide a nonthreatening environment for the resolution of conflict, issues, minor procedural and process problems, and related challenges to the success of a team or department.

3. *Identifying problems and issues:* Not only is the informal meeting a good place to resolve issues, it is also a good setting for identifying concerns, issues, and problems in the first place. Identification of an issue in this setting provides an opportunity for more rapid response than in a formal setting due to the impromptu nature of the informal meeting.

4. *Facilitating contributions:* Often informal meetings occur without the presence of a senior manager, so the intimidation factor of higher level supervisors may also be absent. The opportunity to engage in the free flow of ideas without having to check for agreement with the supervisor removes a major inhibiting factor in workplace innovation.

5. *Following up:* One of the pitfalls of the more informal meetings is the lack of a useful record. Few people take notes appropriately in the informal meeting—sometimes because they become highly involved in the conversation—so care must be taken to create the opportunity for follow-up and feedback. These can be easily handled if participants take a few notes immediately

after the meeting (especially if it occurs over a meal) or a note or two during the meeting. A follow-up communication, either an e-mail or a phone call, helps move the ideas from a meeting stage into an action process.

Check Point—Section A

Directions: For each question, circle the correct answer.

A–1. Which one of the following involves a formal meeting where a group is formed to investigate a particular event or problem within an organization?

    A) Standing committee
    B) Ad hoc committee
    C) Public forum
    D) Conference

A–2. Martinez wants to get professionals from a number of companies and agencies together to share ideas about a new innovation. The appropriate meeting format would be a/an

    A) informal meeting
    B) conference
    C) general meeting
    D) public hearing

A–3. Without an agenda or a regular meeting schedule, informal meetings

    A) tend not to be successful
    B) rarely get tasks finished
    C) allow the sharing of ideas freely
    D) have inconsistent follow-up

B. Purpose of Meetings

Meetings can be scheduled for a wide variety of purposes, ranging from the opportunity to obtain needed information to perform specific tasks to information relating to the organization of the company. Here are some of the primary purposes for using meetings as an important communication strategy within the organization.

1. *Information:* Meetings are held to present information to a group of people who have a common interest in this information. An informational meeting should be conducted by an executive or supervisor who is very knowledgeable about the matter and thus can pass along the information to the participants. Another important factor is the leader's ability to respond to questions that are asked about the information presented.

   a. *Types of information:* The types of information presented at meetings include the following:

      1. *Conveying information:* Meetings represent an excellent venue to disseminate information either as a report by the chair or a member assigned duties to report the information. The presenter can address questions and offer comments that may clarify the information and its impact.

      2. *Receiving reports:* Meetings provide an opportunity for the entire body to hear the work of a subcommittee. Often meetings are set as a place for several subcommittees to present reports and hear about the reports of other committees, and the entire meeting is a series of oral presentations of reports. External reports are often presented to a group in a meeting.

      3. *Explaining new procedures:* Another common type of information is that of procedural changes. Managers often call staff and workers together to hear

about new processes, procedures, schedules, goals, etc. A meeting is an efficient way to present such information, and questions can be answered quickly.

b. *Types of meetings:*

1. *Informal:* Informal informational meetings can be large, but usually will address one issue or a small set of information issues. Usually informal informational meetings are small group meetings.

   EXAMPLE: *A manager calls the department together to give copies of a new procedures manual to each unit and describe a few of the key changes.*

2. *Formal:* Formal informational meetings may follow strict guidelines required by the bylaws of a board, or they may follow a regular reporting cycle, like monthly progress reports. The formal nature of the meeting allows a larger slate of items to be covered. An agenda or list of topics is typically provided.

2. ***Evaluation or Performance Review:*** Meetings may be held between a manager and a subordinate to discuss the employee's ratings, salary increments, promotion, or possible transfer as a part of the organization's plans for evaluating employees. In addition, meetings are scheduled for a supervisor or a manager to discuss employees' evaluations with superiors.

   a. *Office meeting:* A performance review or an evaluation is almost always delivered in the context of an office meeting.

   b. *Informal review:* Fortunately, informal does not mean unimportant. A performance review or an evaluation is a serious matter, and the meeting is informal by nature of the discussion that occurs. Usually, the supervisor meets with the evaluated worker and reviews an evaluation that is prepared prior to the meeting. Discussion may lead to mutual agreement that results in changes in the final evaluation or performance rating.

3. ***Decision Making:*** Every level of the organizational hierarchy is involved in problem solving. Sometimes meetings are called so that people who are having difficulty in making a decision or solving a problem can call upon others in the organization with expertise in specific areas to help with the solution. Participatory management strategies include employees in some of the decision-making meetings that are scheduled within the firm.

   a. *Formal, organized processes:* Final decisions may follow a series of informal and formal meetings during which any number of issues have been discussed and resolved. However, most important decisions are made in more or less formal circumstances. Some companies employ techniques like total quality management or the quality circle because they provide an organized and formal process that leads to recommendations that can be accepted or rejected.

   b. *Informal processes:* Group meetings that explore solutions using brainstorming (see below) or even organized group problem-solving techniques are informal in nature, though they may result in formalized recommendations.

4. ***Inspiration:*** Meetings that are intended to motivate employees to become more enthusiastic and loyal to the firm or to be morale boosters are called *inspirational meetings.* Employees may be asked to perform unusual services or to get more involved in

company activities. Sales and marketing meetings are examples of inspirational meetings. At such meetings a common practice is to schedule an outside consultant or one of the top executives to present the inspirational message.

a. *Regular inspirational meetings:* Some companies have regular, daily, weekly, or monthly meetings that look and sound like pep rallies. At these pep rallies, employees who have reached targeted goals for performance, sales, productivity, and so on are recognized and applauded for their accomplishments. For this to be truly successful over time, there must be a sense of authenticity and felt appreciation.

b. *Occasional inspirational meetings:* Impromptu informal meetings can appear more authentic to the workers involved, and thus can inspire them more effectively.

EXAMPLE: *An impromptu pep talk just before the opening of a holiday shopping season can help emphasize crucial aspects of customer service and friendly atmosphere, thus improving sales and customer loyalty.*

5. ***Reorganization:*** When changes are being made in the organizational structure of the firm, the staff, or specific assignments that will affect employees, it is necessary to schedule a *reorganizational meeting.* Employees have the right to be informed about changes that affect their positions as well as the company.

a. *Types of reorganization that bring about change:*

1. *Merger:* Sometimes, reorganization occurs because of a merger, and departments may be redundant. Certainly, hierarchies of power will be realigned.

2. *Unit dissolution:* Some reorganization means that new departments will be formed and others will be dissolved.

3. *Unit rearrangement:* Reorganization may mean only a shifting of responsibilities and lines of reporting.

b. *Meetings everyone dreads:* Rarely do people look upon dramatic change as a good thing. People depend upon stability in their work and are often frightened by change that reorganization brings.

c. *Information as power:* The more informed the employees are, the more cooperative they hopefully will be when the changes are implemented.

d. *Required informal and formal meetings:* A series of formal and informal meetings are needed to assure employees that their concerns will be addressed during a reorganization process.

6. ***Education:*** Some meetings are held so that a select group of employees can learn new procedures, new information, or changed processes. Many organizations stress the importance of education for their employees and pay for all costs involved in education for employees. Sometimes in-company educators and trainers conduct these meetings, and other times they are conducted by outside professional consultants.

7. ***Brainstorming:*** A specific type of problem-solving meeting is the brainstorming meeting, which is used to generate as many solutions to a specific problem as possible. The meeting is held merely to generate ideas, with evaluation of these ideas later.

Check Point—Section B

Directions: For each question, circle the correct answer.

B–1. Evaluation or performance reviews are regularly conducted in

A) office meetings
B) inspirational meetings
C) unit rearrangement meetings
D) general meetings

C) performance review meetings
D) informal meetings

B–2. Regular meetings that look and feel like high school pep rallies are called

A) inspirational meetings
B) office meetings

B–3. Topics like merger, the dissolving of a unit, or the reorganization of a unit are discussed in what is called a/an

A) brainstorming meeting
B) educational meeting
C) inspirational meeting
D) reorganization meeting

C. How to Conduct Meetings

Administrative professionals, especially those at the level of manager, are frequently required to chair or lead a meeting in some way. Conducting a meeting requires calmness and fairness, and with a few thoughts given to planning and arranging the meeting, they can be very successful.

1. *Arranging and Planning:* Many factors must be considered in holding meetings for any of the foregoing purposes. Costs, planning, scheduling, presentation of issues, and techniques are some of the concerns that managers have in preparing for meetings.

   a. *Costs:* Meetings are costly to hold. The person in charge must consider the costs for materials and equipment, space utilization, outside speakers, transportation, and indirect costs that must be absorbed by the company as a result of the meeting. Such items as the time taken from the work of the people involved, the value of the information presented, and the frequency of meeting times are major concerns.

   b. *Planning:* Another important part of holding meetings is the planning that must precede any other action. To make sure that the meeting is effective, the planner must decide the why, who, when, where, and how of the meeting.

      1. *Purpose:* Why is it necessary for this meeting to be held? One of the problems managers have is "too many meetings." Sincere consideration should be given to other ways of communicating besides the meeting. A meeting is usually the response if other communications strategies would be less effective.

      2. *Participants:* The audience is very important. Who are the people who should participate in the meeting? The number of participants will influence the types and locations of facilities used for the meeting. Notices of the meeting must be sent out in advance so that all participants will have adequate information about the meeting.

3. *Date and time:* The scheduling of the meeting is of utmost importance. If the meeting is designed for a particular group of people, the person in charge will want to be sure that the meeting is scheduled at a time when these people can attend. Sometimes, meetings must be scheduled during regular working hours to ensure that the largest number of participants will be available.

4. *Location:* Conference rooms or meeting rooms located within the company may not be large enough to accommodate the number of people involved in the meeting. To have adequate space for the meeting, arrangements may need to be made with a local hotel or conference center. This is another reason why companies have very few general meetings.

Many organizations are now focusing attention on telecommunications and videoconferencing in scheduling meetings for people who are in diverse locations.

EXAMPLE: *The GenWay Company has 16 branch offices across the country. Bimonthly videoconferences are now providing the opportunity for people at all locations to meet without incurring travel expenses to get to the meeting. Specially equipped conference rooms in each branch office provide the communications technology needed to conduct the meetings (such as electronic blackboard and video recording equipment).*

5. *Meeting arrangements:* A number of questions need to be answered regarding the meeting. How will the meeting be conducted? What is the agenda? Will the arrangement of the room facilitate the kinds of discussion to go on during the meeting? Electronic technology with audiovisual components will be helpful in presenting information to the participants, especially if there is a large group. The use of handout materials during the meeting should be coordinated with the audiovisual presentation so that participants will be able to follow presentations easily.

EXAMPLE: *Presentation software enables the preparation of visual slides for computer projection during the meeting. In addition, the presenter can opt for copies of the visual images (in reduced format) for inclusion in a handout for participants. Sometimes extra space can be left to the side of the images for the participants to write notes or comments.*

c. *Scheduling:* Regular meeting dates and times should be coordinated within the company and announced to everyone. Conflicts in scheduling can arise easily, especially if people find out "on the spur of the moment" about meetings in which they are involved. Often, a week or two is adequate notice for a departmental or work group meeting. For a more formal meeting, one or two months may be required so that people can make plans to attend, especially if travel is involved.

d. *Presentation of issues:* Meetings are sometimes called to resolve issues that are complex. Adequate time needs to be scheduled in which to present the details so that everyone can understand the importance of the issue being presented. The manager who "does her or his homework" will have an easier time representing a complex issue than will one who comes unprepared. Time should also be scheduled to field and respond to questions that participants might have.

2. *Leading and Chairing Meetings:* The most critical role in managing any type of meeting is that of the chairperson, unit head, or team leader. The **chair** leads the meeting, keeping it on track, on time, and efficient. The chair diffuses tensions and encourages collaborative and supportive efforts.

    a. *Techniques for managing informal meetings:* Sometimes the chair of an informal meeting is the person charged with convening the meeting participants and reporting any recommendations or decisions made by the group to the person or office that asked for the meeting. Even the leading or chairing of informal meetings requires care if the meeting is to be successful. The following should be useful guides to informal meeting leadership:

        1. *Full participation:* Make sure that everyone is heard and each point of view is given full attention. Everyone should contribute; otherwise the noncontributors may not have their opinions included or they may be inappropriately included.

        2. *Negative tactics:* Quick management of the negative tactics some people employ will help the group reach its goal. Sometimes people use negative tactics when they cannot control the outcome themselves, and sometimes people are just pessimistic.

        3. *Summary and review:* A method of keeping the group on task and moving the group forward includes summarizing contributions and restating the ideas and points made by group members. The chair should check that all participants understand the points being made and the recommendations that the group will be making.

        4. *Distractions and negative attitudes:* The chair will be expected to cope with negative and/or distracting participants at the meeting. People who dominate the discussion must also be held in check, as people who do not contribute must be helped to understand their roles.

    b. *Techniques for managing formal meetings:* The manager should use certain techniques to increase the likelihood that the meeting will be effective.

        1. *Agenda:* An **agenda** is a plan for the meeting, with the items to be discussed during the meeting listed in order of presentation. Copies of the agenda should be distributed before the meeting so that participants will be aware of the business to be discussed and have an opportunity to suggest additional new business items.

        2. *Promptness:* Meetings should start and end at pre-announced times.

        3. *Stated times for agenda items:* It is helpful to assign the approximate amount of time to be allotted for each item on the agenda. Participants can gauge their remarks according to the time allotment.

        4. *Parliamentary procedure:* The use of parliamentary procedure keeps a formal meeting on target. Such procedures allow everyone an equal opportunity to be heard and provide the opportunity for all views and concerns to be aired. See the section on parliamentary procedure below.

        5. *Motions or ideas presented:* Motions must be stated correctly and in language that everyone understands. The presiding officer (or leader) of the meeting should repeat motions or ideas presented so that everyone present understands the meanings being conveyed.

6. *Summary:* A summary of the meeting should be prepared and distributed to all who attended, usually within one week. The major points of discussion, motions made, or ideas presented should be included so that everyone who attended will have a clear record of what transpired during the meeting.

7. *Minutes:* **Minutes** are a written record of the main points of a meeting and how members voted on motions and other actions, as well as a verbatim record of each motion statement. Minutes are kept by the secretary of the group.

Techniques such as these will help a meeting run smoothly and allow business to be transacted or information presented in an efficient manner. The more preplanning that goes into the meeting, the fewer number of problems there will be.

c. *Parliamentary procedure:* Formal meetings generally follow **parliamentary procedure,** a formal set of rules that guide the conduct of the meeting. Actions follow an agenda that is shared prior to the meeting. Some meetings must follow prescribed rules according to the group's bylaws. The most common set of rules used is that of *Robert's Rules of Order* (first published in 1876). The parliamentary procedures outlined in this handbook serve as the basis for acceptable parliamentary procedures followed in formal meetings. The chair should appoint a parliamentarian (someone who is familiar with parliamentary procedures), who will be responsible for ensuring that the meeting is conducted according to *Robert's Rules of Order.*

1. *Core principles of parliamentary procedures:* Meetings controlled using parliamentary procedure are first and foremost orderly examples of fairness and courtesy. The centerpiece of the procedure is that one item will be discussed at a time, and both minority and majority views are heard. Typically, everyone has a right to speak. To allow all to speak, however, time limits should be set. Sometimes the time is allotted to each person, sometimes to each side, and sometimes for discussion of the topic. Rules govern every aspect of the discussion and voting.

   EXAMPLE: *Jones offers a motion to limit debate to three minutes per member. Smith seconds the motion. After discussion, the chair calls for a vote.*

2. *Actions resulting from motions:* Action can occur only following a motion, the formal statement of the proposed action. Other activities of the formal meeting include reports from subcommittees and officers (like the treasurer). Usually a meeting involves approving the agenda, approving the minutes, hearing and accepting reports (by vote), new and old business, and adjournment. Items brought to the meeting as a part of a regular report are considered motions, and they do not need a second. A second to a motion affirms that at least one other member is interested in considering the proposed action. A motion must be made by a voting member who has secured the floor by being recognized by the presiding officer for the meeting. If a second to the motion is required, the motion must receive a second by a voting member other than the member making the motion. Nonvoting, ex officio members may participate in the discussion, but they may not vote.

   a. *Types of motions:* The agenda governs the order of discussion of items. They are discussed each in turn, and the chair keeps discussion focused on the item that is "on the table." Reports are considered motions, so discussion begins as soon as the report is complete. For other motions, a motion is first made and seconded, and then the group discusses the item.

There are five different types of motions: main motions, subsidiary motions, incidental motions, privileged motions, and unclassified motions.

(i) *Main motions:* A *main motion* is a motion that states an item of business. The motion can be debated and amended. Amendments are motions, and they must be voted upon prior to the main motion. Subsidiary motions can interrupt the action being considered on the main motion.

EXAMPLES:

Jones: I move that we accept the plan to increase membership through a membership drive.

Smith: I second the motion.

(ii) *Subsidiary motions:* A *subsidiary motion* may support, modify, or dispose of the main motion. The body must act upon a subsidiary motion before continuing with any other activity. The subsidiary motion may be: to table a motion (to lay aside the item and motion until later); to call for the vote; to refer the motion to a specific committee for further consideration; to amend a main motion; or to postpone action on a motion indefinitely.

(iii) *Incidental motions:* Like a subsidiary motion, an *incidental motion* requires immediate action. However, it must be introduced before the main motion to which it applies is decided. One cannot have a motion to table a main motion if that main motion has already been passed. Common incidental motions are (1) to suspend a rule temporarily, (2) to close or reopen nominations, (3) to raise a point of order, (4) to modify or withdraw a motion, and (5) to appeal a decision make by the chair.

(iv) *Privileged motions:* Recess, adjournment, setting a meeting time, and dealing with an interruption are motions called *convenience motions.* They are related to the comfort of the group and must be acted upon immediately and thus take precedence over all other motions.

(v) *Unclassified motions:* Taking a motion from the table, reconsidering a motion, and making a motion asking the group to rescind (change its vote) are motions considered *unclassified.*

(vi) *Quorum:* The organizational bylaws specify the number of voting members who must be present in order for business to be conducted. Usually a quorum is half the voting membership plus one, but sometimes a group may require two-thirds of membership to be present. This number is called a *quorum.*

d. *Meeting chair:* The chair of a meeting is the person in charge who has been given the authority to manage the meeting, enforce rules, keep order, and direct others to perform supportive roles. The role is important for the success of the meeting.

1. *Chair selection:* The first order of business for any formal and most informal meetings is the selection of a chair or leader.

2. *Characteristics of a chair:* This person must be able to gain the respect of all meeting attendees. Also, experience with leading meetings is helpful. The leadership characteristics associated with being chair of a group that meets

regularly include conscientiousness with regard to planning and executing plans, keeping others informed, excellent listening skills, responsiveness to the interests of others, and so on.

3. *Basic chair actions:* The following items summarize duties that the chairs of committees are expected to assume. Someone who chairs the meeting (if the regular chair is absent) would be required to undertake only items (f) through (i):

   a. Set meeting time and place.

   b. Notify participants in a timely manner.

   c. Monitor the preparation of materials to be shared at the meeting.

   d. Confirm plans to attend the meeting.

   e. Prepare the agenda.

   f. Start and end the meeting on time.

   g. Provide a summary of recommendations and review of motions, checking for understanding and agreement.

   h. Review the minutes and send them to participants for review prior to the next meeting (the group will approve the minutes at the next meeting).

   i. Confirm time for the next meeting and remind participants of any follow-up assignments and due dates.

e. *Responsibilities of the chair:* In addition to performing the basic actions necessary to guide a meeting from setting the time and place through to monitoring follow-up assignments, the chair of a meeting has several other important responsibilities.

   1. *Know the membership:* If possible, the chair should research the members of the group so that familiarity is established with their interests, personal style (are they shy or are they outgoing?), and office politics. If the chair knows the other projects on which members are working, the chair may be able to discern the level of participation that will be comfortable for them, and possibly understand prior to making assignments the specific or special interests they have.

   2. *Be prepared with appropriate research:* A knowledgeable chair is a powerful chair. If the chair is charged with a task that requires information about a new procedure, new manufacturing process, or new service, the chair can be prepared with current research to help inform the participants and speed the work of the meeting.

   3. *Employ effective people skills:* At all times, a chair must be an effective listener and a diplomat. Those who speak must be allowed to have their say, yet prevented from monopolizing others. An effective listening skill for meetings is the ability to restate the issues and concerns expressed by others in brief, concise terms. Restating should ensure that others understand the points being made and demonstrate that the contributor is being given full opportunity to make contributions. Another important personal skill is that of flexibility. Things happen that may affect the progress of the meeting (an accident, an illness, or worse). Flexibility may be invoked to postpone the meeting or end it abruptly.

   EXAMPLE: *Cano was in a committee meeting at 9:30 A.M. eastern standard time on September 11, 2001. The cochairs of the committee, who had not completely informed everyone of the purpose of the meeting and who were very disorganized, continued the meeting until noon. No one paid any attention.*

Having an interruption like the terrorist attacks on 9/11 is very uncommon; however, as we experienced, it does happen. For sure, whatever the meeting was about, it could have been continued the next day (no one was going anywhere, anyway).

4. *Manage distractions and control tactics of others:* The single toughest duty faced by a chair is to cope with one or more participants who dominate the process. This can include the "know-it-all," a person who has an answer for everything and an example for every circumstance. Another control tactic includes subterfuge by confusion—someone who does not seem to be keeping with the agenda and regularly goes back and forth on the list. These are just two tactics that might appear. Other tactics are discussed in the following section on resolving group conflict.

5. *Keep the meeting on track and on time:* Pacing a meeting is one of the greater challenges to a new chair. Often people will either try to rush through an agenda or stall the meeting with distractions or sidetracked issues. Invariably someone will be unhappy with actions taken in past meetings and try to return the meeting to the now past topic. Many of these efforts are quite innocent, yet they reflect the concerns of the members involved.

6. *Acknowledge the efforts of members:* One way to encourage group solidarity is to recognize the contributions of others and use praise as often as seems reasonable. Acknowledge the efforts even if they may have caused distraction. The distraction may not have been intentional, and the acknowledgment can remind the distracter of the goal of the group.

f. *Control of meeting progress:* The primary duty of the chair is to manage the progress of a meeting. This requires keeping the meeting on track, observing the reactions of participants, focusing the discussion, and reaching conclusions.

1. *Keep the meeting on track:* Both a formal and informal meeting should start on time and end on time. A formal meeting should follow the agenda as closely as possible, while an informal meeting may stray from an action list or agenda without harming the meeting goal. However, both formal and informal meetings can be side tracked onto topics that are not relevant to the meeting goals. The chair should remind participants of the topic being discussed when the discussion begins to depart from the focus.

   a. *Summarize regularly:* Summarize the progress of a long meeting at regular intervals, such as when moving from one agenda item to the next. This can help keep everyone focused.

   b. *Give breaks in long meetings:* Meetings that extend more than 90 minutes require breaks. A two-hour meeting, for instance, should have a break at 60 minutes.

   c. *Watch the cycle of interest:* Participants are eager and receptive at the beginning, tired and ready to move on at the end.

   d. *Pace the meeting:* Sometimes the chair will need to move the meeting more quickly, perhaps by skipping items that are not essential or that can be tabled until the next meeting. Skip those items only if everyone agrees that they can be dealt with later.

2. *Watch for nonverbal communication:* Participants will express themselves nonverbally before making positive or negative verbal responses. Watch for the negative signs and help diffuse negative reactions by giving an opportunity to be heard. Positive responses can be used to strengthen a current point or even redirect and refocus the discussion. Negative expressions can forecast stronger reactions if not dealt with quickly.

   a. *Watch for potential contributors:* Sometimes people are eager to speak, but they cannot break into an ongoing debate or dialog. They will have many nonverbal signals, so the chair should ask for a pause in the debate at an appropriate moment and ask for input from the eager participant.

   b. *Watch for withdrawn noncontributors:* Oftentimes a participant is not comfortable with making a contribution. These individuals should be given an opportunity to respond, but should not be forced into the discussion.

3. *Stop private conversations:* Rude as they may be, someone always has additional side comments to make about any topic. A chair can end these with a simple comment about giving everyone a chance to be heard or a comment about respecting the meeting process itself.

4. *Use the powers of the chair to keep order:* The chair can use a number of simple tactics to maintain or regain order. They include:

   a. *Identify a breach of order:* When people talk out of turn, carry on private discussions, raise irrelevant points, and otherwise alter the order, the chair can stop the discussion and refocus the meeting. One method is to ask the out-of-order individual to make the point relevant to the agenda item or defer to a relevant time in the meeting.

   b. *Defuse arguments by taking control:* If an argument becomes heated, stop the discussion and restate the points as they are understood and without any personal or emotional tone. Check that the two sides agree with the description. If they do not, the chair can ask that the points be put in writing for later review.

   c. *Adjourn the meeting:* The chair can adjourn the meeting, or a member can make a motion for adjournment. An **adjournment** stops the meeting activity for a specified period of time. It can be for a brief break, for another day, or indefinitely. A 30-minute break may allow tempers to cool and reason to return. A day or two may allow for the points to be researched and supported in a reasonable rather than emotional manner. A complete adjournment without setting a new meeting time effectively ends the work of the meeting. This last option should be used only in the most irretrievable circumstances.

5. *Create a subcommittee:* When complex issues develop, or new concerns are introduced, a simple and effective tactic for the chair is to create a subcommittee that will examine the topic and report back at the next meeting or a meeting in the near future. If it involves a debate, ask a neutral party to chair the subcommittee and be sure that representatives from the differing sides are on the subcommittee.

3. **Resolving Conflicts within Meetings:** At times people will disagree in a meeting situation. Disagreement can have a positive effect, resulting in some needed change. Or disagreement can lead to conflict, with the result being very negative. Conflict can cause communication to deteriorate and people to become openly hostile toward each other. The goals of a meeting in which conflict occurs cannot be achieved effectively.

   a.   *Types of conflict:* Conflict can occur when people disagree about the topics being discussed, when people genuinely dislike each other, or when both of these situations are present.

     1. *Topic conflict:* Two people like each other, but they disagree on the topic being discussed.

     2. *Interpersonal conflict:* Two people dislike each other, but they agree about the topic being discussed.

     3. *Combination or multilevel conflict:* Two people dislike each other, and they disagree about the topic being discussed.

   b.   *Problems that occur in meetings:* Several types of problems occur regularly in meetings and have several options that will be effective in reducing the conflict. They include:

     1. *Unprepared participants:* For one reason or another, a key participant may arrive at the meeting unprepared to make a report or deliver an assignment made prior to the meeting. The chair can cope with this by:

        a. *Delay the report:* The report can be delayed until the next meeting or the person can submit it in writing. Reminding the person before the entire committee may help encourage more effective participation.

        b. *Appointing another participant:* Another person may more effectively complete the task. Also, the chair can appoint someone to supervise the action.

     2. *Sabotage:* Some people may not want the action of the meeting to be complete. They will undermine the work of the group by "ambush" or another form of **sabotage.** Sabotage generally refers to any obstruction of work or other normal operations.

        a. Isolate the saboteur.

        b. Adjourn the meeting.

        c. Eject the ambusher from the meeting.

     3. *Direct challenge:* Usually this type of action has a purpose, but it can be one of many things, like wanting to take control and redirect the meeting to another purpose, or even being angry at not being put in charge.

        a. Remind the challenger of the purpose of the meeting.

        b. Draw attention to the inappropriate behavior and ask for the common courtesy of respect.

        c. Use humor.

4. *Breakdown of control:* Many actions can result in serious **breach of order,** sometimes they are accidental, sometimes humorous, and sometimes a result of anger. Accidents and humorous events can be handled smoothly, while anger presents a problem.

Breach of order occurs when rules are ignored or not followed, someone speaks out of turn, or when the decorum of the meeting is lost.

a. Call for order.

b. Ask the angry person to leave and calm down before returning.

c. Adjourn the meeting.

c. *Resolution of conflict:* Other kinds of conflict may develop in addition to the four specific types just described. This conflict often results from differing views. Business to be conducted during a meeting can be stalled as a result of conflict. Therefore, conflict must be resolved. Here are some basic steps used to resolve conflict:

1. *Fact-finding:* Do the people in conflict disagree with the topic, or do they dislike each other, or both?

2. *Isolating factors creating the conflict:* It may be necessary to move to the next agenda topic rather than trying to solve the conflict at this time. This depends upon how heated the argument might be. A compromise might be discussed to bring out the elements that are important to each individual.

3. *Defusing the causes:* The presiding officer (or leader) must take steps to ensure that a similar conflict will not occur again. More information about the particular topics can be gathered and disseminated to the participants so that they will understand the topic better. Interpersonal differences will take a little longer to resolve.

Conflict must be resolved for the business at hand to move forward. The causes of the conflict must be determined for final resolution to take place.

Check Point—Section C

Directions: For each question, circle the correct answer.

C–1. Which one of the following items should be available prior to the meeting?

A) Motions to be presented
B) Parliamentary procedure
C) Summary
D) Agenda

C–2. Meeting chairs use parliamentary procedure to control a meeting so that

A) motions will be passed
B) minutes will be read

C) one item will be discussed at a time
D) majority speakers will be heard first

C–3. Jones is chairing a meeting in which two members begin arguing angrily with each other. To regain control, Jones should

A) use humor
B) adjourn the meeting
C) call for order
D) table the motion

For Your Review

Directions: For each question, circle the correct answer.

Case 1: Meetings to Go

Goliath Hotels International has been so successful at marketing its business centers to hotel guests that it has expanded its service to nonguests. Each business center has all the necessary office equipment; and the adjacent meeting rooms can be configured for any type of meeting, from a small informal meeting of a company and client representatives to major, international conferences. Rankin manages one of these centers for Goliath. Rankin guides a small staff, called the business team, and tries to meet each customer's needs without any complications. Some local entrepreneurs have abandoned having an office of their own because Rankin and the business team can offer the occasional space they need more economically. In fact, Rankin has expanded the team to include temporary office personnel to type, file, and serve as receptionists for these local business people.

Meetings appear to be a specialty for the Goliath business support teams, and with just a short description, Rankin can configure the meeting to fit the clients' needs exactly.

1. Global Industries has decided to expand the annual meeting of its management staff to include shareholders and a board meeting. Rankin will need to prepare for what is called a/an

   A) external general meeting
   B) conference
   C) general meeting
   D) public hearing

2. The local city and county government is planning to form a merged municipal government. Neither the city nor the county has a facility large enough to accommodate open meetings with citizens from both the city and the county in attendance, so they turn to Goliath Hotels. A meeting space is needed that includes microphones for the public to ask questions and make comments. The type of meeting being planned by the merger group is called a/an

   A) external general meeting
   B) public rally
   C) public forum
   D) conference

3. A national teacher organization plans a meeting for which all its membership is invited. Textbook and instructional aid vendors will also attend and set up displays. This type of meeting is called a/an

   A) company-sponsored conference
   B) business association conference
   C) professional association conference
   D) community association conference

4. The idea to provide administrative, receptionist, and clerical support to locate businesses came from Rankin talking with the owner of a temporary service. Immediately after that encounter, Rankin assembled the entire staff to talk about the idea. This meeting would be called a/an

   A) committee meeting
   B) impromptu meeting
   C) business conference
   D) general meeting

5. After each meeting with a client, the client completes an evaluation. Rankin reviews each evaluation and discusses the results with each staff member individually. This type of meeting is called a/an

   A) office meeting
   B) evaluation meeting
   C) committee meeting
   D) impromptu meeting

Case 2: Better Body Works, Incorporated

The personal health and hygiene company, Better Body Works, Incorporated, holds monthly executive meetings attended by department and division heads. Some of the attendees are present via teleconference technology that connects them with those physically present at headquarters in a technology-equipped conference room. Ramsey is responsible for preparing the meeting agenda and delivering packets of information to all participants. The regular executive meeting is often preceded by a series of less formal planning meetings. The costly time of the executives is considered too valuable to waste on unproductive meetings. Many kinds of activity can take place during the meetings including external vendors making presentations, special project reports, and discussion of regular business cycle issues. Ramsey briefs the external presenters so that their presentations will mesh with the technology. Ramsey must also establish ground rules for anyone presenting materials to the group.

6. The monthly meeting of the department and division heads at Better Body Works is most similar to a typical

   A) business conference
   B) external general meeting
   C) board meeting
   D) departmental meeting

7. Since the main business of the monthly meeting is to convey reports, hear proposals from internal and external presenters, and explain new procedures, the main purpose of the meeting would be considered

   A) decision making
   B) information
   C) inspiration
   D) evaluation

8. The informal meetings that Ramsey conducts with external vendors prior to their making presentations at the monthly executive meetings have the purpose of

   A) performance review
   B) inspiration
   C) brainstorming
   D) education

9. After any meeting in which a problem occurs—whether it is with technology, someone talking too long, or any confusing incident—Ramsey gathers the staff in an impromptu and informal session in which anyone can offer analysis or solutions. The central purpose of this session would be

   A) brainstorming
   B) inspiration
   C) information
   D) education

10. Which one of the following represents a common pitfall of informal meetings that may occur at the Goliath Hotel business center?

   A) Inability to share ideas
   B) Intimidation by senior managers
   C) Lack of a useful record
   D) Failure to identify concerns

Case 3: Meeting Manners

Gracy's Department Stores, Incorporated has a division at its headquarters with a primary task of planning the inventory and promotions for each annual season, for holidays, and for special sales periods. Every Monday at 10 A.M., department head Douglas holds a staff meeting.

These events are notorious for digression, rancor, and ambiguous results. Robinson, for instance, likes to talk about every issue. Gutierrez has a set of pet peeves that somehow always enter the discussion. Quire interrupts someone at almost every meeting with what sounds like irrelevant ideas that require lengthy explanation. Oleka will raise an issue, get an answer, and then raise the issue again later in the meeting. People suspect Hughes of being an alcoholic, and sometimes Hughes's comments become overexaggerated and almost belligerent. Douglas wants to take control and has asked Gaines to help devise some methods for better meeting management.

11. Gaines notes that Douglas lists a couple of items on a whiteboard and then starts the meeting. Gaines suggests that Douglas would be more successful if the meeting had a/an

   A) summary
   B) agenda
   C) follow-up
   D) prompt beginning

12. Which one of the following should Gaines recommend as a means of keeping participants focused on the meeting agenda?

   A) Stated times for listed items
   B) Repeating motions
   C) Parliamentary procedures
   D) New location

13. To cope with Oleka, Gaines recommends

   A) allowing discussion only after a motion has been made
   B) summarizing what each person has said

   C) asking Oleka to record the minutes
   D) having stated times for each item and sticking to them

14. Which one of the following participants does Gaines recommend that Douglas ask to leave when his or her typical behavior reoccurs?

   A) Hughes
   B) Oleka
   C) Quire
   D) Robinson

15. Which one of the following participants engages in a breach of order that could be solved by Douglas asking to make the point relevant?

   A) Hughes
   B) Gutierrez
   C) Quire
   D) Robinson

Solutions

Solutions to Check Point—Section A

Answer:	Refer to:
A–1. (B)	[A-1-a-(3)-(b)]
A–2. (B)	[A-2-a]
A–3. (C)	[A-3-b-(1)]

Solutions to Check Point—Section B

Answer:	Refer to:
B–1. (A)	[B-2-a]
B–2. (A)	[B-4]
B–3. (D)	[B-5-a]

Solutions to Check Point—Section C

Answer:	Refer to:
C–1. (D)	[C-2-b-(1)]
C–2. (C)	[C-2-c-(1)]
C–3. (C)	[C-3-b-(4)-(a)]

Solutions to For Your Review

Answer:	*Refer to:*

Case 1:

1. (A)   [A-1-a-(1)-(b)]
2. (C)   [A-5-b]
3. (C)   [A-2-b-(3)]
4. (B)   [A-3-a-(1)]
5. (A)   [A-3-a-(3)]

Case 2:

6. (D)   [A-1-a-(2)]
7. (B)   [B-1]
8. (D)   [B-6]
9. (A)   [B-7]
10. (C)   [A-3-b-(5)]

Case 3:

11. (B)   [C-2-b-(1)]
12. (C)   [C-2-c]
13. (D)   [C-2-b-(3)]
14. (A)   [C-3-b-(4)]
15. (A)   [C-2-f-(4)-(a)]

Chapter 10
Communication

OVERVIEW

Management succeeds only through effective communication. A sender communicates a message to a receiver. The receiver acknowledges having received the message, completing the feedback loop. This communication cycle takes many forms. Effective communication within organizations requires the use of many forms. Some organizational communication must take place in person, whereas other communication must include a written form, such as an employee evaluation. Successful human relations among people in organizations depends upon good communication skills. Quality and productivity also depend in large part on the good communication skills of employees, managers, and executives. Successful business and organizational practices depend upon effective communication between the organization and its clients.

Beyond the basics of communication are many subtle, yet powerful nonverbal means of strengthening communications. Since the manager must frequently be the receiver of a message, nonverbal listening skills are critical. Formal presentations require careful attention to the nonverbal aspect of communication if the goal of the presentation is to be achieved.

As the use of new communication technologies continues to increase in organizations, personal communication skills will have a greater role in contributing to individual success. Communication skills increase the effectiveness of relationships within the organization.

KEY TERMS

A. Understanding Communication

Communication is the successful transmission of a message between a source and a receiver. Usually the source is a person—a sender—who is trying to send the message; the receiver is the person listening to the message. The success of the sender, the clarity of the message, and the effectiveness of the receiver depend on many factors that shape the basic communication process. Managerial communication is a special case because of the specificity of the role of communication. Not only is the sender attempting to send a clear message, but the desired goal is to control or manage the actions of the audience to an extent not common in other communication contexts.

1. *Communication as a Process:* By its nature, communication requires that information move from one place to another. This information begins at a source. The source gives form to information, shaping a message that can be sent through some medium. The information arrives at its target, a receiver. For the most part, the source and the receiver are people, and the message usually takes the form of language. But, there is more to communication than language. The basic model of communication involves two or more people talking to each other; at times one sends and the other receives, then roles may switch. All communication must have some form of a source, some form of a message, and some form of a receiver. Feedback informs the sender that communication has occurred. This process is illustrated in Figure 10–1.

    a. *The source:* Fortunately, most communication sources are human speakers. There are some very easily identified sources that are not people, however. A poorly maintained machine may produce too many rejected parts. A worker may decipher the quality problem by examining the messages the machine has been sending. Signals from nonhuman sources, like the marketplace, are equally meaningful. A market specialist must find the hidden messages that customers may send. The organizational "lines of communication" also support certain kinds of messages and responsibilities for communicating. For instance, the job position of floor manager in a department store may carry the communication responsibility for handling difficult customers.

        1. *Sender:* The **sender** is responsible for encoding the message in a manner that can be decoded by the receiver.

        2. *Encoding:* **Encoding** refers to putting information into a form or code that can be sent and understood by the receiver. Making a thought into a sentence

FIGURE 10–1   A Model of Communication. The sender encodes the message; the message is sent; the receiver decodes the message. The receiver then becomes a sender and encodes feedback (a message) that the first sender uses to check whether the original message was properly decoded. Source: Mark Garrison and Margaret Anne Bly-Turner, *Human Relations: Productive Approaches for the Workplace* (Boston: Allyn & Bacon Publishers, 1997), 35.

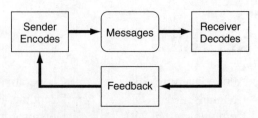

Feedback becomes a Message, and the Sender and Receiver switch roles.

requires that the thought be encoded into language. Converting a thought into a typed memorandum requires encoding in language and in the particular form of written and typed documents. Encoding may also mean using special symbols to make the message meaningful to others.

> EXAMPLE: *A government employee might be required to encode a device as a "non-mechanical instrument for the manual installation or deinstallation of metal alloy fastening units." To a carpenter, the device is a hammer. A carpenter on a government contract might have great difficulty ordering a hammer without the government supplied "lexicon of encrypted common nomenclature" (that is, dictionary).*

b. *The message:* A **message** is the specific physical form given to information so that it can sent to a receiver.

   1. *Channels:* The message can be transmitted over one of three basic types of communication modalities or **channels:** oral, written, or nonverbal. Most interpersonal communication occurs with a mixture of these three channels.

   2. *Channel effects:* Each channel has particular advantages and disadvantages, and understanding them is important for human communications to be effective. How the channels are used and how the message is encoded will reflect the skills, knowledge, personality, and cultural background of the sender.

c. *The receiver:* The **receiver** is the target of a message.

   1. *Decoding:* The receiver must decode the encoded message. Proper **decoding** requires that the receiver determine how the message was encoded, why it was sent, and what to do with it once it is received. Decoding requires listening or reading and placing the message in context.

   2. *Context:* The context changes the meaning. Just as the message is affected by the sender's level of skill, knowledge, and background, the receiver is limited by the same factors.

   > EXAMPLE: *A manager walking the floor late on a warm afternoon shouting "Wake up" is saying the same thing that a talking alarm clock is saying.*

d. *Feedback:* When a message is received, the receiver usually acknowledges the message by providing some form of feedback. **Feedback** is itself a message back to the sender acknowledging the original message. An energetic "We're awake" may satisfy the manager, but the alarm clock will require a finger on the snooze button. Feedback completes the circle of information, allowing the sender to determine if the message was properly decoded by the receiver. This completed circuit is often called a feedback loop to suggest the interactive quality of most communication.

2. ***The Goals of Communication:*** To understand a message, the receiver must know the goal of the sender's attempt to communicate.

a. *Personal and organizational communication:* There are two basic arenas of communication: personal and organizational.

   1. *Personal communication:* Personal communication takes place usually between two or more people acting as individuals. It may take many other forms such as an e-mail, a phone call, a smile, and the like. The sender of a personal communication seeks to affect the feelings of or get a response from another individual.

2. *Organizational or managerial communication:* The organizational arena may involve personal communication at times, but it differs from personal communication in that the goals of the organization are the underlying reason for organizational and managerial communication. Without knowing the goal we might misunderstand the message.

b. *Four goals of communication:* There are four possible goals of organizational communication:

1. *Convey information:* Daily production goals, goals for quality, work schedules, changes in regulations, news, local current events, and news about other employees are but a few of the kinds of messages that serve to inform people. In organizations, employees depend upon information. Providing current and accurate information is one way an organization can increase employees participation in its goals. Knowing how well the company performed yesterday and hearing the forecasts for today's performance help each employee realize personal involvement in the success. This communication assists the employee in being part of the organization while conveying information. The employee now also shares responsibility for continuing the success.

2. *Direct and control action:* Control is a core management function. When supervisors announce goals for the day, they not only communicate information but they also control behavior. The communication directs and controls actions throughout the organization. There are many ways action can be controlled.

a. *Instruct:* Managers use communications to let people know what they must do in their jobs and how they need to perform specific tasks.

b. *Assist in problem solving:* Managers and subordinates can engage in give-and-take discussion sessions to help solve problems more effectively.

EXAMPLE: *One common approach in manufacturing to minimize waste and warehouse costs is by delivering materials and component parts on a just-in-time basis. This means that suppliers must know and adjust to demands daily (and now, in the electronic era, even more often). The flow of information from customer orders, to the manufacturer, and then to suppliers becomes critical in this approach.*

3. *Motivate:* There are many ways to motivate people to perform. A financial reward is just one. Money is a kind of message: it encodes the value of our work in a physical form. Making people feel that they are part of a process, making their sense of personal success part of the corporate success, also motivates.

4. *Express feelings:* Feelings comprise a very complicated set of expressions that range from subtle moods to strong moods such as love, anger, or hostility. Senders add feelings to every message sent. In fact, to hear a message that appears to be without feelings may arouse suspicion. Feelings have both verbal and nonverbal means of expression.

a. *Feelings and goals:* Motivation toward a goal is greatly enhanced when strong feeling, such as loyalty or belongingness, is associated with the goal.

b. *Group affiliation:* Group affiliation is supported by emotional ties, and these must be communicated.

EXAMPLE: *At Motorola, focus groups were used to measure how employees would react to a drug-testing policy. Knowledge of these potential reactions became the foundation for the design of a thorough and appropriate plan of communication to convince employees to accept the policy.*

c. *Effect of goals on both the sender and receiver:* The goal of any particular communication affects both the behavior of the sender and the receiver. When correcting performance errors, the tone and form of a message will differ depending on whether one is correcting a trainee or disciplining a veteran employee. This is true even though the sender's goal of controlling action will be the same for both. How a message is communicated can shape both the sender and the receiver. Politeness usually brings a polite response. Rudeness usually brings rudeness. Indifference generally is met with indifference. The verbal and nonverbal modes used to send messages are the topics of the next section. The character of a message depends upon whether the message is communicated orally, in written form, or through the nonverbal channels.

3. ***Two Basic Factors in Shared Communication:*** Two factors that help determine the amount of information that is shared by the sender and the receiver are common ground and the cooperative principle. When little is shared between people, more effort must be given to developing a basis for communicating. Further, more background information is required.

EXAMPLE: *In an organization like Motorola, the policy of no drug use is understood by employees as a means of identifying and helping people. In an organization with less concern for people, the expectations would be that a drug-abusing employee would be fired rather than helped. Knowledge of which action—helping the employee rehabilitate or firing the employee—would be more likely if an organization requires having an awareness of the company's values. Values are one of many aspects that form the basis of shared information.*

a. *Common ground:* **Common ground** includes the assumptions that we make about each other, about our mutual interests, about shared values, and about our awareness of individual interests.

1. *Daily interaction:* Often, people will talk about work with their coworkers when they meet away from the office. To "outsiders," such as spouses, the discussion will appear fragmented and very short of details.

2. *Shared body of knowledge:* The coworkers share a large body of information that has accumulated in their work setting, and the spouses do not share this information.

3. *Shared assumptions:* Common ground assumptions may get in the way when one person assumes that the other has similar interests because they work in the same place.

EXAMPLES:

If a labor union is about to take an action or negotiate a contract, one worker may approach another with the assumption that the other is in agreement with the union. The worker may begin to complain about the behavior of the management.

Couples talk about their children to each other so much that they assume other couples are interested in hearing all the wild stories that have preoccupied parents for generations.

4. *Crucial role of common ground:* For the most part, though, common ground is very useful because it relieves the speaker of having to account for every detail. When a common ground exists, communication becomes very efficient. In a business environment, the common ground of the employees may be established by management attitudes and corporate culture.

b. *The cooperative principle:* The **cooperative principle** is the belief that someone speaking is making an honest attempt to be understood. The assumption of cooperation between people who are talking to each other is so fundamental that it goes unnoticed. The value of the principle is best seen in cases where it is violated. Unfortunately, there are times when someone in a group is unwilling to participate or believes that the group process has no value. The unwilling participant may sabotage the activity by asking questions or making points that seem to have no relevance to the activity.

1. *Failure to cooperate increases suspicion:* When an official of an organization appears to be communicating only part of the truth or a limited amount of information, those who hear become suspicious. The speaker may be deliberately giving vague responses to avoid sharing information considered sensitive or privileged in some way. This violation of the cooperative principle is interpreted nonverbally, and people begin to hear "what was not said."

2. *Cooperation is critical for success:* If an organization seeks to involve employees in participatory management, its communication with the employees cannot violate the cooperative principle which is the basis for mutual and open exchange. When one side holds back, there is a tendency for the other to hold back as well.

c. *Common ground, the cooperative principle, and nonverbal communication:* Common ground and the cooperative principle are fairly important for the sending and receiving of verbal (oral and written) communication. However, they are critical aspects of the communication that occurs nonverbally. Gestures, body movement, facial expression, space, timing, eye contact, and vocal inflection all have common ground based on the extent of shared experiences.

EXAMPLE: *A sigh will be made with the intent of others hearing it and understanding its meaning.*

4. *Listening:* Listening is the primary receiver role in communication. Listening is also the most critical form of nonverbal communication. Successful organizations have managers, employees, and executives who are good listeners.

a. *The critical nonverbal role of receiver:* Effective management requires a significant amount of careful listening. Research has estimated that managers spend 45 percent or more of their time listening and only about 30 percent talking. Good speakers are not necessarily good listeners. It takes more effort to listen than to talk, and communication absolutely depends upon someone listening. Effective listening requires practice and can improve with training.

1. *The manager as receiver:* Managers must recognize the role of listening. As a receiver, the manager must do more than merely listen. Feedback must be used to indicate that the receiver understands the message. Nonverbal behavior must indicate continued interest and attention.

2. *Attending skills and effective listening:* Effective listening is accompanied by skills that convey the receiver's physical attention to the speaker. These include:

    a. *Posture:* Posture is part of body language. Positive attending skill posture is open, relaxed, alert, and focused on the speaker (leaning toward if sitting).

    b. *Physical distance:* The physical space appropriate to the formality of the communication. Personal space (proxemics) will be discussed later in this chapter.

    c. *Eye contact:* Appropriate eye contact includes focus on the speaker, but without staring or looking away for extended periods.

    d. *Barrier reduction:* How one controls the environment is also an aspect of attending to the speaker. Every distraction is a possible barrier. Calls should be held, the door closed, cell phones and e-mails alerts turned off. Attention to these details strengthens the attention one can give to the speaker.

    These four attending skills are part of the broader concern of nonverbal communication and will be described below. They also support the task of active listening.

  b. *Active listening versus passive listening:* Communication is a dynamic process: a listener must take an active role which requires strong attending skills (just described). In contrast to the passive listening approach that merely hears, **active listening** requires that the listener devote complete attention to the speaker and take responsibility for understanding the message. It takes far more energy than passive listening. Active listeners are also engaged in understanding the point of view of the speaker. This may require identifying how the speaker is aiming the message. Also, it may require identifying the goal and motivation that have shaped the message.

  Active listeners:

  • may take notes
  • restate important points to themselves or to the speaker to make sure that the message was clear
  • ask questions for clarification

  c. *Characteristics of active listening:* There are four characteristics of active listening: (1) intensity, (2) empathy, (3) acceptance, and (4) taking responsibility for completeness.

    1. *Intensity:* People can process spoken language four times faster than the normal individual speaks. The extra capacity available for processing speech can be used to attend to other distractions or it can be focused on understanding the message. The degree to which one focuses on the message is the degree of intensity. Active listeners use the extra capacity to summarize and integrate the message.

    2. *Empathy:* Empathy occurs when the listener takes the speaker's point of view in an effort to understand. This means that the listener is trying to identify the

concerns, pressures, and related interests of the speaker. Above all, empathy conveys the listener's sincerity.

3. *Acceptance:* Active listeners withhold disbelief and judgment until the speaker has finished and the message is clear. Too often people will make a judgment about a message before the message is complete. This is unfair to the speaker and frequently results in wrong interpretations of the message.

4. *Taking responsibility for completeness:* Completeness in active listening is the result of hearing the entire message and making certain that the message is understood properly in context. Active listeners share responsibility for completing the communication.

d. *Improvement of listening skills:* A number of steps can be taken to achieve effective active listening. They are:

- Maintain eye contact and use nonverbal cues to assure the speaker that the message is being followed.

- Pay attention to feelings as well as the verbal message.

- Respond to the feelings by recognizing them verbally or nonverbally.

- Do not interrupt or engage in distracting behavior.

- Put the speaker's message into your own words to demonstrate that you comprehend the message.

- Use questions to clarify ambiguous or complex parts of the message.

- Provide feedback that reflects an understanding of the message or a considered response to the message.

e. *Feedback to the speaker:* Feedback is the means for the receiver of a message to complete the communication process. Feedback closes the communication cycle from sender to message to receiver and back. This is often called a feedback loop. While feedback has been addressed in other contexts throughout this book, its particular role in communication must not be overlooked. Just as communication has goals that account for its character, feedback serves four goals similar to the goals of communication:

1. *Feedback informs:* Feedback provides information to the sender concerning how effectively the message was sent and interpreted. The response "I do not understand" requires the sender to rephrase the message.

2. *Feedback controls:* Feedback can control communication by forcing the sender to modify the message. The comment "I do not agree with what you said" results in the sender either modifying the message, attempting to persuade through another approach, or discontinuing the effort to change another's behavior.

3. *Feedback motivates:* Feedback can have a positive or negative effect on the sender. When feedback is positive and supportive, the sender will be encouraged; when feedback is negative or disapproving, the sender will be discouraged.

EXAMPLES:

"I really like your proposal; when do you think the project can be ready?" will energize and motivate the person making the proposal.

> *On the negative side: "Your proposal will require too large an initial out-lay of resources to get it started, and the project promises only marginal results."*

Note how details of this feedback convey specific reasons for disapproval. Negative feedback is more effective when it is specific.

4. *Feedback expresses feelings:* Feedback can express how the receiver feels about the message. To make the most of the communication process, people must be attentive to the feelings of the audience as well as their thoughts. Feelings can reveal undercurrents of dissatisfaction that might not be evident in the direct verbal response.

The process of communication is fundamental to organizational relations. When communication is poor, organizational effectiveness will be low; when communication is effective, organizations will be effective.

Check Point—Section A

Directions: For each question, circle the correct answer.

A–1. Which one of the following is an appropriately matched set of communication concepts?

A) Message and emotion
B) Receiver and channel
C) Feedback and decoding
D) Sender and encoding

A–2. When the manager shares production quotas, quality targets, and work schedules, the manager is employing the goal of organizational communication known as

A) conveying information
B) directing and controlling action
C) motivating others
D) expressing feelings

A–3. Intensity, empathy, acceptance, and taking responsibility for completeness are characteristics of

A) common ground
B) the cooperative principle
C) active listening
D) feedback to the speaker

B. Using Managerial Communication

The communication process becomes more complex as a manager moves up in an organization. Supervisor-level managers use verbal communication primarily. As a manager moves up in the organization to middle management, writing skills become more important. Upper-level managers must possess both strong verbal and written communication skills.

1. *Features of Managerial Communication:* Managers influence behavior and coordinate planning and implementation of plans within an organization by using communication skills effectively. A manager's or administrative professional's responsibilities for communication include the following:

    a. *Communicating with coworkers and subordinates:* It is estimated that 90 percent of a manager's time involves communication. Communication is the method that accomplishes the "work" of the organization.

b. *Choosing channels to communicate:* Managers need to determine the best channel for communicating different information. There are many choices of channels. For instance, there are policy manuals, directives, employee records, incident reports, letters, e-mails, face-to-face (in person), speeches, and even bulletin boards.

c. *Communicating nonverbally:* While the manager may choose a method of communicating a specific bit of information or directions, the manager is always communicating through nonverbal channels, whether or not the manager is aware of the messages being sent.

d. *Communicating ethics and behavior:* Managers have the primary responsibility to communicate the expected behavior and ethics throughout the organization. Ethics and behavioral communication are transmitted by both verbal transmission and the behavior of the managers. The policies and directives considering ethics must be reinforced by the behavior of management.

e. *Communicating across cultures:* Globalization requires that managers be prepared to communicate with many cultures. There are the cultures of the employees in the organization and the cultures of the environment of the business. This requires becoming knowledgeable about all the cultures that are or may become involved with the organization. Technology is an excellent way to acquire the information needed to communicate with different cultures. Communication with different cultures involves more than obtaining a dictionary to translate.

2. **Types of Managerial Communication:** Types of managerial and organizational communication can be characterized according to many aspects. The communications can be formal or informal, have direction, can go up or down the chain of command, and can have differing purposes. Each means of classifying communication can be associated with a specific product, like a report, an e-mail, a business letter, a contract, or an appraisal. Much of the classification of organizational communication can be made on nonverbal aspects of the method or channel of communicating. A business letter is made more or less formal by the tone of the salutation and the inflection in the style. **Formal communication** refers to written or oral messages that are sent in the context of an official action or otherwise are presented as the directive of an office or officer of an organization or as following the directive or request of an officer. **Informal communication** include all the messages other than official directives or requests.

a. *Directions and types of managerial communication:* Organizational communication may be upward, downward, lateral, or diagonal.

1. *Downward communication:* Information flow from individuals at higher levels within an organization to those at lower levels is **downward communication.** Messages are transmitted from top or middle managers to lower level managers and employees. Downward communication includes the following:

- The major problem with downward communication is *drop-off,* the distortion, or loss of message content that occurs as messages are relayed from one level to another within the organizational hierarchy. Drop-off will occur more often in larger, centralized organizations than in smaller, decentralized firms.

- Other problems with downward communication include the use of improper channels to deliver messages, the lack of consistency between words and action, overreliance on written memos, and information overload.

2. *Upward communication:* Some messages flow from workers at lower levels to managers and workers at higher levels of the organizational structure. This information flow is known as **upward communication.** The most common types of upward communication include the following kinds of information:

   - Reports to supervisors
   - Notices of completed action
   - Inquiries for clarification
   - Proposals for action
   - Recommendation and evaluation of options

3. *Lateral (horizontal) communication:* The exchange of information between peers or workers at the same organizational level can occur within or across departments. One of the main reasons for **lateral communications** within an organization focuses on the need for problem solving.

4. *Grapevines:* In addition to these three directions of communication in the organization, the existence of a system of communicating information, gossip, and rumors through informal networks also exists. The **grapevine** is an informal pattern of communication that moves in any direction. Informal networks are the patterns of communication among people who have regular interactions. Networks and grapevines carry information rapidly and with differing degrees of accuracy. The grapevine is one of several informal ways of communicating within the organization.

5. *Diagonal communication:* Diagonal communication occurs when workers at different levels interact and also in situations where *staff* workers deal with *line* workers. Diagonal communication is a form of lateral communication. However, workers from different levels of the organizational hierarchy, as well as separate departments, may be involved. This is also called *boundary spanning.*

b. *Formats:* Managers communicate through a number of formats. These include written documents, verbal directives, and extensive interpersonal communication. Each format serves a set of specific purposes or objectives related to administration and supervision. In most cases, some form of feedback is expected and requires attention. The verbal communication requires quality listening skills as well as the ability to formulate a verbal response.

   1. Written formats include the following:

      - Weekly, monthly, quarterly, and annual reports
      - Forms
      - E-mail
      - Notices
      - Written announcements
      - Notification of changes, promotions, separations, and so on
      - Reprimands

   2. Verbal directives and related communications include:

      - Specific directions or work instructions to individuals or groups
      - Group or team meetings
      - Daily announcements

- Closed-circuit television, both taped and live
- Telephone
- Public announcement (PA) messages
- Feedback and praise

3. Interpersonal supervisory discussion and coaching include:

- Individual training
- Evaluation and performance review
- Employment interview
- Resolving conflict among subordinates
- Feedback and praise

3. *Nonverbal Communication Channels:* **Nonverbal communication** accompanies virtually every form of oral communication and most forms of written communication. Nonverbal communication includes all the non linguistic elements that accompany a message and contribute to the meaning and interpretation of the message. Gestures, body position, voice inflection, and eye contact occur simultaneously with oral communication and are called *paralanguage.* Written communication can have subtle nonverbal messages in the use of humor or the sense of confidence conveyed by the author. When a supervisor puts a reprimand in writing rather than making a comment in person, the nonverbal message has the quality of making the warning stronger. Other nonvocal messages include the expression of feelings and emotions through body language and facial expression. The most active forms of nonverbal communication are those that accompany oral communication.

a. *Paralanguage:* Paralanguage includes any nonverbal communication that accompanies verbal expression. When oral communication is accompanied by appropriate gestures or facial expressions, the force of the message is intensified. A manager may express disapproval orally and frown while looking at the poorly done work. A stern warning may be accompanied by a gesture to reinforce its message.

1. *Gestures:* Gestures represent a complicated area of paralanguage because some common gestures in North America can be insulting in other parts of the world. The "OK" sign made with thumb and forefinger is an obscene gesture in Denmark. Pointing is offensive to the Chinese. The side-to-side headshake means "no" in American and European expression but "yes" in India. Hands and fingers can be used to emphasize verbal points or to get the attention of others (to gain the "floor" in order to speak). Hands touching face and eyes looking away may suggest uncertainty.

2. *Facial expressions:* The six basic human emotions—anger, joy, surprise, disgust, sadness, and fear—each have a unique facial expression so powerful that they are recognized universally. Cultural experience has modified these basic six expressions to be the basis of a wide assortment of nonverbal messages.

3. *Voice inflection, rate, and pronunciation:* Inflection refers to the tone of voice, which can convey interest, enthusiasm, joy, anger, disinterest (flat tone), and many other qualities. A high rate of speaking communicates eagerness or anxiety, while a slow rate may communicate thoughtfulness or deliberateness. Clear vocalization with good diction (no slurs or mumbling) expresses confidence, whereas mumbling may reveal nervousness.

4. *Eye contact:* Eye contact can be a valuable tool for the astute individual. Eye contact can be used to establish confidence, to make initial contact with someone, to check for the reactions of others, to monitor attention to activity, and to intimidate. Prolonged eye contact in casual situations will most likely make the recipient uncomfortable, and can be a sign of aggression.

EXAMPLES:

> *In interviews, eye contact is important, though too much of a good thing can make the interview and the interviewer uncomfortable.*

> *In customer relations, business meetings, and interviews, prolonged eye contact should be broken occasionally by glances to the focus of the activity, like giving attention to a document or product.*

People find rhythms of eye contact that make them comfortable and help establish a focus appropriate to the situation. Eye contact has important implications in other cultures.

EXAMPLES:

> *People of Latin American descent are taught that direct eye contact is a sign of defiance, and that looking away while speaking to a person of authority is a sign of respect.*

> *Older African Americans tell of their parents insisting that they look at the ground while being scolded—again a sign of respect.*

b. *Body language:* Body language includes the position of our body as we speak or listen to another person. Crossed legs and crossed arms suggest distance, dislike, and possibly self-protective or defensive attitudes. Open, relaxed posture communicates a relaxation and comfort with others who are present. Slumping can communicate fatigue or lack of self-confidence. Uneasiness and anxiety might be communicated through fidgeting or rocking motions. Body language also reflects personal differences and unique characteristics. The better one knows an individual, the better one will be able to read that person's body language to detect changes in feelings or the presence of other concerns. When we speak to people we know, we also anticipate their verbal responses through their body language. If we stay alert to these signals, we will make adjustments in our message as we observe the response of our friends.

c. *Gestures and facial expressions as complete messages:* Gestures and facial expressions can form complete messages. A "thumbs up" sign signals approval. A nod of the head can indicate approval or rejection. A smile can have many meanings, depending upon the context. A raised eyebrow may show interest or concern. In personal communications, gestures and facial expressions often signal meanings understood by both parties instantly. A child knows the special look of a parent's disapproval. A spouse can show exasperation with a gesture. A smile can display a whole range of caring.

In organizations, the meanings of these forms of communication may not and probably should not hold the same personal significance. It is important to know and maintain personal boundaries at work. A supervisor may smile at a subordinate. The smile should communicate approval of the work or friendly concern, but it should not have the same weight as the smile between two family members or friends. In the same way, gestures can be used to indicate a "job well done."

d. *Personal space (proxemics): Proxemics* is the study of the personal space or territory people establish around themselves. Anthropologist Edward Hall has proposed that there are four different zones of space: intimate, personal, social, and public. Intimate is the closest, with the shortest distance, and public has the greatest physical distance. Different cultures and occupations have different physical distances that define these four spaces. Because personal spaces are so deeply conditioned, people from one culture or occupation may feel uncomfortable with the space requirements for people from another.

1. *Intimate distance:* For North Americans, *intimate distance* is from actual physical contact to about 18 inches. The space that falls into this distance is reserved for people who have an intimate relationship. A person interacts with children and spouse in this space. When people who do not have this close relationship come closer than 18 inches, both will turn their heads and look away. This behavior can be seen on a crowded elevator or in a crowded subway train—people do their best to look beyond the intimate space. When two people are trying to talk in noisy conditions, they will alternate turning away while the other talks. Communication in this intimate range affirms the nature of the relationship.

2. *Personal distance:* In tight or close working conditions, such as in a small utility space, or in the close quarters of machinery being repaired, invasion into intimate distance is tolerated, but at soon as the situation is ended, the standard of personal distance resumes. *Personal distance* is from 18 inches to about 4 feet. Friends and coworkers will form groups that sustain these distances. When three people are talking together and have established the appropriate distance, and another friend joins the group, the first three will (if possible) move to expand the space in order to maintain stable distance.

   EXAMPLE: *A conversation between a Saudi Arabian and a North American can appear quite comical. If neither has lived long in the other's homeland, the two will appear to move around the room with the American backing up and the Saudi moving forward. The person from Saudi Arabia will be constantly moving within about 12 inches of the American's face while the American will be constantly trying to maintain a distance of about 18 inches. The efforts on the part of both are to establish what for each is a physical distance appropriate to their experience of a space for interaction. People in Latin America, the Middle East, the Far East, and India share this spatial difference.*

3. *Social distance: Social distance* is from 4 feet to 12 feet. When people must communicate with casual acquaintances or strangers in an informal manner, like in a seminar or conference discussion, the preferred distance is from 4 to 12 feet. If a group discussion is being lead by someone who is walking around the room, then interaction between the leader and one of the participants will usually draw the leader to within 12 feet of the participant. At parties or during coffee breaks, casual conversation will draw people together, but they will avoid breaking the 4-foot barrier.

4. *Public distance: Public distance* is from 12 feet and beyond. This distance is a very formal distance, and it often is the distance of a formal speaker from the closest member of an audience. Speaking skills and gestures appropriate to public speaking become important at this distance because facial expressions become more difficult to interpret at the 12-foot range. Speakers should

increase their projection or use a microphone to amplify normal voice tones for people farther away.

4. ***Qualities of Nonverbal Communication:*** No gesture, sigh, inflection, or any other nonverbal cue goes without some interpretation. All nonverbal activity has some meaning, thus it contributes to the message in some way. Some nonverbal methods of communication can be very specific, while others can be vague. However, all nonverbal behavior communicates something. Nonverbal communication has several key qualities:

   a. *Powerful:* The initial impressions of others that people form are based almost entirely on nonverbal cues. Nonverbal elements of any message can have as much power as the verbal message. If the nonverbal message is opposite the verbal message, then the value of the verbal message can be diminished significantly.

   b. *Ambiguous:* Nonverbal messages are potentially ambiguous because they usually have more than one meaning. A gruff tone of voice in the morning can suggest either someone is angry or did not have a good night's sleep. A completely distracted person may be daydreaming or may have just received horrible news. The receiver of a nonverbal message is often promoted by the message to explore further for clarification, often by switching to a verbal channel.

   c. *Expresses attitudes and feelings:* The nonverbal message that accompanies a verbal declaration is the means by which emotion and feeling are conveyed in a message. Nonverbal is the primary channel for expression of emotions and feelings, and the verbal expression of an emotion is meaningless if accompanied by a contradictory nonverbal message. A flat tone will not work to express joy.

   d. *Reflects culture and ethnicity:* Nonverbal expressions have a style and quality that is shaped by culture and may be specific to a culture. Culture and ethnicity provide the first area of common ground that people learn from birth on. One must actually make an effort to override culturally ingrained nonverbal behaviors. They shape the nonverbal behavior almost like an accent will reveal a country or region or origin.

5. ***Verbal Versus Nonverbal Communication:*** The nonverbal and verbal channels of communication can occur independently of each other, or they can occur in coordination with each other. Usually, all the various channels of communication are working together to communicate the same message. Even without any training in how to "read" nonverbal communication, people detect the contradictory messages of speakers who are trying to hide something, are lying, or are otherwise uneasy. If the nonverbal messages disagree with the verbal messages, the receiver can lose trust or confidence in the speaker very quickly. A manager expresses verbal sympathy to a worker who has just relayed information about an ill family member. However, the manager remains physically unresponsive. The worker will not accept the manager's superficial effort and will believe that the manager is insincere.

   a. *Precision and clarity:* Verbal communication has the quality of being precise and comprehensive. While moods, feelings, and emotions can be communicated in the nonverbal channels, their interpretation may be just as vague as the mode in which they are sent. Words have a remarkable capacity to generate meanings and convey specific information. They can, intentionally or unintentionally, create vagueness as well. Formal communications can specify complete instructions, data, timeframes, and who should receive the information. Nonverbal communication cannot convey this kind of precision very often or with much consistency.

b. *Hidden Message:* An important difference between verbal and nonverbal communication is that the nonverbal includes a message about information that was "not shared."

   EXAMPLE: *The director of a plant comes before his employees with a small army of executives behind him and proclaims that the plant is not in danger of a shutdown and that people should stop worrying. However, the presence of the support force and the formality of the presentation convince the employees that there must be more that is not being said.*

   Suspicions increase, rather than decrease. Omitted messages are detected in a range of subtle forms, which include everything from the structure of the spoken or written message to the place the message is presented.

c. *Written communication:* When verbal and nonverbal channels are involved, it is most likely that spoken verbal communication and nonverbal communication will be mixed. However, written communication can have nonverbal components as well. People may consider the "tone" of a letter when referring to qualities of style or the ever important "what was not said." In attempting to develop effective human relations habits, one must be alert to the presence of these major channels of communications at all times.

Check Point—Section B

Directions: For each question, circle the correct answer.

B–1. When workers at different levels interact and in situations where staff workers deal with line workers, the communication is considered

   A) downward
   B) diagonal
   C) grapevine
   D) formal

B–2. Nonverbal communication that accompanies verbal communication is known as

   A) body language
   B) paralanguage
   C) proxemics
   D) common ground

B–3. Friends and coworkers form groups that maintain a communication distance described as

   A) public
   B) social
   C) personal
   D) intimate

C. Employing Presentation Techniques

Advanced organizational management requires presentation skills and techniques that go beyond the formal technology-assisted presentation. These requirements include reporting, media relations, public speaking, negotiation, conferring, and others. The effective senior or midlevel manager will be an excellent communicator capable of employing a well-practiced set of written, oral, and nonverbal techniques to convey a message. These skills and techniques not only help convey an effective message, but they also help remove barriers to communication.

1. *Hierarchy and Communication:* Moving up the organization, each level of management has different communication tasks.

a. *Supervisor:* A line or staff supervisor typically conducts most communication in a downward manner, with some communication upward. Downward communication is for the purpose of directing employees and guiding work processes. Upward communication is typically routine reporting and some problem solving.

b. *Midlevel manager:* The midlevel manager communicates in both upward and downward fashion. Written communication will be more common than at the supervisor level. The midlevel manager will be required to make reports and communicate some with external clients.

c. *Upper- and top-level managers:* The higher up the chain, the larger the audience becomes. Upper-level managers will also write more, but the writing will be less routine and involve more analysis. At the top level of management, writing diminishes except for special projects, and usually a team of writers supports the top level. The audience continues to get larger, and oral presentations have less concrete language as messages become more abstract and less detailed. Upper and top managers will address the public more frequently.

2. ***Presentation:*** Managerial communications require frequent presentations to subordinates, other managers, and upper management, external authority (auditors, accreditation teams, government inspectors and licensing agents), clients, customers, and the public. Generally, the higher in the organization the manager is, the more presentations he or she will need to give. Advanced organizational managers (mid- to top-level managers) typically will have staff who prepare the technical materials used in a presentation. The manager will be responsible for a clear and well-designed presentation, so not being part of the development will require the manager to spend time preparing for the presentation, usually in the form of review of basic concepts, data, and proposals.

a. *Types of formal presentations:* There are hundreds of specific types of presentations that can be made. They may involve the transmission of a formal or informal report or proposal; and, in both formal and informal contexts, the presentation may itself serve as the entire report.

1. *Persuasive internal:* A persuasive internal presentation can address any topic of interest to the organization. This can be a budget proposal, proposed projects, reorganization, procedures, strategic plans, and so on. The general objective is to persuade the audience to accept the point of view of the presenter and to undertake a proposed action.

2. *Informative:* An annual budget report may be merely informative. Other types of informative presentations include performance reports, cyclic progress reports, audit reports, and so forth. A consultant might make an informative presentation at the conclusion of the consulting activity. Informational presentations may be made to the public as well. Sometimes these might accompany a press release or product announcement.

3. *Selling:* A special form of presentation is to the client or customer. This is of course a persuasive presentation, but the audience should be more focused on making an informed decision about a product or service being offered. Complex product or service offers may lead also to the process of negotiation, which will be discussed later in this chapter.

b. *Roles of the presenter:* The presenter has several very clear roles. Remember, the presentation is often developed by a team, and the presenter is just one of the team members. Often the other team members will be present, but the presenter is responsible for a smooth and successful presentation.

1. *Establish clear objectives:* The presenter must have clear objectives. These must be conveyed to the audience early in the process. If they are vague in the presentation, the presenter must direct the team to make the objectives more understandable or accessible to the audience.

2. *Be fully informed:* The presenter, perhaps more so than any one of the team members who helped develop the presentation, must be fully informed about the data, analytic processes, proposals, and even the approaches that were rejected. Questions will follow either during or at the end of the presentation, and the presenter must be able to answer them quickly and confidently.

c. *The presentation:* The care put in developing, organizing, reviewing, and practicing a presentation shows in the results.

1. *Formats:* There are several possible formats a presenter can follow.

   a. *Manuscript:* For presenting complex concepts, a prepared manuscript may be necessary. However, if the manuscript will be read, much practice must precede the delivery in order for the delivery to appear natural. The narrative of the manuscript must also sound as if it were an oral presentation.

   b. *Extemporaneous:* This format involves presenting from notes. The presenter must be practiced and confident.

   c. *Impromptu:* When a manager holds a Monday staff meeting, the points made may be or appear to be impromptu. An impromptu presentation is entirely spontaneous and unplanned. Given the rapid pace of some businesses, this may not be as rare as one would think.

   EXAMPLE: *An unexpected visiting client may receive a tour and presentation made by a manager without any preparation.*

   d. *Memorized:* A brief and frequently repeated talk works well if memorized. Long presentations are difficult to make appear fresh when memorized and frequently repeated. If an audience member hears the presentation more than once, memorization can have negative results.

   e. *Teleconference or Web-based:* A Web-based presentation involves an audience viewing a screen with the presentation material prepared as a Web page or similar format and the presenter speaking, unseen, over a telephone connection. In a teleconference, a presenter appears on the screen and has little or limited contact with the audience.

2. *Technical details:* Technical details of the presentation include all the warnings, suggestions, and directions for preparing pages and charts. The manager who must make the presentation should review the electronic format in the physical situation where it will be displayed. Several problems occur when viewed only on a laptop or desktop monitor.

   • Color wrong (nice on monitor, ugly on the projector)
   • Too many lines on a slide
   • Too verbose
   • Too many slides

- Difficult graphs and charts
- Transitions that distract

3. *Preparation for technology failure:* Be prepared for the technology to fail at the worst possible moment. Handouts and overhead transparencies are good to have for formal presentations. For the informal presentation, it is acceptable to trust the audience's ability to follow uncomplicated oral presentations.

d. *Effective delivery:* Effective delivery will not win the contract or convince the senior executive, but ineffective delivery has a strong chance of undermining success.

1. *Confident and poised:* The best means of ensuring that the presenter will be confident and poised during a presentation is for that person to be confident and poised prior to the presentation. Though some people are natural public speakers, most people succeed only through practice and experience. Repeated practice and years of public presentation have no substitute.

2. *Controlled nonverbal expression:* The nonverbal channel is paramount for the presenter. Just as effective vocal delivery may not win the contract, effect nonverbal communication does not provide a guarantee. However, poor nonverbal presence can and will ruin the effort. Paralanguage elements of posture, body language, gestures, eye contact, and space must be considered and, where possible, practiced with the oral part of the presentation.

e. *Response to questions:* The presentation always closes with an opportunity for audience inquiries. The presenter must be open to inquiry.

1. *Odd questions:* Frequently, an audience member will ask a completely "off-topic" question. The question will require treating the questioner with dignity and not dismissing the odd question. It may be that an answer does relate to the presentation and simply has not occurred to anyone. However, the question may require a gentle, suggestion to discuss the point after the presentation has concluded.

2. *Domineering interrogators:* Another common experience in formal and informal presentations is the person who asks a question in order to control the event. Often the person has an elaborate point to make and uses the question as a time to make it. Though this is unprofessional on the part of the questioner, the presenter must maintain professionalism and find a way to regain control. The presenter can emphasize that others have questions also, and that the concern can be addressed in follow-up communications.

3. *Follow-up:* Follow-up can take the form of offering a more detailed answer to a complicated question, or it may be a follow-up to explore the acceptance or rejection of the proposal made in the presentation. Specific types of follow-up depend on the type of presentation.

3. ***Removal of Barriers to Improve Organizational Communication:*** Top management must actively support efforts to improve organizational communications. The leaders of an organization must do everything in their power, as well as empowering others, to improve organizational communication. Specific ways to accomplish this include creating an open climate, developing information-sharing systems, restructuring the organization, and treating employees equally.

a. *Creating an open climate:* Top management must take action to create a climate of openness and trust. Top-level managers need to practice an open-door policy, share more information about pending events with organization members, and delegate more meaningful tasks and responsibilities to supervisors and other first-line managers. By creating such a climate, the most important organizational communication barrier will be eliminated.

1. *Visible and tangible signs:* Establishing an open-door policy, more information sharing, empowered employees, and decentralized authority are some of the visible and tangible signs and actions that top-level managers must take to help create an open climate. Developing such a climate is a prerequisite for improved effectiveness in organizational communication.

2. *Open-door policy:* Middle-level and first-level managers must also be encouraged to establish and keep open doors, a climate of trust, and more empowerment of responsibility and authority to their subordinates.

b. *Developing information-sharing systems:* Top management should ensure that a system for increased information sharing is initiated and maintained. Some of the more progressive firms in the United States today are sharing financial statement results and operations information with workers at all levels. The key is to ensure that every worker knows as much about the inner workings and financial operations as do stockholders, financial analysts, and reporters.

1. *Fostering communication methods:* More attention should be given to fostering methods of upward, lateral, and diagonal communication. Local area networks, with the capacity for electronic mail, enhance internal communication in all directions.

2. *Creating suggestion systems and grievance procedures:* Formal suggestion systems and grievance procedures should be utilized more often and in more effective ways.

3. *Participating in organizationwide meetings:* More companywide, plantwide, and unit meetings should be held, with all employees provided with appropriate incentives to actively participate.

4. *Seeking support from informal organization:* Managers at all levels should seek the support of the informal organization, trying to work actively with it, and ensuring that information is made readily available before formal requests are initiated. This involves keeping in touch with workers and anticipating their needs and actions.

c. *Improving interpersonal communication:* Interpersonal communication problems result from ineffective interactions among people. The greatest cause of ineffective interpersonal communication is poor listening. Other steps that can be taken to improve interpersonal communication include elimination of stereotyping, treating employees equally, and encouraging more favorable environments.

1. *Eliminating stereotyping:* Managers need to encourage all employees to view others as individuals, not as members of specific groups. When people begin to view each other as individuals with distinct personalities, needs, behaviors, and preferences, instead of categorizing their actions according to a group to which they belong, stereotyping will start to be eliminated.

2. *Treating employees equally:* Training programs can be developed to share the information that all employees in all positions are needed and have credibility. Employees need to realize that they will be treated equally.

3. *Encouraging more favorable environments:* Some business settings are more conducive than others for interpersonal communication. Many settings and channels fill with noise, which detracts from the communication process. Some ways in which organizations can encourage more favorable environments for communication to occur include:

   a. Planning training sessions to make people more aware of the problem that noise creates in the communication process.

   b. Encouraging people to try to share information during what is determined the "best time" to remove noise barriers and improve interpersonal concentration on messages that need to be exchanged.

   c. Stressing the need for increased communication accuracy by taking such steps as training people to write, to speak, and to serve on teams more effectively.

4. *Teaching effective writing techniques:* Varying amounts of noise are associated with the messages that many people write. Writing skills can be improved with these steps:

   a. Encouraging people to practice simplicity in writing. Shorter words and simpler sentences enhance readability.

   b. Urging people to write concisely. Being direct and to the point enhances the decoding of written messages.

   c. Reinforcing the need to use basic rules of grammar and composition. Appropriate training programs help people to relearn basic writing principles.

5. *Teaching the effective use of technology:* Electronic communication systems are essential to doing business today. All employees should be trained to use the systems that the organization is using.

6. *Teaching managers how to speak publicly:* Taking one or two speech courses in high school or college does not guarantee that someone will be able to speak with others in an understandable manner. People need to be encouraged to learn how to speak more effectively. Training programs need to be available that will enhance oral communications.

7. *Training people to be more effective group members:* Meetings occupy a significant part of almost every manager's time. Many people have never received formal training on how to participate in group meetings. Training employees to serve more effectively on committees and other work-related groups and to lead group meetings will improve interpersonal communications. Training people how to share on local area networks, including instilling knowledge of "netiquette," is an essential part of this communication form.

8. *Creating awareness of cultural and language difficulties:* Many people are unaware of the many ways that cultural language differences can impede effective interpersonal communication. Providing information and training about cultural differences can be an effective way of improving interpersonal communications, especially as organizations become more involved in global ventures and employ people from various cultures. Specific cultural training should be provided whenever an organization starts a new venture with a new culture.

9. *Helping people with language:* Countless people forget the problems associated with semantics (different meanings assigned to the same word) or nonverbal action. People need to be encouraged to be more aware of how their words and actions can be decoded and understood by others. More precise use of language can clearly improve interpersonal communication.

10. *Creating more awareness of channel usage:* People will often select improper communication channels because they lack awareness or time. In so doing, senders encode messages properly but use the wrong communication channels, thus often making the information shared meaningless.

    a. More training is needed to help people learn to use appropriate communication channels in given situations.

    b. People should be reminded that improper channel selection impairs interpersonal communication efficiency and effectiveness. When sharing information, haste can make waste.

d. *Improving managers' personal communication:* The primary personal communication barriers are psychosocial differences and selective perception. Several methods are recommended to improve personal communication effectiveness.

1. *Use empathy in communication:* Empathy is the ability to put oneself in another person's shoes and understand his or her needs, background, values, and expectations.

    a. Learn to consider the backgrounds, needs, motivations, and expectations of the audience. If this is not done, it results in improperly encoding words and symbols or selecting inappropriate communication channels.

    b. Evaluate the purposes of a message before it is encoded and transmitted, the sender can select the most appropriate channel so that the meaning intended is the same as the actual meaning to the receiver.

2. *Be aware of differences in communication:* Individuals need to become more aware of the differences between verbal and nonverbal communication and the results when there is lack of consistency between the two. *Actions* speak louder than *words!*

3. *Use more feedback:* Very often, communication problems occur because one person is unaware of the responses of the other. The number of levels in the hierarchy can impede feedback from upward and downward communication. *Distortion* is modifying news, usually to make it more positive. *Filtering* is screening out news sent to a supervisor or subordinate, usually negative news.

4. *Managers need to use follow-up: Follow-up* is the process of ensuring that all messages sent were understood. Follow-up is used when the source tries to determine if the intended message was decoded with the same meaning by the receiver. Quicker feedback and follow-up are even expected when the Internet or other forms of electronic communication are used.

5. *Managers need to use simpler language:* Common words and simple phrases can be understood more easily and properly than complex terminology. The use of simple language enhances communication, especially when cultural and language difficulties exist or if follow-up or feedback is also utilized.

6. *Use assertiveness frequently: Assertiveness* is a personal communication skill that can be learned, characterized by displaying honesty, directness, respect, and confidence in oneself while sharing information. When using assertiveness in communication, a person shows more respect for his or her own rights and the rights of the receiver(s).

7. *Managers need to understand emotionality:* People often let their emotions speak for themselves. Becoming more sensitive to one's emotions and emotional state can lead to a reduction of unnecessary displays of feelings, which may impede effective communication.

8. *Suspend judgment to overcome distrust:* Very often, people encounter situations where they get hurt, physically or emotionally, and become distrustful of others. The key to overcoming distrust lies in the ability to suspend judgment, looking at and listening to every communication in a new light, without carrying forth preconceived views.

9. *Managers need to overcome perceptual differences:* Selective perception is probably the greatest source of personal communication difficulty. Overcoming perceptual differences is a difficult task. Perceptual differences can be overcome in a number of ways.

   a. Information from varying sources will be helpful. Instead of relying only on selective perception, people should try to view persons or objects in different ways, depending on the sources of information. This will require more time and effort, but the benefits will offset the cost.

   b. Making quick ("snap") judgments should be avoided. Initial impressions due to perceptual problems can lead to stereotyping and the halo/horn effect (good people have halos, and everything they do is good; and people have horns, and everything they do is bad).

   c. Helping others overcome their misperceptions is an important task. When one sees or hears another using selective perception, this problem should be called to the other person's attention so that more accurate decisions can be made by both parties.

Check Point—Section C

Directions: For each question, circle the correct answer.

C–1. Which one of the following members of an organization conducts most communication downward?

    A) Upper-level manager
    B) Midlevel manager
    C) Supervisor
    D) Line employee

C–2. Which one of the following formats of presentation involves making the presentation using notes?

    A) Extemporaneous

    B) Impromptu
    C) Manuscript
    D) Informative

C–3. The ability to put oneself in another person's shoes and understand his or her needs, background, values, and expectations refers to

    A) suspended judgment
    B) the use of more feedback
    C) extemporaneous responses
    D) the use of empathy

For Your Review

Directions: For each question, circle the correct answer.

Case 1: Preferred Printing and Packaging, Incorporated

Preferred is a printing and packaging company with a couple hundred employees. The owner is Peterson. Peterson recently hired a vice president, Smith, with experience in big corporations. Preferred's operation manager, Gonzalez, has a number of years of experience working with Peterson. Consultants were hired because Peterson had run into some problems with expansion. The consultants discovered that bulk mailings were not being completed on time. The machine operators were not clearly instructed on the order in which they were to complete their jobs.

Every morning in a staff meeting Smith announced the priorities and mailing dates for upcoming jobs. Gonzalez communicated the jobs to the senior operator. Consultants discovered that the machine operators were not getting clear information on the order for performing the jobs.

For a mailing to be prepared, as many as 30 pieces of material had to be copied and collated. Copy machines had to be set up with different colors and configurations.

Consultants were not sure where the communication breakdown occurred. It was recommended that Smith prepare a list of priorities for printing. Gonzalez would then assign the list by color and machine capability. This worked.

1. Because there are many new employees at Preferred Printing, they shared few experiences. To improve communication, the consultants recommended activities that would build

   A) diagonal communication
   B) encoding
   C) feedback
   D) common ground

2. The purpose of the daily staff meeting was to

   A) assist in problem solving
   B) motivate
   C) convey information
   D) express feelings

3. Which one of the following actions would have had the effect of reducing a communication barrier?

   A) Peterson hiring Gonzalez
   B) Smith preparing a list of priorities

   C) Smith's daily briefing
   D) Peterson contracting the consultants

4. The primary channel for communication though flawed at Preferred appears to be

   A) oral
   B) written
   C) nonverbal
   D) decoded

5. The consultant suggested that those who attend the staff meeting should take notes, ask questions, and take responsibility for understanding what is being said. This recommendation is a suggestion that everyone

   A) become more active listeners
   B) use feedback more effectively
   C) increase their personal distance
   D) express feelings more directly

Case 2: Lindstrom and Associates

Morella is the office manager at Lindstrom. Morella has worked with Lindstrom, the owner, since the business was started 20 years ago. Morella has a "difficult" personality and does not know how to delegate work to the office staff.

Lindstrom recently hired an accounting graduate to work in the office. Morella, who does not have a degree, feels threatened and refuses to give the accountant the checkbook. The new accountant is considering leaving. The turnover rate in the office is much higher than would be expected for a business like this.

6. Though Morella is still dedicated to Lindstrom and Associates, the negative feelings toward the new accountant will still be communicated through

   A) paralanguage
   B) oral channels
   C) written messages
   D) nonverbal channels

7. Which one of the following features of managerial communication suggests that Morella should not express the sense of being threatened by subordinates?

   A) The responsibility to communicate ethics and appropriate behavior
   B) The fact that nonverbal communication is continuous
   C) Communication across cultures
   D) Choosing channels to communicate

8. When talking with the accountant, Morella's body language may be expressing anxiety through

   A) crossed arms and legs
   B) the six basic emotions
   C) relaxed posture
   D) frequent eye contact

9. The increase in turnover begins with the arrival of the new accountant. Though Morella has never said anything, tension has been communicated. This event is a result of

   A) confused encoding of oral messages
   B) the power of nonverbal messages
   C) others being threatened by the accountant also
   D) the loss of intimate distance in the work group

10. Morella has always kept tight control over the work and has basically assigned menial tasks to others in the office while completing critical tasks alone. The accountant views the refusal to grant access to the checking account as a direct affront or challenge. The presence of these two different interpretations shows how

   A) much better written communication would be
   B) nonverbal messages have hidden messages
   C) oral messages have precision and clarity
   D) nonverbal messages can be ambiguous

Case 3: Custom Art and Design, Incorporated

Adams, the vice president, is director of the art department at Custom Art and Design, Incorporated. The company uses highly technical equipment to produce art and designs quickly and inexpensively. Of all the custom art companies in the country, Custom has a reputation for creativity and quality.

Designers need both an artistic flair and the ability to design using computers. The art department is small and includes a number of full- and part-time artists. One of the part-time employees, Luria, is skilled at using the computer programs to prepare the high quality of design needed for the artwork. However, Luria lacks creativity. A new, full-time employee, Sanchez, is an excellent artist and is good at working with the sales staff, but lacks experience with the computer.

The department needs to promote or hire another manager for the art department. Luria wants to convert to full time and move up to the manager's position. Luria also believes technical ability ensures the new position. The department clearly needs Luria's technical expertise.

11. Luria and Sanchez have the potential for working together, so they are assigned to make an important presentation to a client. Which one of the following formats would work best given their lack of shared work experience?

A) Impromptu
B) Extemporaneous
C) Manuscript
D) Teleconference

12. For their presentation, the fact that Luria has excellent technical skills and Sanchez has worked with the sales staff means that together they should be well equipped to handle

A) odd questions
B) technical difficulties
C) domineering interrogators
D) nonverbal expressions

13. As the art department begins to grow, Adams needs to find ways to keep the members working as a team. One method requires developing information-sharing systems that foster teamwork such as

A) using extensive follow-up
B) focusing on clear, downward communication

C) seeking support from the informal organization
D) making a formal, persuasive, and internal presentation

14. After observing an early run-through of Luria and Sanchez's presentation, Adams establishes a workshop for the art department that is intended to help all artists improve their writing ability. To which one of the following does this activity specifically relate?

A) Establishing clear objectives
B) Making more effective presentations
C) Creating an awareness of cultural difficulties
D) Improving interpersonal communication

15. Luria discovers that Sanchez wants the manager's position. Luria then gets the job. A potential conflict can be avoided if Luria

A) asserts authority by overcoming perceptual difficulties
B) learns to suspend judgment to avoid distrust
C) uses simpler language when talking to Sanchez
D) eliminates stereotyping

Solutions

Solutions to Check Point—Section A

Answer:	Refer to:
A–1. (D)	[A-1-a-(1) (2)]
A–2. (A)	[A-2-b-(1)]
A–3. (C)	[A-4-c]

Solutions to Check Point—Section B

Answer:	Refer to:
B–1. (B)	[B-2-a-(5)]
B–2. (B)	[B-3-a]
B–3. (C)	[B-3-d-(2)]

Solutions to Check Point—Section C

Answer:	Refer to:
C–1. (C)	[C-1-(a)]
C–2. (A)	[C-2-c-(1)-(b)]
C–3. (D)	[C-3-d-(1)]

Solutions to For Your Review

Answer:	Refer to:

Case 1:

1. (D)   [A-3-(a)]

2. (C)   [A-2-b-(1)]

3. (B)   [A-2-b-(2)-(a)]

4. (A)   [A-1 (b) (1)]

5. (A)   [A-4-(b)]

Case 2:

6. (D)   [B-3]

7. (A)   [B-1-(d)]

8. (A)   [B-3-(b)]

9. (B)   [B-4-(a)]

10. (D)   [B-4-(b)]

Case 3:

11. (C)   [C-2-c-(1)-(a)]

12. (A)   [C-2-e-(1)]

13. (C)   [C-3-b-(4)]

14. (D)   [C-3-c-(4)]

15. (B)   [C-3-d-(8)]

Chapter 11

Legal Issues in Communications

OVERVIEW

Communication within an organization is governed by laws and regulations that are meant to protect the employer and the employee. The employer has certain obligations to protect the employee from discrimination, harassment, unsafe conditions, and unfair separation, to name a few. The constitutional rights of free speech, due process (the right to fair and equal treatment in law and organizational policy), and privacy protect workers as well.

Prejudice is an attitude about an individual or group of people that is based on a selected set of characteristics rather than the entire person. Prejudice is usually the result of stereotypes about people who have noticeable differences, like skin color, national origin, religion, gender, age, and special needs.

Employment practices are also governed by laws and regulations, and discrimination must be avoided in recruitment, selection, and separation.

KEY TERMS

Affirmative action, 289
Discrimination, 288
Doctrine of comparable worth, 296
Drug-free workplace, 301
Employment-at-will (EAW), 308

Equal opportunity employment (EOE), 295
Glass ceiling, 288
Hostile environment, 292
Inbreeding, 303
Prejudice, 288
Quid pro quo sexual harassment, 291

Recruitment, 302
Separation, 308
Sexual harassment, 291
Termination, 308
Tokenism, 289

A. Legal Issues and the Workplace

The workplace has become more contentious in the past several decades. Managers and other administrative professionals must be fully informed about the rights of employees and employers as they communicate with their staff and workers. Among the most significant concerns are prejudicial and discriminatory actions, and sexual harassment.

1. *Prejudice and Discrimination:* **Prejudice** is an attitude about an individual or group of people that is based on a selected set of characteristics rather than the person. Prejudice is usually the result of stereotypes about people who have noticeable differences, like skin color, national origin, religion, gender, age, and special needs. Often, prejudice leads to views that a group is the cause of many of society's problems, a view called scapegoating. The causes of prejudice include competition, physical and social separation, modeling, and thinking processes. **Discrimination** occurs when people act on their prejudices and treat other people unfairly. Workplace discrimination occurs in testing practices, evaluation practices, promotion and hiring decisions, tokenism, pay differentials, and reverse discrimination. The government and the courts have worked to end workplace discrimination through a number of laws and court decisions that seek to achieve fair treatment of everyone. Affirmative action is a common course taken to remedy past and current barriers to employment. One approach to eliminating prejudice is through increased social contact and workplace interaction. Contact with people who are different helps eliminate the other causes of prejudice.

   a. *Types of workplace discrimination:* Workplace discrimination can occur in areas of performance appraisal, pay, promotion, job selection—virtually any area of work. The following are some of the specific forms that this discrimination can take:

      1. *Testing and evaluation:* The criteria used for testing and evaluating minorities and females have long been considered suspect. In schools, the differences between the average scores of minority groups and the general population are often significant. Even with knowledge of this kind of variation, employers have used standardized tests to make job selections and promotions. The most serious aspect of the problem is that the test may have little relation to the job. The highest scorer may not be the best performer. Some tests do measure minimum standards for performance, and these tests are often used to create the job or promotion applicant pool. Once placed in the pool, other methods can be used to make a fair selection. A prejudiced evaluator can still prevent selection or promotion.

         EXAMPLE: *A fire department of a midsized city illustrates the difficulties faced by those who work to change discriminatory practices. The fire department faced three problems in recruitment: the Emergency Medical Technician (EMT) Certification, a low number of minority applications, and a range of tests, including physical agility tests. The physical tests are crucial because of the need to lift and carry the injured or ill. To solve the problems, they began a program to encourage more minorities to enroll in EMT classes and provide physical training and exercise classes to build strength and agility.*

      2. *The glass ceiling:* The **glass ceiling** occurs when a member of a minority group or a female reaches what appears to be a limit to further promotion. Tests and performance evaluations may create roadblocks, but usually the perceived cause is some form of the "old boy's network."

EXAMPLE: *One of the more male-oriented fields is construction. A contractor hires 10 women to serve as a committee called the Female Employment Initiative. Their role is to increase training opportunities and also to make construction jobs friendlier by minimizing sexual harassment.*

3. *Tokenism:* **Tokenism** occurs when one or a few minority or female candidates are promoted, and the management takes the attitude, "Now we have met our responsibilities." These few are "tokens" of efforts to end active discrimination. However, such tokenism discriminates against those not chosen and casts a shadow over the few who were selected. Another form of tokenism is the use of a quota system, where a set number or percentage of promotions and new employees must have a minority status or be female. Quota systems have been used to correct severe discrimination, but they can be misused, creating discrimination against members of both the minority and the majority groups.

4. *Pay differential:* Pay differences still persist between male and female average pay and between majority and minority pay. While most people believe that those who perform the same tasks at similar levels of quality and productivity should be paid the same, actual pay differences continue. New pay systems might help by making pay contingent upon skills and group performance as well as individual performance, the opportunities to acquire additional skills may be limited by the testing and evaluation discrimination practices. Discriminatory selection practices can have effects throughout an organization.

5. *Reverse discrimination:* A subtle yet very real form of discrimination occurs when a member of a minority group receives preferential treatment in an effort to be fair. An evaluator may actually apply different, sometimes less stringent standards of performance to members of a minority group. This is unfair to everyone. It gives the impression that some groups do not have to work as hard, or that they are having it "handed to them on a platter."

EXAMPLES:

Researchers found that teachers would rate an essay of poor quality higher if they thought that an African American had written the paper, and then rate it lower if they thought it had been written by a white student. This kind of differential treatment can perpetuate prejudice.

Quota systems have a potential for reverse discrimination. The quota system that was being used at the University of California Davis Medical School led to an African American being selected over a white male with better qualifications. Bakke, the white male, sued and eventually took the case to the U.S. Supreme Court. The Supreme Court ruled that a quota could not be used to correct racial imbalance unless there was a history of intentional discrimination.

b. *Affirmative action as a remedy:* **Affirmative action** is not a law, but has evolved through presidential executive orders and a number of court cases intended to remedy discriminatory practices. The constitutional rights of free speech, due process (the right to fair and equal treatment in law and organizational policy), and privacy protect workers as well.

1. *Type One plans:* Type One plans focus on improved recruitment and hiring of minorities and women.

EXAMPLE: *A Chicago truck and bus maker began a program that focuses on recruiting minorities and women at 10 major universities. The truck maker saw this approach as an effective way for them to increase the minority and female applicant pool and to identify top recruits early.*

However, small companies cannot send recruiters all over the nation, and they face greater difficulty getting applications and qualified applicants because they are less visible.

2. *Type Two plans:* Type Two plans focus on how decisions will be made in hiring and promotion. These plans are used when minorities and women are underrepresented in the position.

   EXAMPLE: *If two individuals have equal qualifications for a position, then the job offer will go to the minority or female candidate.*

3. *Type Three plans:* Type Three plans set hiring and promotion decisions on the basis of minimum qualifications. If a minority or female candidate meets the minimum qualifications, the minority or female candidate will be given the position even if a non-minority or male candidate has higher qualifications. Type three plans tend to have difficulties in court.

   EXAMPLE: *The director of a major hospital needed a chief financial officer, and the CEO insisted on hiring a minority. The CEO believed the notion of "best candidate" does not necessarily mean white male.*

4. *Type Four plans:* Type Four plans state that a female or minority will receive the job. The search will continue until a female or minority is found who meets the qualifications. No Type Four plan has ever been allowed by the Supreme Court.

2. **Laws Regulating Discrimination:** Centuries of prejudice and discrimination have been addressed in the last few decades through affirmative action, the Equal Employment Opportunities Commission (EEOC), and laws focused on establishing fair and equal practices. These laws include the Civil Rights Acts of 1964 and 1991, the Americans with Disabilities Act of 1990, and the Age Discrimination Employment Act of 1967. These specific laws are described in following sections.

3. **Sexual Harassment and Hostile Environments:** Sexual harassment includes a range of actions from comments to actual assaults, and it can be a series of actions or a single act. Quid pro quo harassment involves sexual coercion of an individual as a condition for special treatment, promotion, or job. In addition to employees, clients of a company and individuals who have other special relationships with people, such as teachers, physicians, counselors, and so on, may be engaged in quid pro quo harassment. The existence of a hostile environment has been recognized as a source of sexual harassment. Coworkers, clients, and customers, as well as supervisors can create hostile environments. The consequences for victims of sexual harassment include shame and guilt, physical symptoms, and anxiety and helplessness in addition to lost productivity. Sexual harassment can be addressed through individual effort, sensitivity training programs, clear corporate policies, and serious efforts to enforce the policies.

   a. *Forms of workplace harassment:* The workplace has become sensitive to sexual harassment. Several conditions apply to sexual harassment: the victim or the harasser may be of either sex; the harasser does not have to be the victim's superior; the victim and the harasser need not be of the opposite sex; the victim does not have to be the person to whom the sexual advances are directed; the victim does not have to complain to the harasser or inform the employer; and the victim need not suffer a concrete economic injury as a result of the harassment.

1. The actions that might be included in sexual harassment range from comments to actual assaults.

2. The harassment can be a series of actions or a single act.

3. It may be as severe as rape or physical assault, yet the more common forms include demands for sexual intercourse, pressure to date, touching, leaning on or over, sexually charged comments, and teasing.

b. *Definition of sexual harassment:* **Sexual harassment** includes any conduct involving the "unwanted imposition of sexual requirements in a relationship of unequal power." According to the EEOC's 1980 definition, *sexual harassment* is defined as:

Unwelcome sexual advances, requests for sexual favors, and other verbal or physical conduct of a sexual nature constitute sexual harassment when (1) submission to such conduct is made either explicitly or implicitly a term or condition of an individual's employment, (2) submission to or rejection of such conduct by an individual is used as a basis for employment decisions affecting such individual, or (3) such conduct has the purpose or effect of unreasonably interfering with an individual's work performance or creating an intimidating, hostile, or offensive working environment. (29 C.F.R sec. 1604.11 (a), quoted in McWhirter, *Your Rights,* p. 121)

c. *Interpretation of the guidelines:* The first two components of these guidelines establish what has been called *quid pro quo* harassment. The third component has been identified with claims of hostile environments.

1. *Quid pro quo harassment: Quid pro quo* means simply, "Do me a favor and I'll do one for you." In **quid pro quo sexual harassment,** a sexual favor is exchanged for promotion, favorable or special treatment, or even the job itself.

a. *Supervisor–employee relationships:* In 1986, the Supreme Court held that sexual harassment by a supervisor constituted sex discrimination covered by the 1964 Civil Rights Act. When expectations or demands are made of a sexual nature, then the actions of supervisors become coercive for reasons other than the supervisor's legitimate responsibility and authority.

EXAMPLE: *About 30 years ago, Senator Bob Packwood of Oregon was considered a leader in defending women's rights. Many young women wanted to work for his Senate office. In 1992, Senator Packwood was accused of sexual harassment by a number of women who worked in his office during the previous 20 years. It seems that he engaged, by his own admission, in a number of inappropriate behaviors. The women felt harassed and did not feel able to come forward at the time. Now the laws have changed—due in part to the senator's own work—and the reporting climate is more favorable to the acceptance of women's complaints. In 1995, after Senate hearings, Senator Packwood chose to resign.*

b. *Client relationships:* Quid pro quo harassment can occur in client relationships as well. Imagine a situation where a client expects sexual favors—or at least some form of flirting—before signing a contract or as a matter of doing regular business. A female on a team dealing with such a client can feel particular pressure to help secure the account. However, sexual favors for a client are not part of anyone's job description.

c. *Teacher–student sexual relationships:* Teacher–student sexual relationships are particularly sensitive to quid pro quo harassment. Teachers can easily coerce students into sexual relationships. There may be implied or outright promises of improved grades or help preparing papers or for tests. Even relationships that are avowed by both parties to have been freely entered can be tainted by the appearance of sex for grades. Almost every public and private school, college, and university has clearly stated standards for sexual conduct between teacher and student, usually as an extension of sexual harassment polices.

2. *Hostile environment:* A **hostile environment** is more difficult to define and has been more difficult to prove in court cases. By 1991, a federal judge had determined that photographs of nude or partially dressed women constituted sexual harassment in the workplace. A hostile environment may be an extension of the sexual harassment to the entire environment, or it may be a sustained atmosphere of threat, discrimination, hostility, and discomfort not related to sexual aggression.

    EXAMPLE: *A hostile environment case developed in allegations against Hooters, a restaurant and bar franchise based on a concept of females dressed in jogging shorts and T-shirts and a menu filled with double-entendres (statements that have two meanings, like "more than a mouthful"). Former "Hooters Girls" have claimed that the concept encourages customers and male employees to harass the servers.*

3. *Client relationships:* Just as with quid pro quo harassment, clients can create hostile environments.

    EXAMPLE: *McCarthy, an advertising account representative, was constantly offended by the obnoxious behavior of a client. While anxious not to lose the account, McCarthy tolerated obscene behavior at meetings, parties, and client dinners as long as possible. Finally, McCarthy asked to be removed from the account. Fortunately, the supervisor understood the situation and replaced McCarthy with another account representative.*

    When clients mean profits, the problem can produce difficult, ethical choices for a company to make.

4. *Coworker involvement:* The hostile environment form of sexual harassment is more likely to involve coworkers than is the quid pro quo form. Coworkers tell jokes and interact as friends, but they can also tell jokes and interact as a means of harassing other coworkers. No longer merely bad taste or boorish behavior, insults and taunts like these create an atmosphere that makes job performance suffer.

d. *Impact on victims of harassment:*

1. *Shame and guilt:* Both submission and refusal can result in a sense of guilt. By submitting, the victim knows that she or he stands to gain an unfair advantage. If the advance is refused, she or he can easily blame him or herself for not handling the situation better and then avoiding all the problems connected with the refusal. In either choice, virtually every event can be reinterpreted as a result of the sexual coercion.

2. *Physical disorders:* The stress that a harassed individual feels, both because of a fear of being found out and a fear of the consequences for refusal or for standing up to the harasser, causes stress. With the stress come stress-related physical disorders. Specific health problems observed in victims of harassment include headache, chronic fatigue, nausea, sleep problems, appetite problems, and increased number of colds and urinary track infections. These problems then have another cost in the lost work time and the increased health care costs.

3. *Anxiety and helplessness:* Since sexual harassment creates a "damned if you do and damned if you don't" situation, the individual is quite prone to experiencing a sense of helplessness. Feelings of helplessness are associated with mild and severe depression. Depression can require clinical intervention to overcome. The no-win choice also causes anxiety, which itself can be compounded with the anxiety about how others view the activity. Self-esteem and self-confidence suffer greatly in these conditions.

4. *Hypersensitivity:* The harassed individual experiences the worst of the symptoms, but the workplace can have symptoms too. Public accusations of sexual harassment have changed workplaces across the country as they become charged with anxiety about saying or doing the wrong thing. Rather than becoming sensitive to the issues, people have become hypersensitive. When a legitimate complement about a man's new tie or a woman's new dress is offered, the half-joking "Oh, was that sexual harassment?" has become a frequent response.

5. *Defensive responses:* Rather than find other ways to include each other in office or workplace conversations, a choice remains to exclude for fear of accidental harassment. While complete refusal to recognize people of the opposite sex is unlikely, the environment can be tainted with a wariness that will affect productivity.

e. *Legal remedies—individual rights and corporate obligations:* People readily accept the definition of sexual harassment as covering a supervisor or other person of higher status making unwanted advances toward a person of a lower status. In the stereotypical conception of harassment, the supervisor is male and the victim is female. According to EEOC regulations, other conditions apply and make a much broader application to individual rights and corporate obligations. These conditions are as follows:

1. *The victim or the harasser may be of either sex:* The larger numbers of victims of harassment are women, but the number of men filing complaints is increasing.

   EXAMPLE: *A notable public case occurred when a male aide sued a female St. Paul City Council Member and the City of St. Paul. The aide charged that harassment by the council member had occurred over a 20-month period.*

2. *The harasser does not have to be the victim's superior:* According to a national survey of readers and of the human resource directors of the *Fortune 1000* companies by *Working Woman* magazine, more than 80 percent of the cases reported by respondents involved a harasser who was in a position superior to the victim. The remainder involves coworkers.

3. *The victim and the harasser need not be of the opposite sex:* The defining characteristic is whether gender is used as the basis of differential treatment. Same-sex sexual harassment is included by the EEOC.

4. *The victim does not have to be the person to whom the sexual advances are directed:* When one person is being harassed, the environment can become hostile and sexually intimidating. Others in that environment become victims too. Special favors and threats change the political balance of the workplace.

5. *The victim does not have to complain to the harasser or inform the employer:* The victim can sue the employer because of the liability the employer has in providing a harassment free workplace. If the harasser is a nonemployee, like the client described in the case of McCarthy, the employer has the responsibility, if informed, to protect the employee from harassment during the course of normal work.

6. *The victim need not suffer a concrete economic injury as a result of the harassment:* Interference with work or the existence of an intimidating workplace is sufficient to bring suit.

Naturally, organizations need to protect themselves by developing clear policies against harassment and then to enforce the policies. The primary obligation of the organization is to provide a work environment free of harassment.

f. *Approaches to dealing with sexual harassment:* A combined effort of the individual and the organization is required. Many companies and public agencies have initiated training programs focused on sensitivity to gender issues. The focus of the sensitivity programs is to teach men and women to respect each other and treat each other with dignity.

EXAMPLE: *A major chemical company has a four-hour workshop that has been attended by most of its 95,000 employees. Employees receive basic information about policies and procedures related to sexual harassment and then watch video depictions of situations. Many companies have programs designed to make sure that employees know the procedures that are followed to make complaints and the potential penalties for harassers.*

Check Point—Section A

Directions: For each question, circle the correct answer.

A–1. Sousa, a member of a minority, takes an employment examination that has been standardized for the general population. Sousa can expect

A) fair placement based on actual performance on the test

B) better than average chances based on the test results

C) scores ignored as required by affirmative action

D) less likelihood of success than the majority population

A–2. Which one of the following is *not* considered sexual harassment?

A) Teacher–student relationships

B) Employee–employee relationships

C) Quid pro quo

D) Hostile environment

A–3. Seals works in an office where the supervisor is having an affair with a subordinate. The subordinate is at the same level in the hierarchy as Seals. Seals is most likely to

A) be completely unaware of any consequences

B) suffer distress because of the increase in anxiety in the workplace

C) be sued by the victim for not interceding to stop the affair

D) receive special favors from the victimizer

B. Laws Affecting Management and Employees

Laws cover much of the activity in the workplace, and the administrative professional must be aware of these laws and the impact they have on being an effective contributor to the flow of work. Managers must be particularly well informed concerning laws that cover compensation, benefits, workplace safety, and drug use and abuse, in addition to the laws already addressed.

1. *Laws Related to Compensation and Benefits:* Many laws at the federal, state, county, and municipal levels influence human resource management practices dealing with compensation and benefit issues of all sizes and types of organizations. While most widely known laws have been developed at the federal level, legislation that is often further reaching and more binding exists at the state and local levels. This section includes some of the major laws at the federal level.

    a. *Equal employment opportunity (EEO):* Perhaps the most widely known laws affecting compensation and benefit policies and practices today exist in the area of equal employment opportunity. The term **equal employment opportunity** refers to the responsibilities and obligations that organizations have to ensure that all human resource management objectives, policies, procedures, and specific rules are developed and administered to ensure that every potential and present employee is treated fairly, regardless of race, gender, color, age, religion, or national origin. This pertains especially to the awarding and administration of compensation and benefits. Organizations are also mandated to maintain records that are subject to public scrutiny in such areas as:

        1. Orientation, training, and development programs

        2. Direct and indirect compensation and benefits

        3. Work requirements, workloads, work shift assignments, and overtime benefits

        4. Promotions, demotions, transfers, temporary layoffs, and terminations

    b. *Title VII of the Civil Rights Act of 1964:* The keystone of equal employment opportunity and affirmative action activities at the federal level is Title VII of the Civil Rights Act of 1964, as amended by the Equal Employment Opportunity Act of 1972. The act created the Equal Employment Opportunity Commission (EEOC) to promulgate (make known or announce publicly) and enforce employment discrimination regulations for employers with 15 or more employees. EEO provisions pertain to virtually all organizations and individuals. Some of the major provisions of this legislation include the following:

        1. Title VII prohibits discrimination based on race, color, religion, gender, or national origin in any form of employment.

        2. An employer may not discriminate in hiring, retaining, promoting, or laying off employees.

3. In very limited situations involving reasonable business necessity, an employer may apply a bona fide occupational qualification defense whereby an employer may legally discriminate based on gender, national origin, or religion but not race or color.

4. The role of the EEOC is to investigate complaints, attempt to reach administrative solutions with employers, file suits against employees on behalf of claimants, and dismiss complaints.

c. *Equal Pay Act of 1963:* The Equal Pay Act of 1963 prohibits wage discrimination on the basis of gender. This act mandates that employees holding equal jobs should receive equal pay.

1. In reality, women still are paid only about 80 percent of the wages that men receive for doing the same work.

2. Many women hold positions that do not involve identical tasks compared to men but have seemingly equal workloads and responsibilities. In these cases they usually receive lower wages unless a shortage of qualified workers exists in the labor market.

3. Women in some traditionally female-dominated occupations have more responsibilities and require greater knowledge to perform their work than men in traditionally male-oriented jobs.

EXAMPLES:

Nurses and truck drivers

Elementary school teachers and miners

Executive administrative professional and construction workers

d. *Doctrine of comparable worth:* The **doctrine of comparable worth** states that people holding different jobs that require comparable knowledge, skills, and responsibilities should receive the same pay and benefits.

1. The doctrine of comparable worth has still not been accepted as official law by the U.S. government.

2. Many foes of comparable worth argue that the differences are too great or difficult to be evaluated equally.

3. Many proponents of comparable worth suggest that the arguments concerning difficulties in measurement are a smokescreen designed to keep wage and benefit costs lower even when strong evidence supports the position that "comparable" jobs have "like" tasks and responsibilities.

e. *Pregnancy Discrimination Act of 1978:* The Pregnancy Discrimination Act of 1978 prohibits firms from dismissing women solely on the basis of pregnancy and protects their job security during maternity leave. The act mandates firms to treat pregnancy and maternity leave the same as other types of leaves of absence. While this federal act pertains primarily to larger firms, some states have extended it to apply also to employers of very small organizations. This act specifically protects fringe benefits and job seniority.

f. *Age Discrimination in Employment Act of 1967, as amended:* The Age Discrimination in Employment Act of 1967, as amended, prohibits employment discrimination on the basis of age. This act especially protects people 40 to 70 years of age, particularly in pay and benefit issues.

    1. Some firms may increase the physical and mental workloads of long-term employees as they approach retirement age. The insidious goal of at least a few of the firms using these policies is to try to get the workers to quit before they can retire with full pension and benefits, a very devious way of trying to save some dollars.

g. *Mandatory Retirement Act of 1974:* The Mandatory Retirement Act of 1974, as amended, prohibited organizations from enforcing mandatory retirement before the age of 70. Now there is no mandatory retirement age in many professions and organizations, although some notable exceptions exist.

h. *Employee Retirement Income Security Act of 1974 (ERISA):* This legislation guarantees certain pension vesting rights to employees.

    1. Vesting is the policy that makes individuals entitled to collect pensions that they may have earned previously with an employer. They may or may not still be in that organization's employ when they retire.

    2. ERISA guarantees vesting and also sets certain standards of conduct that individuals who direct organizational pension programs must follow to avoid fund mismanagement.

    3. ERISA does not require organizations to offer pension programs to employees, but if the firms do so, they can be required to meet specified rules and regulations.

i. *Veterans Readjustment Act of 1974:* This law prohibits discrimination against disabled and Vietnam War veterans. Its provisions apply to persons participating in Operation Desert Storm and similar incursions.

j. *Vocational Rehabilitation Act of 1973:* The Vocational Rehabilitation Act of 1973 prohibits organizations from discriminating in hiring, promotion, pay, fringe benefits, or other HRM practices on the basis of physical or mental disability.

k. *Social Security Act of 1935, as amended:* The Social Security Act provides a guaranteed minimum income to persons who are retired and disabled. The Social Security Act provides income from Social Security funds for countless retired persons in the United States.

l. *Fair Labor Standards Act of 1938, as amended:* The Fair Labor Standards Act, as amended in 1938, includes provisions establishing a minimum wage, requiring the payment of overtime for many people who work over 40 hours per week, and setting standards regarding the use of child labor.

m. *Health Maintenance Organization (HMO) Act of 1973:* This act was passed to stimulate the development of prepaid health care systems.

    1. An HMO is an organization of physicians and other health care professionals that provides treatment and preventive medical care to subscribing members.

    2. Persons who belong to an HMO must use the organization's providers or pay for the services of outside professionals, unless granted permission to do so in a genuine emergency.

3. HMOs are viewed as a viable alternative in reducing health care costs. While the choice of providers is limited to those within the group and many physicians do not join HMOs, participants in full-service organizations often view them as being very favorable.

n. *Family and Medical Leave Act of 1993:* This act was passed to ensure that employees who need to take care of family members will be able to do so, under specific circumstances, without the fear of losing their jobs.

1. Eligible employees are entitled to 12 weeks of unpaid leave, under specific circumstances, during any 12-month period.

2. Employees are entitled to a leave to take care of a child, which includes birth, adoption, and placement of a foster child with the family.

3. Employees are also eligible for a leave when care is needed for a spouse, a parent, or a child with a serious health condition.

4. The employee who is unable to work due to a serious personal health problem is also eligible for a leave.

The Family and Medical Leave Act applies only to employers who have at least 50 employees within 75 miles of a worksite.

o. *State and local laws affecting HRM:* In many instances, state and local laws are much more stringent than federal legislation in the broad field of human resources management. When state or local laws are more rigid, they have to be followed. When no federal legislation has been enacted pertaining to a specific topic but state or local laws do exist, they have to be followed. Organizations having operations in various states and localities are required to keep abreast of and in compliance with the HRM laws in all jurisdictions in which they function. Three areas to be mentioned are minimum wage, children's work hours, and family leave.

1. *Minimum wage:* Some states have higher minimum wage laws than the current standard as specified in the Fair Labor Standards Act. Firms operating in these states must pay the higher minimum wage.

2. *Children's working laws:* Some states and localities have more stringent laws regarding children's work activities than those contained in the Fair Labor Standards Act. In such cases the state or local laws must be followed.

3. *Family and medical leave laws:* The federal government has passed legislation regarding family leave in specific situations to protect employment and fringe benefits. However, the trend is for more states and local jurisdictions to have stricter laws regarding family leave. If both federal and state or local laws exist, the more stringent laws apply.

EXAMPLES:

In California, employers with 50 or more employees are required to provide 16 weeks of unpaid leave over a two-year period for birth, family illness, or foster care. Similar laws exist in Connecticut and the District of Columbia.

In Washington, employers of 100 or more employees must allow 12 weeks of unpaid leave or accrued sick leave to be used for birth, adoption, or the care of an ill child.

In Minnesota, employees working for firms of at least 21 workers can take up to six weeks for birth or adoption, as well as use accrued sick leave days to take care of sick children. Also, employees can receive 16 hours of unpaid leave per year to attend school conferences.

Wisconsin permits employees at firms that employ at least 50 workers to use up to eight weeks of unpaid leave a year for birth, adoption, or family or personal illness.

In Dade County, Florida, employers of 50 or more workers must permit up to 90 days of unpaid leave every two years for employees to deal with childbirth, adoption, or the serious illness of a close relative.

2. ***Workers' Compensation Laws:*** Through workers' compensation laws, benefits are provided for injured workers or their dependents regardless of who is at fault. With workers' compensation, workers do not have to prove the employer's negligence or culpability. If a worker is killed or injured on the job, the worker or the worker's dependents collect according to a schedule based on the severity of the injury. The employer pays the total cost of workers' compensation insurance. All states require businesses to have workers' compensation coverage through state or private insurance companies. The premiums are based largely on the risks involved in performing various jobs.

   EXAMPLE: *The workers' compensation fees for loggers and police officers are much higher than those for office workers or food service workers.*

3. ***Health and Safety:*** While the immediate responsibility for the health and safety of each worker rests with the line supervisor or immediate superior, concerns for the continued wellness of all employees must be shared throughout the organization—from top management, HRM experts, and the individual worker. Each worker has to bear some responsibility for his or her own safety. Total responsibility cannot be placed on each supervisor, especially if attempts are made to hide specific conditions or problems. An error by anyone in the production or service processes occurring because of problems caused by any factor within the organization can have reverberating effects. Through the proactive support of immediate supervisors, the administrative professional is in a unique position to assist with a health and safety prevention program that will provide safe and sound working environments. Improper practices, leading to health and safety problems, can be avoided or minimized with oversight, proper planning, and continuous reminders. Resources (money, time, work produced) are lost by employees who are away from the job for health reasons as well as those who are working at less than optimum efficiency because of health-related problems.

   a. *Benefits of health and safety programs:* When a viable health and safety program is in effect, organizations gain through such ways as:

      1. Reduced health insurance and workers' compensation insurance premiums

      2. Reduced litigation costs to pursue injury claims

      3. Less money paid out for lost work time

      4. Fewer expenses involved in training and orienting new and replacement workers

      5. Less overtime pay for workers who remain at work while others are out due to illness

6. Greater productivity and quality when workers are well and performing on the job

7. Greater productivity, quality, and customer satisfaction stemming from high morale and pride that usually result when workers realize that management is providing safe working conditions

b. *Health and safety legislation:* Organizations should be responsible for ensuring that working conditions are up to standard. Legislation administered through public agencies plays a key role in seeing that working conditions are not health or safety hazards for employees. The Occupational Safety and Health Act (OSHA) of 1970 (as amended) directs employers to develop and to implement health and safety programs for workers. Mandatory workers' compensation laws require that all employers have coverage.

1. *Occupational Safety and Health Act of 1970:* The specific provisions of this legislation include the following:

a. Requiring employers to provide their workers with a place of employment free from established hazards that can lead to serious physical harm or even death

b. Mandating that employers follow specific health and safety standards as determined by OSHA

c. Establishing enforcement mechanisms to ensure that employers maintain safe working conditions for their employees, at the risk of facing serious fines and even possible imprisonment

EXAMPLE: *The newly appointed administrator of a midwestern health clinic group became concerned about the safety of employees after observing a frayed electric cord on an examining room light in one of the offices. The administrator requested a voluntary inspection by the state's OSHA agency of the physical facilities under his supervision.*

A team of inspectors studied the facilities and presented the administrator with a list of recommendations: replacing a few rods on stairways, repairing broken ladder rungs, replacing a defective refrigerator, and replacing inoperative fire extinguishers. The administrator quickly had the recommendations implemented. Costs involved were minimal, particularly when compared with possible losses that might have resulted from unsafe and unsanitary conditions that inspectors identified.

Complaints are sometimes made about OSHA's intrusion into the operations of organizations. However, given the fact that an organization's most valuable resource is its people, OSHA performs a vital role that should not be overlooked. When an inspection is requested voluntarily, the organization is usually given time to make any needed health or safety corrections without fear of penalty.

c. *Smoke-free workplace rules:* The issue of smoking in the workplace has resulted in dramatic changes. Most government agencies now declare smoke-free buildings. The costs of smoking have made other companies place strict penalties on smokers. The potential insurance costs and law suits from people who suffer secondhand smoke has led many employers to declare the workplace smoke-free.

1. *No-smoking policies:* No-smoking policies have developed in public and private organizations. Aggressive codes, such as the California state labor code, have provisions that state if a worker like a firefighter develops lung disease, then the employer is presumed responsible. These aggressive policies and the numerous implementations of smoking bans in buildings have made non-smokers very happy. Perhaps one of the most extreme policies developed in 1986 and continues to this day: Atlanta-based CNN (now a division of Time-Warner) adopted a "no smokers need apply" rule.

2. *Smokers' rights:* On the other side of the issue is the smoker. Smokers believe that they have the right to smoke cigarettes if they want to do so. Some believe they have the right to do so in closed spaces when nonsmokers are present. The American Civil Liberties Union has begun a Workplace Rights Project to investigate where the line should be drawn. At what point do the rights of privacy end and the rights of others become primary? Most states protect the worker from discrimination for behavior when not at work, and most of these apply specifically to smoking.

3. *Costs of smoking:* Even when smoking does not occur at work, the non-smoking workers pay for the nonwork behavior of smoking workers through higher group health costs. When an employer is considering a no-smoking rule or establishing smoke-free buildings, smokers and nonsmokers can become quite emotional about the options.

4. **Drug Use and Abuse:** The Drug-Free Workplace Act of 1988 led to an increase in testing for drug use in the workplace. The law directly addresses employers who have contracts with the federal government.

   a. *Drug-free workplace and testing:* Employers are required to ensure a **drug-free workplace,** that is, a workplace in which illegal drug use is not tolerated, and the employer is able to claim that illegal drugs are not being used. The extent to which an employer can test employees continues to be challenged and tested in the courts. It is clear that when safety or national security is involved, testing is likely to be allowed.

   b. *Limits:* Corporate control of drugs in the workplace has raised many issues that spread to the privacy of a worker when not at work. Drug traces can persist from one day to the next, and yet the drug may no longer affect performance.

Check Point—Section B

Directions: For each question, circle the correct answer.

B–1. Chung has filed a grievance with the EEOC. Which one law established this body and governs the grievance?

A) Title VII of the Civil Rights Act of 1964

B) Equal Pay Act of 1963

C) Fair Labor Standards Act of 1938

D) Americans with Disabilities Act of 1994

B–2. Simmons's mother is quite ill, and she lives in the house with the Simmons family. Which law would be most helpful to Simmons in caring for the mother?

A) Social Security Act of 1935

B) Health Maintenance Organization Act of 1973

C) Pregnancy Discrimination Act of 1978

D) Family and Medical Leave Act of 1993

B–3. Patton, a smoker, takes frequent breaks to smoke outside the building following new regulations requiring no smoking in the workplace. Pat-ton's employer has most likely taken this step for which one of the following reasons?

A) Complaints by nonsmokers

B) Costs of smoking

C) Political correctness

D) Mandates by the federal government

C. Employment and Separation

Recruitment, hiring, and separation from employment are activities that have legal protections and regulations that must be followed very carefully to avoid litigation.

1. *Legal Issues in Recruitment and Selection:* Establishing sound policies for recruiting and selecting employees is paramount to a firm's ability to survive in a competitive business world.

   a. *Recruitment:* Recruitment and selection procedures need not use sophisticated techniques. But the use of practices that are fair and nondiscriminatory and able to match people to available positions is imperative.

      1. *General purposes of recruitment:* As soon as an organization has determined that additional human resources are required, as identified during the HRM planning process, action must be initiated to identify applicants who might be interested in filling the position vacancies.

         a. *Recruitment:* **Recruitment** is the process of locating, identifying, and attracting qualified applicants to fill positions within an organization.

         b. *Sources of applicants:* Sources of potential applicants can often be identified easily, but the potential candidates must be enticed to apply for the vacant position(s) that the organization is seeking to fill.

         c. *Qualifications for positions:* Organizations must seek to identify the potentially most qualified individuals to apply. The qualifications for any position are identified in the job specification. Sometimes the job specification is included as a major section in the overall job description.

         d. *Applicants from minority groups:* Active efforts must be taken to ensure that potentially qualified applicants from minority groups are informed about the vacancies to ensure compliance with equal employment opportunity and affirmative action laws. Persons responsible for recruitment should apply special measures to be able to prove that minority-group members were sought out actively as potential applicants. Recruiters should reach and notify recruitment sources that minority-group members might utilize to learn about job openings.

      2. *Internal recruiting (recruiting from within):* The most common approach of many organizations to recruit potential candidates for vacant positions is the use of internal sources.

a. *Recruiting from within:* Recruiting from within the organization is accomplished by:

    1. Notifying present employees about job vacancies and encouraging them to apply for positions for which they are qualified.

    2. Asking present employees to identify or to refer persons whom they know to apply for the positions. Sometimes these employee referrals are viewed as an external recruiting resource. However, asking current employees to recommend persons whom they know and consider qualified to apply typically results in recruiting from within.

b. *Inbreeding can occur:* **Inbreeding** can occur when too many people of the same background, interests, and cultural orientation become associated with an organization. This can result in a paucity of new ideas and new blood being infused throughout the organization.

c. *Qualifications:* Sometimes lesser qualified people are accepted as the organization tries not to offend its present employees. As a result, training and development costs may also be greater.

d. *Equal opportunity:* Recruiting from within can lead an organization to violate equal employment opportunity or affirmative action laws because most existing employees will usually not be members of minority groups that the firm should be actively trying to get to apply for job vacancies.

e. *Promotion:* Promoting from within can also be in violation of EEO and AA laws if the organization then seeks to fill primarily just the entry-level positions through external recruitment methods. The reasoning is that women and members of minority groups should have a fair chance to attain higher level positions within the organization. If they are only "let in on the bottom floor," the perception can be that the upper levels are reserved for the old boys' network.

3. *External recruiting (recruiting from without):* The HRM policy of using external recruiting is very effective in many situations. This strategy does have its pros and cons, however.

a. Attracting the most qualified people for the job is a major advantage. Very often organizations that have highly specialized positions do not have adequately trained replacements available to fill vacancies that arise. Also, internally generated employee referrals may not generate the most qualified applicants for specialized positions.

b. External recruiting is highly recommended if an organization does not have an adequate share of women and minority-group members in its employ or in the more specialized, higher level positions.

c. Sometimes the "recruit from within" policy results in women and minority-group-member employees being relegated to mundane, first-level nonmanagerial or specialized jobs.

d. External recruiting often affords an organization the opportunity of identifying women and minority-group members who clearly have the qualifications for more specialized, higher level, and managerial positions. The organization may find less internal resistance to bringing in qualified outsiders, regardless of their gender, race, religion, color, or national origin, when an external recruitment policy is utilized.

   e. More risks are taken in recruiting and hiring outsiders than in promoting and appointing people who are already known within the organization or to its members.

4. *External recruiting resources:* A number of different external sources can be used to locate, identify, and attract capable persons to apply for positions within any organization.

   a. *Newspaper want ads:* Want ads in the classified section of the newspaper are probably the most commonly used external recruitment resource.

   b. *Specialized journals and publications:* Specialized publications are a less widely used but more effective means of attracting qualified applicants.

      EXAMPLE: *Some employers receive hundreds of applications from one classified ad placed in a city or urban newspaper when they are actively seeking persons to fill administrative professional positions.*

   c. *Professional associations:* Another feasible source of potential applicants, especially for specialized positions and those requiring persons with higher education preparation, is the professional association most closely related to the type of position.

      EXAMPLE: *The Midwest Business Administration Association has been holding annual meetings for the past 30 years, many of these at the Palmer House, a prestigious hotel in the heart of downtown Chicago. Organizations interested in finding possible candidates for teaching, research, or specialized professional positions can pay a nominal fee to have job vacancies listed at the conference. Persons seeking jobs can have their resumes made available to prospective employers at the meetings by paying a nominal fee. There are always areas where organizational representatives and applicants can meet. The regularity of this organization's conferences and the same centralized location each year make it a highly conducive setting for selective recruitment activities. Countless other professional organizations offer similar services.*

   d. *Educational institutions:* Placement services within educational institutions help link employers with students and alumni. The services can range from simple listings of possible candidates to full-scale data searches for specifically qualified applicants and the opportunity to interview individuals in professional settings. Some institutions hold career days for their students, at which time organizations set up displays and have the opportunity to meet a variety of potential applicants from a large or limited number of disciplines.

   e. *Public employment services:* Public employment services are of value to local and state organizations in the recruitment and screening of possible applicants for positions.

   f. *Private employment agencies:* Private agencies can be very effective in finding high-caliber individuals because of usually extensive knowledge of select fields.

g. *Labor unions and trade associations:* These organizations are excellent referral sources for skilled and semiskilled employees.

h. *Walk-ins and mail-ins:* Another group of external recruitment resources comes from walk-ins and mail-ins, individuals who are inquiring about the possibility of job openings.

i. *The Internet:* Many organizations are now utilizing the Internet and the World Wide Web (WWW) to attract, recruit, and select employees from a vast pool of individuals, including those not seeking active employment. Virtually all the selection functions including credentials checks, reference evaluations, paper-and-pencil tests, and even interviews can be conducted over the Internet. Promising anonymity, firms are able to attract persons who normally might not be seeking new positions.

j. *The combined approach:* Most organizations tend to use a combination of internal and external recruiting methods.

   (i)   Some organizations promote only from within while hiring persons from the outside to fill beginning and entry-level positions.

   (ii) A few firms try to get beginning and entry-level positions filled through employee or community referrals, maintaining the exclusive recruitment-from-within approach through the organization.

   (iii) Very few organizations rely exclusively on external recruitment human resource procedures.

   (iv) After recruitment activities for particular positions have ceased, the selection process must begin.

b. *Selection:* Many different selection methods are available. Common practices include screening applicants through formal applications and employment tests and the use of personal interviews.

   1. *Screening of applicants:* The selection procedures should include screening techniques. The amount of screening done will vary based on the company's needs. Because of the work involved, some firms need a particular type of person.

   2. *Employment tests:* Any instrument or informational device used by human resources personnel to make an employment decision may be considered an employment test. Federal and state governments have been actively seeking to determine whether employment tests being used have potential for adverse impact.

      a. *Job skills tests:* Some businesses find it necessary to design exercises that are validated to test for skills the applicant must apply to specific job tasks. If these tests are job related, they are typically better predictors of job success and the chance for adverse impact of the testing will be minimized. Job skills tests are commonly used in the staffing process.

         EXAMPLE: *An applicant for an administrative position may need to demonstrate expertise in working with specific software applications, such as word processing or databases as a part of the application process.*

      b. *Personality tests:* Another type of test often used during the selection process is the personality test or inventory. These inventories may be most helpful in selecting candidates for sales and customer relations positions. Most often these personality inventories provide a self-rating by the applicant indicating the degree to which he or she thinks he or she possesses certain personality characteristics.

Projective tests like the Rorschach Test or the Thematic Apperception Test require the individual to respond to stimuli in situations that have no right or wrong answers. These tests are used primarily with specialized diagnostic procedures.

   c. *Reference checks:* Even reference checks are considered tests. The applicant supplies a selected list of references that the interviewer can contact for information verifying education, work experience, or personal characteristics or traits.

   d. *Resumes:* Some organizations depend on resumes submitted by the applicant as a preliminary test or screening device. Hiring companies now use computer programs in two ways to reduce costs of hiring and to make resume information more accessible to company personnel:

     (i) *Tracking of incoming resumes:* Software programs are used to help large companies track incoming resumes. Optical-character recognition is used to scan incoming resumes, identify job categories, and rank applicants. Letters may then be prepared offering job interviews or rejecting the application. All information obtained from scrutinizing the applications can be stored for future use.

     (ii) *Developing resume databanks:* Smaller companies generally turn to resume databanks that store thousands of electronic resumes submitted by job applicants. An electronic search of a databank can yield possible job candidates at much less cost to the employing firm.

Human resource management should have information ready for job applicants letting them know if resumes will be scanned electronically. If so, some simple directions might be given to the applicants for creating an acceptable electronic resume (with specific key words), in case they are not aware of this new strategy.

3. *Personal interviews:* One technique used universally is the personal interview. Although not considered as such, the interview is perhaps the most widely used personnel test. The interview matches an individual's personal fitness, communication skills, ability to relate under stress, personality traits, and flexibility with the needs of the organization.

The interviewer is able to compare the information obtained through the application and testing procedures with a face-to-face discussion with the applicant. In turn, the applicant has an excellent opportunity to inquire about the organization and its particular employment needs. Often the applicant has the opportunity to meet with individual members of the work group or team so that each one can evaluate the applicants fit with the position.

4. *Matching of organizational and individual goals:* The goals of the organization wishing to attract suitable candidates for job openings and the individual seeking suitable employment are comparable. The prospective employee probably hopes to secure a position that will not only pay a competitive salary

but also offer personal job satisfaction. The firm's goal is to employ the individual who best matches the job.

5. *Objectivity versus subjectivity:* In recent years, it has become very important for employers to carefully scrutinize their human resource management practices to be assured that they are being implemented objectively. The Civil Rights Act of 1964 and other federal legislation have mandated employers to establish objective, nondiscriminatory recruitment and selection procedures.

EXAMPLE: *Davis, 47, applies for an administrative professional position. Davis has 25 years of experience working in supervisory positions with several companies. The firm cannot discriminate against Davis because of age. In addition, the law requires the firm to stress job qualifications in their employment practices. Thus, Davis will be given an equal opportunity to get the job.*

c. *Legal restraints:* During the 1960s and 1970s several federal laws were enacted that intended to prohibit employers from implementing discriminating personnel practices. The Civil Rights Act of 1964 was a major piece of legislation having broad implications for personnel management functions. This legislation prohibits employers with 15 or more employees from implementing personnel practices that discriminate on the basis of race, color, gender, national origin, or religion. The following laws have an impact on recruitment and selection, and were discussed in an earlier section.

1. *Equal Pay Act of 1963:* Employers under coverage of the Fair Labor Standards Act must abide by the Equal Pay Act of 1963. This act states that discrimination on the basis of sex is illegal.

2. *Age Discrimination in Employment Act of 1967:* The Employment Act of 1967, Age Discrimination Section, mandated that employers with 20 or more employees may not discriminate in the employment of persons between the ages of 40 and 70.

3. *Equal Employment Opportunity Act of 1972:* This act is an amendment to the Civil Rights Act of 1964, specifically Title VII. The employer was defined as a person with 15 or more workers, engaged in an industry affecting interstate commerce. The Equal Employment Opportunity Commission is identified as the regulatory agency of the act. Selection devices, such as tests, application forms, or interview sheets are subject to challenge if they appear to be discriminatory to classes of people identified in Title VII. If challenged, an employer must prove that a test or other selection device is not discriminatory.

4. *Vocational Rehabilitation Act of 1973:* This landmark legislation precludes discrimination in employment on the basis of physical and mental handicaps. This act recognizes employment as a civil right of the handicapped. Basically, it prohibits employers from denying a qualified person a job, requires employers to make "reasonable accommodations" for workers with disabilities, and prohibits discrimination in federally funded programs.

5. *Americans with Disabilities Act of 1990:* This extension of the Vocational Rehabilitation Act of 1973 went into effect in 1992 and 1994. The act guarantees the right of employment to any job applicant who can perform "essential" job requirements and requires that firms make "reasonable accommodations" to help persons with disabilities be able to act, as long as the alterations can

be made without "undue hardship." This legislation also gives these persons greater rights to access public facilities.

6. *Other acts and executive orders:* Many other federal, state, and local acts govern employment, including selection and recruitment. In addition, the executive branch of the federal government issues orders as needed. While most executive orders pertain to only federal employees and organizations engaged as federal contractors, they also have spillover effects into the private and nonprofit sectors. Executive orders often overlap federal and state acts, filling gaps and specifying penalties for noncompliance.

2. *Termination and Separation:* Organizations may discharge employees using the employment-at-will doctrine as long as contracts and work provisions are not being violated. Some jurisdictions require notice of separations be given to terminated employees, after a specific period of employment service. Also, organizations may often deem conditions desirable to try to get people retained under contract or law out of the organization and may offer special settlements to induce them to leave. **Termination** usually refers to the act of being discharged from an organization ("fired") where **separation** is a more global term and refers to any discharge by the employer or voluntary act by the employee, such as moving on to a new job, retirement, or furlough.

EXAMPLE: *While many teams sign coaches to multiyear contracts, after one or two losing seasons, the organizations may desire a change in coaching staff. Buyouts may be permitted in the provisions of such contracts. Even when they are not, organizations may offer incentives that the coaches find hard to ignore, such as being paid full salary for not continuing on during the remainder of their contracts.*

a. *Involuntary separations:* Organizations may require people to leave an organization as a result of downsizing or plant closures. The organization may be required to do the following:

1. Pay severance allowances

2. Give time and assistance to help people find new jobs

3. Offer outplacement services

4. Provide job retraining for displaced workers

5. Permit displaced workers to have health insurance for up to 18 months, without a physical examination, as long as they pay the full premium (COBRA)

Note: COBRA can be a valuable benefit, especially for older persons and those with pre-existing health conditions. After COBRA expires, the ex-employees are usually given another more expensive option, with no "preexisting" clauses. This is also very helpful until the ex-employee is eligible for Medicare coverage or other health plans.

b. *Employment-at-will (EAW):* **Employment-at-will (EAW)** is a common law doctrine that states that employers have the right to hire, fire, promote, or demote any employee they choose at any time, unless there is a law or specific written contract to the contrary.

1. *Background and historical developments:* EAW was adopted during the 19th century as a part of the industrial revolution and was viewed as a necessary provision with laissez-faire capitalism.

a. *Effect of organized labor and public sector:* EAW remained intact until the 1930s when organized labor gained protection from arbitrary employers' activities through grievance procedures in the union contracts. At the same time, many public-sector employees started getting due process protection under civil service regulations, paralleling the rights granted to union members. However, most nonunion private employees remained under EAW.

b. *Effect of state legislation:* In the 1960s state courts began creating exceptions to EAW for all employees. The exceptions were established because the courts, influenced by public pressure, expanded their questions about the employers' action to fire employees without due process or just cause. Today almost all states have statutes that limit employers' rights to discharge employees on an arbitrary basis using EAW.

2. *Basic premises of EAW:* Here are some of the basic premises of EAW.

a. *Private ownership of business:* The right of private ownership of business includes employment-at-will. This extends to public management by caveat.

b. *Maintenance of organizational efficiency:* Tampering with employment-at-will reduces organizational efficiency and effectiveness.

c. *Defense of workers' and employers' rights:* Employment-at-will defends workers' rights to change jobs as well as employers' rights to hire and fire employees at any time.

3. *Exemptions from EAW:* Certain employees are generally exempt from EAW: government employees, union members, contract employees, and members of management.

4. *Restrictions on use:* Employees covered by EAW are also protected by specific restrictions on its use.

a. *Discrimination:* Firing employees on the basis of race, age, gender, or national origin is specifically prohibited in the provisions of Title VII of the Civil Rights Act.

b. *Good faith and fair dealing:* This approach implies a covenant of good will between employers and at-will employees. It presumes employees and employers work together in good faith. Actions by employers to arbitrarily break this covenant by unfair behaviors, including firings, allow the affected employees legal recourse to challenge the dismissals.

c. *Implied employment contracts:* This restriction holds that employees will not be fired as long as they perform their jobs properly. It includes oral pledges by employers to employees regarding lifetime employment at the time of hiring.

d. *Public policy exception:* This restriction holds that an employee has recourse to sue if he or she was fired for a reason that violates public policy.

EXAMPLE: *The Wisconsin Supreme Court expanded the public policy exception in the case of Hausman vs. St. Croix Care Center. In this case two employees were fired after reporting to the Bureau of Quality Compliance that the employer, a nursing home, was guilty of abuse and neglect of its patients. Before going to the bureau, the employees had reported their concerns to the center's director of nursing. The employees were legally obligated under Wisconsin laws to report the suspected abuse and neglect of patients.*

While the Circuit Court and the Court of Appeals upheld the employer's firings under EAW, the Wisconsin Supreme Court reversed this decision. The Supreme Court ruled that EAW did not apply when employees were complying with a legal obligation to report such behaviors.

In other public policy exception cases, workers discharged because of refusal to perform illegal actions, such as cheating in the preparation of IRS or OSHA reports or publicly dispensing restricted products, have had their jobs reinstated after lawsuits. Refusal to perform illegal activities is protected under the public policy exception in most cases in most states.

c. *Violations of agreements:* Even persons working under union contracts or nonunionized written agreements may violate specific employment conditions and rules that lead to dismissal or discharge. Special care must be taken to ensure that any employees are not forced out of the organization by practices that are illegal: violations of public policy exceptions, demotions, or transfers. When employees perceive that they have been wrongfully discharged, lawsuits may be brought against the organizations. Very often the costs of wrongful discharge greatly exceed the opportunity costs lost by not retaining the employees.

d. *Effects of separations:* Downsizing and other forms of discharge can lead to decreased employee morale as well as lowered productivity and quality as remaining employees experience feelings of job insecurity.

1. *Additional voluntary separations:* Sometimes firms discharge employees with less experience and skill but then find that their more experienced workers leave to work with competitors because they fear losing their jobs.

2. *Sharing of organizational information:* Organizations need to explain to remaining employees what their status will be. When any changes are being considered, especially at the higher echelons of an organization where the power to make structural decisions lies, the proposals should be shared with employees as promptly as possible. Trying to keep "employees in the dark" does not work because the grapevine does not require light to flourish. Very often, notifying people ahead of time of pending changes can lead to very positive results as the workers begin evaluating possible career changes while they still have some security.

3. *Varied employee productivity:* In contrast to the notion that bad news leads to reduced effectiveness and efficiency, employees generally can sense what is occurring. They appreciate honesty and will continue to be productive as long as they receive fair treatment and are kept informed by the organization. However, firms usually do not keep the remaining employees informed. Moreover, usually the remaining employees have to perform more work at the same rate of pay, due to having fewer workers available.

4. *Coping with organizational change:* Mergers and acquisitions do lead to layoffs, despite messages from top-level management to the contrary. Even changes in ownership can lead to rearranging and restructuring, promotions and demotions, layoffs, and transfers. The keys to an effective separation

process are to keep the employees informed and involved. There are long-term benefits gained from treating retirees and dischargees fairly and equitably.

EXAMPLE: *Dissatisfied former employees can cause great short- and long-term harm to an organization, even if they were "simply overlooked" during the separation process, as illustrated in the movie Barbarians at the Gate, which focuses on a leveraged buyout and the downsizing that eventually occurred.*

Unfortunately, many organizations do not follow this procedure because they might have staged reduction cycles. The end results can be disastrous in terms of organizational efficiency and ineffectiveness during these change periods.

Check Point—Section C

Directions: For each question, circle the correct answer.

C–1. When compared to recruiting for vacant positions from outside the organization, internal recruiting results in

  A) lower training and development costs

  B) higher numbers of qualified female candidates

  C) greater likelihood of affirmative action problems

  D) fewer equal opportunity complaints

C–2. Which one of the following acts first addressed discrimination on the basis of physical and mental disabilities?

  A) Equal Pay Act of 1963

  B) Fair Labor Standards Act of 1938

  C) Equal Employment Opportunity Act of 1972

  D) Vocational Rehabilitation Act of 1973

C–3. Which one of the following workers would be exempt from the employment-at-will doctrine?

  A) Williams, a restaurant chef

  B) Mason, a technology consultant

  C) Osada, a sales clerk

  D) Assibey, a stock broker

For Your Review

Directions: For each question, circle the correct answer.

Case 1: Goodfood Restaurant Corporation

Goodfood Restaurant Corporation runs a nationwide chain of restaurants catering to families. Though traded on the New York Stock Exchange, the only child of the founder still runs the organization with modest success and an encouraging "family" approach to the business. Like the founder, the junior Goodfood is well liked by business associates and appears to be a fairly savvy executive and CEO. Goodfood regularly visits restaurants throughout the chain and greets long-term employees by name. However, Goodfood is such a micromanager that the regional managers anticipate the visits with some anxiety and dread. Goodfood picks all the district and regional managers from within the organization and even sets their salaries and other compensation.

There are few minorities and females in the main office except in low-level jobs. The corporation has very few regional or district managers who are not male. There are only a few minorities and women who have risen to the store manager level. The human resource office and the legal office have begun to raise concerns about potential litigation for discriminatory hiring practices. They have proposed developing a program of recruitment and internal advancement to remedy the situation and ward off potential suits.

1. At Goodfood, internal promotion has lead to an old boys' network for males and, for females, the result has been
   A) reverse discrimination
   B) the glass ceiling
   C) tokenism
   D) quotas

2. One proposed plan is the use of tests to qualify candidates for promotion rather than CEO Goodfood's personal selection process. The problem with employment tests is that they
   A) cost too much to administer to the entire company
   B) require everyone to be able to read and write
   C) cannot be administered to external candidates
   D) may not be fair to minorities and women

3. Goodfood believes that everyone works for the company and for the CEO, Goodfood. This view reflects the concept of
   A) employment-at-will
   B) quid pro quo
   C) tokenism
   D) reasonable accommodation

4. While investigating the problem of minority and female advancement in the company, the human resource department discovered that females and minorities who advanced receive far smaller salaries than males in similar positions. This is called
   A) pay differential
   B) tokenism
   C) Type Four plan
   D) reverse discrimination

5. Which one of the following would provide the broadest basis for employees to sue Goodfood Restaurant Corporation?

A) Affirmative Action
B) Equal Pay Act of 1963
C) Equal Employment Opportunity Act of 1972
D) Doctrine of Comparable Worth

Case 2: River Technology International

River Technology International supplies high-technology components to a wide array of industries. It produces a large number of stock components and custom designs and manufactures components for a range of customer needs. Management must communicate regularly with customers to ensure that the components manufactured continue to meet the customer needs and standards. Relationships with customers are very important because even with high-quality parts, clients bid each new component for competitive contracts.

Chief executive officer Johnston and vice president for sales Murphy have engaged in an extramarital affair for several years. Though both are married, the relationship evolved during constant travel together and sales presentations away from the headquarters of River Technology. Murphy is a fairly aggressive sales manager, but as the affair becomes more obvious to office personnel at company headquarters and to other vice presidents, questions about why Murphy was promoted begin to circulate. Senior executives are also unwilling to confront Johnson for fear of their own jobs. Executives also express many concerns regarding how clients react to the relationship between Johnston and Murphy and are especially concerned whether or not the affair has jeopardized sensitive contracts.

6. If Murphy was promoted as a result of having an affair with the supervisor, the sexual harassment situation is known as

A) mutual consent
B) unwanted imposition
C) quid pro quo
D) hostile environment

7. Senior executives have anxiety about confronting Johnston because

A) they work for Johnston in an employment-at-will situation
B) sexual harassment often leads to job discrimination
C) the hostile environment can result in retribution
D) sexual harassment involves only the people engaged in the affair

8. Even if Murphy fully consented to the affair, the situation is considered sexual harassment because

A) Murphy has not had other affairs before
B) the spouses are affected by the affair

C) Johnston does not let the affair interfere with work
D) the work relationship is one of unequal power

9. Office workers could be considered victims of harassment to the extent that they

A) think Johnston and Murphy should be fired
B) experience compromised work relationships
C) oppose the affair
D) become jealous of Murphy

10. Murphy can be further victimized by

A) being divorced after having an affair with the boss
B) coercing coworkers to comply to requests
C) coercing Johnston for a salary increase
D) being expected by clients to provide access to Johnston

Case 3: Commonwealth Health Systems

Commonwealth Health Systems manages health and related benefit packages for large employers. The company customizes health insurance plans of major insurance providers and then negotiates annual health plans for their clients. It serves as the contact between human resource managers and health insurance companies once a contract is in place. Essentially, Commonwealth manages the benefits contract for the client while advocating for the client's employees. The success of the company has resulted in significant growth.

Commonwealth needs to recruit and select a large number of new employees. It needs information technologists, customer service representatives, office managers, and claims representatives. Miklavcic has been placed in charge of the recruitment program.

11. Miklavcic should create a plan that recruits new employees from outside

    A)   at all levels of the company

    B)   for entry-level positions only

    C)   as a last resort

    D)   before considering current employees for promotion

12. Newspaper ads, Internet announcements, radio promotions, and employment agencies support

    A)   internal hiring

    B)   minority recruitment

    C)   external hiring

    D)   entry-level hiring

13. Miklavcic wants to have aggressive minority recruitment and hiring component of the plan. Which one of the following is the law governing this plan?

    A)   Equal Pay Act of 1967

    B)   Equal Employment Opportunity Act of 1972

    C)   Health Maintenance Organization Act of 1973

    D)   Americans with Disabilities Act of 1990

14. Which one of the following techniques for screening can actually result in discrimination if used in the minority recruitment plan?

    A)   Personal interviews

    B)   Employment tests

    C)   Resumes

    D)   Job references

15. As the recruitment phase begins, Miklavcic has several highly qualified information technology people apply who are wheelchair-bound. If hired, what must Commonwealth provide for these people?

    A)   Reasonable accommodations

    B)   Access without undue hardship for the employees

    C)   Opportunities that include transportation

    D)   Complete and unrestricted access

Solutions

Solutions to Check Point—Section A

Answer:	Refer to:
A–1. (D)	[A-1-a-(1)]
A–2. (C)	[A-3-c-(2)]
A–3. (B)	[A-3-c-(4)]

Solutions to Check Point—Section B

Answer:	Refer to:
B–1. (A)	[B-1-b]
B–2. (D)	[B-1-n]
B–3. (B)	[B-3-c-(3)]

Solutions to Check Point—Section C

Answer:	Refer to:
C–1. (C)	[C-1-a-(1)-(b)]
C–2. (D)	[C-1-c-(4)]
C–3. (B)	[C-2-b]

Solutions to For Your Review

Answer:	*Refer to:*

Case 1:

1.	(B)	[A-1-a-(2)]
2.	(D)	[A-1-a-(1)]
3.	(A)	[C-2-b]
4.	(A)	[A-1-a-(4)]
5.	(C)	[B-1-a]

Case 2:

6.	(C)	[A-3-c-(1)]
7.	(C)	[A-3-c-(2)]
8.	(D)	[A-3-b]
9.	(B)	[A-3-e]
10.	(D)	[A-3-c-(1)-(b)]

Case 3:

11.	(A)	[C-1-a-(2)]
12.	(C)	[C-1-a-(2)]
13.	(B)	[C-1-c-(3)]
14.	(B)	[C-1-b-(2)]
15.	(A)	[C-1-c-(5)]

Chapter 12
Professional Protocol

OVERVIEW

The interactions within organizations, between organizations, and among the professionals generally are governed by rules and codes of conduct that are defined by general business etiquette and specific protocols. Individuals at all levels of an organization and at all levels of professional accomplishment strive to make the most effective presentation of who they are and what they represent. In business and professional circles, this effort to manage the impression people form of us governs all initial contacts and ongoing interactions, and it results in mingling of the person and the organization's image. Good impression managers can be successful at all corporate communication, from interview to negotiation, personal contact to public speaking.

To make effective presentations of oneself in diverse, multicultural settings and in international business, one must be aware of the differences culture can make. The differences from one country to another can be described using several dimensions that help the international businessperson succeed. Administrative professionals must have appropriate skills for navigating customs, etiquette, and business protocols in a foreign country as well in a diverse workplace.

KEY TERMS

Bypassing, 327
Co-culture, 327
Courtesy, 341
Entitlements, 321
Ethics, 325

Ethnicity, 331
Ethnocentrism, 329
Etiquette, 325
High and low context, 328
Impression management, 322

Negotiations, 338
Protocol, 325
Representation, 320
Self-disclosure, 320
Self-presentation, 320

A. Managing How Others View Us

Communicating with others involves more than presentation of language in its many forms. It involves the total presentation of self through verbal, nonverbal, and artifactual (physical items) means. How others perceive someone can be very crucial to their appraisal of the person's worth as an individual and value as a contributor to the group. Even as the individual personally identifies with the company for whom he or she works, others will make the same identification even more strongly. Where a person works or the profession one has is often the strongest basis for identification that other people will have of that person. In turn, the personal qualities an individual expresses will influence the extent to which employees and customers will trust, follow, or support the business with which the individual is associated.

1. ***The Importance of What Others Think:*** The role of how one is perceived by others is significant in all walks of life. Important factors in the home, at work, and in social life, impressions guide how others view an individual's most important qualities. These impressions control the extent to which people will trust someone, respect that person's authority, accept their leadership, and accept affiliation. These views are the foundation of critical employer, employee, client, and customer relationships.

    a. *Family:* An individual's spouse, brothers and sisters, children, and parents form lasting, accurate opinions of who they are and their importance to them. These opinions and expectations are based on detailed interactions and a long history of actual performance. The impression this group forms is probably beyond the individual's short-term control.

    b. *Coworkers:* People who do not know someone as intimately as a family member or a long-term friend form opinions of that person over a much shorter period of time. With some coworkers one may have only a few minutes of contact a day, if any at all. With a supervisor, one may have only a few minutes of contact a week.

    c. *Social acquaintances:* With people met through charitable and professional organizations, at church, at children's schools, and in other public places, one has even less contact. For this group of acquaintances, which includes people both inside and outside of the workplace, one can control the impressions other people have. Most people want to convey a positive self-image. The image others develop is mostly based on how one looks and acts rather than on the deeds one performs. The image that acquaintances develop of a person can be influential in many kinds of interactions.

2. ***The Role of Impressions in the Workplace:*** In the workplace, positive impressions can influence hiring, performance appraisal, and promotions. In the workplace and elsewhere, positive impressions can influence one's ability to acquire personal power and authority. Impressions influence how others perceive a person's honesty and integrity and affect the ability to persuade others over whom one has no direct control. How impressions work requires careful examination.

    a. *Hiring:* The image an interviewer develops of a job applicant can actually give an applicant with lower qualifications an edge over a better qualified candidate. Even when objective performance ratings and testing situations are used, most companies rely on a face-to-face interview in making the final selection. If the applicant shows desirable characteristics, takes responsibility for accomplishments, and conforms to the opinions and attitudes of the interviewer (letting the interviewer talk), then chances of being selected are highest.

b. *Performance appraisal:* With an improved performance appraisal comes better salary increases, greater chance of promotion, and improved choices of assignments. If conveying a better image improves the appraisal above what would be received for good performance alone, then whatever can be done to improve others' impressions certainly helps. Apparently ambiguous or uncertain situations can be more easily influenced by the image that a person projects. Part of performance appraisal includes attitudes, demeanor, willingness to contribute to the team effort, or some other qualitatively defined measure. Also, the less specific the performance appraisals, the more these kinds of factors count. These measures will be influenced by the impression that the evaluator develops.

c. *Promotion:* Promotions will often require that an individual develop new skills and increase knowledge about work and the organization. As a result, the observed performance and performance history of an individual will offer only certain predictions of the ability to perform in the new position. The opinions held by people responsible for a promotion decision will have a significant influence on their final outcome. Like the job selection process, these opinions may give a candidate with lesser qualifications a chance. The appearance of conforming to the opinions and attitudes of the decision makers is clearly an important quality. Likewise, being accountable for successful projects also suggests that the individual will be accountable once promoted.

d. *Personal power and authority:* While many elements of personal power and authority may come from position and accumulated support from others, the ability to utilize the power must be communicated to others. This ability should remain an impression; otherwise, an outright exercise of power over others may actually be detrimental. If people have acquired the image of someone as capable of exerting power, and when the time comes that person is unable to control events or make things happen; the results can be disastrous for the individual.

    EXAMPLE: *Consider a manager who constantly threatens his employees with disciplinary action, yet never follows through. Employees become particularly disgruntled when they see someone who should be disciplined, but is not. They lose respect for the manager.*

e. *Honesty and integrity:* Honesty is a characteristic that one hopes never has to be proven. However, individuals are always proving their honesty and integrity by keeping promises (no matter how small), by returning found items, by giving credit to people for their good work, and by taking personal responsibility for actions. Unfortunately, years of honest behavior can be undermined by one failure—even a misplaced accusation. People often interpret unintentional negative actions as signs of the inner, true person.

f. *Persuasion:* The ability to persuade others to accept one's point of view or proposal requires that one be knowledgeable, prepared, and articulate. More than these characteristics, however, one must also appear believable. The ability to persuade others depends heavily upon the consistency between the impressions others have and the message being communicated. A person who frequently "cries wolf" will have difficulty convincing others when the real wolf shows up. When a person who never shows any alarm or concern seems alarmed, others will pay attention.

3. ***Impression Formation:*** People form impressions in the first few minutes of an initial meeting, and these impressions appear to linger. Body language, voice inflection, dress, the extent of formality, and eye contact all directly influence first impressions.

The extent to which an individual can control all these aspects of behavior may differ from one person to another, but most people can attend to significant details. One can choose what to wear and should be able to anticipate whether the situation will require formal clothing, business dress, work clothing, or casual dress. With practice, most people learn how to be comfortable in new situations. Most important, one should try to be oneself. People will often, and sometimes subconsciously, detect the inconsistency between the real person and any artificial façade being presented. The resulting impression will be based on the inconsistency, and on neither the real nor the presented person.

a.   *Presentation or manipulation?* Communication has two distinct roles that relate to efforts to convey a particular image of oneself to others—representation and self-presentation. Whenever people communicate facts about the world around them, whenever the source of information is not the self, then people are communicating through the **representation** of these other phenomena. Whenever the source of information is the self, or an aspect of self that others know, one is engaging in **self-presentation.**

   1. *Self-presentation:* This distinction is particularly relevant to presentations of the self that attempt to control the information and attitudes that others have. These presentations of the self, or self-presentations as they are called, are often idealized notions about ourselves. We take them quite seriously, and we expect others to take them seriously as well.

       EXAMPLE: *If Mason refutes the accusation of going through other employees' mail, then Mason expects others to believe the denial. Unfortunately, the self-presentation contradicts the evidence of representation that others have received from the person who saw Mason at the message boxes.*

   2. *Self-presentation and self-disclosure:* Self-presentation can occur in a number of very casual ways. Whenever we share with a coworker or a friend what we like and dislike or our opinions of things, we are making presentations of ourselves.

       EXAMPLE: *On several occasions, Vakes tells a coworker about movies watched in the evenings. The coworker builds an image of Vakes as an avid film watcher. The coworker then begins to ask Vakes's opinion of films: "I thought I would get a video for the children to watch this weekend. Vakes, do you have any suggestions?" Even if Vakes does not watch children's films, Vakes would probably offer some form of advice to continue to build the image of thoughtful video interests. "I don't watch many children's films, but the sales clerks at the Video Place really seem to know their stuff. I would ask them."*

       The self-presentations from this contact include *Vakes's* personal interests—film, but not children's film; honesty—"I don't know children's films"; and willingness to help others—"Though I cannot provide direct information, I know which source to trust [the sales clerks at the Video Place]."

       The self-presentation also begins to open the door for additional **self-disclosure.** The revelation of intimate, personal details. In fact, self-disclosure is a component of self-presentation. However, self-presentation includes information about the self that would not necessarily require intimate disclosure. Instead, it refers to the wide array of information that pertains to who we are, what we can do, our values, and our public as well as private thoughts.

b. *Leadership and self-presentation:* In organizational leadership, self-presentations can influence others by establishing the norms of behavior and clarifying the values of the organization. This influence process is important for the organization as well as for individuals within the organization. It is one of the means by which organizational culture is communicated. A study of managerial communications reveals at least seven different, common kinds of self-presentation. The seven kinds of self-presentations are:

1. *Self-descriptions:* Self-descriptions would include conversations like the one described above between *Vakes* and the coworker. They can be more formal. A manager can address employees and describe a style of management. A new acquaintance might talk about family, a new job, interests, and so on.

2. *Accounts of events:* People frequently give accounts of events to others who were unable to witness the event. The account might include descriptions of motivations for actions or explanations related to the event that were not part of the event. These interpretations disclose information about the interpreter.

3. *Apologies:* An apology can be a way of taking responsibility for an action or event as well as it can establish credibility and honest. Sometimes apologies can be used to distance oneself from an undesirable action: "I'm sorry, but upper management has insisted that we cut your responsibilities . . . " The apology places the person who apologizes in a sympathetic light. It works as a means of defending against anxiety-provoking thoughts or feelings for both parties, but especially the person making the apology.

4. *Entitlements:* **Entitlements** refer to a person's proclamations regarding rights and obligations of a position in an organization.

   EXAMPLE: *A father may insist that he make the final decision about spending money he earns, or a supervisor may claim the right to set schedules and make performance appraisals as the supervisor "sees fit."*

   These claims to certain rights and perks are entitlements. Entitlement also suggests responsibility for an action, as a group member may claim responsibility for a group action.

5. *Flattery:* Flattering others can have the effect of ingratiating them to the source of flattery. Overdone flattery, especially unjustified or exaggerated praise, can produce an aura of insincerity. Flattery can place the person giving the praise in the position of an evaluator and, if overdone, can produce a sense of superiority. In a positive light, flattery can be a means of friendly support that entices the recipient to offer reciprocal praise at some later time.

6. *Favors:* Performing favors, or at least making others think that favors you are giving them, creates a situation of direct reciprocity. Once a favor is given, the recipient feels obligated to give a favor in return. Initiating the favor can convey an image of selflessness and unselfishness.

7. *Organizational descriptions:* For managers, team leaders, and team members of any organization, the self-presentation that provides knowledge about an organization also aligns the presenter with the organization. The representation of the organization can be used to show points of identification and points of disagreement. The stated allegiance to the group conveys the identification. Managers and corporate leaders must offer a convincing presentation if

they expect their employees to follow their lead. In public or volunteer organizations the leader may be less concerned with profit, efficiency, and productivity and more concerned with the mission of the organization. In fact, the leader or future leader may see an opportunity to change the mission to become more consistent with his or her vision and goals.

c. *Basking in reflected glory:* As the previous seven kinds of self-presentation might suggest, there may be a fine line between self-presentation and manipulation. A special kind of self-promotion is called BIRGing, or "Basking in Reflected Glory." In BIRGing, the self-promoter reflects glory through association with a desirable person or deed.

EXAMPLE: *Gruber was a friend of Ted Turner (of Turner Broadcasting) when they were both in high school—they sailed together during the summers. Though their association was long ago, an aura still persists. In fact, as Gruber tells the story, one wonders if Gruber and Turner merely shared the same harbor.*

4. **Impression Management:** Some people actively manage their self-presentations more than others. These people are vigilant in their efforts to determine the appropriate dress, behavior, and conversation for any particular situation. They always want to know "Who will be there?" "What will Parker think if I show up wearing this outfit?" "I know Santiago likes professional basketball, maybe I should know scores and standings for the last few weeks," and so on. This effort to manage self-presentations actively and intentionally is called *impression management.*

a. *Impression management defined:* **Impression management** was first introduced by Erving Goffman, a well-known sociologist, in *The Presentation of the Self in Everyday Life.* The prevalent view of impression management is that it is a kind of drama, a process of acting out the image one wants to present to others. William Gardner, a professor of management and researcher into the impression management phenomenon, has elaborated the theatrical qualities of impression management. In his view, impression management is a kind of dramatic performance. As a kind of theater, impression management has an actor, an audience, a stage, a script, a performance, and even reviews (Gardner, 1992). A brief examination of these qualities can be instructive:

1. *The actor:* The actor has a number of roles he or she "claims." Jobs, family, or even aspirations may define these roles. The roles help individuals determine which images can be presented.

2. *The audience:* The audience has identifiable characteristics that influence the acting. According to Gardner, they include "power, status, attractiveness, and familiarity." Children require an act different from the one for the boss.

3. *The stage:* The stage is the situation, which is both the place and the occasion. An evaluation review is one kind of stage; a boardroom is another. Each calls for a different drama.

4. *The script:* The script includes the accumulated experiences an individual has of given situations and what to expect from them. Upon meeting someone for the first time, an individual may begin a script of casual conversation that leads through a number of necessary topics: occupation, marital status, children, home, region of origin, and other details. What an individual reveals at these times can be tightly controlled. Corporate culture can also define a script. While a sales clerk and a sales associate are the same thing, the

term *sales associate* is meant to convey a sense of professionalism not apparent in *clerk.*

5. *The performance:* Gardner identifies three elements of the performance: verbal behavior, nonverbal behavior, and artifactual behavior. By *artifactual,* he means dress, business cards, office decor, and other signs that reflect the intended impression.

6. *The reviews:* Reviews are the responses the audience makes. Favorable reviews result in positive outcomes for the individual actor: positive performance appraisals, promotions, and pay raises.

These parts of the dramatic presentation combine for each individual performance. If an individual wishes to recognize the drama, then one should pay close attention to each of these elements. One might ask, "To whom is this person playing?" or "Am I the audience?"

b. *Impression management behaviors:* Impression management can be used positively to gain an advantage or defensively to protect an image. Positive impression management would typically be considered an assertive use of impression management. All of the self-presentations described earlier, including self-descriptions, accounts, apologies, entitlements, enhancements, flattery, favors, and BIRGing, as well as others, such as conformity and making excuses, can be used in combination to achieve a given strategy. The five assertive strategies identified by Gardner are:

1. *Ingratiation:* This strategy calls for flattery and favors as well as conforming to the opinions of the target audience. Ingratiation involves frequent compliments (flattery) and praise. Nonverbal behavior can include frequent smiles and supportive eye contact. One of the problems of ingratiation has been called the "ingratiator's dilemma," the problem of becoming transparent to the target audience. The possibility is that the ingratiation may backfire, resulting in the target being disgusted with attempted manipulation.

2. *Self-promotion:* Self-promotion is necessary for someone who is interviewing for a job or trying for a promotion. It may involve BIRGing, explaining events in such ways that they make the self-promotor look best (enhancement), and self-descriptions that focus on the positive.

   EXAMPLE: *Self-promotion may involve rephrasing activities to make them sound more important. For instance, an individual who reviewed several grant proposals for the federal government may list his job title as Consultant for the U.S. Department of Education.*

3. *Intimidation:* This tactic can be successful for getting people to perform duties, but it may be costly over time. The intimidator essentially scares employees or coworkers into action through threats, emotional displays, and a cultivated fear of reprimand or reprisal. Intimidation is a popular behavior among students and teachers. Students (especially in high school) will attempt to intimidate a novice teacher by testing every possible rule. Teachers, on the other hand, may create testing situations that are particularly challenging and sometimes even frightening. The more subtle the intimidation, the more effective it will be in the long term.

   EXAMPLE: *An anecdote about a third-grade teacher tells of the teacher placing tape on the floor to identify the proper location of desks. At the beginning of each class period, or when activities changed, the teacher would make sure that the students had their desks in place. This would involve cajoling a few whose desks had gotten too far out of line. The students were extremely well behaved, and the story goes that via the student grapevine "If the teacher is that mean about desks, you had better not cross the teacher at all." Is this any different from the manager who insists that employees follow procedures exactly and at all costs?*

4. *Exemplification:* Exemplification occurs when one is trying to provide an example of (exemplify) a desirable behavior or characteristic. People may consciously try to be a role model or achieve recognition by striving to be the best.

EXAMPLES:

> *An administrative professional strives to know technical details of a word processing program.*
>
> *A consultant strives to establish expertise in special areas.*
>
> *A trainer works toward offering a seminar with established objectives that earn high ratings by the attendees.*

5. *Supplication:* Supplication involves apologies and excuses with open admission of inability to perform a task. The goal is to get another person to help with—or actually complete—the task. The supplicant may also use flattery and favors to get the audience to comply with a request for help.

c. *Defensive behaviors:* Defensive behaviors are used to avoid having to do something or to avoid responsibility. The idea of the defensive behavior is to save face or to protect or restore a damaged image. Blaming a scapegoat can avert the dangers of an error from both an individual and a group. In fact, by identifying a scapegoat, good impression managers can both avoid blame and ingratiate themselves with a superior who may have also been in danger of receiving blame. "Passing the buck" and forcing someone else to make a decision or complete a task can aid in the avoidance of taking action. When a supervisor overdelegates—charges all or most of his or her responsibilities to others—the term *off-loading* describes the excessive use of delegation. When the actions are not completed, the subordinates take the blame. The tactic will not work for long, though, because it is the supervisor's responsibility to make sure the work is done.

Check Point—Section A

Directions: For each question, circle the correct answer.

A–1. Which one of the following characteristics should one never have to prove?

A) Authority
B) Entitlement
C) Self-presentation
D) Honesty

A–2. When one shares likes and dislikes, anxieties and important feelings with a coworker, the act is called

A) BIRGing
B) self-disclosure
C) representation
D) entitlement

A–3. Which one of the following can be viewed with insincerity when overdone or exaggerated?

A) Flattery
B) Favors
C) Exemplification
D) Self-description

B. Learning International Professional Protocol and Etiquette

Knowledge of the basic differences in how one interacts with members of one's own culture and how one interacts with members of another culture is crucial for translating business activity from the familiar culture to the unfamiliar culture. No review book can cover all details of all cultures of interest. Instead, the basic groundwork can be reviewed so that an administrative professional will have the skills to undertake a systematic preparation for working with any particular culture. Proper business etiquette and professional protocol must be observed.

1. ***Protocol and Etiquette:*** **Protocol** refers to specific rules or rituals that govern a particular action or process. For instance, protocol governs the steps that would be taken to deliver a contract for signature to a company. A protocol will govern the steps of a negotiation that would apply to any team member in the negotiation process. The act of following the chain of command is a protocol. For the most part, protocol refers to the rules governing processes or procedures. **Etiquette** refers to the rules that govern the conduct or behavior of an individual in any given setting. How one greets another person, shakes hands, dresses, uses silverware, offers gifts, among other behaviors would be described as etiquette. Protocol and etiquette are often used interchangeably, but they do actually refer to different aspects of interactions between and among people.

   a. *Why it matters:* Together, appropriate behavior in business and related interactions (for instance, the social interaction that accompanies business) and common activities results in successful business transactions. Etiquette guides an individual's conduct during interactions, while protocols define the shape of the interactions themselves. Proper conduct means that the interactions will be predictable. Participants can be comfortable with the interactions if it all goes smoothly.

   b. *Common barriers:* Lack of knowledge about business processes and procedures can imply an unwanted lack of concern for the desired outcome. In venues where members are unfamiliar with each other's cultures, the lack of proper etiquette or protocol will be interpreted as a signal of other problems. Worse, misinterpreted actions can be insulting in one way or another. The most significant barriers are:

      1. *Lack of knowledge:* Ignorance of the culture of a company with whom one is negotiating or entering into a contract is unforgivable in all cultures.

      2. *Assumptions of power:* Sometimes the more powerful party—the larger company, the group with the scarcest commodity, or the individual with the needed skill—acts as if the power is all in their hands. This may result in the appearance of disrespect, pompous behavior, or other insulting actions. The misbehaving individual or group may be in power today, but they cannot act as if the situation will always be so. Insulted parties always have a long memory.

      3. *Miscommunication:* More than any other barrier, outright miscommunication is the common source of communication breakdown, especially between members of cultures foreign to one another. Whether caused by lack of knowledge or unintended misperception of culturally specific behaviors, the problem is one that can be easily avoided with a small amount of effort.

   c. *Ethics and professionalism:* **Ethics** refers to a code of conduct that governs the behavior and actions of individuals that subscribe to the code. A particular code of ethics may be defined by a social order, religious view, political entity, or a professional group. When a profession, such as a medical or business group, defines a code of conduct, the ethical code states what is required of the behavior of members of the profession.

1. *Ethical codes:* Sometimes a specialized code of ethics will be written and published to cover specific areas of conduct.

2. *Ethical conduct:* A broader and less well-articulated code of conduct is assumed to govern members of the profession.

3. *Professionalism:* Professionalism refers to abiding by both the written code of ethics and the less well-defined unwritten code. Those who profess to be a professional endeavor to project that they are a member of a particular profession by abiding by the stated codes at all times. Furthermore, professionals take personal responsibility for their actions.

4. *Professionalism and etiquette:* A professional would accept as a personal responsibility the need to understand appropriate business etiquette and professional protocols necessary to conduct successfully the business of their profession. This applies to situations involving unfamiliar cultures.

5. *Caux Round Table Principles for Business:* Business leaders from Japan, Europe, and North America have joined to create a universal business ethics code called the Caux Round Table Principles for Business. Elements of the code include treating employees and business associates with respect, honesty, and integrity; avoiding discrimination; being fair to customers; and not engaging in corporate espionage.

   a. *Two core ideals:* Caux Round Table Principles for Business are based on two core ideals, one of living and working together and the other of respecting human dignity.

   b. *Seven principles:* The Caux Round Table Principles for Business have seven principles. These principles are discussed in detail at the Caux Round Table Web site. The seven principles are:

      (i) *Principle 1:* The Responsibilities of Businesses: Beyond Shareholders toward Stakeholders

      (ii) *Principle 2:* The Economic and Social Impact of Business: Toward Innovation, Justice and World Community

      (iii) *Principle 3:* Business Behavior: Beyond the Letter of Law Toward a Spirit of Trust

      (iv) *Principle 4:* Respect for Rules

      (v) *Principle 5:* Support for Multilateral Trade

      (vi) *Principle 6:* Respect for the Environment

      (vii) *Principle 7:* Avoidance of Illicit Operations

   c. *Participants:* The Caux Round Table Principles for Business also identify the stakeholders in the business principles. They are customers, employees, owners and investors, suppliers, competitors, and communities. Any stakeholder can endorse these principles and choose to be guided by them.

2. ***Culture and Etiquette:*** Culture influences communication rules in more than just verbal ways. The paralanguage rules differ significantly from one culture to another. In

highly diverse cultures such as the North American society **co-cultures** (cultures co-existing in the same society) have significantly different interpretations of body language, space, even silence.

EXAMPLES:

> *Native Americans consider silence a sign of respect, while European Americans may take the silence as a sign of boredom or refusal to interact.*

> *Latino/Latina culture considers avoidance of direct eye contact a sign of respect, while others may interpret it as a lack of attention.*

The etiquette rules that govern these paralanguage behaviors are not easily learned. Misinterpretation can be avoided if the receiver of the message takes a moment to reflect on the possibility of alternative interpretations rather than presuming that the vantage point of their own culture is always correct.

a. *Common ground:* Successful business and social interactions occur when both parties work to find or establish common ground (a concept discussed in Chapter 10). This is true of local community businesses as much as it is of international business interests. It is more difficult on the international stage. Sometimes business social interaction—such as dining, night-life, or a brief walk on the corporate grounds—is intended to help create a common ground for interaction.

 1. *Lack of common ground:* If no effort has been made to educate various subcultures or diverse ethnic groups within an organization about the feelings and attitudes of each group, then no common ground has been established. By itself, work can become part of a common ground, but many cultural groups have different attitudes about work.

    a. *Building common ground:* Diversity training has become a popular means of educating members of an organization, but the trainers must be well prepared and familiar with a variety of situations. For such training to succeed, everyone must be reached. Unfortunately, training activities can divide groups into the oppressed minority and the oppressing majority. This can actually increase tensions.

    b. *Using diversity training methods:* Diversity training is commonly approached by presenting scenarios and building from the reactions of participants to the scenarios. Often, if there are primarily two cultures involved, the trainers will focus on stereotypes each group is thought to have of the other. Great care is taken to balance the presentation. A primary goal is to help participants identify their stereotyping of others, their automatic prejudices, and to begin to see the presence of a common ground with the other group.

 2. *Bypassing:* When a statement has two meanings, whether from different perspectives or from different cultures, the event that occurs is called **bypassing.** In bypassing, a message has one meaning for the sender and another for the receiver.

EXAMPLES:

> *In a Japanese company, a request for "all orders for more than 100 items" would mean that all orders of 100 and up should be sent. "More than" includes 100, the number that establishes the margin.*

In an American company, "more than" would mean that all orders for 101 items and up should be sent.

Even when everyone speaks the same language, bypassing can occur. When a policy states that an employee shall be evaluated "at least every three months," problems can develop. If an employee is evaluated twice in one month, can he claim that the rule has been met so that evaluation is unnecessary until six months have passed? The employee has read the rule to say "at least twice every six months."

b. *International differences:* Countries and cultures have been rated as a means of helping understand the degree of differences between two cultures and the impact that differences may have on conducting business. Differences have been studied concerning dimensions such as high versus low context, individualism versus collectivism, nonverbal behavior, and specific particular behaviors including time-orientation and dress. Understanding several ways of distinguishing characteristics of cultures will serve as a foundation to understanding differences in etiquette and protocol. These characteristics influence how members of the culture behave and understanding the characteristics should influence how someone foreign to the culture interacts with members of that culture.

1. *High context versus low context:* "Context" refers to the situation or background of communication. Communication in a **high-context** situation means that many of the cues necessary for understanding the meaning of a message come from the context, which can be nonverbal, physical space, time, authority of the speaker, office of the speaker, and so on rather than strictly from the message itself. **Low-context** communications depend more on the message content than the context, with the lowest being entirely based in the message.

   a. *Cultures:* Cultures are distinguished as high- or low-context cultures. The meaning conveyed in communication will be interpreted by most members of the culture according to the appropriate contextual cues. High-context cultures may employ highly indirect messages filled with metaphor, poetic language and little direct, concrete expression. Everyone from that culture will have a reasonable sense of the extent of the context that must be "read" to understand the message. This is part of the cultural common ground. Even if the culture is a low-context culture, members know that the focus is on the content of the message more than its context.

   EXAMPLE: *In a tribal culture, a man may enter the house of his son's future wife to discuss the dowry for the daughter with her father. He enters and says something like "Beautiful birds are flying high today, and the sun will set with them still in the air." This could mean "It is time to talk," and everyone in the culture would know exactly what had been said.*

   b. *High- and low-context business exchanges:* Context can affect decision making, problem solving, and negotiating styles.

      (i) *Decision making:* High-context cultures influence decisions by requiring all details to be worked out with care. Low-context cultures seek to reach the decision quickly and economically, with details worked out later.

(ii) *Problem solving:* High-context cultures have less tolerance for arguments and attach negative feelings to them. Low-context cultures enjoy debate.

(iii) *Negotiating:* High-context cultures take negotiation personally and must work to establish negotiation elements like trust and fairness through contexts other than negotiation. Low-context cultures do not take negotiations personally and trust what is said (at least at first).

c. *Countries exemplifying high- or low-context cultures:* The United States and Canada are examples of low-context cultures. Members of the main cultures in these two countries count on the specific information contained in the message to understand its meaning. In contrast, Middle Eastern and Asian cultures, including China, Korea, and Japan, depend on varying aspects of context to evaluate a message. These aspects include authority of the speaker, rank, age, gender, and relationship (father or father-in-law, etc.). Tribal cultures throughout the world tend to be high-context cultures.

2. *Individualist versus collectivist cultures:* Another important dimension is the difference between cultures that hold individualism and individual accomplishment in high esteem and those that consider family, society, and groups more important than the individual. Group-oriented culture is called collectivist, while individual-oriented culture is called individualist.

EXAMPLE: *The major cultures of the United States, Canada, and northern Europe are highly individualistic, while Middle Eastern, eastern Asian, and African cultures are highly individualistic. Mediterranean cultures may fall more in the middle; tribal cultures tend toward collectivism.*

3. *Nonverbal behavior:* Cultural differences vary significantly in nonverbal behaviors. Similar behavior can have multiple meanings throughout many cultures. Every dimension of personal space, gestures, eye contact, body language, dress, posture, and details of physical activity can have different implications from one culture to another.

4. *Global dimensions of difference:* The perspective of **ethnocentrism,** the belief in the superiority of one's own ethnic group or culture, is easily strengthened by a number of factors that set a group apart. Ethnocentrism is one of the main barriers to international and intergroup communication. These factors include:

a. *Formality:* The degree of formality of a culture is expressed in the etiquette that governs any kind of interaction. How parents are addressed, the use of titles, naming conventions (such as whether the mother's name is combined with the father's name, as in many Spanish-speaking countries) must be recognized. The formality dimension is very common and widespread and often has particular forms associated with a given culture.

b. *Social customs:* Social customs refer to the rituals and rules that govern interactions in social life. In some countries an invitation to the home of another is quite an honor and is a signal of friendship. Other cultures might invite almost any stranger into the home.

c. *Dress:* Manner of dress often identifies not only cultures and countries but also regions of countries.

    d.   *Time:* Few countries in the world follow the time-consciousness of North American and northern European societies.

    e.   *Tolerance of conflict:* In some cultures, conflict can lead to a loss of self-esteem or self-worth, and members of the culture strive to "save face" and will compromise at all costs. Others see failure to win in the same manner and consider some compromises as a loss of face. Conflict can be unpredictable and, thus, culturally particular.

    f.   *Gender:* Gender relations run the gamut of variation. Highly traditional cultures have specific views of the roles women can have, while industrialized cultures tend to be far less restrictive in the options for women. In the extreme forms, women are treated as second-class or even third-class (behind the children) citizens.

c.   *Geert Hofstede dimensions:* A major method of distinguishing characteristics of culture that has been based on rigorous research and widely accepted is that proposed by Geert Hofstede. The dimensions he offered have been quite popular since their introduction about 20 years ago. Hofstede (2001) developed his ideas about cultural differences through an extensive study of the national cultures in 64 countries. As a researcher for IBM, he studied the people from countries in which IBM had subsidiary offices. The initial study was followed by studies of students, airline pilots, consumers, and civil service managers. He developed five dimensions along which natural cultures could be differentiated. These five dimensions are often used to clarify cultural distinctions in communication and business texts. The dimensions are (1) power distance, (2) individualism, (3) task versus social orientation, (4) uncertainty avoidance, and (5) long-term versus short-term orientation.

    1.   *Power distance:* Power distance refers to inequalities within a society. Inequalities are always the concern of those without power or access to power. The degree of acceptance of the power inequality is important. A society that has high power distance will have strong class systems and that are fairly difficult to cross (like the caste systems of India). Low power distances means that people can move up in status and power (like the notion of promotion based on merit in North America and northern Europe).

    2.   *Individualism:* This is the dimension of individualism versus collectivism described earlier. Hofstede puts the dimension on a scale where countries with high individualism place more emphasis on individual success and responsibility. An important consequence of high individualism is that the person will have more relationships that are less intense or less strong. The collectivist society finds people with fewer relationships, but those few are based on intense and strong bonds.

    3.   *Task versus social orientation:* This is the gender-based dimension focused on the difference in the values of men (task oriented) and women (social oriented). Evidence suggests that women seem to have more similar values from culture to culture, while men have greater variation. In more task-oriented masculine cultures, assertive and competitive behaviors define masculinity and values are focused on strength and success. In more social-oriented feminine cultures, the male values are more similar to the female values of caring. Low task-oriented cultures treat women on a more equal basis with men than do in high task-oriented cultures.

4. *Uncertainty avoidance index:* Some cultures appear to have a very low tolerance for uncertainty. The lack of structure is one form of uncertainty and ambiguity that appears in some workplaces, especially where the self-managed team approach is used. Societies that avoid uncertainty depend heavily on rules, regulations, controls, and laws. Low-avoidance cultures tolerate differing opinions and views and minimize the use of rules.

5. *Long-term orientation:* Long-term orientation addresses the dimension of valuing long-term commitments and hard work that is rewarded later. Short-term orientation focuses on respect for tradition and meeting obligations. Change may be easier in short-term orientation because the long-term commitments are not seen as barriers.

3. ***Multicultural Issues at Work:*** The globalization of the workplace has resulted in increased conflicts arising from minor tensions that often lead to major disputes. Most workplace barriers can be addressed with appropriate training and increased tolerance and acceptance. A core issue is the perceived threat of competition that arises between differing cultures and ethnic experiences. These issues are now entering individual offices and plants, where the tension can be intense and potentially damaging.

a. *Co-cultural issues:* When two or more cultures are represented in a workplace, the term *co-culture* is applied. Co-cultural issues differ from issues related to someone visiting a foreign country because members of both cultures usually require the same treatment by supervisors and company policies. So, instead of one group representing a foreign or alien group, both groups have full rights of membership within the organization. Co-culture can arise from several factors:

1. *Regional subcultures:* These co-cultures may arise simply by the difference associated with geographic location. A common original language may be shared, but differences in attitude and style may distinguish someone from the American South from an American New Englander. Larger countries like India or China can have significant regional variations that even involve language and religious differences. Regional differences can have subtle effects. Some parts of the United States have much slower patterns of speech, more relaxed approaches to dress, and more or less tolerance for differences.

2. *Ethnicity:* When the differences include country of origin, subcultures based on race, language, or religion, the dimension is called **ethnicity.** Ethnic differences can result in different social rituals, different religious practices, and so on. These differences can be manifested in attitudes toward authority, regulations, time, and work habits.

3. *Consequences of co-cultural workplaces:* Co-culture can influence how people get along and work together on a daily basis. Some cultures encourage talk while others interpret silence differently. Conflict is handled one way by one group and another way by others.

EXAMPLES:

Direct confrontation is avoided by the people of northern European, Asian, and African descent, while southern Europeans will engage in conflict openly. Formation of friendship varies from one group to another.

How should someone approach a person from another culture (or subculture) who has experienced the death of a family member? Each group has a set of topics that can and cannot be discussed with anyone who is not a close friend or even a family member. The only solution is to ask that person if a particular behavior is inappropriate. Most people appreciate the opportunity to discuss how their cultures deal with adversity.

   b. *Diversity:* Diversity refers to more than ethnic and racial differences, and it includes gender, sexual orientation, physical or mental disability, and religious practices. The Americans with Disabilities Act (ADA) has contributed significantly to improving awareness of the needs of individuals who are disabled or challenged with physical or mental differences.

      1. *Do not depersonalize:* Too often, people view a person as the disability they have. Someone might refer to an individual as the "blind person" or the "deaf person." This depersonalizes both the individual and his or her interactions with others.

      2. *Use common sense:* When meeting a blind person, state who you are. When speaking to someone who requires a helper such as a signer, speak to the person, not the helper (this is true of language translators also).

      3. *Treat support equipment or helping animal respectfully:* The wheelchair should be considered an extension of the person's physical body; the assistive dog is not a pet.

      4. *Be relaxed and natural:* Talk normally, relax, and interact with the person. Do not presume the person needs assistance. Offer and wait for the offer to be accepted. Accept directions for the assistance.

Check Point—Section B

Directions: For each question, circle the correct answer.

B–1. The rules that govern conduct or behavior of an individual in any given setting are referred to as

    A) protocol
    B) etiquette
    C) ethics
    D) professionalism

B–2. When a culture tends to understand the meaning of a message based entirely on the content of the message, the culture would be identified as

    A) collectivist
    B) task oriented
    C) low context
    D) high avoidance

B–3. Which one of the following describes the situation where long-term local employees share work with new immigrants?

    A) Low context
    B) High avoidance
    C) Individualism
    D) Co-culture

C. Improving Professional Behavior Through Etiquette and Protocol

Successful professional interactions require effective use of etiquette to control behavior, and the many protocols that must be followed in every aspect of work. No one can know every detail of protocol and etiquette. Protocols for some communication tools change as rapidly as the technology that supports them. Professionals endeavor to stay as informed as possible.

1. *Civility, Ethics, and Legality:* The primary purpose of etiquette and protocol is to make the activity of the organization and the individual's professional work be effective, productive, and civic. The rules of conduct and interaction must include the necessity for ethical and legal conduct. Etiquette and protocol also provide a civil basis for an individual to make ethical choices and conduct business legally. Successful administrative professionals will experience a continuum from etiquette to legality that governs the actions and work of the professional.

   a. *Dealing with etiquette and protocol workplace issues:* Appropriate protocol or etiquette can actually make work more productive and prevent serious blunders.

      1. *Interacting with supervisors:* It may not be imperative to keep subordinates and colleagues completely informed about what one is doing, but supervisors must be regularly updated on even the most routine tasks. Managers delegate work to subordinates, but the manager remains responsible for that work. Some managers prefer being informed only about exceptions to the routine, but most will want to be fully aware of a subordinate's progress toward completed work.

      2. *Managing meetings:* Every company has a set of expectations for what is accomplished in meetings and how those meetings are managed. Etiquette for how to behave in a meeting might be different for each company. For the most formal meetings, parliamentary procedures control the meeting protocol and etiquette. Courteous behavior should always be involved, including advance notice of topics, civil discussions even during disagreements, and follow-up notes of appreciation and thanks.

      3. *Using telephone etiquette:* One should always return telephone calls, even if it is to inform the caller that an inquiry will require more time to respond. Messages should be clear and have all the information required for someone to return the call. Too often callers leave messages in such a way that the telephone numbers they recite are inaudible, making it difficult for the recipient to return a call. Courtesy on the telephone should not be made a victim when using new communication technology.

      4. *Using e-mail:* E-mail requires special attention because so often people ignore the fact that e-mail should be approached as any other business communication. Proper subject lines, carefully worded sentences, as well as review and proofreading prior to sending are just a few of the important aspects of properly prepared electronic messages. The sender must also recognize that the receiver does not necessarily know the sender's e-mail identity; therefore a full signature line should be added. Sometimes, the recipient might not recall the purpose of the original message to which the current message is a response. Including prior messages will be helpful, but even a reminder within the current message can be sufficient. The proper etiquette for e-mail and the protocol governing to whom and under which conditions the message should

be sent or "copied" have been addressed frequently. It is the responsibility of any professional to be aware of the protocol's specific to his or her work environment. Generally, e-mail is more informal than the business letter, and the following are true:

- This informal communication is focused, short, and to the point.
- The message is transmitted immediately over the network.
- E-mail is an easy method to use in providing input to and receiving input from all relevant individuals.
- E-mail has lowered the cost of communication.

E-mail message fundamentals include being concise, correct, complete, and courteous. E-mail systems that are already programmed into the business' computer network include a space for the sender, receiver, copies to, subject, and the message. The e-mails may also carry an attachment. This system allows for all kinds of materials to be transmitted including Web pages, potential materials for research use, abstracts, official reports, word processed documents, contracts, and so on.

5. *Dealing with interruptions:* Work is regularly interrupted with calls, customer visits, emergencies, coworkers stopping by, and so forth. While some interruptions are violations of the etiquette of courtesy, one should not respond to these with similar discourteous behavior. Sometimes an interruption requires a firm insistence that one is busy, and other occasions may be well served with a gracious "I have a few minutes to spare."

a. *Guests:* Guests are common in the workplace, and introducing them to others is appropriate and necessary. If a guest is expected, be sure to inform coworkers and others that the person is coming, who the person is, the importance of the person's visit (it may be, for instance, a subcontractor, a vendor, an interviewee for a position, even an inspector). Ask whether the visit will bother anyone or interfere with the completion of critical duties.

b. *Introductions:* Introductions of guests, customers, and clients to coworkers or other visitors is the responsibility of the host. Commonly, first and last names, affiliations, and purpose of the visit are included in an introduction.

c. *Giving credit:* One of the greatest and most unprofessional actions one can engage is to take credit for work done by another person. Thus, even an accidental oversight that results in a failure to acknowledge the contributions of others is a major insult that requires extensive recovery. Credit, recognition, and acknowledgment to those who contribute to a project should be given even if the credit is overstated. People tend to believe that their role in any given activity was more important than what others contributed. The tendency to overrate one's own contribution must be acknowledged.

b. *Improving workplace protocols:* One duty of the administrative professional is to contribute to improvement of workplace protocols. It may be difficult to change manners and etiquette displayed by others, but a systematic approach can be used to define appropriate protocols for various work exchanges. Protocols can be of value when encountering barriers and can serve as opportunities for improvement.

1. *Barriers:* There are many barriers to the effective use of commonplace protocols used to make work progress more smoothly. Here are just a few:

- Personalities
- Underprepared and unprepared employees
- Undeveloped procedural plans
- Co-cultural tensions
- Staff versus line tensions
- Fault-finding
- Unstated objectives
- Turf problems
- Insufficient reward and punishment systems

2. *Opportunities:* Every breakdown in communication—whether it is caused by the absence of a guiding protocol, the lack of etiquette on the part of participants, or the shear complexity of a problem—is an opportunity for learning. Learning organizations not only quickly acquire new technologies, new skills, and new approaches to work, but they adapt new protocols for interaction quickly and without faltering.

3. *Barriers:* Identifying the barriers and then recognizing the opportunities for adaptation and change can be completed only by establishing new protocols for interactions. The following are strategies for developing and implementing new protocols.

   a. *Marketplace approach:* Let those who must use the new technology format work through a reasonable protocol. The marketplace of interaction will gravitate toward the most reasonable method. This natural technique has led to the creation of "emoticons" used in instant message systems. This approach leads to the development of conventions in widespread phenomena like the Web log and the Instant message. In co-cultural situations, people can be encouraged to work through their concerns without outside intervention.

   b. *Standards:* A new purchasing system may have several paths for processing purchase orders. The purchasing department can select and declare the required protocol and refuse to accept any order not properly processed. A similar declaration may be made by a committee or a task force. For procedural actions, this approach reduces conflict and eliminates time for negotiating a method.

   c. *Special training:* Training techniques such as diversity training, sensitivity training, and problem-solving techniques such as the Delphi and nominal group techniques can be used to identify barriers and then to propose solutions for improving the workplace protocol. Often ideas that emerge from the group having the problem are more likely to be accepted than other solutions.

c. *Dealing with technological change and protocol:* Technology has changed the way people interact with each other, and it has changed work in fundamental ways. These changes have resulted in different protocols for work. Using technology may lead to overload of information.

   1. *Telecommuting:* With the explosion of technological advances, telecommuting is a growing trend. This trend can be beneficial to the employee, especially in

terms of employing mothers with small children at home or persons with disabilities who have the intellectual talent, but have difficulty traveling from home to office. In some cases, telecommuting consists of a portion of the workweek being spent at home, with some time spent at the office. Companies and employees are receiving cost benefits as a result of reduced commuting and reduced physical space requirements.

2. *Networks:* Information systems are integrated. Voice, data, image, text, and video communication systems are being merged. Small and large businesses use networks internally. Managers and employees can access the corporate network from any site in the world that has the available technology. Cell phones and laptop computers keep managers in instant contact to keep traveling or offsite employees in touch with the office. Information can be exchanged freely and safely in real time, and business can be conducted more efficiently. Communication is a key to using these technologies to enhance the business.

3. *E-commerce:* The Internet is a major part of retail commerce. The electronic market links buyer and seller in order to exchange products, services, and payments. The Web page becomes one of the firm's marketing tools.

   EXAMPLE: *A small car repair company accepts electronic payment from all major credit cards. At the end of the workday, a backup service provider logs and stores all transactions. This protects the company's records in case of failure at the point of the transaction.*

4. *Teleconferencing:* Teleconferencing is used by organizations to enable people to meet face-to-face while actually being located in different places. Teleconference originally referred to conference calls that were strictly based on audio connections, often using speaker phones. Two or more people could participate in the audioconference. Streaming video and dedicated video connections have added the video teleconference, or just videoconference. This format requires more technology and broader bandwidth than closed circuit television (one-way video).

   a. *Audioconferencing:* The problem with this format is that people have difficulty determining who is talking if more than one person is at the other end of the line. Few nonverbal cues transmit very well in a setting with more than three people in the conference call.

   b. *Videoconferencing:* Videoconferencing provides an improvement over audio-only methods because the participants' actions can be viewed. The camera is not as complete as being in person. Cues are missed that are clear in person meetings. There is still social information that is conveyed in an in-person conferencing situation that is missing when technology is used for the meeting.

      (i) *One-way videoconferencing:* This teleconference allows information transmission of the participant(s) from one location to another but not vice versa. This form of videoconference is used for educational lectures, training, and product promotion where seeing the presenter is important to the audience. The audio communication is usually two-way, whereas the video communication is one-way. However, the audio communication may also be one-way.

(ii) *Full-motion videoconferencing:* Two-way conferencing where all participants can see one another in motion and hear one another is videoconferencing at its optimum. This is also called an interactive videoconference. The teleconferencing center must be fully equipped with cameras, overhead microphones, and acoustically treated rooms so that the audio and video transmission is of the highest quality. The participants sit at a conference table as they would at a face-to-face meeting and confer with the other participants as they are viewed on video screens. This is the most complex and the most expensive form of teleconferencing. The ability to observe the reactions of others is still limited to the capabilities of the camera and upon which person it is focused.

EXAMPLE: *Some hotels specializing in conferences and conventions are creating conference theaters as available meeting rooms so that teleconferencing can be included as part of the meeting programs. These theaters include the latest in teleconferencing technology to accommodate the needs of a wide variety of business and professional organizations.*

5. *Changes in protocol:* The technological changes and the increase in telecommuting require the preparation of workplace and meeting protocols that previously had been left unspoken. At the beginning of a teleconference, the host will review how interaction will be handled, including how someone gains the floor, who will record the actions and discussion items, and what each participant should expect after the conference is concluded. For distance workers, the employer sets some work rules, but the primary change is that the employee has become self-regulated. To protect the employee and the employer, methods of submitting work and reporting time must be clearly stated. Both these technological advances require more use of communication tools like e-mail and cell phones.

d. *Developing an ethical standard:* Perhaps the best approach is one of continuous learning and continuous improvement. The desire to be a trusted colleague and dependable employee is not enough; it must be supported with thoughtful and reflective self-awareness. Sometimes an error can occur because the guidance was not in place to help a person avoid the mistake; sometimes an entire group takes a wrong turn, behaving according to standards that emerged in a crowd mentality. Mistakes can be overcome, and forgiveness must always be an option. However, the professional always makes the effort to review actions and set the course for the next time the circumstances present themselves.

1. *Loss of privacy:* The addition of new forms of participating in work, completing projects, submitting completed tasks, and so on also expose the employee to greater invasion of privacy. Clear lines between work-related activities and other activities must be established. For instance, can the employee use e-mail for non-work-related activities? Can the employer have access to the personal computer, or is it like the desk, considered part of the personal space of the employee?

2. *Loss of security:* Recent accidental loss of data and transport of secret information has caused a stir about the security of electronic information. Security protocols must be formulated for all levels of data and for the employee as

well. Passwords, access cards, fingerprint and retinal scans all provide differing levels of secure access.

2. *Negotiation:* Negotiating represents a special place for the careful use of both etiquette and protocol. Etiquette errors can reveal an unintended hidden agenda or be perceived as a slight against the other party in the negotiation. Inappropriate body language, gestures (like yawning), poor eye contact, and others can send signals that may undermine one's negotiating position. Failure to establish a workable protocol for a negotiating session may give the other party an opportunity to take control by digressing, dominating time, or refusing to move forward. Protocol can create an orderly process that leads to successful negotiation for both or all parties involved.

a. *Types of negotiations:* **Negotiations** occur every day in the workplace and are interactions that lead to an agreement or cooperate effort. This may be in the form of asking for support or help on a project, interviewing for a position, or reconciling different interpretations of an event. More formal negotiations include the following:

1. *Employee–Employer contracts:* These negotiations can be union related or just the talk between an employer and employees about health and other benefits. Union negotiations are special enough that most unions and employers with union contract utilize special negotiators and arbitrators.

2. *Vendor agreements:* For existing products, negotiations may occur to set a price; for services, negotiations may define the service to be provided, for how long, and at what price.

3. *Customer orders:* This is the other side of the vendor agreement. Customers want to pay as little as they can for services, and the sales agent wants to get as much as possible.

4. *Legal resolutions:* Attorneys control both sides in this kind of negotiation, and they follow recognizable negotiating strategies and rules.

5. *Mergers:* Though governed by attorneys, many aspects of a merger (or separation) require careful exchanges, compromises, and conciliations.

b. *Preparation:* More than for almost any other interaction, preparation is key. Both sides in a negotiation must have clear understandings of what they are after and what the other party wants, and what either party will accept. Preparation may include

- Collecting data
- Assessing the opposition
- Observing other negotiations
- Developing reasoning and logic
- Analyzing strengths and weaknesses of both parties
- Identifying common ground
- Examining previous encounters, successes, and failures

1. *Objectives:* Objectives must be clear and unambiguous, as they are the basis of any good strategy. They may or may not be disclosed to the other party, but they must be known by all members of the team. A good team will also devote time and research to determining and thus anticipating the objectives of the other party as well. Objectives may include priorities organized around:

- Price
- Time
- Quality
- Quantity
- Priority
- Service

2. *Acceptable results:* Both parties must be aware of what would constitute acceptable results. In most cases, a win/win result is the preferred outcome, and the second option is that of both sides compromising.

c. *The negotiation process:* The style of a negotiation is shaped by the attitude of the negotiators. Someone out to win for his or her side will take an aggressive approach, and possibly not even engage in a completely fair or even-handed approach.

1. *Choosing a negotiation style:* There are several styles commonly seen in negotiations. They are:

a. *Competitive:* Parties are opponents and thus engaged in a win/lose perspective. One side will win; the other will lose. Sometimes the nature of the necessary outcome will dictate this approach (in a criminal case, a plea bargain is just this kind of negotiation).

b. *Cooperative:* Mutual success is the purpose of this kind of negotiation. A customer and a vendor may be mutually aided by one providing a service or product that the other needs. A win/lose strategy may cause the customer to go to another vendor. Likewise, a customer who expects more than can be given may lose an opportunity for a fair exchange of a product with the highest quality and be forced to settle for less or lower quality.

c. *Power-oriented versus trust-oriented:* Power and trust are not compatible in negotiations. Power leads to competition, while trust leads to cooperation.

d. *Open:* Some negotiators may be perceived as holding back, revealing only a part of the intended objectives. Fully disclosed expectations and objectives would be considered an open approach.

2. *Presenting a proposal:* The presentation of a proposal is governed strictly by a predetermined protocol.

EXAMPLES:

Proposals for a price contract may be required to be submitted in triplicate, with operational details in one package and financial details in a second package.

A union may be required to submit a counteroffer to the company within 48 hours.

3. *Hearing a proposal:* Each proposal and counterproposal should be given a fair hearing. A predetermined timeframe can be established as part of the negotiation protocol. Each side should have an opportunity to review each proposal carefully.

4. *Acknowledging nonverbal elements:* During the face-to-face negotiation, nonverbal communication elements, both paralanguage and those of the

listeners become highly charged and powerful signals. These nonverbal elements can include or be influenced by the following.

    a. *Atmosphere:* One of the parties will often serve as host. Food, water, physical space, and so on should be adequate and comfortable. Sometimes a remote, neutral location is chosen to provide a balance.

       EXAMPLE: *Negotiations in the corporate headquarters may be intimidating to union representatives.*

    b. *Seating:* Seating is always a charged item. Sometimes the negotiations for the shape of the table and the placement of people can take weeks for diplomatic events.

    c. *Stalling or rushing:* Stalling or rushing can give signals that may be seen as reflecting an effort to take control. Time is a factor that plays a big role in deliberations.

    d. *Emotional responses:* An emotional response can sometimes reveal more than the negotiator wants to reveal. Likewise, emotion can be used to bluff or test an opponent negotiator.

    e. *Facial expressions:* Facial expressions can give away a likely response to a proposal or counterproposal. However, poker players and jury watchers have been notoriously unable to read the facial expressions of someone who wants to distort or disguise a reaction. Other nonverbal behaviors can be equally nonpredictive.

       (i) *Closing:* A negotiation is closed when all parties have agreed upon one of the proposals. This should be determined by a prearranged protocol. Once accepted, a reading of the proposal should be made to confirm that all understand the terms and the conditions that have been negotiated.

3. ***Research and Preparation for International Business Contacts:*** When a business assignment is made involving a new country, unfamiliar location, or the local offices of another company from a foreign country, the appropriate approach is to study the situation just as one would any new encounter or challenge. Being informed is most critical for success. Today, the Internet provides nearly endless resources for discovering information about how to conduct interactions with people from other nations and cultures. Below are areas of communication that should be examined for one to become knowledgeable of the etiquette or protocol necessary for any given international contact.

    a. *Basic etiquette issues and concerns:* Etiquette is about communicating and interacting with people. The rules that govern personal conduct govern all aspects of the interaction, from start to finish.

    1. *Making introductions:* A sequence of introductions governs each beginning. One must know whether the entire party is to be introduced to everyone, or whether a social and power status will govern who must be and who should not be introduced.

       a. *Business cards:* A business card is a critical part of one's identity. When visiting a country where your language is not the first language, print the information on one side in you language and on the other side in the language of the country.

b. *Handshakes and other greeting rituals:* Handshakes differ somewhat, but a firm and quick handshake at the beginning and end of the meeting is appropriate in most European countries. The equivalent bow is common in Asia, and other countries use a perfunctory kiss on either cheek. The handshake convention is becoming more common worldwide.

c. *Titles:* Titles are a good indicator of the formality of a country. First name use is rare, and in most cases requires an invitation from the other person. Mr., Mrs., Doctor, Professor, and so on are expected.

2. *Making progress:* Without understanding a culture, one may not be able to recognize the signs of progress or lack of progress toward a goal. This can be disastrous.

3. *Ending and following up:* Another problem is ascertaining when a conclusion has been reached. Clear signals are required, and these are governed by social and business rules that may not be self-evident.

b. *The business of courtesy:* The key to interacting with all cultures is **courtesy** (being polite to others). Courtesy and manners govern business etiquette, meetings, diplomatic and political dealings, networking, and socializing with business contacts. When the right action or behavior is unknown, then one cannot go too far astray by showing courteousness. Honesty helps as well, for example, in a situation where one does not know the proper way to address the persons who have just been introduced. Admission of ignorance often leads to a brief, informative, and kind lesson from a well-informed teacher.

c. *International venue negotiations:* How negotiations take place and the circumstances under which they occur vary from country to country. For important negotiations, a consultant can prove invaluable. Even for small negotiations, some kind of training will prove beneficial.

d. *Appointments in unfamiliar countries:* The means of establishing appointments will vary from one culture or country to another. For an international contact, especially in a foreign country, the following questions should guide one's preparation. In this country:

- Are appointments always made by a receptionist or other administrative professional?

- What is the appropriate amount of time or number of days in advance is it necessary for the appointment to be made?

- What are the expectations of keeping an appointment and being on time?

- Does one even ask for a specific meeting time, or is "Thursday afternoon" enough?

The etiquette of meetings will vary from one culture to another. Appointment details should be learned in advance of the visit, though a confidant can help.

e. *Business dress:* International guidelines for acceptable business dress can be found on the Internet. Foreign embassies are also eager to help potential business ventures with etiquette and protocol information and guidance. It may help to locate someone from the country or region and ask. Clothing choices will generally be influenced by the following factors and conditions:

1. *Occupation:* Occupation or profession will often determine the appropriate attire in any country. When in doubt, the more conservative approach is always the safest.

2. *Appropriate apparel:* Some cultures have different dress for each major time of the day. Business attire for the work period, evening attire for formal social gatherings, and casual attire for in-between and after is a general rule.

3. *Dress:* In many parts of the world, occasional casual dress for men still includes wearing a tie and coat. Typically, for men a suit is required for the business transaction, but a change to a sports coat for other occasions is acceptable as well as to formal evening wear when appropriate. For women, the rules may be more specific. However, a more conservative approach will be the best strategy. Females should consider the following:

   • Observe other professional women and follow their lead.

   • Wear skirts below the knees and long sleeves.

   • Wear skirts for outings—no shorts unless one is confident of the occasion.

   • In Muslim countries shirts or dresses should have closed necks; and the longer the skirt or dress, the better.

   • Jewelry should be minimal. Do wear a wedding ring or band, but do not wear excessive or expensive items.

   • Make-up should be very conservative, and no perfume is best as many people have allergies or perhaps a cultural taboo.

   • Tight and short are typically not good ideas.

f. *Communication:* The whole point of etiquette is to facilitate communication.

   1. *Conversation:* Conversation is critical to success. In some cases, business before pleasure is an absolute error. In other cases it is the rule. For instance, Japanese business people expect to socialize and become familiar with the representative of another business before discussing contracts.

      a. *Learning appropriate topics:* One must learn what topics can be approached and which cannot. The best strategy is for the visitor to let the host guide the conversation topics. In just a short period of conversation, the range and depth of appropriate topics will become evident.

      b. *Being informed:* It is imperative for one to learn enough about the culture to ask questions and show interest in the other culture. Research time used prior to a visit must include a thorough exploration of the culture, its history, geography, other trading partners, major industries, political circumstances, and so on.

      c. *Addressing others with respect:* During a conversation, respect is a mandatory element. Do not interrupt and do remain attentive. Always use appropriate titles and terms of respect. Overdoing it makes the visitor appear quaint; failing to be respectful is rude in every language and culture.

   2. *Listening skills:* Effective listening skills differ from culture to culture. Identify and learn appropriate nonverbal behaviors that show attentiveness to the speaker. These can be used even if a translator is involved in the conversation.

3. *Telephone, correspondence, and e-mail etiquette:* Rules that govern conversation and negotiation continue on to the follow-up of a telephone call or other correspondence.

g. *Gift giving:* North Americans send gifts to corporate clients during the holiday season, but would rarely bring a gift to a regular business meeting without some special circumstance. Holiday gifts might include flowers, food, candy, or local products. For other countries, the appropriateness of a gift depends upon the culture. Selecting and presenting an appropriate business gift is an important step that does require research.

h. *Entertaining:* Table etiquette is a topic about which many people remain uninformed. To entertain properly and effectively, entire books have been written on manners related to social entertainment.

1. *General dining etiquette and manners:* In some cases common social dining etiquette may differ from business etiquette. In most cases, one should wait for the host to initiate discussion of business at a meal. Many cultures do not discuss business at meal time. One should always accept a dinner invitation. Dining is considered in most countries and cultures as a sign of generosity, and the host will cover the check. Again, active research of a country's specific dining etiquette prior to going to the country is the only safe approach.

2. *Business dining and entertaining:* Learn what is appropriate entertaining for business clients both for entertaining foreign visitors to one's own country as well as learning what will be expected of someone who visits a foreign country.

4. ***Tips for Preparation:*** There are many books and Web sites that offer tips for preparing to work with people from other cultures or preparing for a visit to another country. These tips include both pleasure travel and business travel, as well as how to acquire information about business etiquette and protocol. As stated earlier, any preparation requires study and investigation. The following tips represent a few of the best.

a. *Understand one's own tendencies:* If one knows the tendencies of one's own culture, then some of the differences between the home culture and the foreign culture will make more sense.

b. *Anticipate the need to be respectful:* Some people announce their ignorance through loud talk and an overbearing presence. This is unnecessary and calls attention to one's lack of respect.

c. *Accept offers of help:* People do like to help strangers. Accept this help.

d. *Learn some of the language:* A few words can help communicate even if all one learns to ask is for help.

e. *Do not make comparisons:* This is an insult in any country at any time. It implies criticism at best and superiority at worst. Discussion of religion and politics can result in accidental insults that may be irreversibly damaging.

f. *Be aware of time differences:* Few people move as fast as Americans, and the North American sense of urgency is unique. Learn to be patient, accept silence, and wait calmly.

Check Point—Section C

Directions: For each question, circle the correct answer.

C–1. Which one of the following is referred to as an informal communication that is focused, short, and to the point?

A) Teleconference
B) Introduction
C) Meeting
D) E-mail

C–2. Collecting data, developing reasoning and logic, and identifying common ground are all elements of the preparation for

A) negotiations
B) teleconferences
C) privacy rules
D) networking

C–3. In preparing to visit a foreign country and undertake business activity, the appropriate approach is to begin with

A) the basic etiquette rules
B) introductions
C) study
D) making appointments

For Your Review

Directions: For each question, circle the correct answer.

Case 1: First Job

The very first impression in a hiring situation is often the most important. In a small New England town, a local shoe store typically hired two 16-year-olds each fall for part-time, after-school work. One family with three children supplied two of their children as workers for a number of years. After the two had worked successfully at the store, the turn came for the youngest child, Casey, to apply for the job. Casey was not hired. Surprised by the decision, the parents pursued this issue with the shoe storeowner. Their intent was not to make them hire Casey; they merely wanted to know what they observed in the interview with their youngest child. The owner explained that Casey seemed to "have an attitude." This attitude overpowered the owner's experiences with the child's two older siblings' work records and desirable work ethics. Apparently, impressions count immensely to the owner and are a major determining factor as to whether or not a candidate is hired.

1. The revelations to the parents could be a surprise if there are major differences between their experiences with Casey's attitudes and the storeowner's impression derived during the interview. Long-lasting and accurate impressions of an individual are typically formed by

    A) supervisors
    B) coworkers
    C) family members
    D) social acquaintances

2. On the subject of Casey, the parents sought from the storeowner a/an

    A) impression
    B) representation
    C) self-presentation
    D) self-disclosure

3. Which one of the following would account for Casey's attitude?

    A) The job was an entitlement
    B) Casey was using flattery
    C) Self-description is more honest
    D) Casey was attempting ingratiation

4. The parents later discovered that Casey perceived that the job was being forced onto him, so Casey purposefully sabotaged the interview. This is a highly successful form of

    A) self-promotion
    B) ingratiation
    C) impression management
    D) performance appraisal

5. Given the importance of following proper protocol, the effort of the parents to investigate as to why the job was not offered to Casey may have been a/an

    A) effort at ingratiation
    B) scripted event
    C) effort for honest appraisal
    D) violation of privacy rights

Case 2: Promotional Transformation

A major publisher of electronics books in Canada has an opening for an experienced editor who is well trained in computer technology. This individual would be required to communicate effectively with a number of authors and representatives from other countries, as the publisher uses names available from an international list. Most of the writing is prepared in English. Jackson, the editor-in-chief, personally favors a young, talented assistant named Martin for the position. The vice president expresses strong reservations. Martin has extensive computer knowledge, but the new job would involve public appearances at conventions and meetings along with important company meetings, which includes foreign visitors and nationally famous authors. Martin usually wears jeans and T-shirts and does not have a professional appearance.

Jackson is not certain what to do and does not want to insult Martin. Instead, Jackson goes to Martin's direct supervisor, Olivier, and explains the situation. Wanting to assist, Olivier speaks with Martin and explains the opportunity for promotion, but warns that Martin has an image problem that needs to be solved first. Martin seems to be responsive. Imagine the supervisor's surprise when Martin appears with a haircut and in a brand-new suit the very next day. Martin goes on to become a successful editor. As soon as Martin's appearance changes, attitudes expressed by other people toward Martin change, too. Martin grows more confident, and it even helps job performance.

6. Martin's preference for jeans and T-shirts clashes with the expected formality of interaction with important people from other countries. This difference may be described as a lack of

A) protocol
B) ethical code
C) etiquette
D) common ground

7. When the vice president tells the editor-in-chief Jackson, who in turn speaks to the supervisor Olivier, about Martin's chances for the promotion, the protocol that is followed is the

A) assumption of power
B) chain of command
C) Caux Round Table Principles for Business
D) Geert Hofstede dimensions

8. Considering the types of international clients and authors Martin would likely work with if promoted, the dimension that appropriate dress relates to most is that of

A) formality
B) time

C) gender
D) power distance

9. Martin's willingness to change habits immediately suggests an approach that is clearly driven by

A) power distance
B) uncertainty avoidance
C) long-term orientation
D) individualism

10. The publishing firm has a number of offices internationally, and Martin will be required to communicate with employees in those offices who are natives of those countries. The company's headquarters has a large group of individuals *who have come* from foreign offices who work for extended periods at headquarters. Conflicts and miscommunications that might occur between Martin and employees from other nations would be called

A) high-context
B) co-cultural
C) ethnocentric
D) collectivist

Case 3: Burneko and Fox Security Systems, Incorporated

Burneko and Fox Security Systems, Incorporated has developed a sophisticated array of security devices that help keep computer and network devices secure from physical and electronic intrusion. The product line is unique and highly successful, which has resulted in rapid global growth for Burneko and Fox. The founders, Burneko and Fox, have always employed partners worldwide, but now they find it essential to have sales representatives and product specialists prepared to travel anywhere in the world on short notice. They have begun hiring people from many countries while boosting employment of local, well-educated specialists.

Burneko and Fox decided that a handbook for etiquette and protocol is needed for both internal communications and external contacts. Furthermore, a similar handbook is needed to address the differing concerns in different parts of the world—a primer of security threats that may appear in some countries, but not others. Canard has been assigned to lead a team to prepare both of these handbooks.

11. Canard starts by having the team undertake a brainstorming session and then develops ideas further by having employees from throughout the company participate in focus groups. This approach used to develop protocols is called

    A) declaration
    B) giving credit
    C) marketplace
    D) problem solving

12. Canard discovers that resources for learning about different cultures served by Burneko and Fox already exist within the company and through its partners. To conduct training for employees, Canard uses the broadband electronic and satellite connections available to the company and has participants share information. This approach is called

    A) telecommuting
    B) interactive videoconferencing
    C) audioconferencing
    D) face-to-face teleconferencing

13. Canard and the team discover that from country to country the rules for employee and customer privacy and security differ. Because of this, Canard will need to direct the team to prepare handbooks for each country describing the differing

    A) changes in protocol
    B) professional etiquette
    C) ethical standards
    D) vendor agreements

14. Canard has been directed by Burneko and Fox to include clear directions for negotiating, which have become their hallmark. Canard must find ways to explain to differing groups with differing attitudes that the desired negotiating style places mutual success above other considerations. This negotiation style is

    A) cooperative
    B) competitive
    C) trust oriented
    D) open

15. Canard and the handbook team settle on a theme that focuses on the central role of etiquette as one of guiding

    A) communication
    B) negotiation
    C) ethical codes
    D) dress

Solutions

Solutions to Check Point—Section A

Answer:	*Refer to:*
A–1. (D)	[A-2-e]
A–2. (B)	[A-3-a-(2)]
A–3. (A)	[A-3-b-(5)]

Solutions to Check Point—Section B

Answer:	*Refer to:*
B–1. (B)	[B-1]
B–2. (C)	[B-2-b-(1)]
B–3. (D)	[B-3-(a)]

Solutions to Check Point—Section C

Answer:	*Refer to:*
C–1. (D)	[C-1-a-(4)]
C–2. (A)	[C-2-(b)]
C–3. (C)	[C-3]

Solutions to For Your Review

Answer:	*Refer to:*

Case 1:

1. (C)   [A-1-(c)]

2. (B)   [A-3-(a)]

3. (A)   [A-3-b-(4)]

4. (C)   [A-4]

5. (D)   [C-1-d-(1)]

Case 2:

6. (D)   [B-2-(a)]

7. (B)   [B-1]

8. (A)   [B-2-b-(4)-(a)]

9. (C)   [B-2-c-(5)]

10. (B)   [B-3-(a)]

Case 3:

11. (D)   [C-1-b-(3)-(c)]

12. (B)   [C-1-c-(4)-(b)-(ii)]

13. (C)   [C-1-d-(1) & (2)]

14. (A)   [C-2-c-(1)-(b)]

15. (A)   [C-3-f-(1)]

References

Gardner, W. L. "Lessons in Organizational Dramaturgy: The Art of Impression Management." *Organizational Dynamics* 21, no. 1, (1992): 35–42.

Goffman, E. *The Presentation of the Self in Everyday Life*. New York: Doubleday Anchor, 1959.

Hofstede, G. *Culture's Consequences: Comparing Values, Behaviors, Institutions and Organizations Across Nations*. 2nd ed. Thousand Oaks, CA: Sage Publications, 2001.

Final Review Exam

Directions: For each question, circle the correct answer.

CASE 1: Light Power Industries, Incorporated

Light Power Industries, Incorporated makes laser trimming devices. The basic company philosophy includes participatory management. This has led the company to a "matrix structure" of management. Each division is run by consensus. All employees are encouraged to communicate likes and dislikes with everyone including the president. This open communication has resulted in a profitable company with a stable, happy staff.

Expansion presents a problem for the company. Wessin and Dalia are president and chief operations officer, respectively. They face the challenge of growth while maintaining the successful approach of minimal management structures.

1. Expansion is a problem shared by everyone. In the tradition of the consensus approach to decision making with full participation by all employees, Wessin gathers the staff in an impromptu and informal session in which anyone can offer analysis or solutions. The central purpose of this session would be

    A) information
    B) inspiration
    C) brainstorming
    D) education

2. In order to expand effectively, Light Power Industries must undertake careful planning prior to expansion, so for the first step it needs to

    A) focus its plan on internal operations at this time
    B) perform a complete analysis of internal and external environments
    C) emphasize external changes in the environment
    D) create a company policy on professional behavior

3. Dalia has been charged with creating a transition team for the expansion. There are many potential problems, including likely anxiety that will be faced by all brought about by the impact of the expansion. Which one of the following steps will provide Dalia with the means of reducing the possibility of hidden agendas taking control of a transition team?

    A) Pay strict attention to the team's goals
    B) Allow members to showcase their skills
    C) Avoid any conflict over misunderstandings
    D) Have only one leader, whether formal or informal

4. Wessin and Dalia already believe that group leaders have begun to show signs of mistrust toward each other because of the lack of progress toward expansion and the possible appearance that some workers are getting more resources than others. Which one of the

following will provide a means of reducing mistrust and building trust with any new group leaders added during the expansion?

A) Adventure training
B) Nominal group techniques
C) Assertiveness training
D) Quality circles

5. For Light Power, most of the work units in the matrix structure are flexible and change membership as needed; however, a few of them are permanent, with specific leaders who do not change. These units perform regular, routine, and repeating functions like accounting and payroll. These units would be called

A) special-purpose teams
B) horizontal teams
C) task forces
D) command groups

CASE 2: Closed Circuit Success

Jankins, a district manager for International Travel, starts the workday with a cup of coffee and the viewing of a short, five- to ten-minute company-produced, closed-circuit television program. Through the short in-house program, Jankins learns that the organization is doing quite well. The program suggests that customer complaints are down by 5 percent. Quarterly profit reports show an improvement over the previous year. Every employee at every office of International Travel has the opportunity to watch the closed-circuit program. It is broadcast in each language of the company's international offices. Eager to communicate a message with as much clarity, immediacy, and impact as possible, International Travel turned to closed-circuit television as the media of choice.

The program may include information about the previous day's performance and the level of business activity as well as company news and announcements. The program remains available throughout the day to be watched. International Travel wants to expand on the success of the program.

6. Closed-circuit television can be an excellent training medium, particularly for the travel agents who are required to deal with customers, and transportation carrier sales representatives, and especially for workers who need training in

A) technical skills
B) interpersonal skills
C) basic literacy skill
D) certification skills

7. Since people are receptive to audio and visual elements of television, Jankins could improve staff communication skills by using the daily program to

A) address critical issues with new personnel
B) give instructions to office personnel
C) foster practice of listening skills

D) test the knowledge of company performance

8. Which one of the following best describes the type of meeting that the daily television show represents?

A) External general meeting
B) Ad hoc meeting
C) Inspirational meeting
D) Committee meeting

9. When any of Jankins staff talk with other offices of International Travel, even if staff members are not proficient in the language of the other office, they still have a basis for exchanging key instructions or requests because the daily closed-circuit television broadcast has established

A) a grapevine
B) nonverbal communication

C) the cooperative principle

D) a common ground

10. The closed-circuit program occasionally offers information about how people visiting a specific country or region should behave in matters relating to dining, greeting a host, appropriate dress for specific occasions, and so on.

This information would be specifically categorized as part of which one of the following?

A) Protocol

B) Nonverbal communication

C) Ethics

D) Etiquette

CASE 3: Office Dissatisfaction at Multiphase Manufacturing Incorporated

Multiphase Manufacturing, Incorporated has just completed a six-month effort to improve productivity and quality throughout the company's main plant. Consultants helped formulate a plan for implementation and guided the transition. Evidence of improvement is dramatic, but shifts in employee satisfaction in the central business office have raised some concern on the part of company president, Landia. The area with the highest shift to the negative is even more striking, because the central office had regularly reported the highest levels of employee satisfaction. Now it reports the lowest levels.

Bright is the manager of the main office. Bright reports directly to Landia. Landia suspects that part of the problem may be personal troubles Bright is experiencing, but is aware of other stresses brought on by the productivity and quality improvement plan. Bright reports increased pressure from "above" because of recent changes that have been undertaken to improve quality. Reporting requirements have increased, and compliance by shift managers has improved, thus making reporting less difficult. The company has changed quite a number of procedures, including moving to just-in-time delivery of resources and order fulfillment. The main office must process each order more rapidly to keep pace with the new system.

11. For the most part, the reporting process is now routinely flowing smoothly through the central office. The heavier workload is part of which one of the following types of plans?

A) Contingency

B) Tactical

C) Operational

D) Strategic

12. If dissatisfaction starts to cause conflict and that conflict divides Bright's division and many of the coworkers in other divisions, the conflict would be called

A) horizontal organizational conflict

B) intrapersonal conflict

C) topic conflict

D) double approach-avoidance conflict

13. Landia believes that the new, just-in-time manufacturing and delivery ap-

proach may be causing the problem of dissatisfaction in the main office. If Landia's assessment is correct, a review of controls is necessary in

A) compensation and development

B) materials procurement

C) grievance procedures

D) quality of services

14. Landia wants to solve the problem, but not without careful investigation. The reason Multiphase Manufacturing relies on systematic research is that

A) qualitative data can be made useful

B) reliability will ensure satisfied clients

C) information and analysis guide effective decisions

D) only experiments can prove cause and effect

15. Landia depends on subordinates working together to solve problems and engage in planning. Bright has always been involved in the process. Landia expects that with some guidance, Bright will find solutions to the satisfaction problem. Which one of the fol-

lowing would be identified as the organizational style used by Landia in this instance?

A) Unity of command
B) Theory Y
C) Informal leadership
D) Participatory management

CASE 4: Working with Disabilities

A prominent school for the deaf approached High Tech Enterprises about hiring one of its students. Both executives and department managers agreed that hiring the student would work out well. The school agreed to provide an interpreter for a few days and to follow the worker's progress. Avery, a 20-year-old, came to work for High Tech Enterprises. The interpreter was a very helpful person named Hocken.

High Tech placed Avery in the camera section of the graphics department. The camera section is responsible for preparing technical manuals for High Tech's products. Camera work involves a lot of stripping or pasting up material in exact positions. Avery seemed bright and eager to work. At first, Avery was very slow and meticulous. The production manager gave Avery a lot of training and even helped with some of the work to keep on schedule. Gradually, after a few weeks, it became apparent that Avery did not have the needed hand–eye coordination to work in the camera department. The managers found they had a real dilemma.

To allow Avery to continue would jeopardize schedules. As a 20-year-old with a challenging disability, Avery needed to work in a situation that had a future. Finally, Conrad, the High Tech vice president, contacted both the school and Avery hoping to work out a possible different work situation. Conrad did not want to dismiss Avery without helping to arrange some other type of work assignment.

The school and High Tech worked with Avery to determine a work preference. Since the state pays for training, Conrad suggested that Avery could train for assembly. Avery is conscientious and careful—two wonderful qualities for an assembler of high-tech products.

16. High Tech Enterprises employs several highly qualified information technology people who are wheelchair-bound. High Tech understands that hiring Avery requires that they must provide, as they do for wheelchair-bound employees, which one of the following?

A) Reasonable accommodations
B) Access without undue hardship for the employees
C) Opportunities that include transportation
D) Complete and unrestricted access

17. Avery had difficulty in performing camera work. His difficulty reflected ability to learn a skill related to the

A) sensory domain
B) cognitive domain
C) affective domain
D) psychomotor domain

18. Which one of the following represents the appropriate etiquette for talking with Avery?

A) Speaking directly to Hocken, the interpreter
B) Speaking loudly, since Avery is not entirely deaf
C) Looking at Avery while speaking
D) Looking at Hocken while speaking to Avery

19. Many employees in the plant have worked with Avery and found Avery to

be warm, generous, and highly likable. Conrad, however, emphasizes that personal feelings must be set aside for

A) effective data collection
B) results that would be considered satisficing
C) proper problem solving
D) organizational success

20. High Tech considers hiring Avery part of a broader diversity plan that includes an aggressive minority recruitment and hiring component. Which one of the following is the law governing this plan?

A) Equal Pay Act of 1967
B) Equal Employment Opportunity Act of 1972
C) Health Maintenance Organization Act of 1973
D) Americans with Disabilities Act of 1990

CASE 5: Paralegal Pitfalls

Patel joined a law firm as a paralegal. Patel recently graduated from a paralegal program at a local community college. The law firm is an extremely busy office. There is little time to train new employees. Soon, Patel begins to feel insecure.

Patel performs a self-inventory of skills by making a list of job tasks that can be accomplished easily and well. Next, Patel lists job skills that are needed to perform tasks that cannot be completed adequately. Patel realizes that about 70 percent of the tasks can be performed right now. Patel needs training to handle the other 30 percent.

There are 10 experienced lawyers, 1 other paralegal, and 4 legal administrative professionals on the staff. Patel finds that Hendricks, one of the legal administrative professionals, is very helpful. Patel discloses to Hendricks the concerns about skills that need improvement.

21. The use of logical reasoning and systematic investigation imply that Patel is using which one of the following approaches to solve the problem?

A) Idea generation
B) Creativity
C) Idea development
D) Scientific method

22. If more of the law firm's employees took responsibility for their work and personal development like Patel, employees' efforts would result in a noticeable change in

A) improved job satisfaction
B) greater efficiency
C) more delegation
D) increased psychomotor skills

23. Patel's individual efforts suggest that a training program for Patel's needed skills would be successful because of a high level of

A) learner readiness
B) conditioned responses

C) types of reinforcement
D) feedback protocols

24. The issue of a reduced training budget should be resolved when the human resource department of the law firm convinces law partners that

A) performance appraisals will pinpoint weaknesses
B) proper training can actually save money
C) hiring techniques can solve this problem
D) computers and technology are the solution

25. When Patel goes to Hendricks and explains a personal shortcoming and asks for help, which one of the following impression management techniques will encourage Hendricks to help?

A) Self-promotion
B) Supplication
C) Intimidation
D) Exemplification

CASE 6: Same Old Story at Elder Care Enterprises

Whiteside is a manager at a long-term-care facility for the elderly. Recent federal cutbacks have taken their toll on employees. Nurse's aides now do twice the work they did before. Morale is low. The one bright spot is that the facility is regarded as a wonderful training ground for geriatric nursing. The facility also contributes to tuition for nursing school. In spite of this, turnover has been unusually high. High turnover has resulted in high cost of training and in providing inconsistent care for residents.

Whiteside needed to develop a plan and attended a management seminar on employee empowerment. Several options were presented. First, many of the aides have families. Whiteside decided that morale would improve if employees control scheduling. Second, Whiteside found much resentment about floor assignments. The more critical care floors require a much higher level of work. There is no distinction between the salaries of those in critical care and those who work on the regular care floors. Whiteside cannot raise salaries at this point. Whiteside comes up with a plan for rotating assignments with individuals working in teams. Third, Whiteside learned that group social interaction is at an all-time low and plans to provide some low-cost social events to raise morale.

26. Whiteside knows that to make an effective change in the morale, good information about morale must be collected. Part of the information must probe into the deeper core of problems contributing to the morale issue. Which one of the following methods will produce the necessary in-depth response data?

    A) Observational qualitative
    B) Split halves
    C) Experimental
    D) Interview

27. Another benefit of the work teams Whiteside plans to use is that the team members often form relationships that extend beyond work. These relationships may help with morale. These teams are called

    A) interest groups
    B) mutual-aid groups
    C) friendship groups
    D) cross-functional teams

28. Whiteside hopes to see changes in nonverbal behavior once proposed changes are in place. With a desire to change the morale of the workplace, nonverbal behavior is important to watch because it

    A) cannot express a lie
    B) has clear and ambiguous messages
    C) conveys attitudes and feelings
    D) transmits well-encoded signals

29. Whiteside has finished planning and has decided to communicate Elder Care Enterprises' revised and reaffirmed values to the organization at large. Which one of the following will provide the next logical step?

    A) Formulate policy to reflect changes
    B) Undertake a gap analysis
    C) Complete the tactical planning
    D) Adjust the strategic plan

30. Which one of the following is an advantage of group decision making that Whiteside could expect in the new assignment for groups to prepare schedules?

    A) More balanced level of energy
    B) An increase in sharing of knowledge
    C) Detection of free riders
    D) Avoiding the high cost of decision making

CASE 7: Training for a Better Workplace

For a number of years, Tillman heard racial slurs broadcasted over the paging system used at a soft drink bottling plant for Soda Bottling Company. Tillman, a manager, took a leave of absence because the slurs were so disturbing. Upon Tillman's return, the unknown perpetrator immediately started the harassment again.

Soda Bottling Company made many efforts to find the worker or workers who misused the paging system. Even law enforcement was asked to help find the perpetrator(s). Other minorities at the plant also began to suffer from similar harassment. Many nonminority workers substantiated details of a number of incidents.

Soda Bottling Company recently appointed Ong, a human resources professional, to work on the root of the problem. Until now, the organization did not specifically offer diversity training at the plant, nor did it clearly acknowledge the problem.

31. The problem experienced by Tillman at the Soda Bottling Company indicates that management has failed to communicate

    A) timely information about cultural changes
    B) through the proper channels
    C) the proper use of technology
    D) appropriate ethics and behavior

32. Which one of the following would provide the appropriate basis for minority employees to sue Soda Bottling Company?

    A) Affirmative Action
    B) Equal Pay Act of 1963
    C) Title VII of the Civil Rights Act of 1964
    D) Equal Employment Opportunity Act of 1972

33. To make all employees at Soda Bottling less likely to participate in the harassment of minority employees, Ong should conduct a series of workshops that focus on using which one of the following?

    A) Quality Circles
    B) T-Group
    C) Nominal Group Technique
    D) Delphi Technique

34. Other workers at the bottling company could be considered victims of harassment to the extent that they

    A) experience compromised work relationships
    B) think Tillman should be moved to another plant
    C) oppose the racial slurs
    D) become jealous of Tillman's special treatment

35. To prevent the situation from recurring, Ong and upper management formulate new policies and procedures regarding items that have contributed to Tillman's harassment. To convey new information to the employees at Soda Bottling Company, Ong should hold a/an

    A) brainstorming meeting
    B) educational meeting
    C) inspirational meeting
    D) reorganization meeting

CASE 8: Kelley Incorporated

Kelley, the owner of Kelley Incorporated, founded the company. Kelley used personal funds for start-up and put every ounce of energy into building a profitable, dynamic business. Management consultants were brought in when the company's rapid growth threatened its ability to deliver product. Kelley readily agreed that the company needed help; however, Kelley did not seem willing to let go of much real power.

Kelley has many good leadership qualities. Kelley is confident, compassionate, smart, and often willing to listen to new ideas. On the other hand, Kelley can be overbearing. As the company grew, Kelley had to delegate some power to Frances, the vice president. Kelley trusted Frances's judgment, and over the years they worked out a reasonable system. Frances would make decisions independently. The two of them managed to handle many clients and much work.

It gradually became clear that some management responsibility needed to move down the line to area supervisors. Neither Kelley nor Frances could continue to watch production as business grew, nor could they oversee the office staff because clients demanded more of their time. They contracted consultants to evaluate the problems and develop a plan of action.

In discussions with management consultants, the fact that Kelley basically distrusted employees became obvious. Kelley had worked out many production problems alone in the past and did not believe that supervisors would handle matters as quickly and as cost efficiently. Management consultants found opportunities for improvement and were able to show Kelley that the president's time was most valuable when spent with clients. If some production costs rose slightly while the staff gained productivity, Kelley would make more money and thus have a smoother running business. Kelley agreed to try the new system with some modifications.

36. Kelley created the company and knows all the jobs and procedures of Kelley Incorporated. The increase in knowledge and responsibility with each new aspect of the expanding company means that Kelley has built personal power based on

    A) creating a sense of obligation
    B) recognizing costs, risks, and benefits
    C) developing expertise and confidence
    D) taking control of power

37. In establishing a goal of "improve operations" in a strategic plan, Kelley wants to measure operations success as a reduction in interventions required by the president. Frances is charged with determining changes in operations. To be sure any measure chosen will be consistent, Frances must determine whether or not the measure is

    A) qualitative
    B) subjective
    C) valid
    D) reliable

38. Kelley and Frances will need to convince employees that steps toward empowerment are good for them. If they have a successful business plan for how work is currently accomplished, which one of the following would be a method that would ensure employee support of the new idea?

    A) Conduct a careful internal audit
    B) Use management by objectives to establish participation
    C) Establish clear rules for the new approach
    D) Prepare a policy manual with guidelines for international operations

39. Which one of the following characteristics of innovative people will make Kelley's company a success at working with customers with unique or highly unconventional problems?

    A) Originality of ideas generated
    B) Monitoring of innovation
    C) Entrepreneurial spirit
    D) Deductive reasoning

40. Kelley and Frances are willing to follow the consultant's advice and em-

power employees by giving them responsibility and self-managing authority. Given the circumstances described in the case, which one of the following might cause efforts of empowerment to fail?

A) Excessive loyalty that results in blindness to problems
B) Use of statistical procedures to track employees
C) Poor training that results in misuse of opportunities
D) Overly eager employees can fail by trying too hard

CASE 9: Crenshaw and Company

As Crenshaw and Company expanded in the late 1980s and early 1990s, the company needed more experienced workers. One of its suppliers laid off an entire division of production people with the experienced needed by Crenshaw and Company. Most of the workers were from Thailand. They had brought relatives and friends into the company as time went on. Generally, they were a good team. They kept the equipment humming and understood the work.

Crenshaw hired most of the displaced Thai workers and found their work exceptional. On the other hand, the CEO had no intention of firing any of the current workers. Success had resulted in a substantially increased business volume, and all the workers were needed. The workers at Crenshaw felt threatened. Kat, the vice president, noticed an increasing friction among different groups of workers. One day Kat heard an African American call one of the Thai workers a name that showed extreme prejudice. Kat told the African American that the next time remarks like that were used, the behavior would result in reprimand and possibly dismissal. Kat also pointed out that the same procedure would be followed to reprimand anyone who made racist remarks about African Americans.

Kat and Crenshaw called a meeting. The entire production staff discussed the issues involved. Kat and Crenshaw heard everyone's complaints; they tried to be fair. Both Crenshaw and Kat had a bottom line—there would be no racist remarks at Crenshaw and Company. Anyone who could not respect the right of any worker to work in a safe, reasonable environment could leave. Eventually, one or two workers left.

41. The meeting that Kat and Crenshaw called does not have a formal agenda, no minutes are taken, and discussion is fairly open. Considering the purpose of the meeting, it would probably be called a/an

A) committee meeting
B) impromptu meeting
C) business conference
D) general meeting

42. Crenshaw and Kat propose training to improve relationships among different groups. To be certain that training is effective and that the new program is working, they plan to use regular, ongoing evaluation. The human resources manager suggests pretesting all employees before training, posttesting after training, asking for employee feedback, and using other assessments.

Evaluations will demonstrate whether or not training is effective because the evaluation method utilizes

A) pretesting participants reactions
B) multiple evaluative measures
C) documentation
D) one-shot design

43. Crenshaw and Company is experiencing a common problem in the contemporary work environment that has been described as

A) co-cultural
B) multicultural
C) polycultural
D) bicultural

44. One suggestion is for Crenshaw to attempt a team approach beginning at the level of workers who are experiencing conflict. As these workers already

know their job tasks, on which one of the following types of activities should team building focus? Activities that

A) take a task-oriented approach to solving problems
B) clarify roles in the team
C) help set and clarify goals
D) build cohesion by examining interpersonal processes

45. Crenshaw and Company has succeeded through employee involvement and self-direction. The presence of a large number of immigrants from one country may jeopardize the new methods being used at Crenshaw. If these methods are successful with new employees, they are so because they are responsive to which one of the following trends?

A) Standardization of practice
B) Security
C) Technological innovation
D) Globalization of the marketplace

CASE 10: Boxed In at Boxes Galore

Boxes Galore, a packaging-machinery manufacturer, has a decentralized structure. Each department is a separate profit center, and each department manager reports directly to the chief executive officer, Amadife.

The decentralized structure has led to a lot of internal strife among managers. Amadife felt that there were too many complaints from managers and other employees. The company's business seemed to focus on this in-fighting and not on customer problems. Each manager felt the most important thing was to protect his or her department.

Amadife decided to change the direction of the company. Teams were developed. Amadife also commissioned customer-focus checks. Most important, to improve internal management, Amadife instituted a weekly manager report system that unclogged the lines of communication. The backbiting disappeared. Instead, reports now focused on managers' perceptions about themselves and their own groups. Managers also asked about relations between groups. None of the reports were used to discipline or reprimand managers. The point was to identify problems and find productive corrections. Managers did receive favorable evaluations for following the process and seeking positive change, As a result, reports remained honest and straightforward. The focus of managers changed. They no longer felt threatened. They looked at their departments honestly and reported what they saw.

46. Customer-focus checks, like focus groups in general, allowed Amadife to get detailed information about customer needs and quality concerns and in turn share that information with managers. This kind of research is considered to be based upon

A) sales analysis
B) job analysis
C) primary data sources
D) secondary data sources

47. The kind of control that Amadife needed to implement immediately was

A) budgetary
B) cost

C) information
D) production

48. To encourage managers to repeat a desired action or behavior, such as preparing weekly reports, Amadife uses evaluation to

A) condition the stimulus for action
B) offer rewards
C) help the learners understand the behavior
D) model the behavior

49. Amadife decided to implement a team approach and make managers submit weekly reports because it just seemed like a good idea. Which one of the fol-

lowing describes the problem-solving process Amadife utilized?

A) Intuition
B) Satisficing
C) Bounded rationality
D) Presence of certainty

50. If Amadife were to utilize the total quality management approach advocated by Deming at Boxes Galore, which one of the following would address the problem of the lack of focus on customer concerns?

A) Eliminating fear of innovation
B) Eliminating useless slogans
C) Inspecting products or services continuously
D) Developing pride of workmanship

Solutions for Final Review Exam

Answer:	Refer to:
Case 1:	
1. C	[Ch 9, B-7]
2. B	[Ch 2, A-3-(b)]
3. A	[Ch 7, D-1-c-(1)]
4. A	[Ch 8, D-5]
5. D	[Ch 7, A-2-b-(1)]
Case 2:	
6. B	[Ch 4, C-5-(b)]
7. C	[Ch 10, A-4-(d)]
8. C	[Ch 9, B-4-(a)]
9. D	[Ch 10, A-3-a-(1)]
10. D	[Ch 12, B-1]
Case 3:	
11. C	[Ch 2, A-1-c & B-3-(c)]
12. A	[Ch 8, C-1-e-(1)]
13. B	[Ch 3, B]
14. C	[Ch 5, A-1]
15. D	[Ch 6, B-2-d]
Case 4:	
16. A	[Ch 11, C-1-c-(5)]
17. D	[Ch 4, A-1-b-(3)]
18. C	[Ch 12, B-3-b]

19. C   [Ch 1, A-1-b-(4)]

20. B   [Ch 11, C-1-c-(3)]

Case 5:

21. D   [Ch 1, B-2]

22. A   [Ch 6, C-3-a-(3)]

23. A   [Ch 4, A-2-a-(1)]

24. B   [Ch 3, E-4]

25. B   [Ch 12, A-4-b-(5)

Case 6:

26. D   [Ch 5, A-5-b]

27. C   [Ch 7, A-3-b-(2)]

28. C   [Ch 10, B-4-c]

29. A   [Ch 2, C-2-c]

30. B   [Ch 8, A-1-b]

Case 7:

31. D   [Ch 2-c]

32. C   [Ch 11, B-1-b]

33. B   [Ch 8, B-1]

34. A   [Ch 11, A-3-c-(2)]

35. B   [Ch9-b-6]

Case 8:

36. C   [Ch 6, A-3-d-(4)]

37. D   [Ch 5, A-4-b]

38. B   [Ch 2, C-3-a]

39. A   [Ch 1, C-1]

40. C   [Ch 6, C-3-b-(1)]

Case 9:

41. B   [Ch 9, A-3-(a)(1)]

42. B   [Ch 4, D-4 & D-5]

43. A   [Ch 12, B-3-a]

44. D   [Ch 7, C-3-a]

45. D   [Ch 2, A-3-e-(1)]

Case 10:

46. C   [Ch 5, B-3-c-(3)]

47. C   [Ch 3, A-1-d]

48. B   [Ch 4, A-1-c-(b)-(i)]

49. A   [Ch 1, A-1-b-(2)]

50. D   [Ch 3, B-1-(1)]

Glossary

Active listening   Form of listening that requires that the listener devote complete attention to the speaker and take responsibility for understanding the message.

Ad hoc committee   Committee that is usually charged with a single task.

Adjournment   An action of the chair or motion made by a member that stops the meeting activity for a specified period of time.

Adventure training   Training in which participants go into a wilderness area and work together to build mutual trust to achieve a common goal. Also called outdoor training, wilderness training, or survival training.

Affective domain   Dimension in which learning is indicated by emotions, feelings, or expressions.

Affirmative Action (AA)   Steps taken to remedy discriminatory practices in the workplace. The plans guarantee employees the constitutional rights of free speech, due process (the right to fair and equal treatment in law and organizational policy), and privacy. AA has evolved through presidential executive orders and court cases.

Agenda   A plan for a meeting, with the items to be discussed during the meeting listed in order of presentation.

Aggregate planning   Involves making decisions about how the firm's capacity will be used to respond to forecasted sales. Requires the production function to be considered as a whole.

Approach-approach conflict   Conflict in which there are two alternatives, one of which must be chosen, and where both have positive consequences.

Approach-avoidance conflict   Conflict in which a decision must be made that has both positive and negative consequences; the conflict arises in the competing desirability and undesirability of the action.

Assertiveness training   A means of self-improvement through learning to express one's feelings and act with confidence.

Assessment   The collection of data and relevant information about a particular program.

Avoidance-avoidance conflict   Conflict involving a set of choices that have few redeeming qualities and mostly negative consequences, making them choices that one wants to avoid; however, one of the choices must be taken.

Behavioral (administrative) theory of decision making   A theory of managerial decision making, based on the work of Herbert A. Simon, that describes how managers actually make decisions in business situations.

Bounded rationality   Managers must make decisions as rationally as possible with only limited information available.

Brainstorming   Several people meet in an unstructured setting to present ideas or offer solutions. Ideas are encouraged, evaluation is minimized, and active modification of ideas is encouraged.

Breach of order   The situation that occurs when rules are ignored or not followed, someone speaks out of turn, or when the decorum of the meeting is lost.

Bureaucratic knowledge   Knowing how to file reports and knowing the procedures and policies for all manner of managerial activities.

Bypassing   When a statement has two meanings, whether from different perspectives or from different cultures.

Chain of command   The organizational design for the flow of communications and decision making.

Chair   Individual charged with leading a meeting, keeping it on track, on time, and efficient. The chair diffuses tensions and encourages collaborative and supportive efforts.

Channel   A modality of communication, or the medium in which the message is sent, such as oral, verbal, or written form.

Circle   A loosely formed and highly informal collection of individuals.

Classical conditioning   Theory that refers to the learning that has occurred when a living organism responds to a stimulus that would normally not produce such a response.

Classical organization theory   Theory that divides organizations into functions with a pyramid-like chain of command, a span of control, and a distinction between line and staff workers.

Classical theory of decision making   Theory of managerial decision making representing an ideal model of decision making, with maximizing outcomes as a primary goal.

Coaching   A trainer serves as coach in one-on-one situations with an employee being trained.

Co-culture   Cultures coexisting in the same society.

Coercive power   Power that stems from a leader's ability to mete out negative consequences or remove positive consequences for not performing desired behaviors. Coercive power results from others' perceptions.

Cognitive dissonance   Conflicting attitudes or behaviors in an individual cause distress and discomfort that motivates him or her to change some aspect of the conflicting elements.

Cognitive domain   Dimension or domain in which the thinking and knowledge skills most associated with the learning process occur.

Cognitive learning   Focuses on examining how people pursue desired goals, interpret work tasks as opportunities to satisfy desires, and reduce perceived inequities.

Cohesiveness   The desire of the members of a group to remain part of the group.

Command group   A formal group created by the organization, consisting of a manager and his or her subordinates.

Committee meeting   When a group of people meet to discuss problems, tasks, or responsibilities.

Committee   A group of people who are brought together from the organization to deal most often with problems that arise on a regular basis.

Common ground   Shared interests, beliefs, or opinions among people or groups who disagree about most other subjects. It includes the assumptions that we make about each other, about mutual interests, about shared values, and about awareness of individual interests.

Communication   The successful transmission of a message between a source and a receiver.

Computer-aided design (CAD)   A designer conceives and designs parts to meet predetermined specifications using specialized computer systems.

Computer-aided manufacturing (CAM)   A finished design is translated into a set of programmed instructions that are sent electronically to production processing machines, instructing them to perform specific steps in a given order.

Computer-integrated manufacturing (CIM)   Develops production systems to help workers design products, control machines, handle materials, and direct entire manufacturing processes in a systematic manner.

Concurrent control   Control that monitors and adjusts ongoing activities and processes. Also called in-progress control.

Conference   A formal meeting of people with a common purpose; typically they are professionals assembled to share information and research.

Conflict   A natural part of human interaction. Conflict occurs whenever there is disagreement, competing interests, different expectations, or incompatible styles between two or more individuals or groups.

Contemporary organization theory   Theory that looks at the organization as a system composed of people, formal structures, small groups, roles, and physical environment.

Contingency planning   Developing action plans to help an organization cope with any unforeseen events that may arise.

Controlling   Evaluating performance according to the plans that have been established to ensure that the goals set forth are realized, even if modifications need to be made.

Cooperative principle   The belief that someone speaking is making an honest attempt to be understood.

Correlation   Shows the extent to which the change in one factor relates to the change in another factor. A *positive* correlation occurs when an increase in one factor occurs with the increase in another factor. A *negative* correlation occurs when the increase in one factor occurs with the decrease in another factor.

Courtesy   Showing appropriate respect and generally being polite to others.

Creativity   The generation of new ideas.

Critical path method (CPM)   The sequence of events that are most critical as to timing—the longest path of activities in a system.

Critical thinking   An approach to evaluating a claim that requires thorough analysis of assumptions and reasoning followed by evaluation based on the argument rather than on assertions.

Cross-functional team   A version of the special-purpose team, the cross-functional team usually consists of members of different departments from the same hierarchical levels working together to ensure that widespread views are shared and more diversity is included in the decision making and acceptance and implementation processes.

Data set Groups of similar data.

Data Information that has been gathered.

Decision making The process through which a manager identifies and solves problems creatively; a process that involves making appropriate and rational decisions.

Decoding The process in which a receiver determines how a message was encoded, why it was sent, and what to do with it once it is received. Decoding requires listening or reading and placing the message in context.

Delegation The process by which authority is distributed downward in an organization.

Delphi technique Problem-solving approach used in predicting future human resource demands. It involves data gathering, surveying of experts, providing input, responding, and prioritizing.

Departmental meeting Meeting that involves departments, divisions, or other work groups, scheduled on a more regular basis.

Development Planned organizational activities that involve individual employees, teams or the entire organization in expending their capacities to meet future opportunities and challenges.

Discrimination Occurs when people act on their prejudices and treat others unfairly.

Distinctiveness The quality or characteristic that sets something apart from other, similar items.

Distributed practice Learning episodes are spread across several practice sessions.

Doctrine of comparable worth States that people holding different jobs that require comparable knowledge, skills, and responsibilities should receive the same pay and benefits.

Double approach-avoidance conflict Conflict in which both choices have good and bad aspects. The decision will require identifying and weighing all the factors.

Downward communication Information flow from individuals at higher levels within an organization to those at lower levels.

Drug-free workplace A workplace in which illegal drug use is not tolerated, and the employer is able to claim that illegal drugs are not being used.

Economic order quantity (EOQ) Equation used to determine how much should be ordered to meet estimated demand at the lowest cost.

Employment-at-will (EAW) A common law doctrine stating that employers have the right to hire, fire, promote, or demote any employee they choose at any time, unless there is a law or specific written contract to the contrary.

Empowerment An extension of delegation in which the power and responsibility for relevant decision making is extended to the employee without supervisory direction or oversight.

Encoding Putting information into a form or code that can be sent and understood by a receiver.

Entitlement A person's proclamations regarding rights and obligations of a position in an organization.

Equal opportunity employment (EOE) The responsibilities and obligations that organizations have to ensure that all human resource management objectives, policies, procedures, and specific rules are developed and administered to ensure that every potential and present employee is treated fairly, regardless of race, gender, color, age, religion, or national origin.

Ethics A code of conduct that governs the behavior and actions of individuals that subscribe to the code; the standards of right and wrong behavior that guide people.

Ethnicity A characteristic of a group based on origin, sub-culture, race, language, or religion.

Ethnocentrism The belief in the superiority of one's own ethnic group or culture.

Etiquette The rules that govern the conduct or behavior of an individual in any given setting.

Evaluation The combination of assessment with a judgment about the effectiveness of a program.

Expert power Informational power resulting from a leader's special knowledge or skills associated with the tasks being performed by subordinates.

Feedback control Control that involves checking a completed activity and learning from the mistakes. Also known as postcontrol.

Feedback Information about how a learner is performing; necessary for both learning and motivation.

Feedforward (precontrol) control Control that actively anticipates and prevents problems.

Formal communication Written or oral messages that are sent in the context of an official action or otherwise are presented as the directive of an office or officer of an organization or as following the directive or request of an officer.

Formal group A group created by management and charged with carrying out specific tasks to help the organization fulfill its objectives.

Formal leaders Leaders who rely on organizational authority or status to influence people.

Formal meeting A gathering of a group that proceeds under the control of a chair, following an agenda, and typically utilizing rules of conduct that specify how action will be taken.

Gap analysis   Measures the gap between perception and reality within the organization as well as between the organization and the broader business environment. A gap analysis might be done on service to customers, or on internal or external communication.

General meeting   Meeting scheduled for all people within the organization, including managers and supervisors.

Glass ceiling   Occurs when a member of a minority group or a female reaches what appears to be a limit to further promotion.

Grapevine   An informal pattern of communication that moves in any direction; a system of communicating information, gossip, and rumors through informal networks.

Group   Any collection of two or more people who share a common goal or purpose, who work together, and who share an awareness of the common goals and work.

Group dynamics   The interactions within a group that characterize the group.

Groupthink   The tendency to conform automatically and uncritically to group judgments even when those judgments have clear dangers.

High and low context   Communication in a high-context situation means that many of the cues necessary for understanding the meaning of the message come from the context. Low-context communication depends more on the message content than the context.

Homogeneity   The sameness of individuals.

Hostile environment   An extension of sexual harassment to the entire environment or a sustained atmosphere of threat, discrimination, hostility, and discomfort not related to sexual aggression.

Impression management   A process of acting out the image one wants to present to others. Introduced by sociologist Erving Goffman.

Inbreeding   Can occur when too many people of the same background, interests, and cultural orientation become associated with an organization.

Informal communication   All the messages other than official directives or requests made in an organization.

Informal group   A group created by the employees themselves rather than by the organization.

Informal leaders   Leaders who rely on their own abilities to influence others; they lack the official support of the formal structure.

Informal meeting   Meeting that can occur anywhere and at any time. Many begin in the employee snack room during breaks. Informal meetings are crucial to individual and team creativity and innovation.

Innovation   The translation of a new idea into a new product, service, production method, or organization.

Interest group   An informal association of people formed because of common concerns or needs.

Interjudge reliability   Checking observational data by having more than one trained observer collect observations.

Interpersonal conflict   Conflict between individuals.

Interval scale   Measures the intervals or differences between data.

Intrapersonal conflict   Conflict within an individual.

Job analysis   A detailed study of the job to determine the exact nature of the work, the quantity and quality of output that is expected, organizational aspects of the job, and necessary personal qualities such as leadership, judgment, tact, and the ability to cope with emergencies.

Lateral communication   The exchange of information between peers or workers at the same organizational level. Also called horizontal communication.

Leadership   The exercise of influence by one person over another in such a way that the follower behaves as the leader directs.

Learning curve   The course of learning that most people tend to follow; depicts how behavioral changes occur.

Learning   Any relatively permanent change in behavior that occurs as a result of practice and experience.

Legitimate power   Power that comes from holding a formal management position in an organization.

Management by objectives (MBO)   A systematic approach to planning and controlling activities whereby superiors and those who report to them (subordinates) collaborate on setting objectives. Originated by Peter Drucker.

Market analysis   The systematic gathering, recording, and analyzing of data about marketing problems toward the goal of providing information useful in marketing decision making. Also known as market research.

Massed practice   Learner attempts to learn everything in one session; also known as cramming.

Master production schedule (MPS)   Sets detailed schedule for individual end products, facilities, and personnel.

Maximizing The process of making a decision that is aimed at realizing the best possible outcome on one dimension—seeking the best answer.

Mean The average, determined by totaling all the data and then dividing by the number of pieces of data.

Measures of central tendency Measures that show the average, the most common number, and the middle data (called the mean, median, and mode, respectively).

Measures of variability Measures that show the extent to which production varies from one day to another. The common measures of variability are the range and standard deviation.

Median The middle score in a set of scores, or middle data in a set of data.

Mentoring An experienced member of an organization coaches, guides, and counsels newer members.

Message The specific physical form given to information so that it can be sent to a receiver.

Minutes A written record of the main points of a meeting and how members voted on motions and other actions, as well as a verbatim record of each motion statement, usually recorded by the secretary of the group.

Mission The most broadly stated objective of an organization; the basic purpose for the organization's existence.

Mode The most common score; often near the middle.

Negotiation Interaction intended to lead to an agreement or cooperative effort by two or more parties.

Neoclassical organizational theory Theory stating that an effective organization follows the workflow and productivity of the classical organization; however, it also meets the employees' needs as they appear in the informal networks and social components of the workplace.

Nominal group technique (NGT) Problem-solving technique in which a group first generates a list of ideas about a given problem, discusses each idea in turn, and then the group ranks the ideas.

Nominal scale Puts each piece of information into a category or class.

Nonprogrammed and programmed decisions Nonprogrammed decisions are decisions that have no precedents and represent situations that have not been dealt with previously, and if so, only on a limited basis within the organization. Programmed decisions are decisions made routinely on a recurring basis and most often do not require huge expenditures and are less complex in nature.

Nonverbal communication Nonverbal communication can be conveyed in both oral and written forms. It consists of gestures, body position, voice inflection, eye contact, the use of humor, confidence, and so on.

Norms Standards of behavior that apply in specific situations. Norms define the boundaries of acceptable behaviors.

Objective data Include factors such as the number of events; measures of time and money; and descriptive qualities like color, size, and shape.

Objective The end results an organization seeks to attain to fulfill the organization's mission.

Office meeting A group gathering that can be by appointment or unscheduled and involves two or more people in an office conferring on a particular task, often between a supervisor and subordinate.

On-the-job training The use of the actual work site as the setting for instructing workers while also engaging in productive work.

Operant conditioning Theory that holds that behavior results from its consequences. Also known as the law of effect; founded by B. F. Skinner.

Operational planning First-line managers conduct day-to-day activities necessary to achieve longer term tactical and strategic goals.

Optimizing Selecting the best alternative from a range of options that have been evaluated within the existing time and price constraints.

Ordinal scale Uses a single dimension like "most to least sales" to rank the data on the scales. Can be used best to show the relative quality based on the customer's perception.

Organizational conflict Conflict within the units of an organization.

Orientation Initial introduction of a new or transferred employee to work itself, the organization and its rules, other members of the organization, and the organization's goals.

Overlearning Repeated practice even after the task has been mastered.

Parliamentary procedure A formal set of rules that guide the conduct of a meeting. The most common set of rules used is *Robert's Rules of Order.*

Participatory management A process where subordinates share a significant degree of decision-making power with their supervisors.

Personal power Power available to any leader through the use of his or her personal resources, including on-the-job expertise and charisma.

Policy A general statement developed by organization management and communicated to managers and supervisors so they can make consistent decisions in handling certain anticipated problems. Policies define the limits within which supervisors must stay as they make decisions.

Political knowledge Knowing the specific interest of others and how to balance competing interests.

Position power Power that is available to someone holding a position by virtue of its legitimacy as well as the rewards and punishments that can be meted out.

Power The motivational factor, or force, that provides the leader with the ability to influence others to change their behaviors as the leader desires.

Predjudice An attitude about an individual or group of people that is based on a selected set of characteristics rather than the person.

Probability The likelihood, or chance, of a certain event occurring.

Problem solving A process of identifying a problem, exploring solutions, and testing a solution.

Procedure A set, or sequence, of steps to be followed in performing specific tasks or actions. Procedures specify behavior for managers to follow in making decisions in specific situations.

Professional knowledge Refers to how people interact with others who have the same skills and capabilities.

Program evaluation and review technique (PERT) A method for project planning by analyzing the time required for each step. Developed by the U.S. Navy to plan and control the Polaris missile project.

Protocol Specific rules or rituals that govern a particular action or process.

Proximity The physical closeness of people to each other in any particular setting.

Psychomotor domain Learning is expressed by the actual performance of specific acts and the capability of operating equipment and technology by moving and manipulating various levers and devices.

Public meeting Meeting that may include public shareholders or stockholders; a news conference or public portion of a board meeting; or a public hearing of a local, state, or federal commission, committee, or legislative session.

Quality circles Small groups of employees meeting on a regular basis within an organization to discuss and develop management issues and procedures.

Quality control A series of planned measurements designed to verify compliance with all specified quality standards.

Quid pro quo harassment Type of harassment in which a sexual favor is exchanged for promotion, favorable or special treatment, or the job itself. Means "Do me a favor and I'll do one for you."

Range In a set of data, the difference between the highest and the lowest pieces of data.

Ratio scale A special form of an interval scale that has zero as a starting point.

Receiver The target of a message.

Recruitment The process of locating, identifying, and attracting qualified applicants to fill positions within an organization.

Referent power Power achieved when workers admire a supervisor or manager because of the way she or he deals with them.

Reinforcement Providing incentive when the learner has attained a specified level of performance. The two primary types are continuous and intermittent reinforcement.

Reliability The consistency and precision of a measure, test, instrument, performance, or other behavior.

Representation When people communicate facts about the world around them, and the source of information is not the self, they are communicating through the representation of these other phenomena.

Resistance facilitation When members of a group support a position resisting change.

Reward power Power that emanates from the leader's authority to bestow formal rewards or favors on others.

Role The task each member of a group or team is expected to perform.

Rule States exactly what is to be done; it allows for no discretion or deviation.

Sabotage Actions that lead to obstruction of work or other normal operations.

Sales analysis A thorough and detailed study of the company's sales records with the purpose of detecting marketing strengths and weaknesses.

Satisficing Adopting the solution that minimally meets the objectives, often found in the first acceptable option that arises without extensive study.

Scapegoating The diversion of blame from a larger group to a few or even one individual. Sometimes out-groups, especially defenseless or minority out-groups, are blamed in order to protect the in-group.

Scientific method The steps of logical thinking, which include identifying and defining the problem; gathering information about the problem; developing alternative solutions; evaluating alternatives; and choosing an alternative.

Self-disclosure The revelation of intimate, personal details to others.

Self-management   Managing one's own behavior so that less external management control is needed.

Self-managing team   A group of employees who work together on a day-to-day basis to produce an entire product (or a major identifiable component) and carry out various managerial tasks related to their jobs.

Self-presentation   When people communicate facts about the world around them, and the source of information is the self, then they are communicating through self-presentation.

Sender   Individual responsible for encoding a message in a manner than can be decoded by the receiver.

Sensitivity training   Technique for reducing interpersonal conflict that focuses on being sensitive to and aware of the attitudes and feelings of others.

Separation   A global term that refers to any discharge by the employer or voluntary act by the employee, such as moving on to a new job, retirement, or furlough as well as the more restricted term "termination" that usually refers to being fired.

Sexual harassment   Any conduct involving the "unwanted imposition of sexual requirements in a relationship of unequal power."

Single-use plans   Plans that may cover an activity such as a technology transition, a physical move to a temporary location during a renovation, installation of complex machinery or systemwide software, or any singular action that requires concentrated planning.

Social learning   Theory that people can learn by observation and direct experience.

Span of control   Principle that recognizes the limited ability and time of an individual manager. It asserts that there should be a limit on the span of persons or activities assigned to one manager.

Stakeholders   All persons whom an organization is dedicated to serve.

Standard deviation   An index of variation that is sensitive to differences found in sets of data. Standard deviation is most useful when comparing two different data sets.

Standard   An expected level of performance. A standard must be very specific and measurable.

Standing committee   Committee in which members are appointed for a definite term such as one or two years. The committee has definite objectives assigned for which it is responsible during the term.

Standing-use plans   Plans that guide regular activity of an organization. Plans may be in the form of procedure guidelines, calendars, report cycles, documents, or other tools that can guide and direct the business routine.

Statistical significance   A measure of the confidence that researchers have in their results.

Status   The relative importance of individuals within a group; the position in which others in a group place each member.

Strategic planning   Establishing long-term goals agreed upon by the entire organization that define the direction in which the organization will go; establishing clear parameters for recognizing and achieving success; and directing a process of continuous adaptation that is within the corporate objectives and resilient to external challenges.

Subjective data   Data that reflect the attitudes and feelings of customers about quality.

SWOT analysis   Stands for *strengths, weaknesses, opportunities,* and *threats;* a system used to scan the environment and understand the factors that will affect the strategy designed.

Synergy   A state that exists only when $1 + 1 = 2+$ (more than the sum); the whole purpose for using team effort.

Tactical planning   Setting short-term goals that show how to achieve the broad objectives specified in the strategic plans. Tactical plans include specific actions to be taken to achieve objectives.

Task analysis   The process of breaking down work into its constituent elements.

Task force   A temporary formal group created by management to solve a particular problem within a limited time period.

Team building   The processes intentionally undertaken by management to strengthen the members of a work unit so that they work together toward a common goal.

Team   A group of two or more people who interact and coordinate their work with each other to accomplish a common objective.

Technical knowledge   Refers to the skills required to complete work tasks.

Termination   The act of being discharged from an organization, or being "fired."

T-group   Refers to "Training Group" in which a trainer leads a group of individuals in an open-ended discussion of problems and concerns focused on improved mutual understanding among the members

Theory X   A theory that assumes people avoid work by their very nature. A manager who accepts Theory X believes the employee is lazy and requires constant monitoring to ensure that performance remains at expected standards.

Theory Y   A theory that purports that (1) work is natural; (2) when people are committed to the organization's goals, self-control will be exercised; (3) the ability to solve problems is widespread and underutilized; (4) organizational commitment depends on rewards and recognition; and (5) people normally seek responsibility.

Theory Z A theory that espouses these dimensions: (1) long-term employment; (2) collective decision making; (3) individual responsibility; (4) slow evaluation and promotion; (5) implicit, informal control with explicit, formalized procedures; (6) career paths that were moderately specialized; and (7) holistic concern, especially including the family.

Tokenism Occurs when one or a few minority or female candidates are promoted and the management takes the attitude, "Now we have met our responsibilities."

Total quality management (TQM) A management theory whose underlying principle is that all activities and operations of any organization should be focused upon discovering and meeting the needs of the customers. Set forth by W. Edwards Deming.

Training The process of providing the opportunity for individuals to acquire knowledge, skills, and attitudes required in their present jobs.

Transactional analysis (TA) Provides a means of conceptualizing the types of interactions between people by using a simple formula of identifying behavior toward others as parent, child, or adult.

Upward communication Messages flow from workers at lower levels to managers and workers at higher levels of an organizational structure.

Validity The extent to which a measure actually measures what it is intended to measure.

Vroom model The most common decision-making tree, which was developed by Vroom and Yetton. The model helps determine the optimal amount of subordinate participation desired in the decision-making process.

Work team A form of task force or group formed primarily to help organizations deal with problems involving rapid growth or the need for increased organizational flexibility.

Zone of indifference When subordinates accept and follow directives almost automatically.